W9-AEJ-528

HUGH SIDEY

JOHN F. KENNEDY, PRESIDENT

NEW EDITION

ATHENEUM

NEW YORK

1964

WINGATE COLLEGE LIBRARY
WINGATE, N. C.

TO ANNE

Copyright © 1963, © 1964 by Hugh Sidey
All rights reserved
Library of Congress catalog card number 63–7800
Published simultaneously in Canada by McClelland & Stewart
Manufactured in the United States of America by H. Wolff, New York
Designed by Harry Ford
First Printing July 1963
Second Printing August 1963
NEW EDITION
First Printing January 1964

AUTHOR'S NOTE

THIS BOOK was to have been the beginning of the story. Now, tragically, it covers, in time, the entire span of John F. Kennedy, President.

What I wrote is an attempt to record honestly the major events of the New Frontier's three years as I witnessed and understood them. I was granted a rare privilege by President Kennedy. In times of calm and of crisis he often talked to me as a journalist, explaining his ideas and reflecting on the state of the nation and the world. I took detailed notes of these meetings, and when I got back to my typewriter, I recorded much of what he had said. He never established any formal rules about how I might use this material. I had covered this extraordinary man for more than six intense years—first as a senator, then as a candidate, and finally as president—and we had reached an understanding without ever having talked about it. If there was a question in my mind, I checked back with him. If I had no question, he accepted my judgment.

And so it was when I came to write this book. We made but one agreement: I would check all direct quotes with him, and he would turn over to me no secret files. When the manuscript was finished, and he reviewed the direct quotes, he asked for only one change. In my last interview with him before that time, I had asked him if he intended to run for re-election in 1964. It was a rather unnecessary question, I admit, but nevertheless he had never answered it on the record. He looked at me with near annoyance, and said: "Of course I am." I quoted this sentence in my final chapter, and when he came to it, he looked up from his rocking chair and grinned, "Let's change that. I'd like to be the one who makes the announcement." He thought a moment, with his fist raised to his chin. "Let's make my answer, 'What do you think?' " he said. "Then go on with the rest of the sentence, 'Politically the country is closely divided, so it will be tough. But then everything is tough.' "

This book is not intended as an analysis. It is rather a journalist's narrative. As John Kennedy's New Frontier recedes into history, there will be more profound and more detailed accounts of his White House years that may alter the record, correct errors, find forces and reasons that did not seem to be there when I witnessed the events. But the facts have been recorded here to the best of my ability.

The reader will have to devise his own analysis. I have always felt that vital details—such as President Kennedy's immediate belief, when told of the existence of Russian missiles in Cuba, that the United States would have to send bombers to destroy the weapons (a fact hitherto unreported)—can tell more of the mood and mind of men than philosophical musing.

Nor is this a book about the late President's administration. Neither is it about the presidency. It is an account of John F. Kennedy, President, a more complete account than has been available before of what he thought, said and accomplished in his Oval Office as he worried over the terribly intricate problems of the world he cared so much about. There were certain areas and events of the administration that I could not and did not cover with the thoroughness I would have preferred, and these omissions are reflected in the book as a result of its personal nature and the circumstance that it was written in a relatively short time in a period of rapidly moving history.

I first met John F. Kennedy in a Senate elevator in 1958. From that moment on, covering him and his family (and the two were frequently indistinguishable) became my full-time job. I followed him through the precampaign period when he was gathering delegates for the 1960 Democratic convention. I watched him during the crucial primaries in Wisconsin and West Virginia. And I stood below him on the floor of the convention hall when he accepted his party's nomination in Los Angeles in July, 1960. I reported his successful national campaign, and the formation of his government. And when he moved into the White House in January, 1961, my assignment also shifted to 1600 Pennsylvania Avenue. I lived his life, traveling with him to meet heads of states, to Hyannis Port and Palm Beach, to Capitol Hill. My files contain more than a million words of research on John F. Kennedy.

I was with him in Dallas, Texas, on November 22, 1963.

The little spiral notebook I kept that day is a series of jumbled shorthand notes. *Motorcade—Main Street*. That was to remind me to write about the heavy crowd in downtown Dallas which had lined the streets four deep to cheer the President. The rest of the page is blank. The next entry says: *Triple underpass . . . The location of the shooting . . . Kennedy in head . . . Connally through chest . . . SS immediately surround Johnson . . . Jackie on top of Pres, slumped down.*

When I began to write the story on the press plane that afternoon as it sped back to Washington, it took me more than an hour to collect my senses and order my emotions. Those of us who had watched this man in Berlin, Vienna, Paris, New York, Chicago and hundreds of other cities could not quite believe that the last story we would file on John F. Kennedy, President, would be this. Like millions of Americans I was trying to hide from the enormity of what had happened. What now? Which way would the nation go? What would happen to Jacqueline Kennedy, Caroline and John, and Robert and Ethel Kennedy? And to all those others who had been so completely committed and dedicated to this president: Kenny O'Donnell, Ted Sorensen, Larry O'Brien, Ralph Dungan, Dave Powers and the rest? For six years I had lived the life of the 34th [1] President of the United States, and I suddenly realized that I had become more familiar with his routine and his habits than with those of my own brother. And I knew more about the history of his family than of my own.

When the President campaigned, he frequently gave his friends in the press corps a knowing glance or just the trace of a nod when eyes met. This was his private code for those who had traveled so long with him. And it was that way on November 22, first at a parking lot in Fort Worth, then at the airport fence in Dallas. Sometimes it would be a swallowed chuckle at what was going on around him. Sometimes it was a look that reflected sheer pleasure at the crowd's enthusiasm. Those visual messages were to remind us to be certain and note that

[1] There is still a debate as to whether John F. Kennedy was the 34th or 35th president. This arises because Grover Cleveland's two terms were not consecutive. Some historians record Cleveland twice; others just once. My feeling is that while John F. Kennedy had the 35th administration, he was the 34th president.

down. There had been both kinds of signals that day as he walked, back straight, hair blowing in the breeze, unfearing among his fellow Americans.

Correspondents, it has been said, have seen so much horror that shock does not come easily. But few correspondents who were there will ever forget that day.

I drove back to Washington from Andrews Air Force Base late that evening. The city looked very much as it had on my return from other trips. The shining dome of the Capitol, which always welcomed us home after a presidential journey, gleamed brilliantly. And the Washington Monument, bathed in floodlight, was the same symbol I had always seen through the windows of the Oval Office as I talked with the President in the evening. From the front drive, the bare limbs of the leafless elms were outlined against the White House, softly aglow after midnight. It was, as it always is, achingly beautiful. But it would be different now.

What will the historians write of John F. Kennedy, President? Was his term of office too short for him ever to receive the mantle of greatness? I do not know. Perhaps contemporary historians too often measure a chief executive's achievements by the numbers of bills passed in the Congress, by the enemies he destroyed, or by the appropriations he was granted. But what of the tendency in recent months toward a calmer world? What of the beginning of a rollback in the tide of communism? What of the strength of the nation itself, its growing ability to build prosperity and promote the cause of freedom throughout the world? And what of the renewed drive to heal the greatest national wound of all—racial discrimination: Progress came in fragments, accompanied by frustration and setbacks, with compromise and pain. But it is my belief that when he is viewed from that distance which scholars deem appropriate, John F. Kennedy will be high on the horizon of history.

ACKNOWLEDGMENTS

THIS book draws directly or indirectly on nearly six years of reporting John F. Kennedy and his family, so the list of all those kind persons who have helped me along the way would be too long to print.

But to them all, in a hundred cities across this land and overseas—Republicans, Democrats, government workers, and just private citizens—I say thanks, deeply and sincerely.

I owe, of course, incalculable gratitude to John F. Kennedy, who as senator, candidate and president took time to talk to me in many crucial moments. To his widow Jacqueline, his father, Joseph P. Kennedy, his brother and sister-in-law, Mr. and Mrs. Robert F. Kennedy, I also owe a special thank you.

Among those who worked for the President I know of no one who has not patiently, and even cheerfully, endured my persistent fact gathering. This group not only includes the immediate staff of the late President but the secretaries, who I am convinced at times really keep this government together; the men who arrange the planes and accommodations in our nomadic existence; the Secret Service; the pleasant White House switchboard operators; and those cheerful, efficient White House police officers.

Among the New Frontiersmen my relationship with Theodore C. Sorensen goes back the farthest and I owe him a special tribute for long years of frank, honest, intelligent and frequent counsel in the mystic art of presidential politics and function.

And to these others more of my thanks: Lawrence F. O'Brien, Ralph Dungan, Kenneth O'Donnell, Pierre Salinger, Maj. Gen. Chester V. Clifton, McGeorge Bundy, Fred Holborn, Arthur Schlesinger, Jr., Jerome B. Wiesner, Richard Donahue, Myer Feldman, Richard N. Goodwin, Lee C. White, Andrew T. Hatcher, Walt Whitman Rostow, David F. Powers, Timothy J. Reardon, Mrs. Evelyn N. Lincoln, Letitia Baldrige, Pamela Turnure, Walter Heller, David E. Bell, Edward C. Welsh, Capt. Tazewell Shepard, Brig. Gen. Godfrey McHugh, Henry Hall Wilson, Mike N. Manatos, Claude J. Desautels, Frederick G. Dutton, Mrs. Lorraine Pearce, Carl Kaysen, Samuel Belk, Michael Forrestal.

Others beyond the bounds of the White House, both in and out of government, who gave me special assistance include: Clark Clifford, Mr. and Mrs. Sargent Shriver, Gen. Bruce C. Clarke, ret., Senator Hubert Humphrey, John Seigenthaler, James Symington, Edwin O. Guthman, John Bailey, Charles Roche, Robert Manning, James Greenfield, Paul B. Fay, Donald Wilson, James Rowe.

To John Steele and Richard Clurman I owe much for their encouragement and help throughout this project. To my colleagues from whom I borrowed some facts a special bow: Neil MacNeil, Loye Miller, Burt Meyers, Mrs. Anne Chamberlin, Charles J. V. Murphy, Jerry Hannifin. The same to the two devoted ladies who sped the manuscript through their typewriters, Mrs. Pearl Carroll and Mrs. Mary Vreeland.

And to Simon Michael Bessie of Atheneum, my deep appreciation for being incurably optimistic, pleasant and helpful throughout this undertaking.

One final note: this revised edition contains an Author's Note and a final chapter written after the assassination of President Kennedy. The rest of the book was written before that and I have left it as it was.

CONTENTS

PICTURE SECTION

BY JAMES B. MAHAN

(following page 212)

JOHN F. KENNEDY, PRESIDENT

CHAPTER ONE

FORMING THE NEW
FRONTIER

THEY came streaming into Washington in January, 1963, the 534 living members of the 88th Congress (the 535th was elected after his death). The veterans, wise in the fraternal rituals, eased themselves back into their government-issue niches in society; the tenderfeet padded through the elegant streets of Georgetown and the comfortable Chevy Chase neighborhoods, looking for housing that would suit their $22,500 annual salaries.

The spectacle of the 88th in its throes of self-creation was new in detail, yet in form it was as old as the Republic. As each Congress becomes a full working body, each chamber is a hall of statesmen, every man's eyes glistening as the oratory soars—while in the back corridors there is the soft *splunk* of Kentucky bourbon into branch water and in the private hideaways, to which a startling portion of the Capitol is devoted, there is the splash of political blood. The law of the jungle applies there. And, of course, the mechanical systems which provide power, food, transportation and tons of paper, the very life juice of the organism, collapse at the first whack of the gavel.

The 88th was no different, even though it received the full midterm blessings of John F. Kennedy, 34th President of the United States of America, and a man often credited with possessing even more luck than that of the Irish.

The House Republicans canvassed and promptly threw out their aging Chairman of Conference, Charles B. Hoeven, 67, Presbyterian, Mason, Legionnaire—Iowa's own, cut down like a row of hybrid corn at harvest. In his place went Gerald R. Ford, Jr., 50, former football star at the University of Michigan, with two distinguished-service awards from the Jaycees.

In the House kitchen on opening day a caldron of bean soup upset in the conveyor, and for a panicky moment, the first time since Uncle Joe Cannon in 1904 demanded bean soup daily, the patrons of the House restaurant couldn't order bean soup (there were those who contended that the seven gallons already consumed were enough to waterlog the 88th for its duration).

The new electric-bell system in the Senate (full and correct name: electronic audio-visual legislative call system) befuddled its operator and he pressed the "vote" button when he should have pressed the "quorum call" button, and the senators poured forth, scared to death that they would fail to be registered on the very first action and the folks back home wouldn't understand.

Joseph C. Duke, Senate Sergeant-at-Arms, simply wilted from the strain of starting the session, and he was carted off to Doctors' Hospital. And Maryland's Senator Glenn Beall, standing on the Senate floor in full fury, demanded that the puny crabcakes served in the Senate Dining Room no longer be called Maryland Crabcakes. "Patrons of our dinning room should be protected from deception. . . . I want the world to know that those crabcakes are not Maryland crabcakes." (It was a bad start in the congressional kitchens.)

Amid this Gilbert and Sullivan atmosphere, John Kennedy went to the Hill. On January 14, 1963, he delivered his third State of the Union message to the Congress. It injected a sense of order, it gave the Congress a reason for being there. As Kennedy viewed it, the State of the Union in the next two years and beyond would depend more than ever on the Congress.

The President left the southeast gate of the White House a little past noon. A fleet of motorcycle police formed a raucous wedge up Independence Avenue, and the strung-out caravan of black Cadillacs and Mercurys took only seven minutes for the trip to the Hill. In the deep cushions of his limousine Kennedy rode with his wife, Jacqueline.

Two years ago, as a new president, he had taken the trip in the same car, and he had fallen into silence, reading and re-reading the phrases of his speech, typed, like pages from a primer, in huge reading letters. Jackie had also been with him then, but so had Theodore C. Sorensen, with a shiny New Frontier title of Special Counsel to the President, but still an adviser and speech writer, the veteran of eight Kennedy years in the Senate; and Lawrence F. O'Brien, a Kennedy political expert, vintage 1952, new caretaker of the Kennedy legislative program.

In January, 1963, Kennedy rode with more confidence in himself and the men around him, confidence born of two years of crisis. The message he carried in a leather folder on his lap would reflect it.

The big car scarcely slowed as it turned sharply over the sidewalk at the House wing of the Capitol and pulled up to the side. (Two years earlier the curbs had been piled with snow left over from the Inauguration Day blizzard and cold had lashed the Capitol Plaza. Now, there was no snow and the sun warmed the earth to springlike temperatures.)

He had been, on his first journey to the Hill, overly self-conscious. He had stepped out of his car and been swept into the building down a corridor past the House Dining Room, where he looked in and felt obliged to wave at the congress-men having coffee. He had met House Speaker Sam Rayburn in his office and hesitated. But Rayburn had known. He had gestured him to his own desk in the Speaker's office, and for a few minutes, as they awaited the summons to go into the House Chamber, Kennedy had worked at his speech.

The route was familiar this time: up in the small elevator and on around the Chamber to the Speaker's office, now the preserve of John W. McCormack of Massachusetts.

If a man who has been elected president does not quite seem to achieve the presidential image in the earlier occasions of his office taking, his appearance before a joint session of Congress washes away the final traces of the outside world. It had, for Kennedy in 1961. There is, perhaps, nothing more governmental in appearance than the Senate and House meeting together, particularly when a president comes to as-sess the state of the Union. The scene is indelible: the two great legislative bodies flow together and their outlines blur, and suddenly they become Congress; and added to this are the Cabinet, the foreign diplomatic corps, the Supreme Court, the military Chiefs of Staff and so many visitors in the galleries that they must stand, scarcely breathing, along the walls and must sit on the steps. By 1963 the scene had become familiar to the New Frontier, but it was still impressive, a reminder of this nation's government.

The floor of the House chamber was a pool of muted grays, blues and blacks as the legislators swarmed in to take their places. There were splatters of sharper colors here and there, where the few women members sat. There was, of course, the announced and regimented entry of the other high officers.

And then Jackie Kennedy came cautiously down the steps in the Executive Gallery. She smiled warmly as she paused for a moment at her seat on the aisle of the front row, to acknowledge the tribute from below and around her. Every man and woman had risen and applauded when she entered.

From doorkeeper William (Fishbait) Miller then came the expected, the practiced but still stirring cry, "Mistah Speakah, the President of the United States."

Two years previously John Kennedy had tried to look as solemn as a 43-year-old man can look. He had not been quite successful. Whether in sheer pleasure from the moment or whether in plain amusement at seeing his former colleagues stand and applaud him as president, he had smiled as he walked down the aisle. Now his nature had grown more somber. The lines around his eyes had deepened, erasing some of his youthful look.

He gave a special nod to his old friends, but his eyes did not meet those of his brothers, Robert Francis Kennedy in the front row with the Cabinet, Edward Moore Kennedy at the side and near the back with the senators. In 1961 Bob Kennedy had felt so self-conscious sitting between Secretary of Defense Robert McNamara and Postmaster General J. Edward Day that he had scarcely looked up and had applauded his brother ever so lightly. He seemed to feel a part of the ceremonies now. Those who watched the scene paid more attention to the new Senator Kennedy. Bob Kennedy and his older brother were a familiar part of the landscape.

The four giant klieg lights for the TV cameras blazed from the corners, and the President for the moment looked more like a movie idol playing the climactic role in a Hollywood spectacular than the leader of the free world. But it was all real. In his left hand Kennedy carried his message, the corners of its pages protruding from the folder.

In January of 1961 he had brought everyone to earth within a few minutes with a sobering appraisal of the deep international trouble that faced this nation. It is doubtful that anyone who had been in the chamber at that time realized just how chillingly accurate his address would prove.

But now he talked in a quieter world. The focus of his message was on the need for tax reduction and reform to unfetter the economy and spark new growth, so that idle plants would again produce, the unemployed ranks would dwindle, profits and wages would swell and our wealth and our will, the very preservatives of freedom in the world, would not begin to rot away.

"I can report to you," he told the Congress, "that the state of this old but youthful Union is good." (The words of 1961 had been: "Before my term has ended we shall have to test anew whether a nation organized and governed such as ours can endure. The outcome is by no means certain.") "But we cannot be satisfied to rest here. This is the side of the hill, not the top. . . . To achieve these greater gains, one step, above all, is essential—the enactment this year of a substantial reduction and revision in federal income taxes." (In his first message, though he had found the economy "disturbing," he had made only one fleeting reference to taxes.)

Slowly, precisely, Kennedy read his program: A cut in tax rates across the board that would reduce taxes by $13.5 billion a year when fully in effect in three years. Reforms in the tax code which, by closing loopholes and shifting inequities, would reclaim $3.5 billion annually.

Congress was cool, but then from the start it had never given Kennedy ecstatic endorsement. For two years he had argued and pressured and pleaded. He had made progress, but not as much as he wanted or even as much as many expected him to make.

"Turning to the world outside," he continued. ". . . In

these past months we have reaffirmed the scientific and military superiority of freedom. We have doubled our efforts in space, to assure us of being first in the future. We have undertaken the most far-reaching defense improvements in the peacetime history of this country, and we have maintained the frontiers of freedom from Vietnam to West Berlin. . . ."

Listen, now, to the younger President, inheriting the legacy of freedom in 1961: "I feel I must inform the Congress that our analyses over the last ten days make it clear that—in each of the principal areas of crisis—the tide of events has been running out and time has not been our friend. . . ." As he spoke, his jaw had thrust out; he had chopped the air with his impulsive right hand. His voice grew slightly hoarse.

Now he spoke with more calm and more sense of the full meaning behind his message. That jabbing right hand was somewhat less evident and his right forefinger, which had drilled at every page in 1961, thumped down less often. His seminar had been hard.

"I think these are proud and memorable days in the cause of peace and freedom," he said.

(Two years ago, in the rear of the Chamber, a cluster of Kennedy's assistants—Arthur M. Schlesinger, Jr., Harvard historian turned White House aide; Budget Director David E. Bell; Deputy Special Counsel Myer Feldman; Presidential Assistant Ralph A. Dungan—had attracted the attention of a Republican, who had spoken caustically: "All they need now is Eleanor Roosevelt to be den mother." Now, the assistants were inconspicuous among the congressmen; and Mrs. Eleanor Roosevelt, to the sorrow of the nation, was dead.)

"My friends, I close on a note of hope," the President said. "We are not lulled by the momentary calm of the sea or the somewhat clearer skies above. We know the turbulence that lies below and the storms that are beyond the horizon this year. But now the winds of change appear to be blowing more strongly than ever, in the world of communism as well as our own. For 175 years we have sailed with those winds at our back, and with the tides of human freedom in our favor. We steer our ship with hope, as Thomas Jefferson said, 'leaving fear astern.'

"Today we still welcome those winds of change—and we have every reason to believe that our tide is running strong. With thanks to Almighty God for seeing us through a perilous passage, we ask his help anew in guiding the 'Good Ship Union.' "

He hurried back to the White House while the wires of the news services clacked out the prosaic facts of tax reduction and the words of hope, somehow not as arresting as the words of warning of January, 1961: "Our problems are critical. The tide is unfavorable. The news will be worse before it is better. And while hoping and working for the best, we should prepare ourselves for the worst. . . ."

The Kennedy voice had held all attention then. His phrases had rolled into a stilled Chamber. They had been, as always, Kennedy phrases. He had sat by the hour going over the drafts of his 1961 message, retooling the sentences, simplifying the images. It was Kennedy who had added the blackest bits. On the Sunday before he had given it he had slumped in his chair in the mansion and furrowed his brow. He had wondered to his new Secretary of State Dean Rusk and to Sorensen what else needed to go into the talk which they had reviewed. He had been silent, then added, ". . . the tide of events has been running out . . ." And again he penciled on the sheets: "The news will be worse before it is better." (Later John Kennedy was to explain why he had so shaped his message. "Nobody knew what the missile age meant. All other estimates of our power had been based on old weapons, old ideas of our superiority. But now they could kill us as well as we could kill them.")

The New Frontier in January of 1961 had already become schizophrenic. Kennedy had accurately sketched the months that lay immediately ahead. But the joy of life in possessing the White House ran too deep for its new occupants to really sense how true his words would become.

For ten and a half weeks the Democratic blood had been rising. In that time John Kennedy formed his government. It was a gurgling infusion of life that was marshaled sometimes on a Georgetown doorstep, sometimes on the palm-lined patio of a cream stucco villa in Palm Beach that looks out to the Atlantic Ocean, and sometimes on the thick carpeting of the thirty-fourth-floor penthouse of New York's Carlyle Hotel, with its wall of glass through which the occupants could look south the length of Madison Avenue.

In the incandescent acres of New York, all turned to peer at that penthouse when the President-elect of the United States of America was in residence. In the vast complex of federal buildings that sprawls beside the Potomac bureaucrats broke out in triplicate goose pimples every time the young owner of 3301 N Street, N.W., stepped out on his frigid doorstep to talk to newsmen. In every foreign capital the men in power watched anxiously when Kennedy, in a knit sports shirt and khaki pants, scuffed along the Florida beach and squinted out beyond the gentle swells of the blue-green ocean.

If Kennedy was not nervous, the country was. It knew him, yet it did not know him. It wanted him, yet it did not want him. The official margin of victory over Richard Nixon was 112,881 votes out of a grand total of 68,838,565—certainly not that unwavering trumpet blast that the Kennedys had expected.

Those who watched John Kennedy in these days felt that perhaps he was the first man in this nation's history to train for the presidency from the cradle. This was not a conscious feeling or spoken by any of the participants in Kennedy's early years. The death of an older brother who was the favored contender for political glory and the near-death of Kennedy himself are elements in the story that cloud it. But there burned within the Kennedy family something that would not stop until one of its members established himself as the first citizen of the land. John Kennedy, while still in short pants, gazed on Plymouth Rock. Later, he was the only fourteen-year-old boy at Choate School to digest *The New York Times* each morning with breakfast. He consumed the vital history books of our civilization. He watched the main actors on the world stage from inside his father's house, which often was near center. With his father's millions behind him he had few duties but those of self-improvement. He traveled the globe, he went through Harvard, he fought bravely in the war, he ran successfully for Congress and then for the Senate and, naturally, he became president.

"No other president in history has been as well prepared for the job," said his father, Joseph P. Kennedy, matter-of-factly one evening in his New York office.

His son possessed a confidence equal to the tribute. In mid-December John Kennedy sat in his Georgetown drawing room before a glowing hearth and looked ahead. "Sure," he said, "it's a big job. But I don't know anybody who can do it any better than I can. I'm going to be in it for four years. . . . It isn't going to be so bad. You've got time to think. You don't have all those people bothering you that you had in the Senate—besides, the pay is pretty good."

The building of a government is a pageant which comes with the regularity but fortunately not the frequency of the seasons. In the two and a half months between election and inauguration, the President-elect sifted through the human resources of this nation. It was a frenzied time, filled with speculation and anticipation and the wonderful flow of the story in the newspapers. There was joy for those who wanted the call and then heard it. There was disappointment for many of the faithful who couldn't be used the way they thought they deserved to be. The people jammed the corridors and tiny waiting rooms of the Democratic National Committee, and those who were anointed traveled to Georgetown where the President-elect wanted to see them. His home had become the seat of the embryonic administration.

Cabinet making came first. In the days after his victory Kennedy called some of his top advisers together, this time in the Palm Beach mansion of his father, where the President-elect had gone for a brief rest.

They sat in the sun around the swimming pool, played nine holes of golf and had dinner, and then Kennedy led a small band into a first-floor bedroom for a long night's work. Kennedy piled up pillows against the bed's headboard, settled back on them, his legs stretched out over the covers. The others ringed chairs around the bed. Kennedy glanced around him at the men who had scarcely had time for a good gasp of air before beginning the new task.

Naturally the family was represented. There was brother-in-law Robert Sargent Shriver, tough, dedicated and tireless, now one of the chief recruiters for the new administration. There was shrewd, calm Larry O'Brien who in the campaign months had talked soothingly to the grassroot politicians; who had fretted about "getting out the vote." Also, there was Clark Clifford, a relative newcomer to the inner circle. He had been Harry Truman's White House counsel. He had been Senator Stuart Symington's friend and closest adviser when Symington sought the nomination which Kennedy won. He had also been John Kennedy's attorney when the senator, angered by Columnist Drew Pearson's television charge that he had not written his Pulitzer Prize-winning book, *Profiles in Courage,* forced a network correction of the statement. So skillfully had Clifford handled the matter that Kennedy never forgot his talent. Shortly after receiving the nomination Kennedy had phoned Clifford. "If the people elect me as president," he had said, "I don't want to wake up the morning after the election and say, 'What do I do now?' " He asked Clifford to prepare a blueprint for taking over the government. On election day Clifford was putting the finishing touches on the report, and that night Kennedy had phoned. "Better send that up here," said the President-elect. "It looks like we've won."

The fifty-page memorandum now lay on the bed beside Kennedy. The President-elect spoke seriously but, as he does so often, with a point of humor sticking through. "I want to get the best men I can for these Cabinet jobs," he said. "I don't care if they are Democrats, Republicans or Igorots."

The meeting lasted four hours, a warning of the work ahead. At 1 A.M. the President-elect sighed wearily, a bit discouraged after considering and rejecting dozens of names for the Cabinet. "At least," he said, "I thought this part of being president was going to be fun."

Not many days later there was another meeting in the Kennedy Palm Beach home. It began in the library, then shifted to the poolside. There were three men—Kennedy, Allen Dulles, head of the Central Intelligence Agency, and Richard Bissell, Jr., one of Dulles' deputies. On November 18 John Kennedy learned about the plans for training Cuban exiles for possible action against Fidel Castro. Dulles and Bissell, with charts and papers, poured out the details to a surprised Kennedy. This was the first time he learned that this government was giving military training to Cuban refugees.[1]

Kennedy found both Republicans and Democrats for his Cabinet. The appointments were announced from the deep-freeze front doorstoop in Georgetown. Icicles clung to the genteelly sagging eaves of the red brick house. From the snow-banked street the nation watched through TV eyes as the President-elect ducked in and out, his breath forming white steam clouds. One by one he selected his men—men from industry, from labor, from politics and, of course, from the family. The icicles did not melt. Georgetown and Washington were in the heart of one of the worst winters of the century. Sometimes, when the sun shone, the crystal drops of water splashed on the shoulders of the men below. But the cold stayed.

Inside the Kennedy house things were cozy. There was the constant gurgle of hot coffee and tea. Wood fires cast their warming flicker across the rooms. Scarcely an hour went by without a new person's arriving. For those Kennedy did not want identified there was an alley entrance at the rear, and many of the interviewees were spirited in that way.

Out front, the growing collection of newsmen shuffled and stamped on the sidewalk to keep warm. NBC rented a complete house across the street. William H. Lawrence, of *The New York Times,* dug up a huge sheepskin coat and lamb's wool hat which he had purchased while on assignment in Bulgaria. With the astrakhan jammed to his ears and the coat at ankle length he could battle the ten-degree blasts. Kennedy once pointed at the correspondent in his weird attire and announced: "He is from Tass."

Though the vigil for the news of government making had been cold, it had been rewarding. A government hierarchy was formed. And it was formed under the singular circumstances of seeking ability first, then political loyalty. If the

[1] In his book, *Six Crises,* published in the spring of 1962, Richard Nixon accused Kennedy of having been told of the Cuban invasion plans in the courtesy intelligence briefings Kennedy received as a candidate, then using this privileged information in planning his criticism of Nixon's own Cuban stand. Dulles then publicly stated that he had not told Kennedy of Cuban plans until November 18, 1960. He also said that he felt the Nixon statement was the result of a misunderstanding.

WINGATE COLLEGE LIBRARY
WINGATE, N. C.

two were happily combined, it was a double bull's-eye; but such was not always the case.

Luther H. Hodges, the Kennedy nominee for Secretary of Commerce, with his white hair and twinkly eyes looked and acted like (and was) a grandfather. Stewart L. Udall, the Arizona congressman with a crew cut, the man who had stolen the Arizona delegation for Kennedy while the sedentary opposition scoffed at the idea, was nominated for Secretary of the Interior.

In mid-December the Ford Motor Company gave up Robert S. McNamara, its president of one month. The McNamara announcement on the Georgetown doorstoop was right out of a Ford plant. A Mark V Lincoln Continental crunched through the snow to the curb. The hatless McNamara jumped out. His black shoes were flawlessly shined. Each hair on his head seemed to have been plastered by a pattern, so that none was out of line. McNamara stepped into the Kennedy drawing room, leaving behind him an aide in his car, motor running, car phone open to the Ford Washington office, which, in turn, had a phone open to Ford in Detroit, which was to relay the McNamara acceptance of a New Frontier job to his wife in Ann Arbor.

In contrast was the long agony of the President-elect's own brother, Robert F. Kennedy, in making up his mind to accept the nomination of Attorney General.

"Bobby's the best man I can get," muttered John Kennedy one day riding up Pennsylvania Avenue to the Capitol. "But that family criticism is the most sensitive there is. We'll see."

For two weeks Bob Kennedy had agonized over the job. "This is kind of a turning point in my life," he told a friend. "I've got to decide what I'm going to do."

In a sense Robert Kennedy had worked for his brother all his life. As Senator John McClellan's chief rackets investigator, he had helped further brother Jack's presidential ambitions almost as much as he had enhanced his own reputation. Done with that, Bob became the master strategist for the Kennedy conquest of the Democratic nomination. Then the younger Kennedy moved in as campaign manager for the nominee. Always, it seemed, the shadow of Jack Kennedy covered Bob.

The situation did not bother Joe Kennedy. Kibitzing from New York, he thought the hesitation ridiculous. "Now if Bobby will just go ahead, we'll really be in good shape," he said.

Joe Kennedy was, in fact, probably as responsible as anyone else that Bob Kennedy eventually became Attorney General. Not only did the father think that Bob should be near the new President but he felt Bob had earned the job by helping his brother win the election. When at first the Kennedy brothers were reluctant to consider the appointment, it was Joe Kennedy who kept the pressure on.

On one December Tuesday, Bob had decided to accept, but he still worried. Head down, he walked the wintry streets, first to visit retiring Attorney General Bill Rogers. For half an hour they discussed the job. Bob dropped by to see his friend J. Edgar Hoover, head of the FBI. This old warrior felt that the war on crime was languishing and that there was a lot the new administration could do.

Eleven blocks further on he sat down for lunch with Supreme Court Justice William O. Douglas, with whom he had traveled through Russia in 1955. They talked about all the possibilities: the Massachusetts governorship, the Senate, the Attorney General's job, Bob's moving to Maryland in hopes of positioning himself for elective office. Douglas did not like the idea of the Cabinet appointment.

Next day Bob Kennedy phoned his brother that he had decided against the job. Jack Kennedy wouldn't take that answer and insisted on having breakfast with him the following morning. Seventy minutes over grapefruit, eggs and coffee changed the scene. Bob Kennedy accepted.

At week's end the announcement came, but not before some Kennedy wit. From his shabby, green-carpeted office at Democratic National Committee headquarters, the younger brother called the elder just a few hours before the announcement was to be made. "When you make the announcement," he chuckled, "why don't you say, 'I know he is my brother, but I need him.' " [2]

[2] In June, 1958, when Eisenhower's assistant, Sherman Adams, was accused of improperly accepting favors from Boston industrialist Bernard Goldfine, Ike defended Adams in a press conference. "I personally like Governor Adams. I admire his abilities. I respect him because of his personal and offi-

The Kennedy team was becoming immensely pleased with itself. It occasionally stepped back to view its handiwork.

Ted Sorensen glowed over the Kennedy Cabinet. "There are two things about this Cabinet," he said. "First, these men are all sacrificing to come to Washington. They are coming because they feel the same way as John Kennedy, that the country needs to move again. Second, they are all innovators in one way or another. Though they may be cautious and careful, they are not afraid to try new things. Hodges demonstrated it in North Carolina when he was governor. Dean Rusk wasn't afraid to express other views when everybody was oriented toward Europe in foreign policy. McNamara showed it with the Falcon." [3]

When John Kennedy sorted through his list of possibilities for Secretary of State, considered by the pundits of the press to be the most important of the Cabinet posts, he brushed aside, after a period of inner struggle, Arkansas' prosegregationist Senator J. William Fulbright, former French and German Ambassador David K. E. Bruce and the two-time presidential loser Adlai Stevenson. One name continued to shine as the Kennedys viewed it from a thousand angles. It was that of Dean Rusk, President of the Rockefeller Foundation. For days it was only a name, as they poked and prodded to find the weaknesses. But the name, which had first been recommended by former Secretary of State Dean Acheson and former Secretary of Defense Robert A. Lovett, endured. Kennedy called Rusk to his Georgetown home for a view in the flesh.

The meeting was brief and Kennedy talked only in general terms about foreign relations, never hinting that he wanted to offer Rusk the job as Secretary of State. When the half-hour was up, Rusk ducked out, convinced he was not in the running. To reporters who saw him hurry away that day he looked bewildered, Kennedy looked embarrassed. Rusk

---

cial integrity. I need him. Admitting the lack of that careful prudence in this incident . . . I believe with my whole heart that he is an invaluable public servant doing a difficult job efficiently, honestly and tirelessly."

[3] While an executive at the Ford Motor Company, McNamara played an important role in bringing out the highly successful Falcon, Ford's compact car. Though he did not originate the idea, he is credited by Henry Ford II, chairman of the board, with handling the "Falcon project" from its infancy.

was put far down on the list of possibilities for Secretary of State.

But he was the man. Son of a poor Georgia cotton farmer, he had become a Rhodes scholar, a political-science professor at California's Mills College. During World War II he had served in the wartime General Staff Office, moved with George Marshall into the State Department as a key aide, helped design the Japanese peace treaty, played a part in bringing NATO and the Marshall Plan to life. John Kennedy studied him and his record closely and decided he liked what he saw. On a Saturday night he put in a call to the Rusk home in Scarsdale, New York, and told the balding scholar that he wanted him for Secretary of State. With a battered suitcase, Dean Rusk next day boarded a plane bound for Florida. By Monday he was headed for a new life.

There was dissent about the Cabinet. But it was generally mild. A Democrat who once had been in the administration of Franklin D. Roosevelt watched in fascination. The flamboyant memories of F.D.R. still lingered. "They're a conservative bunch," he observed about the new Cabinet men. "Too much for me. They seem like good organization men —modern men. They are not a very colorful group. I liked the colorful boys. We'll have to get our color up on Capitol Hill."

Still, even this man could not squelch a deeply felt bit of praise for the way John Kennedy had worked at Cabinet making. "On the whole, though," he added, almost admitting that some of his thoughts were from a different era, "it's a pretty good Cabinet. They are world-oriented men, competent technicians."

At a dinner party a Washington hostess, who had apprehensively watched John Kennedy make out her social register for the next four years, leaned close to Clark Clifford and admitted, "This Cabinet sure doesn't have much glamour."

Clifford, still helping Kennedy make the selections, replied that this was exactly the way he preferred it. "I don't want any mercurial, flashy, brilliant men in there," he said. "I want men who can make things run right, men who can carry out the orders of the boss."

Task forces had been assigned to virtually every major

domestic and foreign problem Kennedy would face. Their missions were to come up with recommendations for policies and programs. But while the task forces, many of them drawing their brain power from the universities of the country, labored in silence, the great manhunt went on.

It was a methodical, exhaustive search. Sarge Shriver and Larry O'Brien were the nominal heads. But every man close to Kennedy worked at it as well—Bob Kennedy, Ralph Dungan, Press Secretary Pierre E. G. Salinger, Ted Sorensen.

For the impatient newsmen, the job of forming a Cabinet seemed to lag. It was because Kennedy spared no effort in finding out about his prospects. Eight years before, when Dwight Eisenhower was going through the same process, there had been less deliberation. Some of the Cabinet prospects were holdovers from Thomas E. Dewey's unfulfilled White House dreams. It was a Cabinet dictated largely by the Republican party, which was separate from Dwight Eisenhower. Contrarily, John Kennedy *was* the Democratic party.

When the Kennedy scouts scoured the archives for notes on David Bell, proposed for Budget Director, they made contact as far away as Pakistan, where Bell had served for four years as an economic adviser.

Dean Rusk's lectures, his memorandums, his written articles were collected by Shriver and brought around to the Kennedy Georgetown drawing room. The President-elect, a great admirer of writing style, read them all.

McNamara's Republican name had recurred in the Kennedy files since the summer before the election. Shriver had hoped to get him on his group of businessmen-for-Kennedy, but he had not succeeded. He had not forgotten the name, however.

One of the most satisfying characteristics Kennedy found in McNamara was his unhesitating decision to give up his Ford job, thus to forego in the next years some three to four million dollars of profits. Each question Kennedy asked got a precise answer. "McNamara was decisive and incisive," said Sarge Shriver. "That's what Jack liked."

Few of the grave and complex defense questions were brought up in detail. Kennedy was taking the measure of the man. The McNamara outlook and manner were more important. The greatest need in the Pentagon, as Kennedy viewed it, was to straighten out the organizational mess, to get it running efficiently. The broad defense policy questions were to be decided in the White House.

McNamara did not hesitate on the time he promised to spend in Washington. He wanted to come for four years, for six, for eight, whatever Kennedy said. And finally McNamara clinched his appointment when Bob Kennedy cautiously suggested that there were perfectly proper ways for a man who must divest himself of great amounts of stock to keep it in the family. McNamara said no, flatly. He said he would not feel right about it, nor would Ford. He would come to Washington without his Ford holdings.

Not every interview went this way, however. From Missouri came Fred V. Heinkel, president of the militant Missouri Farmers Union, and high on the Kennedy list of prospects for Secretary of Agriculture. For this post Kennedy wanted a man who understood the vexing surplus problem and would have the guts to try to solve it. Heinkel proved in twenty short minutes not to be that man. At first Jack Kennedy questioned him and decided that he did not have the right answers to the farm problem. Unbelieving, the President-elect left the room, asked Bob Kennedy to go in and see. Bob Kennedy asked the fundamental questions. How could surplus crops now in storage and costing this government a million dollars a day to store be cut down? Heinkel logically suggested that more of them be sent overseas. But what about the foreign markets, our allies, what effect would such action have on world prices? Heinkel admitted he had no answer for this but felt that surely somebody in the Agriculture Department could solve that end of it. Suddenly Minnesota's Governor Orville Freeman went way up on the Kennedy tote board for Secretary of Agriculture. Freeman was no farm expert. But he was a hard-working man who perhaps would make more sense than the farm experts. In two days Freeman had been summoned to Washington on a special plane and given the Kennedy anointment under the Georgetown porch light at 7 P.M.

While the hard core around Kennedy labored over the

prospective members of the New Frontier, there was little time to let the excitement of the coming January creep in. But when the Cabinet was formed, much of the tension drained away and the frantic movement of the Kennedyites slowed. Then, the thought of the inheritance that was to be theirs on January 20 began to dawn on them.

Sometimes late at night in the Mayflower Hotel's Rib Room, just a block and a half from Democratic National Committee headquarters, they would talk about it over roast beef.

Sometimes in Billy Martin's Carriage House, a Georgetown restaurant, just two blocks up N Street from the Kennedy home, the dreams of the New Frontier would be exchanged over lunch.

And one evening in early December, as winter darkness came on, Joseph P. Kennedy, 72, the father of the President-elect of the United States, put on his black homburg and left his unobtrusive ninth-floor office in the Grand Central Building that looks north up New York's Park Avenue.

He walked unnoticed the block and a half to the grimy 277 Park Avenue apartment house, wound his way through the damp walkways that border the inside court to House Number 10, and then quietly he went to his apartment on the eighth floor.

On this day Joe Kennedy, who over fifty long years of economic combat had amassed a fortune said to be more than $250 million, was more mellow than his Wall Street competitors had ever given him credit for being. His mind was on January 20, when his second son would be sworn in as the 34th President of this republic. Not since Ulysses Grant had a president entered office with both of his parents living. Not since John Quincy Adams had there been one with a more influential living father.

Joe Kennedy marched across the green carpeting of his apartment, a place of such limited size and modest furnishings that one would hardly expect the possessor to be a man who owned vast amounts of the world's real estate. He rummaged in his closet and soon came out with what he sought. Then Joe Kennedy slipped on his long tails and then his cutaway coat. He had not had them on for twenty-two years, since he had left his post in London as this nation's ambassador to Britain. He gave a satisfied glance at himself in the mirror—no alterations were necessary. To himself he checked over the schedule. He would wear the cutaway for the inauguration, probably wear the tails for the big inaugural balls. However, he would reserve judgment on that. If the other men did not wear tails, he certainly was not going to. At this moment in his life Joe Kennedy, his face a healthy pink, his eyes with much of the same old flash in them, stood six feet tall and weighed just 188 pounds, the same as he had in 1921 when he checked himself out in Hot Springs.

He had been an elusive man, Joe Kennedy. Throughout the campaign for the presidency he had remained in the background. Not even when Kennedy stood in the fading light of a Los Angeles evening and told the Democratic faithful in the Coliseum that he would carry their banner to victory had Joe Kennedy been present. He had flown from the seclusion of the rented home of Marion Davies to New York.

Joe Kennedy had edged out into public view a bit more since the victory. The critics howled at the sight of him. Indeed, they said, Joe was the real brains and power behind the new president, Joe would sit in his home in Hyannis Port, Massachusetts, or Palm Beach, Florida, or Antibes, France, and pull the strings.

But the critics, at least for the moment, were wrong. Joe Kennedy was allowing himself the rare privilege of fatherly pride.

Over the phone one day he said to me: "Hell, I don't know how it feels to be the father of a president. These people all ask me. I get letters saying how proud I must be. Of course I am. But I don't feel any different. I don't know how it feels."

The bluff didn't work. In that dim little office of his he sat late one evening, talking. He was soon to go to dinner at the new restaurant, The Forum of the Twelve Caesars. But just for a few minutes he felt something.

"Jack doesn't belong any more to just a family. He belongs to the country. That's probably the saddest thing about all this. The family can be there. But there is not much they can do sometimes for the President of the United States.

"I am more aware now than I've ever been of the terrific

problems that this country faces," the Kennedy patriarch continued, thinking back over his days with Franklin Roosevelt's New Deal. "In 1932 we only faced an economic problem. Now we face an economic problem, a farm problem, a defense problem—there isn't one phase of government that isn't faced with an immense problem."

He told his son that all the time, Joe recalled. "I'd say, 'In your pursuit of this job you will be aware of the fact the problems now are the most difficult ever seen.' Do you know his answer to me? He'd say, 'Dad, for two thousand years every generation, or most generations, have been faced with the most terrible problems ever seen. They all have been solved by humans with God's help. If they can do it, why can't we?' "

He had failed, said Joe Kennedy, in the only assignment that the President-elect had given him so far. That was to take a month and come up with the ideal name for Secretary of the Treasury. "When Jack called and asked me to give him the name, I said, 'I can't.'

"My life won't change much," he mused, glancing out over the darkening city. "I have the notion I'd like to go abroad and stay a little longer than I should—but probably not."

He had resigned himself with mock grumpiness to running the Kennedy fortune. "I have to. There's not a member of the family interested in the business. None of them have done anything here for three years. . . . Business doesn't interest me either, that's for sure. I don't give a tinker's damn about it."

His son was the interest right then, and he turned the conversation back to him. "As a nation we have become too soft. Jack's right. We have got to get moving. Jack understands this. If we lose the brass ring this time, we are never going to get another chance at it. Jack is the fellow who will give his life to this country."

Looking across his battered old desk with the black leather top, his mind drifted a bit. "Jack still writes a letter to his mother about the same way he wrote at Choate. And when he comes over to use the apartment, he still takes my socks if I happen to have some new ones around."

Whenever he could, Joe Kennedy watched the New Frontier progress on TV. One day when the President-elect went to see Eisenhower, Joe sat before the screen with Charles F. Spalding, an old-time friend of Jack Kennedy's. As he watched, Joe Kennedy was silent. Finally he turned to Spaulding and said, "He really looks more like a president every day."

The Kennedy style was becoming evident. And there was no more interesting exercise than assault on the unlikely person of John J. Rooney, a short, balding congressman from Brooklyn. This man was chairman of the appropriations subcommittee for the departments of State, Justice, the Judiciary and related agencies. Rooney was the scourge of diplomats, the terror of the United States Information Agency. He alone, almost, decided if they got their budgets. And he had an uncanny knack of finding misspent funds. He once referred to the skimpy entertainment allowances of our diplomats as "booze allowances." His objective was to keep them down.

The President-elect knew a little about diplomatic life. He had spent the crucial years beside his father in the United States embassy in London. In his youthful Continental wanderings he was lodged and fed at the embassies because of his father's standing in the fraternity.

As Kennedy stumped his way around this nation seeking votes, he seldom missed a chance to cry for reform in the diplomatic machinery. His main plea was to replace mediocre and bad diplomats with men chosen only for their ability, not for their contributions to the party, a system long used by both political parties. To do this Jack Kennedy realized— as does everyone who has been confronted by this problem— he would have to see to it that the nonmillionaires sent to major foreign embassies could get increased allowances.

It cost the diplomats who went to the large embassies as much as $100,000 annually out of their pockets to run them properly. Kennedy did not oppose letting the wealthy men pay. But he did oppose the idea of having to assign wealthy men to these jobs.

He already had promised John Kenneth Galbraith, a Harvard economics professor, the ambassadorship to India. He was considering Charles E. (Chip) Bohlen, a career diplomat, as the man for Paris. Neither had a fortune.

But there loomed immediately on the horizon of the New Frontier an obstacle—John J. Rooney.

Just a few days before Christmas, Rooney came puffing back to Brooklyn from an "inspection trip" of Latin American embassies, and his phone was ringing. It was the Vice President-elect, Lyndon B. Johnson. "John," came that familiar drawl, "the President-elect would like to see you down in Palm Beach next week. Can you make it?" Of course Rooney could.

Lyndon reported back to his boss that Rooney would be there on schedule. As a cover for this venture, Kennedy and Johnson planned to bring in Oklahoma's Senator Robert S. Kerr, soon to take Lyndon's place as chairman of the Senate Astronautics and Space Committee. The excuse for the meeting would be space. From nearby Hobe Sound, Doug Dillon was summoned to add more prestige.

Rooney arrived in his gray fedora and black suit. He put up at the Palm Beach Towers Hotel, as all the visitors and staff did during these southern missions. Apparently Rooney's own booze allowance was adequate. He immediately sought out the Keyboard Lounge, the hotel's bar, and informed the journalists who wanted to listen that his opinion of the State Department had not gone up. His lecture lasted until 4 A.M.

Next morning one of Kennedy's prettiest secretaries met the Brooklyn congressman at the hotel and drove him out to the Kennedy villa shortly before lunch. He walked admiringly beside the attractive girl as she went through the huge oak doors, down the long arcade lined with poinsettia plants and across the patio where the news conferences were being held. She pointed out these landmarks to Rooney as she went. Since there were no Kennedys in sight, the girl guide hurried off to find at least one. Rooney sat a little stiffly in the library alone, but soon Douglas Dillon arrived and then Lyndon Johnson, and Bob Kerr thundered into town on Lyndon's Convair, the "Lucy B.," named for his eldest daughter.

When the President-elect arrived, the men talked business, lunched, then moved to the living room, still inundated with charming Christmas debris—a new glistening leather saddle was under the tree, stockings embroidered "Grandpa," "Grandma," "Mommie," "Daddy," "Caroline," and "Miss Shaw" still hung over the fireplace. The great windows on the back of the house looked out to sea, and the surf rolled easily in against the sea wall. They moved to the patio and talked some more. Joe Kennedy was around but not in on the talks. So was Caroline, wrestling with some of her Christmas presents. The atmosphere was informal, friendly and frank. Even a Brooklyn boy was impressed.

Kennedy's pitch was general. He did not want legislation altering the current diplomatic machinery. What he sought were assurances that if he named the men he wanted to key embassies, Rooney would allow them enough money to run a first-class embassy. Rooney was not easily persuaded. His opinion of many of the State Department career types remained unchanged. But Rooney and Kennedy began to come together when the President-elect agreed fully that there was waste in some of the embassies, too many people who were not good enough in others. Kennedy, who showed Rooney his special task force report on embassy difficulties, did not suggest that a specific amount of money was needed. From the Brooklyn congressman came one concession—he would do all he could to make it easy for qualified men whom Kennedy appointed who did not have the necessary funds. If not totally satisfactory, it was a beginning for John Kennedy.

The day was not ended yet, however. Next on the agenda was a golf game at the Palm Beach Country Club, and Rooney was invited to come along. He declined to play because he had not swung a club since he was fifteen years old. But he did enjoy the company. Joe Kennedy joined the group, and in high humor the five men headed down the fairway.

John Rooney may be the only scorekeeper that the Palm Beach Country Club has had in a gray fedora and black suit. He padded about the course, keeping an accurate count, and later he upheld presidential secrecy. "That's a classified document," he told reporters, referring to the score card.

Rooney stayed for dinner, and at some time during his two days in Florida, Jacqueline Kennedy greeted him warmly. He was even granted a peek at tiny John Fitzgerald Kennedy, Jr.

Rooney's admiration for the tike was expressed candidly later. "I think he looked like a hell of a little baby," said the congressman. There was another golf game with Rooney as the delighted scorekeeper and more talk with the President-elect. When he faced the reporters before flying back north, Rooney cautiously admitted that he would be in favor of some slight increase in the allowances, depending on which embassy and for which ambassador.

Was there a change of heart? Maybe a little softening around the edges. Back in his hotel room, Rooney phoned his wife. "Yeah," he said, "I saw 'em all—Jackie, Caroline and the baby. They were all there. . . ." [4]

For Jackie Kennedy these weeks were as quiet as they could be, living as she did in the maelstrom. She was pregnant during her husband's campaign, and she had wisely avoided any tiring appearances. She spent many hours reading and thinking about the White House and how her family would live there. She was determined that somehow her children were to be shielded from the harsh public glare that by necessity her husband, and less frequently herself, must live in. She also wanted to make the White House genuinely the nation's first home. She wanted it to reflect more accurately its early heritage and she wanted it to be a living museum, a place where parents and their children could come and see and sense the long parade of history.

On Thanksgiving Day, November 24, the Kennedys had somehow stolen a relatively quiet time for themselves and a few friends. They stayed in Georgetown, ate leisurely and talked of their plans for living and for governing. Though the baby was not due for another month, Jackie was being extremely careful. She had lost two others. She seemed in fine condition that evening as Kennedy left Georgetown to fly to Palm Beach to resume building his government, by choice away from frantic Washington.

Three hours after Kennedy left Washington, an ambu-

[4] Kennedy made even more progress with Rooney when in 1962 the Democratic party on the President's urging gave incumbent New York Congressman Victor Anfuso a New York municipal judgeship, thus conveniently eliminating one opponent for Rooney, who had been put into a new district with Anfuso for the 1962 election.

lance was on its way to the Kennedy home. Jackie sat in her bedroom quietly and asked her obstetrician, Dr. John W. Walsh, "Will I lose my baby?"

As the Kennedy Convair, the "Caroline," taxied up the ramp in West Palm Beach, the word was radioed that an emergency phone call waited for the President-elect. Kennedy was told that his wife had been taken to the hospital and as he hurried off the plane to the waiting phone, he turned and said, "We'll be going right back."

For the trip back to Washington, Kennedy got aboard the bigger, faster DC-6 which was flying the press corps. Some thirty minutes after the plane took off, Kennedy moved to the cabin and put on the radio earphones. A few minutes after 1 A.M. Salinger came back and told reporters, "We have just been advised that Mrs. Kennedy has given birth to a baby boy. Both mother and son are doing well." The newsmen applauded wildly.

John, Jr., came by Caesarean section, which meant that there was a long pull back to full strength for Jackie Kennedy. She spent the weeks before inauguration as quietly as possible in the Florida sunshine.

Kennedy could listen with only half an ear to the sounds of the world. But even in limited amounts, they were not pleasant.

There was the crackle of rifle fire in early January along the road from Vientiane to Luang Prabang in faraway Laos. Soviet Ilyushin-14 transports daily roared over the jungle and dropped supplies to the communist guerrillas.

In the Kremlin, Nikita Khrushchev stood before his comrades and delivered a speech which John Kennedy would study as diligently as he would any document that year. "Comrades," said the Soviet Premier, "we live at a splendid time: communism has become the invincible force of our country. The further successes of communism depend to an enormous degree on our will, our unity, our foresight and resolve. Through their struggle and their labor, communists, the working class, will attain the great goals of communism on earth. Men of the future, communists of the next generation will envy us."

Technically it was still Dwight Eisenhower's worry. Kennedy rejected all overtures to associate himself with any actions of the old administration. When General Wilton B. (Jerry) Persons, Ike's assistant, informed Kennedy that the United States planned to break diplomatic relations with Cuba, the President-elect remained silent. Again, when the New Frontier was asked if it wanted to join a European mission headed by Secretary of the Treasury Robert B. Anderson to appeal for help in stemming this country's disturbing flow of gold, Kennedy politely said no. Both he and his adviser, Clark Clifford, felt that it was unwise to make any public policy declarations before they had the actual power of office.

At a closed-door hearing on Capitol Hill, Secretary of State Christian A. Herter made his final report to the Senate Foreign Relations Committee, and Tennessee's Senator Albert Gore best summed it up when he emerged shaking his head: "It wasn't a very encouraging review." Fidel Castro paraded new tanks and artillery in the streets of Havana, and the Russians renewed their offensive to undermine the United Nations efforts to solve the Congo problem.

The Kennedy itch set in as inauguration time approached. He flew north to New York, where he could work in the uptown Carlyle Hotel, nearer Washington but still out of its admiring embrace.

The public clamored for a look at its hero. Police held the crowds back outside the entrance of the staid hotel. Assistant Hotel Manager Gustav Person assured everyone that the hotel was delighted to have the President-elect as a guest. He admitted that the regular patrons had had to make a few adjustments, however.

"It's a great distinction," sighed one elderly woman. "But those horrid men." She gave a limp wave at the fifty or so reporters and photographers encamped in the lobby, all wearing orange badges entitling them to the privilege of sitting on the lobby floor to wait.

The press blocked the narrow hotel passageways, dominated the elevators. When they didn't tie everything up, the visiting politicians did.

"He's leaving tonight, thank goodness," said one elevator

operator. Then he paused and saddened. "But he's coming back Sunday."

Newsmen shucked their heavy overcoats and piled them in the corners of the lobby. The heap got so big that one hotel guest suggested, "It looks like a rummage sale."

Yet things were even worse in the fifteenth-floor quarters of News Secretary Salinger, by now the target of every publicity man and unemployed reporter in the city. In his two-bedroom suite there was a United Press International news ticker that beat out its steady rhythm. Salinger's customary cigars were scattered in profusion on the tables, and the half-emptied bottles of bourbon and scotch marked the room as a haven for the wandering press. Two frantic secretaries tried to maintain sanity and still keep on working, a nearly impossible task.

The high-water mark was reached when actors Frank Sinatra and Peter Lawford came in to see Salinger about their role in the inaugural fund-raising gala. They were early and, as is his habit, Salinger was late. Frankie sat rather glumly in the corner (without his hairpiece) and Lawford paced the floor. The phone jangled incessantly, the two secretaries huddled in a far corner gnawing on sandwiches, lunch hour having passed two hours ago. Economist Dr. Walter W. Heller, new head of the Council of Economic Advisers, came in and staked out a portion of the living room away from Sinatra and Lawford. A journalist buzzed and entered, was shoved into the bedroom with the news ticker. "I think you're too busy," ventured Lawford. He began to answer the door for the girls. Sinatra sat and stared at Heller. A repairman bustled through to adjust the news machine. A phone caller wanted to know if the President-elect would autograph a baseball, and another one wanted money to get her son home on leave from the service.

At some time during this day Xavier Cugat came around, bearing a huge painting by himself that was a caricature of the coming inauguration and included such people as Fidel Castro, Gamal Nasser, Nikita Khrushchev, Richard Nixon, Harry Truman and Henry Cabot Lodge, all blended into one gay landscape around the inaugural stand.

Two composers with a "New Frontiers" march lumbered

through the door with a portable phonograph and a record-
ing of an army chorus singing the piece. Salinger took them
to the bedroom, and for five minutes all other sound was
drowned in baritone voices: "Our country's spirit will prevail, opening New Frontiers. With trust in God we shall not
fail, opening New Frontiers. America, America, land of the
pioneers."

"Great, great," said Salinger, cigar clamped grimly in his
teeth. He gently pushed the musicians from the room. "Here,
give these reporters copies of the music. In fact, they can have
mine."

This was the music of new government, the discordant but
wonderful sounds of the great democracy getting ready for
another change of life.

Kennedy task-force reports rolled in. From Senator Paul H.
Douglas came a volume on depressed areas. Purdue University's Frederick Hovde brought around a massive proposal
for education, envisioning some $9 billion of federal money
to be spent over four and a half years. Adolf Berle's document on Latin America was declared secret because of its
delicate suggestions dealing with Cuba and communist infiltration in other Latin areas.

Space, Health and Social Security, International Youth
Service (Peace Corps), Africa, Disarmament, Foreign Economic Policy, U. S. Information Agency, Department of State
—the reports were framed to a large degree by liberals and
by academicians, who are mostly liberals. There were no
limits set on these mental exercises. Thus their tone was
naturally liberal. Their ultimate use was questionable from
the beginning. They brought out ideas, they united men in
the Kennedy cause, they gave the New Frontier a patina of
intellectualism which Kennedy liked. But just how would
they affect Kennedy? Who makes policy for this man? Even
at this early stage those who had been with the President-
elect knew that to trace the use of this mass of ideas would
be virtually impossible. The Kennedy digestive process is
thorough. An idea rarely comes out the way it goes in. The
liberal cast was misleading. Still, from these policy essays
would come a foundation of ideas on which Kennedy would
build his first year's legislative program.

The White House press corps, transferred from Eisenhower to Kennedy, was learning new lessons. From the $8.50 rooms of the Gettysburg Inn, where they used to bivouac for Ike, they had moved to suites in the Palm Beach Towers Hotel that went for $40 or more a night in season. One careful reporter calculated that it was costing him 30 per cent more to cover the President-elect. The Secret Service was having its indoctrination, too. One night in New York Kennedy careened around the city looking for the new restaurant La Caravelle, and never did find it. He leaped out of his auto on Fifth Avenue, loped the half-block to "21," where he decided to have dinner. In the meantime a frantic search was on for tickets to the musical *Do Re Mi*. Kennedy, as usual, was late for the show, but the management held the curtain. The performance was poor, the cast being too impressed with its guest. One woman in the balcony who climbed on her seat for a better look at Kennedy got stuck and had to be extricated by a carpenter. Kennedy executed one of the most observed trips to the men's room in modern history, but he seemed not the least concerned.

In two days he was back in Florida being massaged in his father's house while talking on the phone and going over the drafts of his inaugural address. One night he and his father went to a reception for Herbert Hoover. If ever there was Republican territory, that was it—the home of Palm Beach banker J. Loy Anderson, his mansion filled with the gilt-edge of Palm Beach. "Hi there, Chief," said Joe Kennedy to Hoover. "Hello, Mr. President, how are you?" said his son.

They stood there in the crowd, the two of them—Jack Kennedy, the youngest man ever elected to the presidency in the history of the country, and Herbert Hoover, the oldest living president of the Republic. "Do you have any advice now that I'm assuming this new responsibility?" asked Kennedy.

Hoover smiled as best he could in the noise and under the hot TV kliegs. "Yes, I have some, but I don't think this is the time or the place to give it to you. . . . Everybody has advice for a new president. You'll have to hear from them all. You'll have to make up your mind on what is good advice."

Final plans for live TV presidential press conferences were made—another New Frontier experiment. Kennedy watched the growing international tension over Laos, decided that another meeting with Eisenhower before inauguration would help illustrate a united America at a delicate time. He had his aides work it out for January 19, the day before the power change.

The Kennedy Georgetown residence was sold (for a rumored $102,000) to Mr. and Mrs. Perry Ausbrook, young, wealthy and with an eye on history. Then suddenly there was the thought that brother-in-law Sargent Shriver might want the house if he moved to Washington for the New Frontier. Attorneys Clark Clifford and Dean Acheson went to work to unsell it, only to resell it to the Ausbrooks a few weeks later. Appointments rolled out, names that meant little now but would be heard later—George W. Ball, Under Secretary of State for Economic Affairs; Arthur Sylvester, Assistant Secretary of Defense for Public Affairs; Angier Biddle Duke, Chief of Protocol; Newton N. Minow, chairman of the Federal Communications Commission. . . .

John Kennedy sold such of his financial holdings as might constitute a conflict of interest, and for the first time the nation had a glimpse of his worth. His income after taxes was roughly $100,000 a year, indicating that his portion of the vast Kennedy wealth was $10 million.

And suddenly the talk of legislative activity like Roosevelt's 1933 "100 days" began to vanish.[5] Before the election there had been such an expectation by some within the Kennedy camp, by journalists even more. But the victory had been too narrow. The temper of the Congress, streaming back into Washington, had been tested. Now came the first clear symptoms that the New Frontier's program would be a hard, foot-by-foot struggle.

There was born a new theory. Kennedy's power would increase year by year until it reached its peak perhaps at the start of his second term, in 1964. This expectation was contrary to every political pattern. But Kennedy had already

[5] Later, when Kennedy was criticized for not acting enough like Franklin Roosevelt, he said, "This period is entirely different from Franklin Roosevelt's day. Everyone says that Roosevelt did this and that, why don't I? Franklin Roosevelt faced the task of passing a domestic program over and against violent opposition. The great issue today is in the field of foreign policy. People don't feel partisan about that."

shattered an assortment of political myths—he was too young, he was too rich, he was Catholic. People would see, the thinking went, how good a man he was. By the 1962 congressional elections, he might reverse the tradition of a loss of seats by the party in power in off-year elections and actually increase the Democratic margin. By 1964 Kennedy would have shown his mettle enough to make further gains in Congress and to come back to the White House with confidence, stature and, yes, power.

Kennedy took the final fling on the golf course before he flew north for the last time as a senator. His special guest was evangelist Billy Graham. Some accused Kennedy of launching his 1964 re-election drive right then. He was out to soothe Graham, who had backed Nixon, and he seemed to do pretty well. Both the Reverend Graham and the President-elect were hitting long, straight balls down the Seminole Club fairways. Kennedy kept the score. So prodigious was the President-elect's performance on the last hole that he won $20 from Senator George Smathers, also in the foursome. If the Reverend knew about this transaction, he kept a ministerial silence.

The press clamored for a word from Graham. He spoke as an American citizen only. "The Bible teaches that we are to pray for those in authority, and I believe that the President, President Kennedy, will become the most prayed-for man in the world, praying that God will give him courage and wisdom, because he is going to be facing some of the most awesome problems that any man in history has ever faced."

Kennedy, in suntans and sport shirt, shifted his eyes down self-consciously. A little of the evangelist's fire blazed and the correspondents quieted in the hot Florida night. "I think the campaign was conducted on a very high level. . . . I think Mr. Kennedy is to be commended for facing it forthrightly. I think that he eased a great many fears that people had, in the forthright statements that he made in the matter of religion. . . . I suspect that the religious issue will not be raised again in the future, at least to the extent that it was raised in the recent campaign. I think that is a hurdle that has been permanently passed. . . ."

To Kennedy he was "Billy" as they walked to the front of

the hotel. There was the quick handshake, the good-bye. Kennedy jumped in behind the wheel of his convertible. A Secret Service man dashed for the other seat. Collar open, hair blowing in the warm night, John Kennedy, President-elect of the United States, disappeared in the dark.

January 17 came, and nothing seemed changed from a thousand days before. It was. For John Kennedy this was the last flight north to Washington as a private citizen. In three days he would belong to the country totally and irreversibly.

In normal fashion, he was half an hour late to the West Palm Beach airport. His motorcade wound over the dusty gravel road and out onto the landing apron, like a hundred other motorcades from the long campaign, now fading in memory. Out of the car came the Kennedy legs, then the rest of the figure. Kennedy walked up to the policemen, shook their hands and thanked them. He had done so in every major city of the United States. Then, as always, he virtually sprinted up the folding metal steps of the "Caroline." He strode back to his private compartment in the rear and flopped in the big easy chair behind the desk. Captain Howard Baird guided the plane down to the end of the runway. It sat there and shuddered for a moment, then leaped into the air. At 2:04 P.M. John Kennedy had begun the last leg of his long journey.

Kennedy lounged on the end of his spine. He slumped loosely, then straightened. He gulped milk and sawed away at a filet of beef. His eyes wandered out the window. Below was the Atlantic, later the snow-sifted ground of North Carolina and Virginia. When his lunch was done, he pushed it back, squinted into the sun, and the wrinkles around his eyes —deepened in the last twelve months—showed plainly. He tapped his teeth with his fingernails, a Kennedy habit of decades. He was in shirt sleeves and he was working on his inaugural address.

Outside the President's cabin Ted Sorensen likewise was hard at work on the words. Amidships Mrs. Evelyn Lincoln rapped out the new versions as fast as they came along.

Kennedy put his feet on the edge of the desk. On his lap he propped a yellow tablet. Over the first three pages he had scribbled in irregular strokes with a blue ball-point pen an opening for the address. I sat beside him and waited for him to speak. This was to be my last talk with Senator Kennedy.

"It's tough," he said. "The speech to the Massachusetts Legislature went so well. It's going to be hard to meet that standard." He read the three pages out loud, his voice rather soft and restrained as heard over the drumming of the engines. Now there was none of the urgency, the stridency that had marked his call to the New Frontier when he had been campaigning. On the stump his voice had best been described as resembling a bagpipe, not exactly pleasant but arresting. He flipped the pages over as he read. The talk had a Kennedy ring to it. The opening paragraphs drew deeply from history. There were the words about our heritage. Then came the message. It was the belief that this country's spirit burned as brightly now as ever. What he was reading was an answer to the Soviet dogma that communism was the wave of the future. At this time neither the Soviet insistence on that theory nor Kennedy's answer were as clear as they would become. Here was the seed of his thinking.

When he finished reading, he paused. He glanced out the window again. He was not satisfied with the beginning, it was too drawn-out and did not get to his point soon enough.

"What I want to say," he explained, "is that the spirit of the Revolution still is here, still is a part of this country." As he spoke, his right arm came up and he gestured in a flat sweep of his arm out the plane window and toward the far horizon. He scribbled on the pad for a moment or two more, crossed out some words. Then suddenly he flung the tablet on the desk and forgot the speech for a few minutes. He turned toward me.

"How do I feel? I don't feel any different." He smiled a little, slapped his middle and rubbed it a bit. There was a new bulge there, just a hint of a spare tire. He had gained almost fifteen pounds in the letdown from campaigning to the sedentary life of President-elect. He weighed now close to 190 and was considering dieting. The new weight, however, had smoothed some of that angular look of youth. If the approaching ordeal bothered Kennedy, he did not show it. He displayed no emotion.

He was upset about the Eisenhower budget. Even Republicans, and even the *Wall Street Journal,* he noted, pointed out that it was balanced with imagined revenue. The budget makers had figured on increased postal rates and gas taxes, both highly doubtful matters before Congress. And the national income had been calculated on a boom economy, while most economic experts agreed that the economy was still in a slump. Red ink, Kennedy figured, would be blamed on him, since with only fairly minor revisions he must live with the Eisenhower budget for a year.

He switched to the troubles in Latin America and gave a discouraged shake of the head. Then he turned to his own Cabinet and to lesser officials. "I've got good men. It looks good."

For a fleeting second he worried about his vice president, about whether Lyndon Johnson could make the switch from Senate Majority Leader. He resolved that problem easily. "Lyndon is good," he said. "He's going to do well . . . we'll keep him busy. He's already got the Space Council job."

Kennedy sat up as if practicing the part of the executive. There would be an executive order—his first—the morning after he took office, doubling the allotment of surplus food being sent to the depressed areas. "I'm going to start seeing people right away," he added.

The big policy decisions faced him, too. The Laotian crisis continued. An immediate decision on nuclear testing might be needed. The gold outflow was still unchecked and action was required.

The President-elect switched off this train of thought as quickly as he had let it flow. He reached to his desk again, picked up a piece of yellow paper and studied it. Typed neatly were some twenty-five passages from the Bible. They had been given to him the day before by Billy Graham. Kennedy had asked the evangelist for some recommendation for scripture to be used in his inaugural address. He read carefully down the list. He paused and read one aloud.

" 'When a man's ways please the Lord, he maketh even his enemies to be at peace with him.' Proverbs 16:7. That's good."

He read it again, nodded to himself. "If you hear that in the speech you'll know where it came from." [6]

Kennedy jumped up, walked out of his cabin to hand this version (the sixth) to Mrs. Lincoln for typing. He looked at Sorensen, declared: "It will be a sensation." The two men laughed.

The world gazed on Washington now—the day before the inauguration. It was a curious day, filled with the most serious business of national security, the unrestrained gaiety of the Democrats, the ludicrous turmoil from having too many people in too small a city and the gray threat of a snowstorm.

The National Park Service had sprayed green dye on the grass around the Washington Monument to add a trace of spring. The trees along the inaugural route were given a coat of Roost-No-More to keep the irksome starlings away. The Secret Service diligently battened down the manhole covers in the street to guard against bomb throwers. A security guard of more than 5,000 was mustered for the big day. The police cavalry trained its horses for the coming din by playing Spike Jones records over loud-speakers.

John Kennedy slept fitfully on the second floor of his Georgetown home. His window was thrown up, blue shutters closed to block the view. A messenger's motorcycle backfired in the chill dawn before seven, and an irritated Kennedy poked his head out, asked the Secret Service for quiet. But the city was too alive. Newsmen began gathering below the window, traffic picked up momentum on N Street. Kennedy gave up trying to sleep. He snapped on his light and dressed.

That morning Kennedy went to see Eisenhower. Jerry Persons stood on the doorstoop at the executive entrance of the White House to greet the President-elect. They moved quickly into Ike's office. For some fifty minutes the two men chatted alone, mostly about procedural matters. Ike summoned a helicopter to the rear lawn of the White House to show Kennedy just how quickly it could be done.

As Ike guided Kennedy into the Cabinet room, he joked to

---

[6] That scripture passage was not used. Kennedy said instead: "Let both sides unite to heed in all corners of the earth the command of Isaiah—to 'undo the heavy burdens . . . [and] let the oppressed go free.' "

the men assembled there, "I've shown my friend here how to get out in a hurry."

This group was a mixture of the old and the new, met to talk about the top international problems. Kennedy's Dean Rusk, Robert McNamara and Secretary of the Treasury C. Douglas Dillon were on hand, as were their counterparts in Ike's administration—Christian Herter, Thomas S. Gates and Robert Anderson.

Subject by subject they went down the agenda, which had been worked out jointly by the aides of the two men: Laos, Cuba, the balance of payments, Africa, and so forth. First Ike would say a few words, then his Secretary would take over with a fuller briefing. Kennedy interrupted each time with questions. Laos took up most of the discussion. And it was at this meeting that Dwight Eisenhower wrinkled his brow as he glanced at the map of Southeast Asia and said, "This is one of the problems I'm leaving you that I'm not happy about. We may have to fight."

Eisenhower's casualness in discussing these monumental problems was something that bothered the President-elect. "How can he stare disaster in the face with such equanimity?" Kennedy wondered to an aide as they drove from the White House. In a few short months Kennedy himself would exhibit much of this same "equanimity" in the face of crisis. It was not disregard; it was simply the art of leading a dangerous world.

Kennedy abandoned his own home. Like a bridegroom, he had been evicted because of the space demands of Jackie, who was preparing for the two great days. The President-elect took up residence in a tiny corner office in the home of William Walton, Georgetown artist and family friend. There he learned some of his duties as commander in chief from General Lyman L. Lemnitzer, Chairman of the Joint Chiefs of Staff. His Labor Secretary, Arthur Goldberg, came by for lunch and in the first flakes of the coming snow echoed the concern from within the House. "With some five and a half million unemployed, it is a bad situation which the new administration will have to do something about."

Then it came—eight inches of thick snow, a present from North Carolina and Virginia. The city became gloriously bogged down in a memorable night of traffic jams. Somehow the storm may have been what was needed to relax the capital. Nothing worked on schedule, but nobody expected it to. Yet everything went ahead. Jackie came out into the night radiant in a white gown, the snow swirling around her, a Secret Service man holding an umbrella over her.

Half the National Symphony was stuck in the drifts when the couple got to Constitution Hall for the inaugural concert. But after half an hour's delay the remainder of the orchestra began to play.

Frank Sinatra's great gala was nearly two hours behind schedule, but it, too, plunged right ahead once the Kennedy clan had gathered. It was interminable, and finally Jackie had to sneak out and return to Georgetown for some sleep. The others stuck it out. At 2 A.M. they began gathering in Paul Young's cavernous restaurant downtown for a special party given by father Joe Kennedy. Not until 3:30 A.M. was Kennedy home, and not until 4 A.M. was he asleep.

Four hours later he was up, and he asked immediately for a copy of his inaugural address. He sat quietly for a few minutes reading it.

There was Mass at Holy Trinity Church. By now the people lined the streets. A cheer rang out down N Street as Jack and Jackie Kennedy came out to get into their bubbletop limousine for the ride to the White House.

Coffee with Dwight and Mamie Eisenhower, then at last the two most important citizens of the United States began the famous mile from the White House to the Capitol. From someplace beside the White House the strains of "America" drifted out over the snow. As he rode to the Capitol, Kennedy listened to Eisenhower at his side. The retiring president told him that somehow he had felt the Russians never would start a war if this country remained firm enough.

At 12:12 John Kennedy stood on the top step, looking out over the Capitol Plaza. He had just brushed by Nixon in the rotunda. They had exchanged greetings rather awkwardly and they had talked for a few seconds about the need for the government to finance presidential campaigns.

Senator Carl Hayden, Senate President pro tem., guided him down to the inaugural stand.

Again Eisenhower and Kennedy talked, this time about D-Day in World War II. Kennedy had just read *The Longest Day*, a book on the great invasion. Ike explained that one of this nation's advantages in the invasion had been the skill of our weather men. The Germans, not nearly so proficient in this science, felt that the weather would continue to be too bad for an assault.

Senator John J. Sparkman spoke. "We are here today to inaugurate the thirty-fourth president of this great Union. . . ."

The sky was a deep and pure blue, whiffs of white clouds scudding here and there. Wind stirred the snow which blanketed the Capitol grounds. It bit deeply because the temperature was just twenty degrees, yet it felt fresh and promising to the people there. The flavor was New England, from Poet Robert Frost to the bareheaded man who became president at 12:51 P.M.

Kennedy stood coatless and gave his message. It came with the Boston accent, with the left hand doubled into a fist and the right forefinger thumping the rostrum.

"We observe today not a victory of party but a celebration of freedom—symbolizing an end as well as a beginning—signifying renewal as well as change. . . ."

Eisenhower sat huddled in his thick overcoat, his white scarf up around his neck, his expression one of parting.

"We dare not forget today that we are the heirs of that first revolution. Let the word go forth from this time and place, to friend and foe alike, that the torch has been passed to a new generation of Americans—born in this century, tempered by war, disciplined by a hard and bitter peace, proud of our ancient heritage—and unwilling to witness or permit the slow undoing of those human rights to which this nation has always been committed, and to which we are committed today at home and around the world." Gone was the rasp of his campaign oratory. These words were read slowly.

Soviet Ambassador Mikhail Menshikov sat impassive. His gray hat was pulled over his brow, he was swathed in a gray overcoat. His gloved hands were clasped in front of him. He did not smile, he did not frown.

"So let us begin anew—remembering on both sides that

civility is not a sign of weakness, and sincerity is always sub-ject to proof. Let us never negotiate out of fear. But let us never fear to negotiate." Just for a moment it was as if he were back in Wisconsin or West Virginia or California. His jaw came up, his voice rose. "In the long history of the world, only a few generations have been granted the role of defend-ing freedom in its hour of maximum danger. I do not shrink from this responsibility—I welcome it."

And then a phrase that might stick with Kennedy for the rest of his life: "And so, my fellow Americans: ask not what your country can do for you—ask what you can do for your country."

In fourteen minutes the speech was over. As Kennedy walked up the Capitol stairs, a quiet figure in black walked down them. Richard Nixon, now jobless, went to the door of his car parked at the side of the steps. He bent to get in when suddenly a few spectators noticed him. "So long," they cried. Surprised, Nixon straightened up. "Good-bye," he shouted back. He ducked again, then he thought of something. He straightened again and raised his left arm. With two fingers he formed the V for victory sign. From the Republicans watching came a cheer. And then Nixon was gone.

Inside the White House, Jackie Kennedy discovered that the fireplaces had not been used for years and were plugged up. The upstairs windows were also stuck from disuse. She wandered by herself through the vast house. She found com-fort in Lincoln's bedroom; there the massive bed seemed the only true link to the past, its huge dark frame almost inde-structible.

John Kennedy waved and smiled through the endless in-augural parade. He visited each of the five inaugural balls in a frantic whirl around the city that night. His final stop, after midnight, was at his friend Joseph Alsop's. It was a last touch of a life that was ending. The Secret Service men waited in the snowy Georgetown street. A caravan of reporters paced up and down out front. This was the pattern of the future.

From a side door of Alsop's came the President. Only the glowing end of a cigar showed in the night. He walked alone out to his car. The caravan moved slowly back to the White

House, and finally the day was over. The north portico, with its massive lamp, formed a bright stage in the dark. Kennedy hurried up the stairs, then he noticed reporters running along the walk below to get the day's last glimpse of the new president. He paused, thrust his hands in his pockets and came to the edge of the porch for a final word. Wind whipped his long tails. He smiled, said good night and walked unhesitatingly through the front door.

CHAPTER TWO

FIRST DAYS

DESPITE his late inaugural night, the President of the United States climbed out of bed at 8 the next morning for his first official day on the job.

By 8:50 he was in his barren office. At 10 former President Harry Truman came up the front drive for his first visit since 2 P.M. January 19, 1953. Kennedy came out to meet him, and as they strolled back to his office Truman explained a presidential phenomenon. "This is the One More Club," he said, poking a cane at the mass of photographers. Turning to them, he asked, "Are you going to elect him the new president of the One More Club? The other fella wouldn't have it."

Chicago's Mayor Richard Daley and six children toured the inner presidential sanctum. No less could be done for the man who delivered Illinois. The White House staff was sworn in and there was a meeting of the top security people. Their mission: to study the Laotian situation and recommend a course of action.

Already Kennedy had been informed that the two Air Force officers, captives of the Russians for seven months after their RB-47 plane was shot down by a Soviet fighter in the North Sea, might be released as a gesture to the new president. Nikita Khrushchev was moving cautiously and Llewellyn Thompson carefully reported from Moscow. There were demands. The main one was that Kennedy must give some kind of public assurance that this country would not resume the U-2 type of reconnaissance flights over the Russian mainland. Another was that this country would not use the released flyers for anti-Soviet propaganda. Kennedy agreed, and his feelings were hastily cabled to Moscow.

Kennedy asked his staff to wheel a stuffed chair into his office from an adjoining room. The new president propped up pictures of Jackie, Caroline and John, Jr., along the office wall. He told his wife to find him a painting of a naval battle for over the fireplace.

In those first days he was restless, roaming about the White House. He delighted in showing it to guests, he marveled at the sights himself time and time again. Routine was a shambles. When he wanted somebody, he went to find him. He poked his head in all the doors he could find, queried secretaries on how they liked things, proclaimed the press room "a mess" when he got his first glimpse.

Jackie was seen in the halls in riding breeches, and a minor convulsion went through the press corps. One night the President slipped out of the White House unnoticed and went for dinner to his brother's house in McLean, Virginia. When the White House reporters learned of this, the dismay was profound. Kennedy let photographers have second chances at pictures, he kept no rules about strolling out to greet his guests. One journalist moaned, "You won't be able to go to the men's room for fear of being scooped."

Another night the President and Jackie delighted in the stories told by Franklin Roosevelt, Jr., as they walked through the mansion. He recalled how his Uncle Teddy Roosevelt's six children had all slept in the huge Lincoln bed crossways. And he remembered that during his father's time that suite had been occupied by Louis Howe.

There were snorts of laughter when the group walked into the Red Room and William Walton, also on the tour, looked up at the portrait of Grover Cleveland and asked, "Who does that remind you of? Pierre Salinger." And indeed, without the mustache, the likeness was unmistakable.

Columnist Joseph Alsop sat in the projection booth of the White House reviewing the television film of the inauguration and cried out to the President of the United States, "My dear boy, look at you with that silly top hat."

The President took a forty-two-page memo on the Congo

from the State Department and read it at night in his quarters. The performance was so unique that the story went along the department grapevine. He read all four task-force reports on agriculture, and he consumed other memos as fast as they could be turned out.

Jackie telephoned to Ethel Kennedy one morning and first got four-year-old Courtney on the line. Courtney rushed to her father's side, then breakfasting with three congressmen. "Daddy, Daddy, I just talked to Jackie and do you know what, she has a swimming pool inside her house." The wonder of it all!

The President ran one caller in and out so fast that the staff did not notice his exit, thus leaving the President alone for a few minutes. The phone rang on an aide's desk in the outer office. "What's going on out there?" asked John Kennedy.

Walking on an outside path, Kennedy skidded on the sand put down over the ice and hurried to find a guard to sweep it up. He trod on the grass when the ground was still wet and, noticing that he had left footprints, made a careful inquiry on whether he had injured the turf.

Even the old hands were taken with the 34th President. Speaker Sam Rayburn, still unbowed by the cancer that would take his life in the first year of the new administration he had helped form, talked about the man in the White House. He hunched forward in his huge black leather chair as the winter's light was fading and the hour of good southern bourbon and talk came on the Hill, the place that he loved as dearly as life itself. "The first thing I want to say about him is that I thought he couldn't have done better through this whole damn jamboree last weekend [the inauguration]. . . . He was the most unhurried man I ever saw—and the most considerate. Why, he took time to talk to anybody, and he was interested in what they had to say. He made a fine impression, a good start. . . ."

As so frequently happened during these days, memories went back to Franklin Roosevelt. They did with Mr. Sam on that January evening. He remembered Texas and the dust bowl and the bread lines and the man who came from Hyde Park. "Why, people were starving to death," he said. "[Roo-

sevelt] was put on this earth at the right instant. . . . This
fellow Kennedy, why he's got a brain—and he knows how to
use it. That speech he made out here"—Mr. Sam waved his
short arm toward the Capitol Plaza, caressing the memory of
years and presidents—"was better than anything Franklin
Roosevelt ever said at his best—it was better than Lincoln.
I think—I really think—he's a man of destiny."

Suddenly the New Frontier was running itself. The government had continued uninterrupted for several days. Only a
few traces of Dwight Eisenhower remained.

There were still many misty-eyed Democrats around Washington who remembered the glorious intellectual binges of
the New Deal. Some still recalled the tinkle of ice cubes at
the Georgetown parties for bright young bachelors. There
were visions still of Tommy Corcoran playing his accordion
and singing at the intimate gatherings of the mental elite.
The New Frontier brought some of this, but perhaps not as
much as some wanted.

Many of the key men around Kennedy did not even live in
Georgetown. They found homes in suburbia, in the modest
but comfortable environs of Bethesda and Chevy Chase. And
though the New Frontier had its share of youth, many of the
Kennedy thinkers were on the lower fringe of middle age, as
was the President himself.

"Most of the men have had experience in government operations before," said MIT's Walt W. Rostow, a White House
staff member. "They know what discipline is. Most of them
are about the same age as the President, a generation that
saw a lot of war and diplomacy."

The Rostows and the McGeorge Bundys and the Arthur
Schlesingers were family people. Children and home duties
sometimes cut into idle moments of good fellowship. "As
quick as we can, we go home," said Budget Director David
Bell, one of the first seven Harvard contributions to the administration. With a 16-year-old girl, a 12-year-old boy and
a wife in Bethesda, his weeknight partying was kept to a
minimum. The Kennedy ten- to fourteen-hour day dominated. "The tempo of this administration is fantastic," sighed
Bell. "The President is a fellow who has a foot-long needle in
you all the time."

Rostow, too, when the long days closed climbed into his car and headed home to a boy, 8, and a girl, 5. On the fringe of the District of Columbia, McGeorge Bundy, the President's Special Assistant for National Security Affairs, put his family ("Three children in school, one in the crib") in a large brick home and laid down a rule that he did not go out at night unless his wife could go with him.

Solicitor General Archie Cox lived in the University Club while he pondered what to do about his family back in Wayland, Massachusetts, on fifteen acres of land. In addition to three children, he had to consider the future of his wife, three horses, twelve hens, a dog and two cats.

The Washington scene had changed since the 1930's, and the constant comparison of the dawning New Frontier with the New Deal was a deep miscalculation. The Washington that Roosevelt came to, despite the immense economic problem facing the nation, was a city that was smaller, far less complex and less hurried than in 1961.

Jackie was stirring, too, in these early days. As an 11-year-old girl she had come to Washington with her mother and had taken the commercial tour of the White House. She recalled in detail its inadequacies and disappointments. She was determined to change things.

"Jackie," explained a member of the family, "wants to be as great a First Lady in her own right as Jack is a President."

She closeted herself with New York decorator Mrs. Helen Parish to go over ideas for the private quarters of the White House. The First Lady set up conferences with artist friend William Walton, John Walker, director of the National Gallery of Art, and David E. Finley, chairman of the Fine Arts Commission. She talked to them and others about changes in the public sector of the building.

Her mind probed further. How would she pay for work she wanted done? Where would she get the rare furnishings she needed? Those people with money or just the strong spirit of patriotism who felt as she did about the White House would be glad to contribute, Jackie reasoned, and reasoned correctly. From the White House or from Glen Ora, the estate the Kennedys leased in the Virginia hunt country for week-end retreats, the calls went out to friends. The President became interested in the project, and he too helped.

Kennedy summoned his legislative leaders to breakfast on Tuesday mornings, a routine that would become firmly established. The leaders of his party on Capitol Hill included Vice President Lyndon Johnson, Speaker Sam Rayburn, House Majority Leader John W. McCormack, House Whip Carl Albert, Senate Majority Leader Mike Mansfield, Senate Whip Hubert H. Humphrey and Senate Policy Head George A. Smathers.

Over scrambled eggs, bacon and coffee, served in the family dining room on the first floor of the mansion, these men talked about the plans of each week in Congress. Kennedy cautiously tried out his new authority in the first meeting, and he told his leaders that he would like to deliver his State of the Union message the following Monday. It was a polite directive and one his leaders acceded to immediately. But this was the first time he had looked at his former colleagues from the other side of the table. Kennedy's transformation from legislator to executive was coming along.

The legislators themselves did not quite know how to act. Mr. Sam brushed by reporters, not saying a word after the meeting. Press Secretary Pierre Salinger was to be the spokesman for the White House, he said.

The newness of the procedure baffled Hubert Humphrey. Asked what room he had eaten breakfast in, Humphrey had to admit he did not know. Then with a flash of his humor and a nostalgic thought about his own efforts for the nomination, he said. "No, I don't know what room it was. I haven't been around here much. I tried to get the floor plan once but I didn't succeed."

Columbia's Professor Richard Neustadt, author of the slim book *Presidential Power, the Politics of Leadership,* which Kennedy had studied, pronounced himself pleased with the first show of the infant administration.

It was to be an executive show. Kennedy had talked about it countless times in the campaign. The power in this country had passed to the White House. Now he was there.

"Kennedy will demonstrate afresh the art of leadership,"

predicted one confident aide. "He's in there early and working away and so is everybody else."

The papers flowed in a widening and deepening stream from the Kennedy office. It was obvious from the start that the President intended to rub himself against as many of the problems as he possibly could. "Jack works as hard as a human can," said Joe Kennedy once.[1]

The warm Kennedy spectacle continued. Caroline's cat, named Tom Kitten, was brought to the White House for official installation by Mr. and Mrs. Hugh D. Auchincloss, Jackie's mother and stepfather, who had been keeping the cat at their estate in Virginia. So entranced with everything in the new government had the press and the reading public become that Tom Kitten got a full interview with pictures. It was dutifully reported by Salinger that Tom Kitten had moved into the playroom on the third floor, which was the room protected with linoleum that had been used by Eisenhower's grandchildren. Further, Tom Kitten's first nights in the White House had been "restful."

Kennedy added another unique touch by appointing Dr. Janet Travell the White House phyician. For years the lady doctor from New York had treated the Kennedys, and the President gave her much credit for clearing up his troublesome back.

Dr. Travell took one look at the chair the President was using at his office desk and declared, "I think I'll make some suggestions." In a few days Kennedy had a new chair.

Kennedy tried an experiment. He put his press conferences on nationwide live TV. No longer would the cramped Indian Treaty Room in the Executive Office Building be used. Instead, the conferences would be switched to the luxurious New State Department Auditorium, a vast chamber with thick beige carpeting and gaudy orange-and-black padded seats. From New York came the young TV consultant William P. Wilson to arrange the staging for the show. Salinger issued orders that the cameras were to give minimum interference to the word men, who would ask the questions.

---

[1] The remainder of this quote was, "And Bobby works a little harder than Jack."

Special phones were installed in a hall outside the auditorium. A reporting service was hired to give instant transcripts of the conference. The White House regulars, reporters who cover the president constantly, were installed in reserved seats down in front. It was discovered that the blue drapes behind the stand were too long, and in the last hours they had to be taken down while two seamstresses rushed in to shorten the thirty-eight panels. A piece of white cardboard was placed on the lectern to reflect light into the President's face to help dispel the shadows.

The day before the first conference, memorandums from all the departments flooded into the White House, posing the possible questions and the answers. These were made up into notebooks and given to the President for study. And just before the afternoon show Kennedy went into a huddle with Salinger, Ted Sorensen and McGeorge Bundy to talk over possible questions and answers. Salinger fortified himself with legions of facts and figures about the current events in case the President might need a stray bit of information. Salinger planned to sit at the side of Kennedy, ready to furnish any data the President might turn to him for. Hollywood could not have done better in preparing a spectacular. In a sense, that is what it was.

The correspondents had the vague feeling that now they were becoming props in a TV drama. They feared that the informality, the close give-and-take of the jammed quarters in the Indian Treaty Room, would be lost and that therefore some of the revealing bits of the personality of the President would be covered up in the great production with cameras and lights and with microphones that looked like howitzers.

What was happening—what, indeed, had happened—was another step in the inexorable evolution of political communication. Kennedy had been, was going to be even more, a creature of television. It had been plainly laid out in the campaign. Kennedy had used TV in the primaries with devastating effect, particularly when he answered the West Virginia religious question. The TV debates with his opponent, Richard Nixon, may have won Kennedy the election. It was through TV that the Kennedy profile, the sincere Kennedy tones, the Kennedy thoughts could get to the people. He did not have to run the risk of having his ideas and his words shortened and adulterated by a correspondent. This was the TV era, not only in campaigning, but in holding the presidency. The regular White House correspondents, who had grudgingly admitted magazine writers to their fraternity but still excluded TV reporters, simply would have to live with it.

For his first press conference the new President had the biggest piece of news since his election. From Russia had come confirmation that the two RB-47 flyers would be released from prison.

Near 5 P.M. on January 24 Kennedy had been handed a pink cablegram from Moscow. It said that Capt. John R. McKone and Capt. Freeman B. Olmstead would be released at 2 A.M. Eastern Standard Time the next day. Thompson planned to put the men on a plane leaving Moscow at 4:30 A.M. (EST), and they would be in Amsterdam at 11 A.M. (EST). For the first time the White House had some hot news to handle.

Salinger rode off to his Lake Barcroft home in Virginia late Tuesday night after leaving instructions that he was to be called and told when the flyers were definitely out of prison. So far the story had been held tightly. But by now more and more people were being told. The Air Force had to arrange transportation. In the State Department more eyes were seeing the Thompson cables.

Almost as soon as Salinger was home, his phone rang. It was the New York *Herald Tribune*'s White House correspondent, David Wise, and he wanted to know what was going to happen around 2 A.M. that morning. Salinger tried to bluff it through and told Wise to go to bed, just exactly what *he* was going to do. But in downtown Washington Wise and the *Herald Tribune*'s aggressive staff were putting the story together. By midnight they had the skeleton of the story and Salinger's phone rang several more times as alarmed government officials called in to say the *Tribune* knew the facts.

Wise called again. He told Salinger the correct story. As the Press Secretary's heart sank, Wise said suddenly that the *Herald Tribune* planned to carry the story unless it was in-

imical to the national interest. Salinger pointed out that the
men were still in prison and that if the *Tribune* went on the
streets before they were released, it might jeopardize their
chances of release. Wise, with authority from his paper,
agreed not to run the story. A crisis passed, and Salinger
slumped wearily back into his pillow. At 4 A.M. came the
phone call he had awaited. The State Department's watch
officer reported that the men had been released.

In four more hours Salinger was at his office. He learned
that the men had been put aboard a KLM airliner but that a
tire had blown out, delaying their take-off. Salinger and General Andrew J. Goodpaster, one of Eisenhower's aides who
was helping to ease the change in administrations, hurried
down the corridor to see the President as soon as he arrived at
his desk.

"That's tough luck," said Kennedy, hearing about the delay.
But then he asked that the wives and families of the men be
notified and flown to Washington to meet their husbands.

The secret was out even though it had not been published.
It ran through the Washington grapevine all Wednesday
morning and afternoon. But it was still a national surprise
when John Kennedy strode across that carpeted stage for his
first news conference, televised to thirty-six million Americans who eagerly watched their sets.

"Good afternoon and be seated," came the Kennedy voice
in low key. "I have several announcements. I have a statement about the Geneva negotiations for an atomic test ban.
. . ." He was deliberate and thorough on this subject.

"Secondly," he went on, as suspense built up, "the United
States government has decided to increase substantially
its contributions towards relieving the famine in the
Congo. . . ."

He was torturing the reporters. Then, finally: "Third,
I am happy to be able to announce that Capt. Freeman B.
Olmstead and Capt. John R. McKone, members of the crew
of the United States Air Force RB-47 aircraft who have been
detained by Soviet authorities since July 1, 1960, have been
released by the Soviet government and are now en route to
the United States. . . ."

*   *   *

With the news out, with the flyers safely beyond Soviet borders, the New Frontier viewed with pleasure its first involvement with Nikita Khrushchev. Though it had been a very simple matter, it meant much to John Kennedy, for this was his first official contact with the Soviet government. Kennedy harbored the bright hope that in some way he could establish communication with the Russians.

Kennedy had never met people with whom he could not establish some understanding. His political success was a monument to persuasion, to "reasoning together," as Vice President Lyndon Johnson liked to say. His collection of the necessary Democratic delegates at the national convention, while it had looked like a power play on the outside, was far more a matter of the Kennedy persuasion. John Kennedy, when asked, could not exactly explain it, it just happened, he said. When you sat down with a "rational" person and you both frankly explained your views, it seemed that always there were greater areas of agreement than either party had thought possible. In countless hotel rooms across the land he had looked into the eyes of delegates and explained what he believed, what he wanted. Time after time the men and women had come from these encounters with new ideas about the young candidate: he wasn't a socialist or a communist, he didn't seem wild or irresponsible, he wasn't uppity despite his millions, he seemed to understand them. He knew their names and their home towns, and something akin to sincere interest in them flickered in those eyes. When face to face, the misunderstandings, the inaccuracies, the false impressions melted away. Two men together could do a lot.

Thus, the very delicate dealing for the return of Olmstead and McKone was the beginning of a dialogue between John Fitzgerald Kennedy of Boston and Nikita Sergeyevich Khrushchev of Kalinovka, the re-establishment of communication between two huge powers which had turned away from each other when the thin-winged U-2 plane, its cameras whirring, had fallen on Russian land.

"I can't see that it will do any harm," said Kennedy, "to hold firm"—he doubled his right fist—"but probe around the edges"—he waved his left hand, fingers open—"to see if we can't communicate in some ways."

*   *   *

In the excitement of the return of the flyers, another important event took place almost unnoticed. It was John Kennedy's first Cabinet meeting.

The Cabinet members, even Adlai Stevenson, new ambassador to the United Nations, filtered through the half dozen entrances to the business end of the White House. They walked over the thick green carpeting in the Cabinet Room and took chairs. In the center of this cool chamber is a massive mahogany table with eight sides. It measures twenty feet from end to end and seven feet at its widest point. Its huge flat surface seems to float in the room, something like the steel acres of an aircraft carrier. John Kennedy sits in the middle, at the widest part of the table. Across from him is his vice president. The table then tapers to smaller ends each way, the other members ranging around so that every member can see the faces of the President and the Vice President. The shape of the table has been compared to that of a coffin. And, indeed, on gray days its dark smooth surface can seem almost sinister.

On this Thursday, however, the atmosphere was light. The President made an opening statement in which he urged his Cabinet officers to discuss their problems with freedom and candor. He wanted their full views, he did not want rubber stamps, he told them. He had read the memoirs of other Cabinet officers from the past, Kennedy continued, and he had sensed from these that some Cabinet meetings in other administrations had not been as fruitful as they might have been had there been greater freedom of thought and discussion at the meetings. Then, one by one, he called on the men to talk about their departments and their plans.

None of them could say much, since they were all so new to their tasks. It was a get-acquainted meeting more than anything else. They were a little self-conscious, sitting there in that famous room, each with a black leather chair with a brass name plate on the back.

Adlai Stevenson spoke up. He gave a short but eloquent tribute to the new President, declaring unabashedly that it was "good to be on the New Frontier." Dean Rusk pledged firmness in an easy voice.

There were some quiet chuckles when the President turned to his brother, lowered his eyes and smiled. "Now," he said, "we'll hear from the Attorney General." What the Attorney General had to say has been forgotten. But the power in this fraternal weld first sensed in that moment still pervades Cabinet meetings.

CHAPTER THREE

PRESIDENT
AT WORK

WHEN RB-47 Pilot John McKone stepped back on American soil on January 28, 1961, he greeted his wife with a long intense kiss in the finest American tradition. One reporter insisted that he had timed it at twenty-seven seconds.

The new President of the United States, feeling somewhat of an intruder at that moment, turned away, scuffed his shoes and looked blankly at the concrete. "Some kiss," he grinned to friends later. And he even kidded McKone: "You had lipstick all over your face."

But the kiss had made history. It marked the culmination of the first Kennedy-Khrushchev negotiations. And it was probably the last thoroughly blissful event in John Kennedy's early months as President of the United States.

His first months were months of crisis. From February to October the news, as Kennedy had predicted, got worse before it got better. Week after week the new administration was battered with trouble, most of it international.

Americans who had lived confidently under the postwar wing of this nation's unchallenged military might suddenly became frightened. The bomb-shelter business boomed. Housewives made pathetic little efforts to store canned goods under their basement stairs. America's faith in herself faltered in this period. That great margin of terror which former Secretary of State John Foster Dulles had used in his global diplomacy no longer was much of a margin—it was a balance of terror now.

In February of 1961, a scant two weeks after John Kennedy had assumed office, the unmistakable signs of what was to come could be detected by even the most casual observer.

Once again the word "Berlin" cropped up in White House talk. Khrushchev had threatened to sign a separate peace treaty with East Germany if the other three powers—the United States, Great Britain and France—would not join in a settlement that would officially end the war after sixteen years.

The stealthy and messy war in Laos, the one which Eisenhower had warned about, kept getting worse. Kennedy summoned his task force and his military chiefs in meeting after meeting. He sought information and more information about the murky jungle kingdom. He saw then, too, the deep trouble ahead for South Vietnam. Walt Rostow, the aide heading the Southeast Asia Task Force, found a report on Vietnam and took it to the President. "This is the worst one we've got," Kennedy said after reading it.

Strife continued in the Congo. One day Central Intelligence Director Allen Dulles sat across from Kennedy and told him that in all likelihood Patrice Lumumba, who had been taken from his prison in Thysville, Katanga, was dead in the eastern Congo bush. The leader had been backed by the Soviet Union in his bid for power against the central government under Joseph Kasavubu, established by the United Nations. On a Monday morning before the President had returned to the White House from his Glen Ora retreat, Salinger was on the phone with the firm news that Lumumba had been murdered. Kennedy listened quietly to the report, then told Salinger to issue the statement already prepared which expressed "great shock." The White House waited for the Russian outburst. It came twenty-four hours later and included a general attack on the United Nations. Kennedy called Dean Rusk and the two of them decided to wait until his news conference at midweek before replying to the Russians, but there was no doubt about the reply. Kennedy remained firmly behind the United Nations and the presence of UN forces in the Republic of Congo. An hour before Kennedy's news conference of February 15, the top-drawer Soviet experts assembled in the Cabinet Room. There were Rusk; former Soviet Ambassador Charles Bohlen; Paul H. Nitze, Assistant Secretary of Defense for International Security Affairs; Harlan Cleveland, Assistant Secretary of State for International Organizations; Kennedy's own national security aide, McGeorge Bundy; and other staff members.

Rusk had brought along a statement for Kennedy to give at his news conference. The President sat in one of the black leather chairs and read the draft. He found it too tough. He wanted to answer the Soviet threats of intervention firmly but not harshly; he still wanted to keep open that delicate line of communication between himself and Khrushchev which had been established by the return of the two RB-47 flyers. The President felt the Russian cries over the Congo were a bit hollow. A battle in the Congo, though an unpleasant place for either nation to fight, would favor the United States. The President got Adlai Stevenson on the phone. (That afternoon, as Stevenson had been talking in the United Nations, a fight had broken out between UN guards and pro-Lumumba demonstrators.) For more than an hour Kennedy and Stevenson hammered away on the statement. Only a short while later Kennedy walked across the carpeting of the New State Department Auditorium clutching the rolled-up paper with the final statement.

Kennedy furrowed his brow, began to read to reporters. "Ambassador Stevenson in the Security Council today has expressed fully and clearly the attitude of the United States government toward the attempts to undermine the effectiveness of the United Nations organization. The United States can take care of itself, but the United Nations system exists so that every nation can have the assurance of security. Any attempt to destroy this system is a blow aimed directly at the independence and security of every nation, large and small. I am also, however, seriously concerned at what appears to be a threat of unilateral intervention in the internal affairs of the republic of Congo. . . . The United States has supported and will continue to support the United Nations presence in the Congo. . . ."

*   *   *

On February 12 the Russians fired another of their massive rockets and sent a projectile toward the planet Venus in a spectacular space probe which once again overshadowed in world propaganda the United States' own more modest efforts. In a resigned voice Kennedy told his news conference at midmonth: "We have sufficiently large boosters to protect us militarily, but for the long, heavy exploration into space, which requires large boosters, the Soviet Union has been ahead and it is going to be a major task to surpass them."

Of all the areas of bafflement when Kennedy took office, space seemed more perplexing than the others. Kennedy seemed to know less about it, be less interested in it. At first he could only reflect the views of the scientists. And the government's scientific advisers were a mystic group, many of whom in the past had tended to scoff at Soviet efforts until they found the Russians surpassing them. The view Kennedy got, heavy on the pure scientific accomplishments of the finer, more sophisticated rockets and gadgetry from the American laboratories, tended to ignore the world's political battle, the immense propaganda war that means so much in conquering uncommitted minds. Russia already had made gains in this respect in being the first nation to launch a satellite. Now came the Venus probe. The government advisers fully expected a Russian to be the first man in space. The scientific answer was a plea to the press to emphasize the superior scientific information being gathered by the United States, not to be wooed by the spectacular nature of the big Soviet feats. It was a naïve appeal and others in the New Frontier understood this. "If we aren't first on the moon," said one of Kennedy's close advisers, "we had just as well give up."

Fidel Castro still stared across that ninety miles of water toward Florida. And one White House staff member, after reviewing the political situation in Latin America, told Kennedy flatly that there were twelve South American countries that could conceivably go communist in six weeks.

Nor was the trouble confined to the rest of the world. On a Tuesday morning John Kennedy held his breakfast meeting with Cabinet and legislative leaders. The topic: nagging unemployment, the sluggish economy. At the meeting's close, Speaker Sam Rayburn came through the White House lobby shaking his head, pushing newsmen aside. "It is the most urgent situation since the great depression," he warned, then hurried back to the Hill.

And then came the crucial vote on expanding the House Rules Committee to allow liberal legislation easier access to the House floor. It was Lyndon Johnson who first sensed trouble. His nose count in the House showed the effort faltering. He hurried back down Pennsylvania Avenue with the bad news. Sam Rayburn was using every bit of his personal prestige, but apparently it was not quite enough. The President called in his best, most trusted political helper, his brother Bob. The two of them and Larry O'Brien drew up a plan of attack. Every House member was to be contacted, every persuasion to be used. John Kennedy phoned key men himself. Stewart Udall, Secretary of the Interior and a former House member, was pressed into service. Such congressmen as Richard Bolling (Missouri) and Frank Thompson (New Jersey) were assigned specific men to plead with. O'Brien drew a chart, checked names as commitments came in. It was just like the Democratic convention in Los Angeles. No detail was left to chance. Everything was recorded on cards. Then came the tally, and the New Frontier won by five votes (217 to 212). The victory was sweet, but to John Kennedy there was a warning in that vote. If on this matter, which had united his strength and had gotten twenty-two Republican votes, the going was this tough, what would happen when sectional interests and economic interests intruded? It was grimly noted that the figures showed sixty-four Democrats from the South and border states aligned against the President.

As Kennedy saw it, one of his main tasks was to battle the pressure groups, to arouse the country for his program, so that the voters would provide a counterweight to the skillful and wealthy lobbyists. "On highways, the truckers already are out against me," mused the President in private. "There's the American Medical Association and the Chamber of Commerce opposed to other things. Some of these pressure groups have become so bureaucratic themselves that I don't believe they represent the majority of people in them. The people are in the middle of the road."

The President of the United States could only reflect that Capitol Hill, too, would get worse before it got better.

Beyond the eighteen acres of White House grounds there were only occasional faint ripples in a calm of complacency. The country had installed its new president with a flourish. It liked his style and his words. Now, the nation would wait a bit to see what he could do.

In the meantime the people studied the man, his wife and his children. Every move was written about. Every word recorded.

After the Kennedys had the new administration appointees over for a Sunday night reception, the Washington society columnists gasped. The evening *Star*'s Betty Beale listed eight social precedents which were shattered in the single evening.

By far the biggest headlines went to the fact there was an honest-to-goodness bar which dispensed hard liquor right out in the open. It was no secret that in previous administrations you could get a little bourbon or maybe even a martini if you knew how to go about it, but never in recent years had the cocktail been given such status. There were ash trays scattered about, too, which meant that smoking was allowed, another break with tradition.

"Naturalness was the keynote of this party," sighed Miss Beale, still shaken by the new look when she got to her typewriter. Children had been invited also, and they romped among the grownups. Fires burned in the fireplaces and small bowls of blossoms decorated the niches and tables.

Still at her typewriter, Miss Beale figured it out: "But obviously, President and Mrs. Kennedy have decided that they are going to offer the same hospitality to their guests when reporters are present as they would naturally do if they weren't, or if they were living back in their own house on N Street."

"The reason for this reception," Kennedy told his guests, "is the desire to see some of the names I have been reading about in the newspaper."

The long hours of the days were filled with work; wearying meetings, thick reports to be read and acted upon. Though so much of the Kennedy life was and is work, the critics of this phenomenal American family sometimes tend to overlook the drudgery which goes into a Kennedy triumph. The writers always note that the Kennedys have money, good looks and power. To mold them into success, however, takes more than a magic word. The new President was invariably awake by 7:30 or 8 in the morning. Sometimes he read newspapers in bed as he ate breakfast, at other times he dressed for a work session while he consumed two poached eggs. Kennedy walked to his office by 8:30 or 9 and plunged into meetings. Seldom did he leave before 7 or 8 P.M., and many staffers would send papers on his telephone demand to the private quarters as late as 11 P.M. So burdensome were the frantic early days that once he looked at an aide and said, "Nixon should have won the election."

The large Oval Office began to look and feel like President Kennedy. The pale-green walls were smothered in a coat of New England off-white. The two couches flanking the fireplace were hurried out and recovered in a light beige. A new stock of oak firewood was rushed in for the fireplace, which now crackled all the time. There were the marks of a Navy man: on the walls flanking the fireplace hung two naval pictures showing the 1812 battle between the "Constitution" and the British frigate "Guerriere," and on the mantle was a model of the "Constitution."

Just before the Kennedy children and the faithful terrier Charlie flew up from Palm Beach to take up residence in their famous new house, Jackie let the public in on how she had decorated their rooms: Caroline's was painted a pale pink with white woodwork, John's white with white woodwork and a blue trim around the door moldings. The information was rushed over the wires and received as much space as the heavier matters of state. Reporters pestered and Jackie reluctantly let out a menu of a dinner served to Bob and Ethel Kennedy: consommé Julienne, filet of beef, sautéed mushrooms, potato balls, mixed green salad, assorted cheese and crackers, crème brulée with strawberry sauce and coffee.

A huge snowman with button eyes and a carrot nose waited for Caroline in the back yard of the White House, the sculpture done by the gardener. She was delighted. In fact, she was fascinated by all her new surroundings. After taking a second look at the snowman, with her father in tow, she toured the President's office. She got a view of the indoor swimming pool, stuck her hand into the water and exclaimed, "It's warm." And when the diplomatic corps was invited to a reception, she helped greet the guests in a fancy party dress ("It's my very best," she told admirers). No doubt there will be many endearing sights in this administration of young people and young children, but few will top the picture of Caroline standing on the red carpeting in the foyer of the White House listening to the President's own Marine Band. Her foot twitched to the music, and when she was granted a special request, she asked for "Old MacDonald Had a Farm," which was rendered with such polish that few of the diplomats noted the tune.

If Caroline was a hit at this reception, so were other Kennedys. Jackie moved slowly among the people in the huge State Dining Room, using her French often. Bob Kennedy, bumping into Soviet Ambassador Mikhail Menshikov, asked him to come to the Justice Department, "where we check up on communist spies." Replied the jolly Russian: "Perhaps I'll come one day and look at the outside."

When the President approached Madame Hervé Alphand, wife of the French ambassador, he greeted her in French, "*Comment allez-vous?*" then he laughed and lapsed into English. "My wife speaks good French. I understand only one out of every five words . . . but always de Gaulle."

Joe Kennedy laughed about the evening he had talked with Caroline on the phone from Palm Beach and she had asked to speak with her cousin Steve Smith, who was in Florida with her grandfather. In the background the elder Kennedy could hear a presidential plea: "Hurry up, Caroline, I want to use the phone."

The Kennedys went unnoticed one night to the home of the Benjamin C. Bradlees, former Georgetown friends and neighbors. But such was not the luck on the evening they were to dine with Mr. and Mrs. Rowland Evans, Jr., New York

Herald Tribune correspondent, and the paper's owner John Hay (Jock) Whitney and his wife. The plan leaked when the Secret Service ordered snow-cleaning crews to get rid of the drifts and ice that clogged the curbs. To the embarrassment of the Evanses, the story soon was on the radio newscasts and, of course, reporters showed up on the sidewalk to photograph the Kennedys as they arrived.

A presidential itch to see the movie *Spartacus* sent the Secret Service scurrying to the Warner Theater one afternoon to check its safety. That evening after the lights were dimmed, Kennedy and his friend Paul B. Fay, Jr., now Under Secretary of the Navy, slipped in undetected. Noting a familiar figure in the row ahead of him, the President tapped Orville Freeman on the shoulder. "This is a hell of a way to write a farm program," said the grinning Kennedy to his Secretary of Agriculture. Freeman, like Kennedy, had sought out the dark theater to escape for a while from the long office hours.

The Kennedy wit itself was becoming legendary. The very night after he had been inaugurated, the President had gone to the all-stag Alfalfa Club Dinner, with its program of lampoons. Kennedy had been the hit of the evening, ribbing the men in his administration. Clark Clifford, went the Kennedy story, had chosen the Cabinet, had chosen the sub-cabinet and had even ridden a buffalo in the inaugural parade. "And all he asked in return was that we advertise his law firm on the backs of the one-dollar bills." He couldn't understand, the President had continued, all the fuss over his appointing his brother Attorney General. After all, he said, he always thought that it was a good thing for a young attorney to get some government experience before going out into private practice.

His spontaneous humor almost always dealt with the matter at hand. Talking to the National Industrial Conference Board, he was in fine fettle. "It has recently been suggested that whether I serve one or two terms in the presidency, I will find myself at the end of that period at what might be called the awkward age—too old to begin a new career and too young to write my memoirs. A similar dilemma, it seems to me, is posed by the occasion of a presidential address to a business group on business conditions less than four weeks after entering the White House—for it is too early to be claiming credit for the new administration and too late to be blaming the old one. And it would be premature to seek your support in the next election, and inaccurate to express thanks for having had it in the last one."

His reading suddenly became a phenomenon. Reporters found that he read their every word, sometimes called them up to praise or complain. He consumed five newspapers with his morning coffee. In voracious glances he could absorb a difficult memo on economics. He read from 1,200 to 2,000 words a minute, maybe faster when the going was light. Attractive magazines and books had to be secreted by staff members. Left out on desks, they were prey for the hungry Kennedy eyes.

When he wanted the facts on Cuba and the rise of Castro, a massive government document was trotted out. Timidly an aide suggested that Kennedy read the synopsis, but the suggestion was halted with a Kennedy wave. He went through the detailed account.

He went after specifics. The front pages of newspapers got first attention. He scanned the headlines, skimmed through pieces of marginal interest, took a moment or so longer with the vital stories while he sucked out their juice. He stopped to browse on the editorial page, taking more interest in the columnists than in the editorials.

Kennedy had a weakness for a fine phrase. One staff member insisted that the New Frontier began in a "French phase," simply because of the eloquent message sent to Kennedy by Charles de Gaulle after the election. Kennedy sometimes wondered how much of Winston Churchill's stature was built on the use of words. Often he read the Churchill memos just to savor their craftsmanship.

Kennedy proclaimed his favorite book to be *Melbourne,* by Lord David Cecil, the story of William Lamb, one of Queen Victoria's prime ministers. Those Kennedy students who rushed to the library for a copy found it described a ruling class of people with remote resemblances to the Kennedy clan.

Though the President generally stuck to nonfiction, he occasionally strayed. It was discovered with some relish by mystery buffs that he was a fan of the hard-drinking, hard-fighting British Secret Service agent James Bond, the creation of Ian Fleming.

Somebody listed the Kennedy print consumption and found that, in addition to his diet of newspapers and magazines in the course of a few days, he read Henry Kissinger's *The Necessity for Choice,* a heavy volume on nuclear war; Elting Morison's story of the life and times of Henry Stimson, *Turmoil and Tradition;* Cornelius Ryan's *The Longest Day;* John Kenneth Galbraith's *The Liberal Hour,* a collection of essays; and selections from a compendium on nuclear testing.

In his Senate days Kennedy had taken a speed-reading course, though even before he was an extremely rapid reader. Nor was he the only one with that talent in his family. Jackie, too, decided to try the speed-reading course. When she took the initial tests for speed and comprehension, her score revealed that she did not need the course.

While Kennedy's reading was gratifying to writers, publishers and government officials, there was another Washington man more pleased than any. He was A. T. Schrot, a Republican who owned the Cosmopolitan Newsstand on 15th Street. It was there that the White House bought most of its papers and periodicals. When Kennedy arrived, Schrot's White House business went up 400 per cent, and, in Schrot's words, "that's a hell of a lot."

Kennedy was a memo man. Soon after he took office, he ordered a dictaphone installed beside his desk. Throughout the day he would whirl and talk into the machine. Toward evening Mrs. Lincoln would rescue the transcriptions and type out the memos.

They were terse messages; sometimes only a sentence or two centered on an eleven-by-eight sheet of paper. There was a low key about them, like Kennedy himself. They had an understated manner, almost a politeness in "suggesting" and "appreciating" rather than demanding. Early in February he fired off this quick sentence to an aide: "I would appreciate it if you would read the Congressional Record— the House and the Senate—every day." In a memo to a staffer concerning letters he planned to send out he displayed his intimate knowledge of what makes a senator or congressman perk up. Wrote Kennedy: "[I will send] these letters so that members of the House and the Senate will see that I am watching their work."

In the thick sheaves of memos was the constant quest for information. "I would like to have more information on the progress of the negotiation with the Germans on increasing their participation in foreign aid to the underdeveloped countries and to defense."

And always his memos reflected his newspaper reading. To Secretary of Defense Robert McNamara he sent a brief reminder: "I note that Congress has once again criticized the Department of Defense for not giving more contracts to small business. This is an old complaint. . . . If it isn't possible for us to do better than has been done in the past I think we should know more about it. If it is possible for us to do better we should go ahead with it and I think we should make some public statements on it. Would you let me know about this?"

The character analysts dug at Kennedy. Despite the fact that he had been on the public stage continuously for four years, they seemed to have just discovered him. It was noted that he was not a vindictive man. After a battle which he won, he picked up his adversaries, dusted them off and offered his hand.

After the House Rules Committee fight, Bob Kennedy made his way up to Capitol Hill to the quiet office of Virginia's Judge Howard Smith, Rules Committee chairman and archenemy of all liberalism. The two sat in the judge's office and talked over many subjects. The judge, who on a Saturday was fond of going to his farm in Virginia and scratching an old red sow behind the ear, talked in his gentle country tones. He allowed as how he felt the younger generation which had taken over the government (he was too courtly to mention John Kennedy by name) seemed to him and those of his era to want to go too fast. He was trying to slow it down a little, in keeping with his own convictions and those he felt sure his people held. The two men, one 35 years old, the other 77 years old, talked about the University of Virginia where they had both gone to school. It was a pleasant chat between two politicians and two Americans, both understanding the business they were about, both knowing that victory and defeat were daily occurrences. They parted on kindly terms. Neither had changed his view—yet some warmth lingered.

From the White House routine came a hint of the Kennedy administrative style. Out was the formal, board-of-directors type of management, with weekly Cabinet meetings and National Security Council meetings at a set time and place. John Kennedy lived and worked informally. He phoned people when he wanted to talk to them. He summoned them to his office when he wanted to look at them as he talked. He did not bother certain men with other men's problems. The Cabinet meetings and the National Security Council meetings in a formal sense withered after the first week. "Why should we bother Orville Freeman or Abe Ribicoff with something they know nothing about?" asked Bob Kennedy, who already was marked as the second most powerful man in this government. Kennedy had a public calendar of appointments and meetings; and there was his own secret list, usually running longer than the public one. Constantly during the day the schedule was rearranged to suit him. He summoned the Secretary of State and the Secretary of Defense to breakfast or lunch or dinner or to his private quarters. There were splinter groups from the Cabinet and from the National Security Council, the men directly concerned with the matters Kennedy wanted to discuss. From the outside, the Kennedy administration took on a formless flow. Because there was no regularity, policy sometimes seemed to be constructed in haphazard fashion. There was less hint of what was going on in the Oval Office because of the relative secrecy of the small quiet gatherings. Journalists, in a first but subdued wave of criticism, began to ask who was making policy. The answer was that Kennedy was making policy. He wanted to know about every problem, every detail of government. He decided to drop the Operations Co-ordinating Board, which had been charged with implementing policy decisions of the National Security Council. To Kennedy it was just another layer of fat in which orders could get lost. Already he had discovered the lag between decision and implementation. He found that he sometimes had to ask three times before action was taken.

Kennedy was reaching for power. He wanted all the lines to lead to the White House, he wanted to be the single nerve center. This characteristic was familiar. To get his party's nomination, he had quietly collected the delegates—the power—and then had turned back easily all the challenges at the Los Angeles convention. Why did he want to be president, he had been asked during the campaign. Because, he had said, that was where the action was, where you could get things done, where the power lay. Once in the White House, John Kennedy did not mean to dissipate the power available to him by passing to others—at least not right away.

Thus, as February closed, Kennedy drifted between two strong currents—the natural ebullience of his New Frontier and the surging darkness of world trouble.

He could chortle to a friend in a light moment, "This is a damned good job." He could throw open the French doors beside his desk and breathe deeply of the cool air, now with a hint of spring in it, and occasionally he could break out of his office for a stroll around the grounds to clear his head.

He got over the hurt at inheriting Eisenhower's problems. At a National Security Council meeting the problems up for discussion were all neatly contained in a folder. Kennedy began, "Let's see now, did we inherit these, or are these our own?"

The entire country was distracted when the Kennedys looked for a new cook. Filipino Pedro Udo had been fine for Ike, but Jackie had other ideas. She installed French chef René Verdon as master of the White House kitchen.

Kennedy from the start took time out to see reporters. And in the lull of one noon he talked to me. He was behind his desk as I first entered, a desk littered with papers, scratch pads, books and thick memorandums. For a few precious seconds as I walked across the rug he turned to the small table behind him on which the day's newspapers and magazines were neatly arranged. He bent his head briefly to scan the headlines, then he whirled and put out his hand.

It all seemed different now as he approached. Doubtless

there was little physical change in the few short weeks of office—perhaps the tan had faded a little, the lines around the eyes were etched more finely from the constant reading. But the real difference in this meeting was in the office which for the moment seemed to be the biggest office in the world. It was bright with its white paint, the temperature several degrees cooler than in the surrounding rooms. The sun cast diffused squares of light on the thick rug after filtering through the drapes. The surroundings were now all Kennedy. Even Eisenhower's old desk bookends—the golden eagles— were perched on the wall bookshelves. In their places were miniature shipboard cannons from Revolutionary War days. They fit with the naval paintings on the walls.

The manners were the same. Kennedy gestured toward a chair and then sat carelessly behind his desk, clasped his hands around a knee.

When the office doors are closed, the silence is enormous. The President sits only a hundred yards from bustling Pennsylvania Avenue. Beyond his office walls the antechambers bulge with secretaries and aides. But suddenly it was quiet, an unusual atmosphere for Jack Kennedy, who for four long hard years never seemed to be out of sight and sound of a huge American crowd of voters.

In the quiet, Kennedy talked about his job. He chafed a bit at the thought that some of the impatient journalists were demanding accomplishment so soon. He simply had not had time to learn as much as he needed to know, to make the firm decisions that he realized must soon be made, to assemble the intricate programs that he had to follow. His action was still reaction. But it would change, he promised.

Kennedy dwelled for a minute on the "export of the communist revolution." This was the challenge before him. "How do you combat guerrillas?" he asked. "That question must be answered."

The President's mind wandered back over other crises of other years. For just a fleeting moment he wondered out loud why we did not do more at the time of the Berlin airlift to show the Russians we meant business. Then we had the uncontested military superiority. He asked with no show of his own feeling if Korea should have been "the right war at the right time," if this country should have gone farther. He seemed to imply that he had inherited something that perhaps could have been controlled by a little boldness earlier.

There was even then a trace of presidential doubt over our ability to wage an effective war in Laos.

Kennedy remarked on the men around him. "Good men," he said. And he revealed that he had just decided to appoint John J. McCloy and Arthur H. Dean to help him with problems of disarmament and nuclear testing. Both men were tough and independent, he said, not wedded to any previous positions, and for this reason he wanted them.

Suddenly the office door flew open. Aide P. Kenneth O'Donnell, the appointments secretary, entered, and with him came the sounds of the outside world.

The words were reassuring, but all the problems remained.

CHAPTER FOUR

COMMANDER

IN CHIEF

JOHN KENNEDY paused a moment on the phone. "What's this about Arleigh Burke being a distinguished combat commander when I was just learning about a PT boat?"

He was talking about a brief item which had chided the President for being critical of Burke, who had indulged in a little verbal muscle flexing in an interview granted before Kennedy imposed stricter policy guides on defense statements. The interview had come out a month after Kennedy's inauguration, and when asked about it at his press conference, the President had suggested that he was glad he had toughened up. A magazine had pointed out that Burke was steaming to combat fame when Kennedy was a naval officer trainee.

"But the point is," said the mildly irritated President, striking every argument down with swift logic, "that is not the way it is any more."

In February of 1961 John Kennedy was commander in chief. And he was a commander in chief with some different ideas—one of particular significance: that the United States of America would learn how to combat communism on its own terms. Gone was sole reliance on John Foster Dulles' massive retaliation. There was, in Kennedy's words, to be a choice between annihilation and humiliation. The U.S. armed forces were to learn to fight the stealthy guerrilla battles. They were to acquire a new flexibility. There were new names for it—counterinsurgency, paramilitary activity; the meaning was the same.

Kennedy had hinted at what was on his mind on that cold January inauguration day. "For only when our arms are sufficient beyond doubt can we be certain beyond doubt that they will never be employed."

He had added a few more paragraphs in his State of the Union address, which tolled out such grim warnings. "On the presidential coat of arms, the American eagle holds in his right talon the olive branch, while in his left he holds a bundle of arrows. We intend to give equal attention to both. . . . I have, therefore, instructed the Secretary of Defense to reappraise our entire defense strategy . . . and the adequacy, modernization and mobility of our present conventional and nuclear forces and weapons systems in the light of present and future dangers. . . ."

And in his special defense message sent to Congress in the closing days of March, he spelled it in clear terms. "We need a greater ability to deal with guerrilla forces, insurrections, and subversion. Much of our effort to create guerrilla and antiguerrilla capability has in the past been aimed at general war. We must be ready now to deal with any size of force, including small externally supported bands of men; and we must help train local forces to be equally effective. . . ."

The idea had nagged at Kennedy for months. As with so many Kennedy ideas, there was no moment of truth, when his concept of military strategy suddenly dawned; it was one of those Kennedy notions that grew from common sense, from his awareness of what was happening in the world. Since we could not use nuclear weapons on a band of ten men in the Laotian jungle, there had to be some other answer, which this nation had not yet found.

The picture of the most famous soldier of our time, Dwight David Eisenhower, seated in the Cabinet Room the day before he left office, deeply worried about the implacable thickets of Laos, haunted Kennedy. The map toward which Ike had gestured stared out at him, the thin country a curving pointed dagger protruding into Asia.

In his private moments Kennedy began to talk about paramilitary activities. He asked for and received a photostated translation from the French of Cuban Ché Guevera's 1950 book on guerrilla warfare (*La Guerra de Guerrillas*). He also sent for some of the selected works of Chinese Communist Mao Tse-tung, who has written on guerrilla tactics. He wanted to see virtually everything in our own military archives on this type of war. Robert McNamara came around with four fat volumes of his own creation that described the new defense directions. This was the reappraisal which the President had asked for. "I've got all that to read?" he asked when he saw the size of the reports. He did not hesitate, however, he read them all.

Nothing was too complicated or too simple for him. Only once did he say anything about the material brought to him. When he was presented with a thin green-jacketed booklet entitled, *Guerrilla Warfare, the Irish Republican Army*, Kennedy laughed, thinking of his own band of Irish politicians who sometimes were called the "Irish Republican Army," and asked, "That's going a little far, isn't it?"

The concept of guerrilla warfare almost magically became a policy. From the casual talk at his desk, from the reading of the skimpy material, came a new military direction.

The immediate problem, of course, was in Southeast Asia, and particularly Laos. From small patrols of rebels (Pathet Lao) who killed at night, the conflict grew into open attack by battalion-sized units. They swept up the northwestern part of the country, fanned out toward the cities. The world suddenly became alarmed.

John Kennedy had directed his first worried thoughts toward the problem in mid-December, when the Soviet airlift of arms had started. Perhaps he had not become concerned enough, but he possessed no power then. The first meeting of his National Security officers had been on Laos—on the day after he was inaugurated.

From then on, almost no day passed in the White House on which he did not ask some questions about the tiny country 12,000 miles away. Twice daily he received his intelligence briefing, and the strange reports of the stranger warfare filtered back to Kennedy. Battles were fought and won with troops firing into the air over the heads of the defenders or invaders. Corruption, indifference, stupidity plagued nearly every military and governmental move. In six years the United States had given Laos $310 million in aid, sent in military men in mufti to help train the Royal Army.

Kennedy called for a neutral Laos, in hopes that the communists would call off their offensive and would agree to let the country have peace. His answer was the whine of communist bullets.

In mid-March he reached the first of a chain of major decisions. No sign of letup appeared in the communist military campaign, indeed just the reverse was true, and the Soviet arms buildup, believed in the White House to be a key element in the offensive, continued unabated. "Who runs this area?" Kennedy asked his military chiefs one day in one of the countless briefings held for him. When he was told that Admiral Harry Felt was the boss, he asked, "What's wrong with bringing him here?" For some reason the military men were reluctant; they had not suggested it themselves. But this was the Kennedy method of action, to which the Pentagon had not yet adjusted. To the President nothing was better than having the man who had been up against the problem come home and talk it over.

Up to then Kennedy's military advice had been murky. The Chiefs of Staff did not want to get involved in a war in Laos. The United States armed forces with their megatons of nuclear blast simply were not equipped for the small fight in Laos. The discouraging history of guerrilla warfare was recited to Kennedy. Nearly half a million first-class French troops had been licked in Indochina.

It was not a fear of fighting which gave pause to the White House. It was the fear of not being able to fight as we should fight. Our military men had concluded that if we committed troops to battle directly, as we had in Korea, we might again face the Red Chinese. Total victory, if it could ever be achieved, would require the massive air power of this nation and it might mean the use of tactical nuclear weapons, the bombing of southern portions of Red China. World War III haunted further thoughts. If there were other ways out of the problem, Kennedy intended to find them.

Again he prodded his advisers. "Wouldn't you like to talk to your Pacific Commander?"

They sent for Felt. And with him came two army officers fresh from the Laotian fighting.

On March 9 Admiral Felt stood in full dress uniform in front of John Kennedy and his chief security aides in the White House and tried, as others before him had done, to make sense out of the situation. But Felt's presentation was not impressive to those in the room. It was a bit pompous and lacked the clarity and detail that the President sought, though perhaps Kennedy at that time wanted answers that could not and did not exist in the Laotian warfare. For two hours the President grilled Felt and the two jungle-war experts. Following this meeting, Kennedy went directly into another session with his top policy men.

At that meeting a seventeen-point course of action was drafted. The program was aimed at propping up the Laotians with more and better supplies and improved troop training and deployment. The great weakness seemed to Kennedy to be the fact the Laotians would not fight or, when they did, would not fight properly. From the White House word of the new decisions was sent to Laos, in hopes that it would spur Premier Boun Oum and General Phoumi Nosavan into greater effort.

One of the facts Harry Felt had relayed to Kennedy was that Phoumi surrounded himself with a personal guard of his best trained officers. Kennedy, as did the military men, was anxious to get the trained officers into the field, where they would do some good. The presidential message to Phoumi was rather stern, in hopes it would create a little action.

But in the days that followed, no action came. The daily intelligence reports from Laos read the same. Phoumi had not been stirred by the Kennedy message. His best officers continued to stay out of the fighting.

John Kennedy grew agitated. His questions to his military advisers became more abrupt. He still did not want to upset the country or the world by openly criticizing the Laotians. Quiet diplomacy was the way he chose to operate. In his office, however, he was less serene.

"Will the Laotians fight for their country?" he asked at one point, totally puzzled by new reports of the Royal Army failures.

"What kind of soldiers are they?" he inquired of his experts.

Sometimes in his wandering through the White House as he pondered the Laotian problem he would mutter, "This is the worst mess the Eisenhower administration left me."

He called for biographies on Phoumi and on Souvanna Phouma, the exiled premier. He wanted to know more about these strange men. He read every fact he could find on the military situation—how it had developed, how the leaders had been chosen.

Kennedy was not happy with the advice he received. Later on he would remark that his military planners optimistically developed plans that never seemed to work. There apparently was little understanding of the jungle fighting among the Pentagon brass. At one point, for instance, Kennedy was told by his military advisers that it would take the communists three weeks to win a specified area. When the communists gobbled it up in three days, the White House wondered if anyone really knew what was happening in Laos.

Kennedy waited a few more precious days before deciding that Secretary of State Dean Rusk should seek a meeting with Andrei Gromyko, then at the United Nations in New York, to make a final stern plea for a neutral Laos. Again the approach hit the Soviet wall of silence and coldness. Minutes after Rusk finished with Gromyko, he was on the phone to the White House. Kennedy, listening to the report of the Rusk-Gromyko talk, made up his mind that quiet diplomacy would, for the time being, have to be abandoned.

The President summoned his National Security men to a special Monday afternoon meeting; Rusk was absent, off in California giving a speech, but Chester Bowles filled in for him. For nearly two hours the deteriorating military situation was reviewed, the diplomatic avenues open to the United States were explored, the military contingencies were re-examined. The time had come for this country to take a verbal stand, if nothing more. There was no final decision at that session. "Let's wait until Dean Rusk gets back," said

Kennedy. He called for another meeting on the next day, when his Secretary of State would be in town.

This one was shorter, lasting about sixty-five minutes. Rusk and McNamara reviewed the plans. "All right," Kennedy said, "we must tell the congressional leaders and the people." He thought a moment longer, squinting a bit, the creases around his eyes deepening as he concentrated. "I want another day to prepare a statement, so let's have the press conference on Thursday." He phoned Pierre Salinger and asked that the press conference be shifted from Wednesday to Thursday. Then he asked Lyndon Johnson to arrange for the congressional leaders to meet in Lyndon's office for a briefing by Rusk and Allen Dulles the following day. McGeorge Bundy and Chip Bohlen were ordered to begin work on a statement.

Thursday morning, March 23, the day of the press conference, the first draft of the statement was brought in. Kennedy was not satisfied. He rarely is on the first try. He sent Bundy and Bohlen back to work. By 4:30 that afternoon, the second draft was ready. This time Kennedy assembled Bundy, Ted Sorensen and Pierre Salinger in his office, and all of them went over the statement, making suggestions. Kennedy read and reread the paragraphs carefully. Just a few minutes before 6 P.M., press-conference air time, he and his aides climbed into the presidential Cadillac for the four-minute ride to the New State Department Auditorium. The car was silent. Because of the Laotian crisis there had been no time to talk to Kennedy about other questions he might be asked. Salinger handed half a dozen memos to the President, and he studied these as the car sped the few blocks in the fading light, policemen at every intersection holding back the straining evening traffic.

In the meantime the State Department technicians had been frantically at work. They had constructed a three-paneled display on which they had tacked three six-by-eight-foot maps of Laos, all drawn in light gray-blue, brown, tan and brownish red, the different colors showing the stages of communist infiltration and domination. Lincoln White, the State Department's press officer, had been assigned the duty of whirling the display as Kennedy referred to the maps.

Now, just seconds before air time, the maps were still covered with cloth, and chuckling reporters called, "Take it off, take it off."

Some 426 reporters, photographers, broadcasters and technicians settled in their places; it was the largest gathering that Kennedy had drawn for a press conference.

Kennedy went into an anteroom, where Dean Rusk met him. They had a quick talk on the Laos statement, and Kennedy sought a few hasty facts on the trouble then developing over Portugal's Angola. The President found a chair and began again to go over his statement. Half a minute past 6 P.M. the knock came on the door; it was time for Kennedy to go into the auditorium. He did not move. He was then on the fourth page of the seven-page statement. He read the last three pages a final time before he sprang up. With the flat of his palm he took a swipe at his forelock to make sure it was pressed down. He walked through the auditorium door, and the correspondents rose. As he strode across the expanse of carpeting toward the speaker's stand, photographers crouched and clicked their shutters rapidly.

Oddly, he wore a vest with his dark-gray suit, one of the few times he has so appeared in public. His shirt was a light tan and his thin tie with the small knot was gray. Most of his Florida tan had faded, yet he looked alert. He neither smiled nor frowned but had an enigmatic expression that he always seemed to wear when he crossed the moat of carpeting to stare at the American citizenry. Each reporter interpreted the expression as he wanted, and frequently opposite views of the Kennedy mood were expressed in the next day's papers.

Then Kennedy gave a slight smile of recognition to reporters in the front rows. He placed his papers on the walnut rostrum and smoothed them down.

Kennedy read quickly. "I want to make a brief statement about Laos. . . . Our special concern with the problem in Laos goes back to 1954. That year at Geneva a large group of powers agreed to a settlement of the struggle for Indochina. Laos was one of the new states which had recently emerged from the French Union and it was the clear premise of the 1954 settlement that this new country would be neutral— free of external domination by anyone."

Kennedy leaned forward on both arms in his urgency to say it just right. "The new country contained contending factions, but in its first years real progress was made towards a unified and neutral status. But the efforts of a communist-dominated group to destroy this neutrality never ceased. . . .

"First, we strongly and unreservedly support the goal of a neutral and independent Laos. . . .

"Secondly, if there is to be a peaceful solution, there must be a cessation of the present armed attacks by externally supported communists. If these attacks do not stop, those who support a truly neutral Laos will have to consider their response. The shape of this necessary response will, of course, be carefully considered, not only here in Washington, but in the SEATO conference with our allies, which begins next Monday . . ."

Kennedy lowered his head, looked into the cameras. "No one should doubt our resolution on this point. . . . We will not be provoked, trapped, or drawn into this or any other situation; but I know that every American will want his country to honor its obligations to the point that freedom and security of the free world and ourselves may be achieved."

Done with his statement, Kennedy called for the regular press-conference questions. In half an hour the time was up, and he walked quickly back out the door. Dean Rusk met him and congratulated him on the Laos statement. Kennedy said little. He dropped back in the chair in the small room, and for a few silent minutes he watched NBC broadcasters David Brinkley and Chet Huntley discuss the press conference. In the dark, John Kennedy returned to the White House.

Kennedy's words were far more stern than his intentions just then. If the communists had launched a major offensive that genuinely threatened the cities of Laung Prabang and Vientiane, and thus the entire country, he probably would have sent in American fighting troops despite all the disadvantages. But he was not yet convinced that matters were so desperate, and he was determined to try to talk the Pathet Lao out of a war before involving American troops.

Russian reaction to his television speech came the next day at a luncheon table in New York. Soviet Foreign Minister

Andrei Gromyko, who had been scheduled to return immediately to Moscow, sought out United States UN Ambassador Adlai Stevenson on the day before his departure. At lunch he asked for an appointment with Kennedy, saying that he had a message from Nikita Khrushchev. In talking to Stevenson, Gromyko said that Moscow shared this country's desire for an independent and neutral Laos and expressed the hope that such a solution could be reached. It was a first "hopeful sign," in American diplomatic parlance. Stevenson phoned Washington immediately, and the meeting was set for the following Monday, March 27.

But even before that time another matter had to be straightened out. As Kennedy sought allies for whatever action might be needed in Laos, he had naturally turned to Great Britain. He had received sympathy but little else at first. Prime Minister Harold Macmillan had cabled Kennedy that Britain would give this nation its "moral" support in whatever we decided to do. This was not enough for Kennedy. Since the Prime Minister was in Bermuda, the President decided on his first major meeting with an allied head of state. Arrangements were made to meet in Key West on the following Sunday. Kennedy flew to Palm Beach on Saturday, and on Sunday morning he was standing on the warm apron of Boca Chica field, waiting for Macmillan's jet Comet to land, the plane having detoured around Cuba on its way up.

At first the British and American teams met separately, to get their papers in order. Then they met together in a severely functional room in the Navy base's headquarters building. An important reason for the meeting was to let Macmillan get a look at Kennedy, so that he would be reassured that the President of the United States was no rash kid who would throw the world into a war. But Kennedy's main mission was to seek actual military support from Britain in case intervention in Laos became necessary.

Macmillan was reluctant. At one point in the conversation he remarked calmly about the course an engagement in Laos might take, "When the others stop cheering, you and I will be out there alone." Yet Kennedy did get what he sought. Macmillan did agree to commit a Commonwealth force if intervention became necessary.

They talked about other troubles, but not too seriously. There was lunch in the white cottage that Harry Truman had made famous when he used to vacation in Key West. And as they prepared to depart, Macmillan kidded the President a bit about Cuba. "I'll fly over Cuba," he said. "If they shoot me down, you can have your incident."

But if one ally was willing, another was reluctant. Back in Washington French Ambassador Hervé Alphand was waiting at the airport for Kennedy's jet. He carried a letter from de Gaulle. At the President's invitation, Alphand climbed into the presidential limousine as it sped through the darkness toward the White House. Kennedy ripped open the letter, read it hastily in the car. It said that under no circumstances would France join in armed intervention in Laos.

The tulip trees around the White House grounds were just burgeoning. The waves of tourists clung to the iron fence, and a warm sun bathed Washington in spring languor the following Monday.

Just six minutes before noon a motorcycle officer, flashing his two red lights, turned off Pennsylvania Avenue and entered the White House yard. Behind him came a 1956 black Cadillac. It moved quietly up the drive and braked in front of the executive wing.

Some seventy-five newsmen and cameramen jostled on the front-door stoop. President Kennedy's military aide, Chester Clifton, stood waiting for the guest. Out hopped Andrei Gromyko, behind him came Ambassador Mikhail Menshikov. Gromyko, with only a slight smile, gripped Clifton's hand and headed immediately for the door. He was in a somber black suit and black hat. The three men walked quickly through the lobby and down the corridor to the President's office.

There were no surprises in the Oval Office, where Dean Rusk and Adlai Stevenson also waited. Professions of a strong Soviet desire for peace in Laos poured from Gromyko. The Soviets wished to work for a truly neutral nation. Kennedy outlined again the history of the small nation and the need for neutrality. Then suddenly he suggested that just the two of them go for a walk in the Rose Garden outside his office windows. The grass was beginning to freshen in the spring sun. A white bench on the other side of the small panel of grass in the middle of the garden looked inviting. The two men strolled through the spring air, Kennedy with his hands in his pockets. Then they sat on the bench. In the twenty minutes they were alone Kennedy did most of the talking. He told Gromyko that many of the wars in the past had come from misjudgments of others' intentions, and he warned him not to miscalculate the will or the fiber of this country. We would not, he said, sit idly by and see the communists sweep up the land in Southeast Asia. To misread his intentions would be a grave error. Gromyko did not say much. Caroline came bounding out of the house, Jackie behind her. Kennedy introduced his wife to the Russian, then they sat again and talked.

At 12:40 the meeting was over, and newsmen were herded out on the White House drive where the TV microphones had been set up. Gromyko pushed through the journalists and halted before the cameras. He fingered the brim of his black hat nervously. Though he knew English, he spoke slowly in Russian, his translator writing frantically on a pad, then carefully giving it in English. Gromyko called the talks "useful and interesting."

"Naturally the question of Laos was touched upon," he said. "The President and I after our conversation expressed the hope that possibilities would be found of settling the Laotian question peacefully."

What about a cease fire? "We touched in conversation on this subject. I have nothing to say at this moment publicly."

With two short choppy waves of his right hand, not unlike the familiar Kennedy campaign gesture, Gromyko walked to his car and disappeared into the Pennsylvania Avenue traffic.

For all the drama of these days, the Laotian problem was still cloudy. No one knew the Russian intentions, and America's own mind, despite Kennedy's words, was not understood.

The mighty U.S. Seventh Fleet, its Marines primed for battle, its aircraft in operating fettle, steamed into the South China Sea. The ships hunkered there, gray and threatening. But the Pathet Lao cared little about power at sea. They marched on. And the United States did nothing. Only John Kennedy's phrases were thrown at the enemy.

Had the United States resolve slipped? Where was the Kennedy courage? For the first time editorial criticism developed. He was scolded by certain pundits for talking tough, then not acting tough—in fact, not acting at all. Faith in this country had been destroyed in Southeast Asia, some said. How could Thailand or Vietnam or other allies again take our word?

While Kennedy's reluctance to send United States troops into Laos was evident, it was not endless. While Kennedy was attempting a bluff, it was a limited bluff. Despite the military disadvantages, despite this country's relative lack of preparedness for guerrilla war, Kennedy in the weeks of April concluded that he might have to commit fighting troops in Laos if the communists swept on dangerously toward Vientiane, the one city which the President felt could not fall.

He did not draw a line beyond which the communists would run the risk of war with the United States. Plans for the formless type of war being fought in Laos had to be formless themselves. Too much depended on circumstance, on what might happen at the given moment.

The broad scheme of action finally developed was called "Plan Five," because in the end five nations had agreed to send in troops if it became necessary—the United States, Great Britain, Thailand, the Philippines and Pakistan. The plan called for troops first to move into positions in the Mekong River Valley to relieve Laotian Royal Army units, allowing them to go to the front for direct combat. If the enemy still came on, John Kennedy had made up his mind that there was no other choice but to fight. It was his first decision to use force.

Had the critical moment ever arrived, it would have been primarily a United States fight. The President had generally been disappointed in the response of the allies to his pleas. But there were a few reasuring moments. For instance, Pakistan President Ayub Khan, a tough old soldier himself, brushed aside the idea of sending only a token force; if Pakistan fought in Laos, she would do it right. Ayub promised Kennedy 5,000 of his best troops. Kennedy never forgot this act of faith. Whenever Ayub wanted to talk to the President after that, Kennedy was ready to listen. When Ayub visited the United States the following July, he was given a state dinner on the lawn of Mount Vernon, the most glamorous social affair of the administration's first year.

Laos in the last days of April simmered in a confusing mixture of jungle fighting and calls for a cease fire. Kennedy and Macmillan had asked for a cease fire to be followed by a fourteen-nation conference and eventual coalition government including members of the Pathet Lao. But apparently rather than submit to the Anglo-American demand for the immediate cease fire, Moscow called for talks forthwith and said vaguely that the Laotian belligerents should work out their own cease fire.

But there were hints from the Kremlin that the communists also wanted to give up the messy business. Nikita Khrushchev said to Ambassador Llewellyn Thompson, "If we all keep our heads and do nothing provocative, we can find a way out of our problems in Laos."

For further confusion one only had to turn to Vientiane itself. Along the Mekong River there were foot races, boxing and wrestling matches. At night the temple courtyards were filled with dancing girls. A torchlight parade wound through the city, and the best floats were those of the Royal Army. The celebration was in honor of the eleventh anniversary of the founding of the army, and most of the troops had been pulled back from the field to celebrate. Though the troops looked fit and eager as they paraded, the army warned the people not to wander outside the city for fear of the Pathet Lao.[1]

On May 3 it happened: from Laos came word of a tenuous agreement by both sides to stop shooting to seek a truce. It was the thinnest kind of promise, and in the weeks to follow it nearly vanished as fighting continued, as the communists captured more ground. But eventually a vague, unsettled peace did prevail. For the time being, at least, John Kennedy had stopped the offensive with words.

[1] Only a little less confusing was an American phenomenon. As Kennedy waded deeper into the Laotian mystery, his popularity in the nation went up. In April, some 73 per cent of the voters thought John Kennedy was doing a good job of running the country.

CHAPTER FIVE

SOMETHING FOR

THE BOYS

EVEN while Laos bubbled, John Kennedy could not forget any of his other problems. Beneath the more glamorous burdens of international politics were the everyday garden-variety political fights, none more difficult than that in New York State.

Most of the Democratic faithful in the fifty states of the union on the day of November 9, when that thin margin of victory was finally established, relaxed a bit and went quietly on planning what federal patronage should come their way. For the most part the Kennedy brothers, who were the chief spoils dispensers, did not argue much. The Kennedy workers generally knew what the Kennedys wanted and made recommendations in line with these wants.

When the Kennedys asked for the patronage nominations from the state chairmen, they did not make any promises, but politics and the Kennedys being one, if the nominations were good, the chances were excellent the men would get the jobs.

The patronage leverage of the federal government is probably overrated in terms of political power. The population of this country is too big now, and too many voters are needed to swing an election, the president is too far removed from the state organizations, for any vast machine to be welded from the federal jobs which can be handed out. Yet to a key state or county chairman the say-so on who gets what in his area is a factor in his political stature.

The Department of Agriculture had an estimated 500 appointive jobs. There were openings for 190 United States marshals and United States attorneys. The Defense Department had some 200 jobs around the country that a new administration could appoint. There were 200 U.S. Savings Bond Administrators, 11 Bureau of the Mint officials, 52 customs collectors and controllers. There were bank examiners, judges, civil defense administrators and so on.

Most of the state recommendations came in on time. But not from New York. Its party hierarchy was fragmented. Only the common effort of electing John Kennedy had held any semblance of a party together in New York before the election. Within hours after the Kennedy victory, the volatile mix had blown up. Nobody would work with anybody else.

The state party was headed by Mike Prendergast, who was Carmine DeSapio's choice, which on paper made Carmine top Democrat. But the Kennedys had tiptoed around Carmine whenever they could, for a number of reasons, among them the fact that Carmine and his dark glasses reeked of big-city bossism, something the New Frontier liked to avoid when possible, although it was not always possible.

For the five months after his election Kennedy adopted a hands-off attitude toward New York. He hoped that some kind of political Messiah would appear and get the party back together or that at least a strong man would come forth who could dump Mike Prendergast and perhaps DeSapio to boot. Kennedy waited and nothing happened; the situation got worse.

New Yorkers dawdled more over patronage. When they finally submitted names to the National Committee in Washington, Bob Kennedy took one look at the list and found most of the recommendations unacceptable to the New Frontier. This message was flashed back to New York in Bob's own style, which was simply to go looking elsewhere for the appointees.

Democratic National Chairman John M. Bailey, Larry O'Brien and Bob Kennedy began to submit names of New Yorkers which they got from the congressional Democrats. Still there was no visible effect. The squabbling between the five New York City borough presidents got worse. The liberals, under former Senator Herbert Lehman and Mrs. Eleanor Roosevelt, declared their own war, and Mayor Robert Wagner proclaimed himself the anointed one. Prendergast and DeSapio yelled more loudly about their political rights.

Finally, in a sequence that resembled a Marx Brothers movie, DeSapio & Co. came down to Washington for a private seance with John Bailey. Carmine and Herbert Koehler, borough leader from Queens, and Joseph McKinney of Staten Island flew through fog and rain to meet Bailey. Joseph Sharkey (Brooklyn) came by train, having less faith in air travel, particularly in bad weather. Bronx leader Charlie Buckley had developed a mysterious virus disease and stayed home in bed. Strangely he had been the lone and staunch Kennedy supporter from the onset of the campaign.

For an hour and a half they talked with Bailey, who told them precisely what they thought he would: if the borough leaders would get their own situation straightened out and come up with an acceptable list of patronage candidates, the Kennedys would do business with them.

Once the message from the White House had been delivered, the four men sped through the rain to Congressman Emanuel Celler's Judiciary Committee headquarters, where the New York Democratic congressional delegation was assembling.

Carmine described the meeting with John Bailey to reporters as "informative, interesting and very satisfactory in every way."

"There was a bottle of scotch that was very interesting," chimed in Koehler. Carmine glanced nervously at his companion.

"I hope they have food here," continued Koehler. "I haven't eaten."

They indeed had discussed patronage with Bailey, said DeSapio, ignoring Koehler, but that had been only the secondary reason.

What was the primary reason, someone asked. "The good of the administration," said DeSapio sweetly.

"Did you ever see a politician that wasn't interested in patronage?" snorted Koehler, as Carmine steered him toward the committee door.

All this proved to the Kennedys exactly what they had

learned from the campaign. Not only was there a lack of the kind of talent they sought in the existing New York party apparatus, but DeSapio's bunch were not planning on changing their style. Still the Kennedys could find no solution until New York Mayor Robert Wagner won re-election over the bosses' opposition in the fall and took shaky command of the party.

New York State was an exception, fortunately. There were small patronage sore spots all over, particularly in Ohio, Nebraska, Vermont and California, but for the most part the jobs were handed out without trouble.

The Kennedys made no secret of the fact that they liked Democrats who had been Democrats throughout the campaign, and they liked friends of Democrats who had been Democrats.

Under the watchful eyes of Bailey and O'Brien, the Kennedy appointments were squeezed for every bit of political goodwill. Once a name had been settled upon, the technique was to check immediately with every Democrat connected with the man. The list often included six layers—senator, governor, congressman, state chairman, national committeemen and committeewomen, and county chairman. Sometimes Bailey and O'Brien even made sure the ward boss knew what was coming.

For those of both parties who had watched the Eisenhower administration frequently ignore the Republican party machinery, the change was welcome. Politics was back in style.

GOP senators and congressmen sometimes during the eight Eisenhower years used to pick up the paper and learn for the first time of new White House appointees in their states. One veteran professional Republican employed by the GOP Republican Senatorial Campaign Committee sighed with envy as he watched the appointments being made. "They're passing out the jobs to the party workers," he said. "That's the way it should be done. I'm for it. If we'd done it, they wouldn't be here now."

But Kennedy searched beyond the ranks of the party to fill many of the secondary jobs.

The Kennedy friends were called into service. From San

Francisco came Paul B. (Red) Fay, a wartime chum of the new President's. Fay was appointed Under Secretary of the Navy, his primary qualification being a four-year hitch in PT boats, just like Kennedy.

Earl E. T. Smith, a Florida golfing companion of the Kennedy family and a former ambassador to Cuba, was slated to be ambassador to Switzerland, but the name leaked out and the Swiss objected. Though angered by the leak, Kennedy dropped Smith, who in his Cuba days had been far too friendly with Batista to do him credit now.

John Seigenthaler, former Nashville, Tennessee, reporter and friend of Bob Kennedy's, who helped Bob on his book *The Enemy Within*, was named Bob's administrative assistant. David Hackett, a Milton Academy friend of Bob's, took over a new division of juvenile delinquency in the Justice Department.

On Capitol Hill the Kennedy team found talent. A total of thirty-nine people who had been employed in congressional procedures, many as administrative assistants to senators and congressmen, answered the call of the executive branch.

Unfortunate political candidates swarmed into Washington after being tossed out back home. Those governors who could not succeed themselves and other state politicians who had fallen into disfavor looked to the east for a job. Orville Freeman, former governor of Minnesota, got top prize in his class: as Secretary of Agriculture, he had Cabinet rank. Iowa's former Governor Herschel Loveless, defeated in his bid for the Senate, was named a member of the Renegotiation Board. Kansas' George Docking, defeated for a third gubernatorial term, became a member of the Board of Directors of the Export-Import Bank. J. Allen Frear, senator from Delaware struck down by the voters, joined the Securities and Exchange Commission. Former Congressman George McGovern, who had unsuccessfully challenged South Dakota's Karl E. Mundt for the Senate, was appointed Director of the Food for Peace Program.

The young, relatively unknown, cadre of amateur politicians who had labored so effectively for Kennedy in the campaign were rewarded whenever possible. Joseph Tydings, son of the former senator of Maryland, got the U.S. Attorney's job in that state as a reward for being co-ordinator for the Kennedys in Delaware and Florida.

Ivan A. Nestingen, mayor of Madison, Wisconsin, answered the call to Washington, became Under Secretary of Health, Education and Welfare. Jerry Bruno, who had been an advance man for Kennedy along that endless campaign trail, was placed in the Department of Labor. Bill Daniel, the brother of the governor of Texas, Price Daniel, became the new governor of Guam. Fred Dutton, former aide to California's Governor Pat Brown, who had worked hard in the campaign on the Citizens for Kennedy and Johnson drive, joined the White House staff.

When the Kennedys could, they liked to soothe sectional feeling and angle for special favor on the Hill. The new Under Secretary of Agriculture was Charlie Murphy, former Truman aide and a native of North Carolina, the state which also produced Congressman Harold Cooley, chairman of the House Agriculture Committee.

There also existed in the Kennedy portfolio of patronage something which became known around the National Committee as "a walk through the bank," from an old legend that to be seen in the bank lobby with J. P. Morgan was enough to assure a man's credit. So it was in its own way with the Kennedys. The friendly handshake with the new president in front of photographers or discreet stories about working with the new administration were enough to increase the demand for a man's talents. Attorney Clifford became an even larger legal figure in Washington when his intimacy with the New Frontier became known. A young Nashville lawyer named John J. Hooker found that the citizens of his good city took a far greater interest in him after he was photographed coming out of Kennedy's front door in the pre-inauguration days.

CHAPTER SIX

HOME NOTES

THE glitter kept shining through. With young people in a young age in the White House, the somber tones of the world could not color everything.

When Jackie gave a party in mid-March for her sister, Princess Stanislaus Radziwill, and her husband, a former Polish nobleman now in business in London, those social historians in the capital were overwhelmed again.

"It was," breathed one of them heavily, "the greatest thing since Andy Jackson."

"It was the gayest evening I've ever had," sighed one participant.

The guests—seventy-two of them—began arriving about 8:30 for cocktails, and they came through the rear and private entrance. There in the flesh were the Aga Khan, the Vice President of the United States, a small, smart selection of United States senators, high society and a cross-section of the rest of Washington. From that moment the city's official society tote boards began to be changed. This was the group that mattered. Since the party was not an official occasion, there were no obligatory guests. These were the people the Kennedys wanted around them for a long gay evening.

It was long. The strains of Lester Lanin's New York society orchestra reverberated through the Blue, Red and Green Rooms until after 3 A.M. The handsome couples, in black tie and long gowns, danced and sipped champagne and gathered in warm clusters to talk about the great adventure in government.

Jackie, in a white sleeveless sheath, was exquisitely beautiful. Her sister, Lee, with her long dark hair loose down her back, was equally striking in a red brocade gown.

The dinner was in the State Dining Room, where nine small round tables were set for eight guests each. There was no formal White House protocol to hinder movement or squelch laughter or ease. It was just fun.

The diners nibbled at their chicken, drank fine wines. Strolling musicians went from table to table to play. The first couple started the dancing, then they split and for the rest of the evening went from partner to partner.

It was, in fact, the kind of evening that Andy Jackson might well have liked. For the Kennedy society blended the rich with those of modest means, the titled with the untitled. There were plain shirt-sleeve reporters, artists, federal bureaucrats, nobility and remnants from the international set.

The irreverent chuckled a bit the next day when the President showed up for work with a small bandage over his left eye and hastily explained he had banged his forehead when he stooped to pick up a toy for Caroline. But nobody seemed to mind.

There was some United States government glitter, too.

For the Italians, Kennedy put on striped pants, and for the Irish he wore a green necktie.

He was the featured speaker at the centennial celebration of Italian unification, which included the red-coated Marine band, Lyndon Baines Johnson and Miss Renata Tebaldi. Jackie came along, wearing a pale green outfit that reeked of spring.

"It is an extraordinary fact in history that so much of what we are, and so much of what we believe had its origin in this rather small spear of land stretching into the Mediterranean," the President told the thousand celebrants. "All in a great sense that we fight to preserve today had its origins in Italy, and earlier than that in Greece. . . ."

The very next morning it was St. Patrick's Day, and Kennedy, wearing a green tie, greeted Irish Ambassador

Thomas J. Kiernan at his door. The ambassador had brought along the Kennedy coat of arms and a brief Kennedy family tree handsomely done on heavy parchment and fitted into a stained-oak box. After the ambassador had read a short poem in Gaelic at the President's request, Kennedy replied in his own native tongue. "Listen, Ambassador, that's terrific."

For some fifty-five congressmen summoned to the White House in the first of a round of special receptions a little of the glamour was left over. Tea and coffee were billed as the official drinks, but a quiet word to one of the waiters produced bolder stimulants. The curious could go to look at the President's office, the insistent could corner the President and press their political requests on him. Kennedy came equipped with pencil and pad to take notes.

"In the four years I've been here I'd only been in the White House twice," said one Republican congressman when it was over. "And I've never been in the President's office. They showed me that. I got to see the putting green for the first time. They even pointed out the swimming pool. I liked it."

The President posed for pictures with small groups of the legislators. Jackie came down for a quick tour through the group.

So at home did Ohio's Republican William H. Ayres feel that he climbed on a new tricycle, a gift left for Caroline, and sped down the red-carpeted hall—something, it was safe to say, he had not done in Eisenhower's tenure in office.

Home life—the life of Jack, Jackie, Caroline and John, Jr. —intrigued the American public almost as much as the new government. There developed a silent struggle between the press and Jackie Kennedy, who had decreed the first family's private affairs off limits for most reporters and photographers. But the readers were insatiable. A picture of Jackie on the cover of a magazine, a word glimpse of family life in the White House, sent circulation soaring.

There had never been a couple like this in the White House. Jack Kennedy and Jacqueline Bouvier, though not bona fide members of international society, at least had hovered on the fringes now and then. Their nomadic lives, their separateness—a phenomenon of great wealth—was not fully understood by the public, which clung to its older ideas of married life.

It could be argued that the Kennedys were a branch of the jet set, people of means and inclination who roamed the world's resorts by plane more easily than the financial lords of the East Coast used to go to Newport around the turn of the century.

The Kennedys, as wealthy as any of them and wealthier than most, added their own peculiar wrinkles. They owned their own resorts in Hyannis Port and Palm Beach (and rented one in Antibes, France) and now they had their own Boeing 707, something that no other members of the jet set could approach.

In the winter Jackie stayed in Palm Beach for weeks. In the summer she inhabited Hyannis Port. On other week ends she went to Glen Ora in the Virginia hunt country. Her trips to New York were often made alone or with her sister, Princess Radziwill. In the months ahead she would vacation in Greece and Italy—sans husband.

Since Jackie did not like political rallies or football games, the President went to these with male friends.

It was an exotic life, which raised the national eyebrow a bit, and there were a spate of jokes about it. ("Good night, Mrs. Kennedy, wherever you are.") Though Eleanor Roosevelt could not be catalogued as a homebody, she had been a vital part of the New Deal itself. Both Bess Truman and Mamie Eisenhower, solid midwestern products, stayed close to the hearthside. These three women were the comparative standards.

There were Jackie's dazzling Oleg Cassini creations and her vivid Pucci pants, which fit her lithe figure snugly, as they were supposed to. She disliked hats but liked bouffant hairdos. She swam, rode, water-skiied, golfed and listened to jazz. She liked color and gaiety and new ideas. Her style was American modern. But she liked to live among things of the past.

There was a stratum of whispered cocktail conversation that insisted the Kennedy marriage was in trouble, but those stories had been around since the day they were married in 1953, as similar reports had plagued previous presidents. Both Kennedys would confess early adjustment difficulties in their marriage, as in most marriages, and there were still obvious tests of will, as in most marriages. But the fact was that as time went on the marriage grew stronger. Those who knew them well found the proper amounts of devotion and respect.

They did not indulge in public displays of emotion, much to the disappointment of the photographers. And they tried to keep their special gifts to each other private matters, though they were not always successful because of publicity-conscious shopkeepers. Their life, however, was, and always would be, a far shot from the pattern in the typical American bungalow. But there were mighty few bungalow denizens who, with the Kennedy millions, wouldn't change houses, clothes, migratory habits and maybe even friends.

As a matter of fact, had anybody bothered to calculate how much time John Kennedy got to spend with his family, he might have been surprised to learn it was as much as the average medium- to high-income man. Kennedy worked and lived in the same place. He saw his family at breakfast; he sometimes was escorted to his office by Caroline. She, her mother and brother often toured the west wing during working hours to say hello. Kennedy lunched with them, and his commute from office to sitting room at night was at the most three or four minutes. On summer week ends he would fly to Hyannis Port on Friday nights, to remain until Monday mornings. In mobile America many jobs sent fathers and husbands away from families more than John Kennedy was away from his family.

The White House at first frightened Jackie—not so much its symbolism as its effect on people and families. It was like a combination of a hotel and a prison. Once you walked in, you did not come out again for four or eight years, and all the time you were there, people stared at you through the iron fence. She had been despondent for a while about losing her anonymity at the age of 32. She had worried about protecting her children from the effect of being the most famous kids in the nation. She drew herself inward to meet the challenge.

She adopted the White House as her project, deliberately

shunning a worldly role. She felt compassion for women who could not find enough in their husbands to stimulate them and interest them so that they themselves had to seek power and dominance. She worried about the little things, too; the President's openness with the press and the public bothered her at first—was he destroying too much of the "presidential aura"? Should he not be more reserved, less exposed? She disliked the term "First Lady" and wanted to be known as Mrs. Kennedy. She was annoyed at the time she had to spend getting her hair fixed for official functions. And she wondered if her hair would fall out from all the setting and drying ("I may be bald in a year," she laughed). She found a five-year supply of red-white-and-blue match books in the White House cupboards. She wanted plain white match books with "White House" written across them, and it gave her momentary pause when she remembered, "The White House budget for matches is shot." But as with other problems, she worked this one out. Little by little, adjustment came. In fact, in the months ahead there were times when she would thoroughly enjoy it. And certainly her husband did already.

CHAPTER SEVEN

THE CORPS

Aफ्T E R the election Charles L. Bartlett, Kennedy's friend and counselor who introduced the President-elect to his wife, had shown up in Palm Beach as a week-end guest.

Nothing would have been unusual about such a visit had Bartlett not been Washington correspondent for the Chattanooga *Times*.

The White House press corps suddenly took notice. The newsmen nervously concluded that things were going to be different under Kennedy than they had been under Eisenhower, who had held a kind of tender dislike for newsmen and tried to avoid them.

Reporters like extremes in high news sources. Those who shun the press provide collective protection. Nobody gets beaten since nobody gets in. Those men who will talk to everybody offer the same protection in reverse. Nobody gets beaten because everybody gets in. But the selective news source who talks to some but not to all shatters this group serenity. Obviously Kennedy and his family were going to talk to newsmen, and they were going to do it selectively.

On one occasion before Kennedy took office, *The New York Times'* Bill Lawrence was summoned to the Kennedy house to get an exclusive story from Ambassador Kennedy on the sale of the President-elect's stock holdings; and while there bumped into United Press International's Merriman ("Thank you, Mr. President") Smith out in quest of an interview with the presidential brother-in-law, Peter Lawford.

Once the New Frontier entered the White House, Press Secretary Pierre Salinger joked that he had to drop into the President's office in order to see reporters. No corner of the building seemed to be off limits. Journalists invaded the swimming pool, the projection room, the presidential bedroom—upon invitation, of course. They came either as friends or in a vague in-between status which Kennedy established with some reporters in which they were blended into the domestic scene or into social activities, so that Kennedy could save time by talking to them while he went about his other pursuits.

On some days more reporters went into the White House offices to talk with staff members than did government workers who had come on federal matters.

To Kennedy, watching and guiding national opinion was part of his job. In the very early days of the administration *The New York Times'* Washington Bureau Chief, James B. (Scotty) Reston, at a luncheon with Salinger advised that it would be unwise for Kennedy to grant exclusive audiences to favored newsmen. Salinger's reply was that Kennedy would see whom he pleased, when he pleased and for whatever reasons he pleased. This doctrine, while it was an open-door policy, was not really an open-news policy.

In the first weeks there were other clues about New Frontier information ideas. Admiral Arleigh Burke, chairman of the Joint Chiefs of Staff, found that a speech he had written urging a more aggressive stance in the cold war was dumped back in his lap with orders to rewrite it and take out the harsh phrases. The speech was scheduled for the night before the RB-47 flyers were to be released by the Soviet Union, and the White House feared Burke's talk might snag the release. For different reasons other brass in the Pentagon experienced similar alterations in speeches. While Kennedy wanted his officials to be seen and heard, this did not mean that they had license in their talk. They were expected to reflect the Kennedy thinking.

Kennedy's ire over news leaks was felt swiftly by a number of people. In the transition period a speculative list of ambassadorial appointments appeared in *The New York*

Times under Reston's by-line. To Kennedy this leak was inexcusable. In most of the cases neither the men nor the countries had been consulted and this sort of premature release caused many more difficulties in the delicate business of finding the right men for the right embassies. Kennedy's anger flared when he read the paper. His own intimate knowledge of reporters and their sources enabled him to narrow the possible offenders to two men. Talking on the phone to one of the men about another matter, Kennedy let off steam about the news leak, knowing that even if this was not the man responsible, the presidential mood would be transmitted to the guilty party in short order. "I don't understand it," he fretted. "Why can't these men just say they don't know?"

To explain the new administration's news policies, Pierre Salinger naturally was chosen and packed off to Chicago, where he spoke to the Publicity Club on March 8. "It has been said—and rightly so—that secrecy is the first refuge of incompetents," Salinger told his audience. "Any administration which allows free access to information is also going to reveal to the public internal debate on policy. This is inevitable. Yet, does America really want policy to be arrived at by unanimous vote? I think not. . . . Once policy is arrived at, however, with everyone having their say, then in my opinion the necessity is there for complete support of this policy by all spokesmen for the administration. . . . What is further needed here, I feel, are a set of definitions. For freedom is not license—and freedom is not without obligation . . . But what of freedom of information? Does this freedom give the right to imperil our nation to aid those who oppose us in the world, to endanger our security? Is freedom of information to become an excuse for inaccurate or sloppy reporting or for the encouragement of the leaking of highly confidential and classified government documents? I think not. I am cognizant of the fact that the mere fact I make these statements here today will again subject me to attack from those who believe no line can or should be drawn. But I do not agree with them and the more I come to understand the maximum perils of today's world and our role in it, the more convinced I become of the validity of my premise. . . . I am a strong advocate of freedom of information—within the confines of national security. . . . Access to information at the White House today is freer than it has ever been before. The people of this country are getting a dimension of the presidency they have never received before. . . . But I will not idly sit by while officials leak information to the press which either endangers our national security or is an outright distortion of the position of a highly responsible government official."

Kennedy had some built-in protective news devices. It became embarrassingly apparent very early that a decision in the New Frontier could not be called a decision until John Kennedy had finally pronounced it. Eisenhower had tended to accept the recommendations of his department and agency heads more than Kennedy. Thus, a glimpse of a new program or a hint of a new appointment from a Cabinet officer was likely to be solid news in the Eisenhower days. But now the final word on all major matters had to come from the Oval Office.

Journalistic speculation tended to subside when one published list of proposed ambassadorial appointees proved, when the appointments were finally made, to be more than 50 per cent in error. New York attorney Fowler Hamilton was listed in cold print as the man who would replace Allen Dulles as head of the Central Intelligence Agency. Eisenhower's former Atomic Energy Commission Chairman John McCone actually got that job, and Hamilton became the boss of Kennedy's new Foreign Aid Agency, which some journalists had already given to New York investment banker George D. Woods, who was later appointed head of the World Bank. It was dangerous journalistic business to plunge too deeply. True, the story might be correct at the moment it went to press, but a Kennedy decision could change course startlingly in the final hours.

When Kennedy held court with reporters, he rarely talked in specifics, even though these conversations were for background only and were not quotable; instead, he kept to generalities that did not yield breathless news beats but gave valuable guidance on the directions of New Frontier policy, the President's own reasoning and thought processes, his mood and feeling.

The vaunted Washington journalistic ritual of holding background briefings for reporters was something Kennedy had learned to distrust early in his career. Theory had it that a group of responsible journalists could gather, usually at lunch or dinner, with an official and talk casually with him on a "background" basis, the material to be used as guidance by the writers or stated on their own authority without the use of the name of the source.

Rarely did this process work properly. If the source was important enough and the story big enough, miffed reporters who were not invited got the news from those who were there and, not being bound by the rule that covered those in attendance, wrote the story with names.

"I figure," said John Kennedy at one point, "that any time I go to one of those backgrounders, what I say is on the record." As a result of this cautious approach, Kennedy was rarely burned by unfavorable publicity in his political career before the presidency. Never was he embarrassed on a major matter because of what he had said at unguarded moments. He was even more cautious as president.

Another very important element in the White House helped immensely in Kennedy's efforts to guide the news: the total loyalty of the staff around him. Only in a few instances were the men who had the minute-to-minute, the hour-to-hour contact with Kennedy new to him. They were old hands, most of them having been with him since 1952 or before. Those who did not agree with the Kennedy thoughts or did not like the Kennedy technique or found other objections, simply did not survive. The men who stayed with Kennedy were absolute in their devotion. A nod of the President's head or a word from him was enough to seal their lips.

While the White House doors remained open to prowling newsmen, once the Kennedy policy had been proclaimed by the President, a reporter could tour the offices of the intimates—Salinger, Sorensen, O'Donnell, O'Brien, Dungan, Goodwin, Feldman—and get precisely the same viewpoint from each man. The front was solid. And it was a Kennedy front. Cabinet members and agency heads by the very nature of their positions were expected to be—and in most cases were—of the same mind and loyalty immediately upon taking office. Trouble usually developed in the lower echelons of the huge departments where the employees were far removed from Kennedy and the White House in both distance and authority.

Kennedy's habit of holding small informal and nonscheduled meetings with his top advisers gave him further control over high-policy news. Most of these sessions were unannounced and unreported. (Eisenhower had scheduled and had held regular Cabinet and National Security Council meetings. The men attending and the subjects discussed were announced publicly, a procedure that clearly marked the news sources and objectives of the day for reporters.) Under Kennedy, days could go by on which reporters had only vague ideas of who was seeing the President and on what matters. For the newsmen who had to meet hourly deadlines, the going was often tough. The advantage went to those who had a week or a month to work on a story, they were able to ferret out the happenings behind the scenes.

But if the back-corridor doings of the President remained distressingly secret, there were compensating factors. While there was a proclaimed ban on reporting the household activities, it never quite worked. Caroline and her friends were spotted on the White House lawn at play. Jackie was seen water-skiing. The President was observed hitting a few golf balls along the fence. The big parties, the small parties, all made news. Kennedy moved around a great deal— to a luncheon to talk, to Hyannis Port for a week end. And each day at the White House hundreds and thousands of hand-out words flooded from Salinger's office. It was the policy to release anything that could be released—task-force reports, the toasts at the state dinners and official lunches, speeches in the Rose Garden to students. Whenever possible, Salinger routed official visitors through the lobby, so that reporters could talk to them after they had seen the President. Much of this great, youthful churning, which had stolen the scene from the U.S. Congress, from the Pentagon, from governors of the states, even from the Kremlin for the time being, was open to be watched and written about. Often just the sights and sounds were more than a reporter could handle in a day.

During the campaign Kennedy had shouted to the crowd that he was tired of getting up every morning and reading in his newspaper what Khrushchev and Castro were doing in the world. What he wanted was to awake and see headlines about what the President of the United States was doing. One morning in the early weeks of Kennedy's White House tenure, Counsel Ted Sorensen came into the President's office with a wry smile on his face and holding a copy of a newspaper with the front page dominated by Kennedy headlines. "People," he told the President, "are tired of waking up every morning and reading what Kennedy is doing. They want to know what Khrushchev and Castro are doing."

The news equation between reporters and the President can never be balanced. Reporters want to know more than they should—in fact, they want to know everything, from military secrets to the color of the presidential shorts. Presidents always want to tell less than they should or could.

Part of the reporters' attitude is a filtered reflection of the public's, the traditional view that the White House and the occupants belong to it, to be peered at whenever and wherever it wishes. Being public property was just part of the job, and any family which was not ready to meet the conditions should stay back home—so the political mythology read.

Since some 183 million people cannot drop in to check up, although there are June days in Washington when it seems that many have come to visit, the self-appointed guardian of the public snooping privilege is something that has grown to be known as the White House press corps.

If Kennedy, hiding several offices away from the area prescribed for reporters (clearly marked with husky Secret Service agents), caused newsmen difficulties, the score was evened by the White House press. Not only must a president come out for a public accounting to this group every now and then, but he must not move outside his eighteen acres unless he is followed in a plane, on foot, in a boat or in a car by a contingent of the press corps, some of the newsmen shouting facts into walkie-talkie radios, others heaving film and dispatches from one moving vehicle to another, the whole scene looking like something between a Ringling Brothers clown act and D-Day in World War II.

Visitors to the nation's capital are often shocked beyond recovery when they attend one of the august ceremonies of the national government, such as the welcoming of a foreign head of state, to find that the view of the spectators is completely blocked by a sweating, shuffling crew of cameramen in parkas and that the presidential words are often drowned by the curses of technicians and the clatter of dropped photographic equipment. Washingtonians take such goings-on in stride. Indeed, if a ceremony is not part shambles, they look around to find out what went wrong.

The White House press includes all those accredited to cover the president. The number currently is near 1,200. But within that group there is a haughty elite—twenty or twenty-five men who call themselves "the regulars." The appelation has nothing to do with breakfast cereal or a term of enlistment; the regulars are those men who cover the president "regularly," who are there day in and day out, who travel with him, who have no other assignment but to watch the man in the Oval Office. Since the big newspapers, magazines, wire services and networks are the only ones who can afford reporters and photographers for such specialized duty, these are by economic evolution "the regulars."

The regulars are the ruling class, and they get the blooded privileges. Some of them claim special seats on the president's plane, which at all times carries a small contingent of reporters from the main group in case something unexpected happens to the president. They get a working table up front in the banquet halls of America, and if the hosts are generous enough, they may even get fed for nothing. They are given the best location from which to watch and hear the president at all public functions. But most important, they get to dwell in that heady atmosphere that accompanies the White House. When they move around the country in the wake of the president, they are ogled by girls, envied by local bank clerks, respected by college journalism students—in short, they are somebodies by association.

Their position allows them to mingle with the great and powerful of the land, who would not look at them if they were not newsmen. Their assignments take them to the places that presidents go on business and pleasure, which are most often the pleasantest or most exotic places in America and abroad. Expense accounts allow them to live at a level that they could never afford on their salaries. "It sure as hell beats working," sighed one correspondent.

All things considered, this may be one of the most undignified careers in the communications business. At airport receptions the corps is pushed inside ropes and there contained like prize Herefords at a county fair. The men must sit in dingy back rooms, halls, streets and locker rooms for hours, waiting to get a glimpse of their president. Strong legs are more of a requirement than big brains. The White House reporter soon finds that much of his job is running across fields to catch the presidential party, which somehow has disembarked a mile away, or he must sprint down a street in pursuit of a motorcade.

Most communities now provide a secondhand bus for presidential motorcades. The White House press is put in the bus, and the bus is often placed so far back in the motorcade that the reporters cannot see the president; or there is a fifty-fifty chance that the bus will be separated from the executive limousine. History has yet to record a motorcade that went off as planned. When, subsequently, Kennedy flew to Paris, buses were banned from the parade route; a special scheme was devised to allow the press corps to see Kennedy land at Orly Airport, then board a bus, take a short cut, and see him arrive at his residence. The bus driver got lost in the back streets of Paris, and the reporters arrived to find the street cleaners already sweeping up after the horse brigade. In Bogotá, Colombia, somebody forgot to measure the bus and just when Kennedy sped off in the distance it was discovered that the bus would not go through an underpass at the airport. With such a record, logic would seem to dictate a change in operation for the White House press. But motorcades go on, precedent being too strong—the idea of the motorcade apparently having come down from the crusades.

The White House press, with all its worldly wisdom and ways, has a high quotient of good old American corn. It has organized itself into something called the White House Correspondents Association, with a seal just like the Kiwanis Club or the Moose and even a blue-and-white flag that is flown whenever the association takes to the water to follow the president's yacht. Once a year it holds a huge banquet which the president and his top men feel they must attend— certainly as boring an evening as any Buffalo civic club can devise.

The White House pressmen are certainly not as good as they think themselves to be. But they are probably not as bad as critics suggest.

The public at large has an overglamorized view of the corps, because of its swagger when it comes to town and because of show business, which bills the White House as the hottest assignment in Washington.

While physically closer to the big decisions, White House reporters seldom learn of them first. The White House sources are few, are protected in the back corridors from unwanted queries, and are so close to the president that they are much more guarded in their talk than other government servants. Most of the big news breaks come from the departments after policy decisions have had time to filter out to many hired hands. Time and again White House newsmen have found stories which originated with a presidential decision just a few feet away from them being written by the men on the Pentagon or State Department beats, because there the news first surfaced.

But even when viewed critically, the White House press has one duty that is vital and that nobody else can perform. It must report hour by hour where the president is, what he is doing and occasionally what he is thinking. It is surveillance reporting. The president's words, the reaction of his audience, his health, his family—these are the things that perhaps matter most to Americans from hour to hour.

A handful in the White House press does it superbly, some even try to get a glimpse of the backstage play. Others do little but sag in the black leather chairs in the White House lobby and wait for the press secretary to hand them the day's news budget. Few men lick the job of being White House correspondent. Mostly, they go off to New Delhi to become foreign correspondents or are pushed into higher posts back

in the office when their legs and stomachs begin to weaken
on the White House beat.

One man has triumphed, however—UPI's Albert Merriman Smith, 49, who has covered the White House since 1941.
His long tenure has earned him the honor of ending the presidential press conferences by shouting, "Thank you, Mr.
President." With that privilege worn like a battle ribbon,
Smitty, with equal parts of showmanship, gall and brains,
turned the beat into money and prestige. He wrote five
books on his experiences, hit the lecture circuit, became
typed by such TV magistrates as Jack Paar as "the dean" of
the White House press corps, and hour by hour, day by day,
he has continued to turn out the fastest and best copy about
presidents that the nation has ever had. He is a man of many
skills, being able to repair a walkie-talkie on a dogtrot, to
find a telephone in the remotest wilderness, to navigate a boat
in Narragansett Bay, to develop a wardrobe that boasts a
suit that looks like a tuxedo or a tuxedo that looks like a
suit in case of an unexpected change in plans. And of course
he is there, always there.

When John Kennedy won the White House and invited
the newsmen to a little party to celebrate his victory, he
took Merriman Smith over to see Jackie. "I want you to
meet Merriman Smith," said Kennedy to his wife. "We inherited him with the White House."

Reporters are an adaptable breed, and they can get used
to almost any conditions. But what would remain most un-
settling to them was Kennedy's awareness of every word
printed about him. Personal references bothered him much
more than did attacks on policy.

So often—for years—correspondents who wrote about the
president had felt they might be writing in a vacuum for all
the reaction their words provoked. But Kennedy changed all
this. Every word, every phrase was absorbed, tested for its
friendliness, dissected and analyzed with scientific precision,
to detect the degree of approval or disapproval. Even at moments of crisis he would not ignore words about himself.
When he was asked why he concerned himself with what
was written, he asked simply, "Would you rather I didn't

read it?" What reporter, correspondent, editor, publisher or citizen could answer in clear conscience, "Yes"? Kennedy continued to read the footnotes, and he continued to care.

For all of Kennedy's cunning about public relations and his profound knowledge of reporters and the American news business, there was trouble ahead for him in his relations with the press.

As a senator, as a political challenger for the presidency, he had been amorphous. You could write about how he looked and what he said and how he voted on the various bills, but none of these facts were a test of the man as president. He had not raised taxes, broadened social security or sent American men to battle. He was a fascinating and charming curiosity who won the interest, if not the sympathy, of nearly every journalist. But before January 20 his words did not mean profit or loss, hunger or plenty, life or death. Now they did, and the basis of his relationship with the press changed. How profound that change was to be neither Kennedy nor the men around him realized at first.

He was under unremitting scrutiny now. Every mistake would be pointed out over and over. Every action would be questioned. Every movement would be treated with suspicion. No statement would be taken at face value. His reasons would often be oversimplified or given too much weight, his motives would be questioned always. He would have to suffer inaccuracies and grotesque distortions, some from carelessness, some from malice. But then, he had not exactly been forced to take the job against his will.

The press and the president—any president—in their natural state are friendly enemies. They both believe in each other, but they both, at some points along the way, disapprove of the way the other one does his job.

CHAPTER EIGHT

SPACE CHALLENGE

THE Washington Senators had just hung up another run on the Chicago White Sox in the season's opener, and most of the 26,734 fans and the new president, John Fitzgerald Kennedy, were feeling good about the 3-to-1 score despite the cold, damp wind in Griffith Stadium.

Kennedy had performed competently the annual ritual of pitching the first ball. He had shed his top coat, hauled back and with a good right arm lobbed the ball over the sixty photographers piled up in front of him. The players, out of the President's sight behind the photographic gallery, had all leaped and clutched for the ball, which had dribbled across a forest of fingers and then dropped into the left hand of Chicago's Jim Rivera.

In the presidential box, surrounded by friends, staff and assorted functionaries from both parties, Kennedy alternately joked and talked serious state business as he watched the play. He straightened up slightly and squinted as Associate Press Secretary Andrew Hatcher reluctantly stirred himself at the end of the second inning and moved over to lean close to the presidential ear.

The United Press International was about to move a wire story reporting a strong Moscow rumor that Russia had sent a man into space and recovered him. Hatcher said he would go check on it and report back. The President listened, nodded without saying a word, then turned back to baseball and a Briggs hot dog.

The Kennedy calm was predictable. The President knew far more than did Hatcher at that moment about the alleged Soviet space exploit. He knew that the Russians had probably not made their man-into-space shot yet; but he also knew that it was due within the next few days.

For more than a month Kennedy had been told by his intelligence units that the Soviet manned space effort would come before April 15, just a few days before the United States had at first hoped to send a man to the fringes of the atmosphere and bring him back in a single looping shot in the nose of an Atlas rocket.

As expected on this Monday, April 10, Hatcher's report was inconclusive. There was no confirmation. Washington went on to lose the ball game, and John Kennedy went back to the White House in his black limousine, speeding through the red lights at sixty miles per hour, a privilege for presidents that some exasperated Washington motorists rate higher than the right to throw out the first baseball. It was the beginning of a week of disappointment, and Kennedy may have felt it.

Late on Tuesday afternoon Press Secretary Pierre Salinger swung his stubby legs up on his desk, lighted another Upmann cigar and welcomed his fellow press aides from the Defense and State Departments and their related agencies. By this time the official intelligence evaluation of the coming Russian space effort placed it within a few hours. Salinger and his colleagues began to draft a statement which the President could release once the Soviet man returned to earth, if he did. There had been a slight argument within the White House on just what to say in such a statement. Running true to the form they had displayed in the Eisenhower years, some of the President's scientific advisers wanted to play down any such Russian achievement. Kennedy would have none of it. His attitude was established at the start: he would pay tribute to a manned space flight for what it was.

As Salinger's group labored over the words for the statement, Jerome Wiesner, top science adviser to Kennedy, came by the Oval Office. He quietly told the President that the best hunch was that the Soviet space flight would take place that night.

A few minutes later Salinger brought in the statement. The President studied it silently, gave it tentative approval, then listened as Salinger outlined his course of action when and if the shot was confirmed.

At 8 P.M. Major General Clifton, the man who sees that intelligence reports go to Kennedy, checked in for the last time that day.

"Do you want to be waked up?" Clifton asked.

"No," said Kennedy. "Give me the news in the morning."

It proved to be a quiet evening for Kennedy and his staff. The President returned to the White House living quarters. Salinger uncharacteristically bowed out of a dinner date and went to his Lake Barcroft home in Virginia for an early supper and an evening of talk with a California friend. Dr. Wiesner turned from space to atomic energy and dined with Homi Bhabha, Secretary of India's Atomic Energy Commission. In the meantime the vast intelligence and communications network of the United States was on a hair trigger.

Few people know for sure when the United States first detected the Soviet space vehicle as it lifted off the pad in Baykonur, near the Aral Sea, with its 153-pound human cargo aimed for successful orbit. But it was within seconds after Yuri Gagarin was airbone that the first sensitive tentacles of the United States detection system picked up the telltale electronic waves from his rocket. At 1:35 A.M. on the following morning the phone jangled rudely in Salinger's slumbering household. The calm-voiced Dr. Wiesner, who had been roused in his own apartment, relayed the expected report: the Russians had launched one of their huge missiles, it was in orbit and believed to be the human space flight. Salinger grunted his acknowledgment, quickly confirmed the publicity plan. Nothing was to be said by the United States until Russia announced the shot. Salinger rolled back into bed to try to get a few precious moments of rest before the inevitable flood of phone calls.

A few minutes after 2 A.M. the next call came. This time it was *The New York Times,* which had picked up the excited Moscow radio announcement of the launch. Before confirming the story for this country, Salinger checked back with Wiesner to make sure Moscow had indeed made its own announcement. Sleep was impossible thereafter. Newspapers, networks and wire services all called for confirmation of the flight. Dr. Wiesner kept the press secretary filled in on the official reports as they trickled in. The President slept undisturbed.

At 5:30 A.M. Wiesner called for the final time to tell Salinger that Moscow had announced the return of Gagarin to the Soviet Union. As far as this country was concerned, said Wiesner, the Soviets had successfully placed the first human in space flight and recovered him.

Shortly before 8 A.M. George Thomas, the President's valet, padded through the long central hall of the second-story White House living quarters. As he does almost every morning, George rapped on the President's bedroom door to make sure Kennedy was awake. He was up and stirring. George Thomas had a special duty this morning—he was to let Salinger know when the President was ready for a phone call. In seconds the white phone—a direct line to the White House—in Salinger's home came alive, and the President was waiting to hear the reports from the night before.

Quickly Salinger told the story. Kennedy listened in silence, still in his bedroom. "Do we have any details?" he interrupted to ask. Salinger could furnish only a few: name, orbit time. Then the press secretary reread the prepared statement while the President listened. Kennedy gave it his final approval. Putting down that phone, Salinger turned to another one and dialed each of the wire services.

Slowly he read, so that the men at the other end could type his words: "The achievement by the USSR of orbiting a man and returning him safely to ground is an outstanding technical accomplishment. We congratulate the Soviet scientists and engineers who made this feat possible. . . ."

Half an hour later Salinger and General Clifton met the President in his office corridor. "Do we have anything more specific?" Kennedy asked. Clifton handed him the yellow intelligence reports that filled in more details. Kennedy studied them without speaking.

There was not much more that John Kennedy could do at that moment. He turned away and went into his office for a day's work on other subjects. Not until that afternoon at 4, then he went to the New State Department Auditorium for his press conference did Kennedy return to space matters. Then he grimly and wearily summed up the United States position in the space struggle.

The question had not been a kind one. "Mr. President," began the reporter, "a member of Congress said today he was tired of seeing the United States second to Russia in the space field. I suppose he speaks for a lot of others. Now, you have asked Congress for more money to speed up our space program. What is the prospect that we will catch up with Russia and perhaps surpass Russia in this field?"

"Well," said Kennedy, "the Soviet Union gained an important advantage by securing these large boosters, which were able to put up greater weights, and that advantage is going to be with them for some time. However tired anybody may be, and no one is more tired than I am, it is a fact that it is going to take some time [to catch up]. . . . As I said in my State of the Union message, the news will be worse before it is better. . . . We are, I hope, going to go in other areas where we can be first, and which will bring perhaps more long-range benefits to mankind. But we are behind."

For those who remembered the flaming days of John Kennedy's campaign for the presidency, the impatience with which he treated the question of our role in space, his answer was disturbing and the pervading calm with which the current Moscow news was accepted in the White House, while the rest of the world marveled, seemed hardly in the spirit of the New Frontier.

It had been in Pocatello, Idaho, in the high-school auditorium, during the fall of the campaign that Kennedy had cried out a harsh indictment of the Republicans. "They [foreign nations] have seen the Soviet Union first in space. They have seen it first around the moon, and first around the sun. . . . They come to the conclusion that the Soviet tide is rising and ours is ebbing. I think it is up to us to reverse that point."

Standing on top of a building at New York University in Washington Square in October, 1960, Kennedy declared: "These are entirely new times, and they require new solutions. The key decision which this [Eisenhower's] administration had to make in the field of international policy and prestige and power and influence was their recognition of the significance of outer space. . . . The Soviet Union now is first in outer space."

It was in Oklahoma City's municipal auditorium five days before the election that he shouted: "I will take my television black and white. I want to be ahead of them in rocket thrust."

But now probably no one was more frustrated by the confining realities of our actual position in space exploration than John Kennedy.

In the rush of his new duties he had never come fully face to face with the immense problem of whether or not to challenge the Soviet Union to a manned space race. He knew well the political realities of continually taking second place to the Russians. Indeed, to a limited extent he had been elected to office on that issue. But the same scientific arguments which made the Eisenhower administration seem complacent were now being given to Kennedy, who in turn was using them to answer the questions.

Kennedy did not come to the White House with the reputation of running from problems. But for a few short days, as Yuri Gagarin's name pre-empted the headlines, it seemed that Kennedy had indeed accepted the leisurely scientific attitude: we had fallen behind in the building of big rockets that could get us to the moon, but our smaller, more sophisticated space instruments were yielding more and better scientific information. Not for a long time, perhaps never, ran this argument, would we surpass the Russians in huge and glamorous space spectacles, but we would know more about what was up there.

In the President's chair John Kennedy was finding it a hundred times more difficult to cope with this problem than on the stump in Oklahoma City.

He could not decide at first if the gain in prestige could possibly be worth the billions of dollars that a challenge to the Soviets might cost. Though scientists work in a world of specifics, when it came to answering his simple question about how and when we might overtake the Russians, their answers were vague and uncertain. Kennedy, who liked to make his own judgments after sufficient study, had not had time to learn about all the space projects on the drawing

ards or all the scientific probabilities. Kennedy prodded
 men. What if the United States launched a crash program
 get a man on the moon first, he asked. Should not the
United States leapfrog its own program, strike out to develop
one of the monster rockets that could take men to Mars or to
Venus?

The answers did not come as Kennedy wanted. The scientists talked about the Soviet Union's ability to loop a man
around the moon and back to earth, to land a human on the
moon, to launch a space laboratory into orbit with several
men on it—all before we could perform such feats.

The thesis went that the United States was doing just
about everything it could do to catch up with the Russians.
More money and more men on the program would not neces-
sarily speed it along. Certain technical breakthroughs were
necessary before more progress was possible. Scientists were
working now at the outer limits of their knowledge, and until more knowledge was available—something that could
simply not be purchased with American dollars, despite their
quantity—this country would have to stay behind Russia in
the manned space race.

There was no unanimity in the scientific ranks, however.
Some of the men at work on the plans for deep probes into
space and landings on the moon and other planets felt the
missing essential in the space program to be the will and desire to be first. What was needed was a presidential decision
that we should challenge the Russians. It was not impossible
to overtake them if we really wanted to. Some of this thought
drifted up through the bureaucratic maze to Kennedy, but
for the most part he got the pat answers.

The problem, explained the space men, went back to
1948, when the scientific community had been debating
whether a nuclear warhead could be put on a missile. Because the art of nuclear war had not been developed to a fine
stage and the nuclear warheads were then so huge, some of
the best scientific minds, including Vannevar Bush, head of
the Carnegie Institution, declared it would be impossible
in the foreseeable future to develop warhead-equipped
missiles which could span continents.

But only a few years after taking this stand, the government's weapons laboratories, in a spectacular breakthrough in nuclear weaponry, found out how to package a bomb in a fraction of its former space. Suddenly the idea of intercontinental missiles became a reality and the United States did begin its missile program, although at a somewhat leisurely pace. But its missiles now could be much smaller, need not have the monstrous power that the original calculations on the old warhead designs had indicated.

The Russians' atomic art lagged behind ours. Their warheads were still the outsized models that would require massive thrust to be lofted into space. Not hindered with any "breakthrough," they went ahead to design the big rockets necessary for the big warheads.

Years later, when the space race developed, the Russians, because of their lack of scientific sophistication, were ready with the huge boosters needed. While the United States, with its far superior space science, had only smaller rockets, splendid for pure space research but inadequate for manned exploration.

John Kennedy is always sympathetic to facts. He appreciated the irony of a situation in which superior achievement in one year meant taking second place a few years later.

Kennedy, however, has never taken kindly to the notion that some problems are insurmountable, that you must sit and accept the inevitable. His entire political success was based on challenging the established theories (such as the one that held that a Catholic could not be elected President of the United States). While he echoed the words of the scientists in his press conferences, he nevertheless had a feeling that something should be done. Under the program that he had inherited there was little hope. This was a fact. The Russians would continue to be years ahead. One alternative was to launch a program like World War II's Manhattan Project, which developed the atomic bomb.

But Kennedy, when he thought in these terms, was stopped almost dead in his tracks by his budget books. The cost estimates were simply staggering—from $20 to $40 billion over ten years—and even this kind of money could not guarantee success by 1968, an optimistic target date for landing a man on the moon. Nor was there a guarantee of winning the deeper space probes later on.

In the years before Kennedy became president, the administration officials faced with these problems chose to do nothing, thereby automatically making a negative decision.

Of all the major problems facing Kennedy when he came into office, he probably knew and understood least about space. In the early weeks of the New Frontier the day-to-day problems of getting along on the surface of the globe dominated his time.

He made one stab at solving the problem. He asked Congress for $120 million more to speed up existing projects. He concluded that the giant Saturn rocket, a cluster of liquid-fueled rocket units of the type already developed, should be hurried by a year. These units lashed together would yield a thrust of a million and a half pounds, enough for the big space ventures. He asked that some of these new funds go to the development of the Nova, the liquid-fueled rocket with a single engine that would develop a million and a half pounds of thrust.

Kennedy moved, too, to make the National Space Council a more effective unit. It had been composed of the President, the Secretaries of Defense and State and the administrator of the National Aeronautics and Space Administration, plus the chairman of the Atomic Energy Commission. But the President had no time to devote to the council. Kennedy substituted Lyndon Johnson for himself, in hopes that the Vice President, with more time for this function, could give the council a spur.

The pressure on Kennedy to finally come to hard grips with the problem of space mounted after Yuri's orbiting. Only hours after the Soviet success, congressmen and senators cried for more action.

"Wait," said one NASA scientist who had been impatient with the previous delays, "until the Russians send up three men, then six, then a laboratory, start hooking them together and then send back a few pictures of New York for us to see."

"Kennedy could lose the 1964 election over this," added another space administrator who had suffered through American missile politics for years.

* * *

Yuri Gagarin seemed to help crystallize some of the fuzzy scientific thinking. Below the top levels, the engineers and physicists who design and see that the missiles work began to show new concern and to talk openly about the need for a political decision. While a few downgraded the scientific results that Yuri brought back to earth with him, most of the space men gave the Russians credit for having achieved far more than just a propaganda victory. "You just aren't ahead if you're behind," said one, summing up his feelings.

America's own Project Mercury continued to fall behind schedule, thus further contributing to gloom. The target time for taking an astronaut into space and back again without putting him into orbit had skidded from late 1959 into 1960, then beyond 1960 into 1961 and from early 1961 to mid-1961, then finally to late 1961. It seemed as if Project Mercury were far from an answer to the Soviets.

Kennedy pondered the crucial decision. One action he took: he ordered an immediate review of our entire rocket propulsion development program. The debate raged in the newspapers for days. The space technicians began to say that a direct challenge to the Soviets would help focus the energy of the country, now expended carelessly in a welter of overlapping space projects with no clearly defined long-range goals.

"Roosevelt was considered crazy when he said we could make 50,000 planes a year, but we did it," said one White House aide, getting the feeling of challenge. "Think what it took to launch the Manhattan Project with no guarantee of success."

Kennedy caught the feel of it. He summoned his space men.

The White House in the evenings along about 7 o'clock sighs slightly and begins to decelerate. It never stops completely, for in the basement of the west wing are the cable machines that are forever writing out their messages from Saigon or London or Moscow. But in the evening the sun slants its rays across the lawn, the oblique lighting bringing a fresh green to the spears of grass, the sprinklers are turned on, bringing soothing dampness beneath the old elms, and inside, the last Boy Scout and the last Rotarian and the last businessman's committee with their plaques and their gold membership cards and their invitations to the annual conventions are shooed out of the corridors. The endless parade of politicians has been slowed; only the select ones come at this hour.

Secretaries begin to drift away, one at a time or in pairs, to their Georgetown apartments. A few of the staff members leave, but not all. For some in the White House, this is the best hour. The phone is stilled, the meetings are over. A man can relax a bit and just think, perhaps drift through the deserted corridors with the black-and-white-tile floor. John Kennedy slows a bit as the sun settles. His regime becomes more informal. He often sees the people he wants to see, and sometimes he schedules those small, vital meetings with key officials. They can talk unhurriedly, and cocktail parties and dinner dates can wait.

A perfect April day subsided, and Kennedy's space advisers arrived. James Webb, NASA head, hurried down the hall, his square jaw set, a firm hand on his brief case, looking on the exterior more like a supersalesman than the government administrator he is. He had once been Under Secretary of State to Dean Acheson. Beside him walked Hugh Dryden, Webb's deputy, the mild-mannered scientist who lurked behind gold-rimmed glasses.

Through the side door and up through the subterranean warren sauntered Jerome Wiesner, his black hair as curly and unruly as ever, the inevitable pipe drooping from his mouth. David Elliot Bell, director of the Bureau of Budget, walked over too. His presence at virtually every vital meeting was becoming habitual. He was the ex-Marine who knew the meaning of that federal document that weighed 4 pounds, 4 ounces, had 1,136 pages and was the budget of the United States, the guide chart for the biggest going business in the world. And Ted Sorensen came too, a quiet force of skepticism. In his office a few yards beyond the domain of the President, Sorensen breathed on his glasses, polished them with his handkerchief in precise and deliberate motions. He turned, in a routine he had already established, picked his coat off the rack and, lifting his arms high above his shoulders, let it slide on. He moved silently down the corridor to the Cabinet Room, where the rest of the men had gathered around one end of the dark coffin-shaped table.

The President entered from his secretary's office, the chamber that connects his oval quarters with the Cabinet Room. He came soundlessly, his quick steps muffled in the thick green carpet.

He did not waste more than a few seconds in the perfunctory greetings. He pulled out one of the black leather chairs on the side and at the end of the big table. Etched in the tiny brass nameplate on the back was "Secretary of the Interior, Jan. 21, 1961." As the others stood, he dropped into the chair, wiggled it back a few inches and then put his rubber-soled right foot on the edge of the table, pushed himself back where he tottered in delicate balance. To his right Dr. Wiesner poked at his dead pipe. Across to his left James Webb leaned forward, ready to press his arguments on the President. Ex-Marine Bell sat like an officer candidate straight across the seven feet of mahogany, and Hugh Dryden leaned his forehead on his finger tips. Sorenson, with a sheaf of papers under his arm, pulled a chair from the wall and positioned himself off the end of the table, like a small tugboat standing by an aircraft carrier ready to dart in and help out when called upon.

Kennedy conducts a restless meeting when he is in quest of information he does not have. He pokes at his men with questions, rushes mentally off, sometimes before they finish, when he catches the gist of what they are saying before they get it out. He did that night.

"As I understand it, the problem goes back to 1948, when we learned how to make smaller warheads that could be carried with smaller boosters," the President said, summing up his own background on the question. "What can we do now?" he asked, rocking back and forth on the rear legs of the Secretary of the Interior's chair.

One by one the experts told their stories. It was a discouraging picture of years and billions of dollars that separated the United States and Russia in space. Kennedy frowned, ran his hands agonizingly through his hair. "We may never catch up," he muttered.

"Now let's look at this," said Kennedy impatiently. "Is there any place where we can catch them? What can we do? Can we go around the moon before them? Can we put a man on the moon before them? What about Nova and Rover? When will Saturn be ready? Can we leapfrog?"

The one hope, explained Dryden, lay in this country's launching a crash program similar to the Manhattan Project. But such an effort might cost $40 billion, and even so there was only an even chance of beating the Soviets.

James Webb spoke up. "We are doing everything we possibly can, Mr. President. And thanks to your leadership and foresight, we are moving ahead now more rapidly than ever. . . ."

But Kennedy did not want to hear praise at this moment. He stopped Webb with a wave of his hand. "The cost," he pondered. "That's what gets me." He turned to Budget Director Bell questioningly. The cost of space science went up in geometric progression, explained Bell.

Kennedy listened between questions. He tapped the bottoms of his upper front teeth with the fingernails of his right hand.

It was not much of a discussion. It reflected precisely the state of the space program at that moment. The one important decision—the political decision—had not been made by either Eisenhower or Kennedy. Would we or would we not get into a head-on manned space race with the Soviet Union?

Kennedy heard from Wiesner that the re-evaluation of the booster program was under way even then. "When can you have it finished?" asked Kennedy.

"Now is not the time to make mistakes," cautioned Wiesner, who pulled on his pipe, looked at the ceiling and asked for three more months.

Light was failing fast now in the White House Rose Garden, which was just outside the Cabinet Room. Beyond the seven-foot iron fence the street lights came on.

Kennedy turned back to the men around him. He thought for a second. Then he spoke. "When we know more, I can decide if it's worth it or not. If somebody can just tell me how to catch up. Let's find somebody—anybody. I don't care if it's the janitor over there, if he knows how."

Kennedy stopped again a moment and glanced from face to face. Then he said quietly, "There's nothing more important."

Suddenly he was out of his chair on his feet. "Thank you for coming by." He strode to the door of Mrs. Lincoln's office, paused a short second for a final few words. Then he ducked back into his own office, beckoning Ted Sorensen to follow him.

Alone with Sorensen, Kennedy thought about the curious dilemma further. The cost was frightening. Yet the threat was there, and Yuri Gagarin's name still lingered in the headlines to emphasize it. To Kennedy it was inconceivable that there was no way to accept the challenge and win this race if it was worth it and the country wanted to do it. "I'm determined to get an answer," he said.

Six weeks later the President stood before Congress for a second time in his four short months of holding office. In a special message on "urgent national needs" he said, "Now it is time to take longer strides—time for a great new American enterprise—time for this nation to take a clearly leading role in space achievement, which in many ways may hold the key to our future on earth. . . . Let it be clear that I am asking the Congress and the country to accept a firm commitment to a new course of action—a course which will last for many years and carry very heavy costs: 531 million dollars in fiscal '62—an estimated seven to nine billion dollars additional over the next five years. If we are to go only halfway, or reduce our sights in the face of difficulty, in my judgment it would be better not to go at all. . . . I believe we should go to the moon."

John Kennedy, and with him the United States, was entering the space race. It was a cautious entry then, but in the next two years the amount spent for space would climb from $531 million to $2.4 billion, and Kennedy's challenge to the Russians in space would be serious.

CHAPTER NINE

THE BAY OF PIGS

FOUR days after Yuri Gagarin sliced through the fringes of heaven, 1,400 Cuban exiles sent by the United States were wallowing toward disaster in Cuba's Bay of Pigs. John Kennedy, with the military power to destroy the world, did nothing as Fidel Castro, gleefully spouting communistic shibboleths, rounded up the prisoners from the beach.

It was a fantastic bungle, and it was a Kennedy bungle. It was the first deep black slash on the New Frontier record. The White House was stunned, embarrassed, angered and confused.

There were clumsy efforts to shift much of the blame to the military planners and to the Central Intelligence Agency.

In the white heat of anger and humiliation there welled up what was defined as Kennedy resolve to avenge this defeat and to beat the obnoxious Castro. But in a few days this resolve had bubbled out to a vague and formless understanding that somehow the Castro infection would have to be surrounded and choked out, rather than cut out in military surgery.

Kennedy learned great lessons. Months later he could look back and see that the military-security operations of the United States government had developed pockets of dry rot beneath the surface. As long as there was no disturbance, there was no hint of trouble in the apparatus. But when Kennedy came along and jarred the calm, he suddenly broke through the shell. Kennedy learned about the use of military power—or rather, he learned what happens in the absence of it. He learned more about the communist enemy. All these lessons came with the Bay of Pigs, but the occasion was still defeat, bitter defeat for a young president who had never known defeat in his life.

Kennedy's own philosophy stated that you did not win by losing. And though even Joe Kennedy time and time again would say to his son that Cuba was the best lesson he could have had early in his administration, the President could never quite accept this view. Men had died needlessly. The prestige of the United States, already dangerously eroded around the globe, suffered more, and more important than any of these was the danger that Nikita Khrushchev might look at the wreckage on the beach and decide that the President of the United States could be pushed to virtually any limit. A war of miscalculation could easily arise from such conclusions, for Kennedy at that moment was not to be pushed in any direction.

The chain of miscalculations and errors that eventually added up to the abortive invasion began upon Kennedy's entrance into the national drama. He had stood on the stump during the campaign and cried out in affronted tones about the communist threat ninety miles from the shores of Florida and about Dwight Eisenhower's lack of action.

But though Kennedy had not known it, Ike had been doing something. Hundreds of Cuban refugees were training in Florida and Texas and Guatemala. They wanted to go back to their homeland and take it from Castro.

When, on November 18, 1960, Allen Dulles and Richard Bissell first laid these facts before Kennedy, the President-elect was more than a little surprised. Under Kennedy the preparations went on, and almost immediately the guidelines for a military operation were laid down. One was that the United States would train and equip the invasion force, help it with plans, advise it in any way that the United States could, but that this country would not at any time intervene directly with its own military might. The Cuban force was to be a catalyst for a national uprising, a core of trained fighters around which discontented Cuban citizens could rally.

Looking back a year later, one Kennedy man who was deeply involved in the action saw that the military and intelligence experts were forced by the change in administrations to be salesmen. They wanted to push on with preparations for some kind of action, and so when the Kennedy amateurs, dreadfully concerned about international appearances, would say from time to time, "We can't do that," or "Take that out," the experts, with only mild sputtering, would go right ahead and say, "Okay, we can still do it." Later, the President would say, "All the mysteries about the Bay of Pigs have been solved now but one—how could everybody involved have thought such a plan would succeed. I don't know the answer, and I don't know anybody else who does."

If there were deep misgivings in the Pentagon or the CIA as Kennedy laid down his regulations for the operation, they did not penetrate to the White House. John Kennedy does not like to lose, and had he been aware of any serious doubts by competent people, it is reasonable to assume that he would have listened.

He was, like the others, quite wary. Yet in a way he was also eager for this adventure. In retrospect, some of his staff think they detected signs that for the first time he lost that cool indifference that he had characteristically brought to every problem.

Army General Lyman Lemnitzer, Admiral Arleigh Burke, Air Force General Thomas White—the Joint Chiefs of Staff —all brave names from a brave era of war when the United States had no military peer, all with ribbons on their chests marking their years of success; these were the men who sat across the table from Kennedy and told about the military plans for Cuba. They, and the immense war machine in the Pentagon and the CIA, selected the Bay of Pigs for the invasion site. They armed the impatient rebels and trained them and gave them B-26's that would have to fight against Castro jets. True, the plan was not like one for an open invasion, where every available force could be used. But the intelligence experts, who hoped for a mass uprising to help throw the dictator out of the country, rated the chances of success better than that for the plan which in 1954 had wrested Guatemala from the oppressions of Jacobo Arbenz.

Kennedy listened to these experts. Why doubt them? There was only one man with doubts who made them known to Kennedy before the adventure. He was Arkansas Senator William Fulbright, and his objections were not based on the military feasibility of the operation but on the more nebulous moral concept that it wasn't consistent with our national ideals.

It was a bold plan, the kind that appealed to the Kennedy spirit. This kind of action, the Kennedy brothers felt, fitted the New Frontier. It was full of chance, certainly, but it was audacious, glamorous and new. It was irresistible.

"Nobody in the White House wanted to be soft," explained one White House aide when the tragedy had occurred. "That was the trouble. There were questions about the plan, but it was a fascinating plan. Everybody wanted to show they were just as daring and just as bold as anyone else. They didn't look at it close enough."

Though calm in the Washington spring as the invasion approached, Kennedy kept turning the proposition over and over to himself. There had been talk that the invasion was going to be launched before it was really ready. But military men are never really ready. And Castro was building his own forces. Even then some Cuban jet pilots being trained in Czechoslovakia were due back home in a few weeks and their ability, plus the Russian MIG fighters in crates on the Havana docks, might tip the balance of power.

Kennedy debated inwardly the morality of the act, the world response, the national response, the Latin American reaction. He sometimes even asked casual visitors how they would feel about some effort to topple Castro, searching secretly for a pulse beat. But his whole inclination seemed to be somehow to soften the military impact of such a venture —the one and only thing that could make it a success.

The exiled Cubans, getting tougher and more competent in their training, were amounting to a skillful fighting force. Their numbers swelled to 1,400, and this army became eager and restless for action. The point had passed when the group could be broken up conveniently or even prevented from acting on its own.

With these facts before him, Kennedy arrived at his own

philosophy for the invasion. It was to be, not a new revolution, but a "revolution redeemed." In all his plans Kennedy
had insisted that most of the old Batista men be kept at
arm's length. He wanted no taint from the pre-Castro days.
The revolution against such oppressive dictatorship was
something that the new administration endorsed. In Kennedy's mind, the mission now was to put the original revolution back on the track on which Fidel Castro had started it.
Kennedy looked to the thousands of young Cubans, all Castro
men in the beginning, who, as they saw Castro pervert his
revolution in the name of communism, left him and came to
this country. The blow was to be struck in the name of freedom, as Castro had originally promised but had since re-
nounced. These philosophical thoughts seemed to prevail
over those of tanks and guns. Kennedy seemed to think that
he could not lose.

He fretted that American businessmen who had lost property to Castro might be the first in line at the White House
in case the upheaval were successful. Such an act would be
damaging to this country's national stature, providing the
communists with another chance to call us imperialists. Kennedy wanted to be sure that, in case of Castro's rout, some
provision was made for a government which would assure
some of the reforms which Castro had promised.

Kennedy's original stipulation that the Cubans at no time
would get direct help from American armed forces apparently was not fully understood by the Cubans. In the week
before the invasion Kennedy sent a CIA emissary to Guatemala to impress the condition on the rebel leaders once
more. The reservation had particular bearing on air power.

Control of the air was part of the invasion plan, but it was
control of the air with old B-26's from the United States, to
be flown by Cuban pilots. No United States jets were to be
committed, even though some would be just over the horizon
on the aircraft carrier "Essex," part of a Navy task force that
would escort the landing party to Cuba.

Further restrictions were made. Kennedy ruled that the
B-26's would not have the right to rove at will in the hours
before the landing, striking at Castro's sitting planes and
dropping supplies to insurgent groups. Instead, he would

allow only two strikes: one, two days before the landing; the other, on the morning of the landing. He was bent on making the operation "unspectacular."

The White House and the State Department rather ridiculously continued to brood about the possibility of the United States' being blamed for the action, which, indeed, she was preparing, as newspapers had pointed out, for weeks. There was even curtailment of some of the propaganda devices, such as leaflets and radio broadcasts, to arouse the Cuban populace. The United States hand was not to be obvious.

On April 4 the last major meeting on the plan was held. John Kennedy polled everyone in the room, and from each came a go-ahead. There were varying degrees of enthusiasm among the men and there were Fulbright's conscience pangs, but there were no real doubters about the ultimate success of the venture. Even Fulbright, at the close of this meeting, came to Kennedy and said that there was more to the operation than he had thought.

The fateful week end came. John Kennedy went to wait at Glen Ora; the White House communications staff 'was ready to keep him informed of progress in seconds.

The rehabilitated B-26's struck out for Castro's airfields, where his planes were deployed as the invasion barges loaded. Castro, who knew what was happening from intelligence reports from the rebel army, screamed to the world, and for the first time it began to listen.

Our story was that Castro's own pilots had defected with his planes and had bombed the fields as they fled. In the United Nations, Cuban Foreign Minister Raúl Roa charged that the attack was the start of an American invasion. Our UN Ambassador, Adlai Stevenson, uninformed of the extent of American involvement, insisted that we had nothing to do with the action.

First reports of the air strike claimed remarkable success, but in fact it had not done well. Castro's air force was estimated at about fifty-five planes of all types, about half of which were of some military threat. There were B-26's and British Sea Furies, obsolete propeller planes and six or seven T-33 jet trainers, which had been armed. It was estimated that only about five or six of all the planes were destroyed or damaged. Nearly all drops of arms to the insurgents missed their targets.

But this state of affairs was not nearly so serious as the developments in the United Nations and New York. The image-conscious planners began to get panicky as the protests poured in. The headlines in the first hours after the air strike exceeded anything that had been anticipated. Kennedy and his men decided that the second air strike should be canceled. Bissell and CIA Deputy Director Charles Cabell protested to Dean Rusk at the State Department, but the Secretary was adamant; diplomacy came first. At one point Rusk asked if they wished to protest directly to the President, who was then on the phone with Rusk, but neither did.

Military men of the lower echelons were deeply disturbed by this development, and Bissell and Cabell became more alarmed as they thought matters through.

At first light on Monday morning, April 17, the landing craft assembled off the Bay of Pigs and headed for the shore. At 5:15 A.M. the President's military aide, Chester V. Clifton, was awakened by a phone call and given the report that the troops were ashore. He ordered the caller to phone Glen Ora and relay the news to the President. John Kennedy was awakened and told the scanty facts.

In the Bay of Pigs four of Castro's jets did their work well. Armed with rockets, they sank two ships with ammunition and communications equipment while the B-26's of the invading force tried unsuccessfully to chase them off.

General Cabell called Kennedy, now in his White House office, to give him the bad news. Kennedy ordered the second air strike reinstated. But he turned down new requests for United States air cover. He still would not alter his basic rule that American military power would not be directly committed. Even then the feeling of failure had crept into the Oval Office.

Suddenly John Kennedy sensed that he needed near him the most trustworthy and reliable person he knew. He put in a call for his brother Bob, who was then in Williamsburg, Virginia, scheduled to make a speech at noon to the United Press International managing editors. The invasion was not going well, he told Bob. "Why don't you come on back and let's discuss it?" As soon as the luncheon talk was over, Bob hurried to the White House.

The country and the world were largely ignorant of the developments. The fact of the skimpy invasion force was established, but no correspondents were on the spot and the news from the other Cubans in Miami was unreliable.

Despite the tragic start, the Cuban rebels had fought well and had achieved some of their objectives. But by Tuesday they were short of food and ammunition, and Castro's tanks and heavily armed columns were on them and his jets still roamed the sky at will, the second air strike ordered by Kennedy having been thwarted by clouds.

The congressional reception, a gay white-tie affair for all congressmen and senators and their wives, was scheduled for Tuesday night in Washington. From 10 P.M. until midnight the champagne would flow and there would be good fellowship in the White House. Most of the guests would know nothing of what had happened in the Bay of Pigs.

As the time approached for Kennedy to dress, he was totally unconscious of the affair. He lingered in his office, did not heed the reminders that the reception was due to start. Only minutes before 10 did his aides literally guide him to the door and insist that he dress.

For two hours there was the old Kennedy, smiling and handsome and as self-confident as ever. He answered questions about the Cuban invasion with a shake of the head and a generality. He chatted about the bills before Congress and about his pleasure that at last there was action on some of them.

He mingled in the crowded public rooms; then, at 11:45, he and Jackie went up to their quarters, the signal that the reception was over. As the congressional couples began to drift away into the cool spring air, Kennedy hurried back to his office, where the lights blazed brightly.

The principal figures had been summoned; the invasion now hung on the edge of total disaster. Bissell appealed for American air power, in a final desperate effort to save the expedition. But Kennedy and his civilian advisers had concluded that the invasion was finished already. They felt that even American air power, the use of which they still opposed, could only prolong the life of the invasion force for a few more hours. Perhaps the men could be helped to escape, but nothing else was of any use.

Furthermore, another major miscalculation in this hapless adventure was becoming starkly clear. The world was not going to pass this off simply as an adventure by a handful of Cubans who had somehow wangled old fighting equipment. Nor were the men, now beaten on the beach, going to be able to make their way fifty miles into the mountains, thus disappearing from sight to join the growing forces gathering to fight Castro in his own backlands.

This was the alternative plan if the beach operation failed, and Kennedy and his men found it, like the rest of the operation, entirely plausible. The idea that the 1,400 men could slip into the mountains was perhaps not so improbable, but the suggestion that the American press would drop the matter in a few days if nothing came of it was such a faulty calculation that almost any person the least familiar with the ways of news gathering could have sounded a warning. That Kennedy, a man intimately acquainted with journalists and journalism, had even considered such a proposition is one of the great imponderables of this event.

All the major men of the government surrounded Kennedy in these hours at one time or another. Lyndon Johnson was in constant attendance. There were Secretary of Defense Robert McNamara and Secretary of State Dean Rusk. CIA Director Allen Dulles with his pipe and brief case and even his unflagging smile was on hand. There were Admiral Burke and General Lemnitzer, Bissell and Cabell, and most of the White House staff. The men gathered off and on in all the rooms—the Cabinet Room, the Fish Room, the President's office. Bob Kennedy lurked in the corners, downcast and silent except when now and then the disaster on the beach would overwhelm him and he would mutter, "We've got to do something, we've got to do something. We've got to help those men."

Coffee was rushed from the mansion to the working men as they pondered. Out of the deliberations came a plan, but not a plan to try for victory. Kennedy agreed that the "Essex" could furnish air cover for one hour the following morning

—from 6:30 to 7:30—while supply ships went in to unload and the remaining B-26's got in another attack. It was near 2 A.M. when these orders went out.

Now Kennedy had to consider the Cuban Revolutionary Council, angry men held prisoners at an abandoned airfield near Miami. Fearing that the fiery leaders might cause trouble at a crucial time, armed guards had been placed around them while they waited for the invasion force to take a part of Cuba, on which they could establish a provisional government. At the White House a frantic call went out for Arthur Schlesinger, Jr. The Harvard historian and Pulitzer Prize-winning author was a part of a drama as spectacular as those he had written about. For weeks Schlesinger had been one of the President's cloak-and-dagger men on the Cuban invasion. Now he and Adolf Berle, Latin American expert who also had worked closely on the plans, were routed out of their beds. Kennedy wanted them to fly to Florida and meet with the council. Schlesinger was rumpled and unshaven and dead tired. Berle wrapped himself in an overcoat and complained of the cold. Air Force Aide Godfrey McHugh at first had trouble finding a plane, but with the full force of the White House behind his calls, he soon succeeded. Schlesinger and Berle took off into that miserable night, fitfully sleeping on the plane which finally got them to their destination at 7:30 A.M.

Schlesinger and Berle had never seen angrier men. One threatened to walk out and let the guards shoot him unless something was done. "We sit here and read the communiqués issued in our names, and we are not permitted to leave," they told the two men from Washington. They had heard the whole tragic story of the failure of the invasion; some of them had sons in the expedition. It was an intolerable situation, and Schlesinger phoned the President and told him so. He advised Kennedy that he should see the council. "If that's what you think, bring them along," Kennedy said.

In the meantime Ken O'Donnell, as composed and faithful a man as Kennedy had around him, sat outside the President's door and watched the night slip by. Pierre Salinger joined him.

The two men felt more anguish for Kennedy, the man

they had followed through his greatest political battles, than they felt anything else. Finally O'Donnell leaned over to Salinger and said, "That's the first time Jack Kennedy ever lost anything."

And then, near 4 A.M. when there was quiet over all of Washington, there was nothing more that these men in the White House could do or talk about. One by one they drifted off into the night. At last only the President was left in his office. He stepped to the doorway a moment to have a last word with O'Donnell and Salinger. Then, alone, he went out the French doors of his own office into the Rose Garden, hands in his pockets. He loitered a bit on his way to the mansion. This was John Kennedy's lowest moment of his months of crisis.

He walked alone through the damp grass on that blue-black April night. The pale globes of the street lamps cast their shadows among the elms, and the gentlest morning breeze was beginning to stir in the leaves of the old magnolias which Andy Jackson had planted at the rear of the White House. There was more than physical loneliness. There was now, without question, about John Kennedy the undefinable and inevitable presidential solitude that comes with the White House just as the ghost of Abe Lincoln still walks there in his bedroom on dark nights.

But the chemistry of the Kennedy soul cannot be explained in a simple equation. When sadness or self-pity or indifference or anger should be precipitated by bad news and bad events, they rarely can be found. Instead, there develops determination. It is not blind and unreasoning, not a flash of passion. It is determination that every faculty must be sharpened and applied with double diligence, that only in this way can success be gained.

Kennedy's mind, when it is so set, looks back only for clues to the future. In the hours preceding this short and lonely walk, the transformation had started. The President of the United States, even before his 183 million citizens knew the grim facts of this disaster, had begun to think about what he had to do to make sure nothing similar would happen in the future.

Early on Wednesday the last gasp came—and even it was

fouled up. The B-26's arrived before the American air cover and were smashed by Castro's jets. Four Americans, who had trained the Cuban pilots and had volunteered to fly on this mission in the place of some of the exhausted rebel airmen, never returned from that strike. In bitterness, Cuban Brigade 2506 laid down its arms and marched toward Castro's prisons.

By noon on Wednesday, Kennedy's ninetieth day in office, a seven-hour meeting had begun. The same team that had spent the night there drifted back into the executive offices. From 12:30 to 7:30 there was no letup. Again the high officials assembled in knots and clusters in all the various offices.

At times Kennedy sat with his military men as they held aimless discussions on what might be done. There was talk of sending in the Marines immediately to conquer the country, of calling on the Organization of American States to go with us. But that proposal was unappealing to Kennedy almost as soon as it was advanced. Castro's men might, under such circumstances, decide to fight to the death. In such a case the United States would be forced to engage in several weeks of bloody battle—the giant stepping on the ant. Castro's cause and the cause of communism might in the end be immeasurably enhanced.

They discussed a blockade of the country, but they thought that this, also, would be an act of war almost as surely as sending in troops.

There was talk of mounting another rebel force, this one better armed, better trained; but in the aftermath of the Bay of Pigs, such an attack would have the same effect on the world as if we invaded with United States troops.

Time and again Kennedy stood quietly off from the others, talking with his brother. It was in these talks that the Kennedys began to see that something was wrong in the White House organization. The debacle could not have happened had the right man been present at the right time to ask the right questions. The President had accepted the advice of the men who should have known. Kennedy was no military and intelligence expert so he couldn't challenge all the conclusions. He needed somebody near him to look over the

Pentagon's advice with a totally independent eye. The Kennedy brothers in these snatches of conversation laid the groundwork for a new and hard look at the White House organization and, indeed, the entire national security structure.

John Kennedy, in shirt sleeves, moved from room to room listening to new facts on the disaster, asking for new ideas. He smoked his usual two cigars after lunch—no more. He did not rebuke his men at that moment nor did he rush. He tried to evaluate every fragment of information. His skepticism of what was told him was now monumental. Probably only his brother had his complete trust in these hours.

What emerged from the afternoon's discussions were the careless and stingy nature of the military planning and the inaccuracy of the intelligence. The retirement of Allen Dulles, long rumored, was now certain. The Kennedy boys liked Dulles and did not fix the blame on him—but the CIA had faulted and Dulles ran the CIA.

In the course of the discussions some of the military men would suddenly slump and blame themselves, asking why they had not thought of certain details before. Kennedy listened to this self-criticism silently. He kept his regular appointments, flinging on his coat at the last second. When the callers were gone, he rushed back to the Cabinet Room or the Fish Room. When one aide came around with a sad face, Kennedy chided him, "There are no long faces here."

Wednesday, April 18, was an American spring day. For Washington it meant hordes of tourists pressed against the iron fence of the White House, waiting with their baby Brownies for the slightest glimpse of the first family. And for thousands of high-school students it was time for the annual spring trip, when they could buy funny hats, walk down Pennsylvania Avenue with their arms around their girl friends, parents being a thousand miles away. Near 5 P.M. the federal office buildings emptied of their legions of workers, and for half an hour there was sidewalk anarchy, the office armies desperately trying to hail cabs and buses and the visitors, equally intent, trying to park their overloaded cars, photograph the monuments and find their directions on the tourist guides.

Though there was national crisis on that evening, it was contained within the walls of the White House. The waning sun filtered through the burgeoning leaves and the heavily fertilized grass was thick and a brilliant green.

On the rim of the eighteen most important acres in the country all was gaiety and curiosity. The circle of lawn from the fence to the building was a tranquil moat of birds and plants. Only near the white walls was the frenzy sensed. At the side entrance to the west wing, photographers and reporters milled, waiting for their prey, the important people whom they knew should and would go in and come out. Bob Kennedy's gleaming Cadillac, which could absorb his entire family of seven children and a dog or two without choking, was parked at the curb, as were a squadron of black automobiles belonging to the mysterious men inside. Along the circular drive in back of the White House another flotilla of official cars rested.

But it was at the other side that another car approached. Edging through the morass of tourists and students and workers, few of them giving it a second glance, it passed hurriedly through the gate and braked to a stop under the columned portico. Six men scrambled out. Miro Cardona, the Cuban revolutionary leader, and five of his council had just flown from Miami in the Air Force plane sent for them.

They strode silently through the corridors of the White House, arriving at the west side and Kennedy's office. Defeat, disillusion and bitterness was heavy among these men. They poured their stories out to the presidential advisers first, then they met with John Kennedy alone for ten minutes. The President told them that the failure of the invasion was his fault, not theirs; they had indeed done everything they could. He extended his sympathy to the men who had sons in the expedition. This country was considering what action was now open to it, said Kennedy. He would keep in touch with the men. Now, free to go as they pleased, they hurried off to New York.

Kennedy had decided that a speech scheduled for the next day before the American Society of Newspaper Editors should be turned into a talk about Cuba. It was one way of stating his mind without interruptions such as occur in a press conference. Sorensen was called, and Kennedy outlined his thoughts.

Then there were more formal doings. This time Kennedy donned a tuxedo and hurried off to the Greek embassy for a reception given for the President by Prime Minister Caramanlis. But by midnight he was back in the offices of the White House, and with him were Dean Rusk, McGeorge Bundy, Chip Bohlen and Sorensen, who since dinner had been at work on the draft of the speech for the editors and the world. It was, Sorensen noted later, the most splendidly dressed policy meeting yet held in the new administration. Everybody but he was in formal wear.

Kennedy roamed Sorensen's large bare office, talking of what he wanted to say. And then again they ran out of words, and the meeting broke up. Last to leave Sorensen's office was John Kennedy, and just before he walked from the room he noted a magazine lying on his speechwriter's desk. He scooped it up and flipped the pages as he walked out. The time was near 1 A.M.

For half an hour Sorensen worked with the words that on the following day would be Kennedy's. He needed help, and figuring that the President would not yet be asleep, he telephoned the mansion to talk with Kennedy. But the President was not there, he was told. Indeed, it was thought that he was with Sorensen, the last place where he had been traced. Sorensen put down the phone receiver and pushed back from his desk to go down the corridor to see if the President was still at work in his office. When he entered the hall, he nearly fell over a figure slumped in a chair, reading. It was Kennedy.

Sorensen, as he had done so often in the past, labored through the night. By midmorning the first draft was completed. Kennedy read it and, as is customary, wanted some changes. He and Sorensen pushed through the French doors and out into the Rose Garden to walk in the sunshine and talk. As they walked, Caroline burst from the White House in a dead run, headed for her swing set on the south lawn. Four little playmates from her nursery school tagged at her heels. The President's eyes brightened as he saw relief from all the tension. He called to his daughter, and she heard.

Without stopping in her child's run, she swerved to where her father stood with Sorensen. He held out his arms and she jumped into them, and without loss of motion Kennedy swung her around in a sweeping and joyful arch. Back on the ground, she ran off again toward the swings, and the President of the United States went back to work.

The hour came. The TV channels were ready to carry his words across the land. He nodded to Turner Catledge, President of the American Society of Newspaper Editors. "The president of a great democracy such as ours, and the editors of great newspapers such as yours," he began, "owe a common obligation to the people; an obligation to present the facts, to present them with candor, and to present them in perspective. It is with that obligation in mind that I have decided in the last twenty-four hours to discuss briefly at this time the recent events in Cuba.

"On that unhappy island, as in so many other arenas of the contest for freedom, the news has grown worse instead of better. . . ."

Incensed by Khrushchev's blathering, Kennedy for the second time in the week answered him: "Any unilateral American intervention, in the absence of an external attack upon ourselves or an ally, would have been contrary to our traditions and to our international obligations. But let the record show that our restraint is not inexhaustible. Should it ever appear that the inter-American doctrine of noninterference merely conceals or excuses a policy of nonaction—if the nations of this hemisphere should fail to meet their commitments against outside communist penetration—then I want it clearly understood that this government will not hesitate in meeting its primary obligations which are to the security of our nation.

"The message of Cuba, of Laos, of the rising din of communist voices in Asia and Latin America—these messages are all the same. The complacent, the self-indulgent, the soft societies are about to be swept away with the debris of history. Only the strong, only the industrious, only the determined, only the courageous, only the visionary who determined the real nature of our struggle can possibly survive. . . . Too long we have fixed our eyes on traditional military needs, on armies prepared to cross borders, on missiles poised for flight. Now it should be clear that this is no longer enough—that our security may be lost piece by piece, country by country, without the firing of a single missile or the crossing of a single border. . . ."

And at the end of this brief but eloquent declaration, Kennedy added: "We intend to profit from this lesson. . . . We intend to intensify our efforts for a struggle in many ways more difficult than war, where disappointment will often accompany us.

"For I am convinced that we in this country and in the free world possess the necessary resource, and the skill, and the added strength that comes from a belief in the freedom of man. And I am equally convinced that history will record the fact that this bitter struggle reached its climax in the late 1950's and the early 1960's. Let me then make clear as the President of the United States that I am determined upon our system's survival and success, regardless of the cost and regardless of the peril."

These were typical Kennedy words. Would there be action? This was the question: would there be the determination that would win the next one?

Kennedy braced for the criticism that rolled in from every corner of the land. "I expected to get my head kicked off over Cuba," he recalled later.

It became a time of rare humility in the White House. "It marks a new phase," said one White House aide. "Kennedy is a man of reasonableness up to a point—until he is made a sap of." Now it was more evident than ever before that reasonableness would not work against communism. Kennedy's dream of quiet diplomacy was fading a bit. His idea that you could "hold firm" and "prod around the edges" seemed to have suffered a setback.

"When it happened, the President was hit hard," said one aide months afterward. "He showed his fatigue for the first time. He looked sad. The exhilaration of the job was gone. He was no longer the young conquering hero, the first forty-three-year-old president, the first Catholic president, the young man smoking his cigar with his friends and telling them how much fun it was. All that was gone. Suddenly it became one hell of a job."

And to another who watched the President most intimately as the Cuban disaster unraveled, the distressing thing was that Kennedy really had asked the right questions. "He got a lot of bad answers," said the aide bitterly. "The President learned you didn't win them all."

John Kennedy accepted the full blame—or almost. In his public declarations, even in private, he admitted his own giant miscalculations. Yet on the Thursday and Friday of the aftermath of the defeat, the White House did its own hatchet work. Reporters were called into background sessions and informed that the Joint Chiefs of Staff had selected the landing beaches and that the CIA had promised the native uprising that never materialized. Some attempts were made to fasten responsibility on the Eisenhower administration. Some statements were considered so far out of line that Salinger personally called reporters to get them rescinded. Secretary of the Interior Stewart Udall in a TV interview took up the cry, almost fully blaming Ike, a charge Kennedy hastily corrected. It was not the most admirable moment for the White House staff, which had gone through one of the toughest political campaigns in history with a minimum of deception.

Sympathy for John Kennedy was genuine without falsifying the record. "I've never had more confidence in the President," said Walt Rostow, who had watched the President take his beating, then spring back.

Coolness had set in at the White House by Thursday. "We don't want to act like some European principality over its colony," admitted one aide, who predicted that time would reveal the consequences from the Cuban bungle not to be as dire as most people thought them at the moment. But any optimism was limited. Bob Kennedy predicted that this was the start of a string of bad news that would be triggered in the next months by the communists.

And Chip Bohlen in a talk with the President advanced the theory that this might be the year chosen by Khrushchev for the showdown.

"Can our society survive, fighting communism the way we do?" Bob Kennedy asked a visitor over lunch.

Kennedy had immediate doubts about the military and security plans for Laos, so shaken was his faith in his generals.

The Kennedy brothers noted that the authority for the world's trouble spots was spread over a dozen men in a dozen departments, and they wondered if they might not need one man with key authority in each area, a sort of cold-war czar for each sore point.

Kennedy looked at his own staff and tended somewhat to slight the professors, who, like himself, had accepted the words of the professionals without question. He asked Ted Sorensen, ever the doubter, to involve himself more in foreign policy.

Kennedy showed a streak of irritation at the public which could remain so apathetic in the total battle against communism. It was a deep Kennedy belief that only the voters could really arouse the government. When their concern was genuine, there was no trouble getting what was needed from the Congress, from the Pentagon, from the State Department and from the White House.

Kennedy asked for more common sense and hard work from his staff, for less theory and more fact.

He decided that there should be a thorough investigation of the disaster, so that he and all his staff members might not repeat the same mistakes. He asked retired General Maxwell Taylor, just then settling in New York as president of the Lincoln Center for the Performing Arts, to head the investigation which was to start immediately. He would be helped by Bob Kennedy, Admiral Arleigh Burke and Allen Dulles.

Even then the Kennedy brothers were forming an opinion that would in the months ahead become their public stand on the Bay of Pigs episode. They held that the plan was doomed before it began from inadequacy, that the whole attempt to bring Castro down was based on a miscalculation. The investigation of Taylor's committee would strengthen that belief until Bob Kennedy would say, "Victory was never close." In his view, ten times as many men were needed and that much more material, at least. He concluded that at no time would the addition of United States airpower have done anything but prolong the inevitable failure of an operation ill-planned, ill-timed, ill-executed. The Kennedys noted gaping information holes once the catastrophe was on them. They had had no idea, for instance, of the lethal qualities of a heavily armed T-33 jet trainer. The fact that T-33's could cause so much havoc had not been discussed, at least on a level that alerted them. Thus no special concern was registered when even the routine measures to destroy the T-33's were curtailed.

Critics, both then and later, would not accept this view. They maintained that the expedition had come closer to succeeding than the Kennedys would acknowledge, and had even a minimum of American airpower been applied at the right time, the invaders might well have held out long enough for a provisional government on Cuban soil to be established and recognized. This event, they argued, would have changed the entire complexion of the operation, for then America and her allies could have applied unlimited power.

As Kennedy fought for air in the flotsam that came in the wake of the disaster, he did not forget politics. He asked to see Dwight Eisenhower at Camp David.

Up in the Catoctin Mountains the trees had not yet leafed out, and the hazy sun of the Saturday morning warmed the bare branches. In front of Aspen Cottage, which hangs on the lip of the mountains and looks into the distance, forty newsmen and photographers waited. Eisenhower and Kennedy came by helicopter and went immediately to lunch. For an hour they talked, Kennedy giving a detailed explanation of what had happened in the Cuban adventure, then asking Eisenhower's advice on what subsequent action to take.

The gesture to Ike, a way of building some unity, so that the nation would not get embroiled in a bitter partisan wrangle, was a skillful maneuver.

After lunch Kennedy and Ike strolled down the mountainside alone for fifteen minutes. Then, in front of Aspen Cottage, Kennedy talked to the newsmen briefly. "I invited the President to come and have lunch so I could bring him up to date on recent events and also to get the benefit of his thoughts and experience," said Kennedy, scuffing the ground with his toe.

Ike, tanned and smiling, parried the questions. "It's very nice to be in a position not to be expected or allowed to say anything," he laughed.

"I'm all in favor of the United States supporting the man who has to carry the responsibility for our foreign affairs," was the only endorsement that Ike could give Kennedy for the mishandled Cuban matter. But it was almost enough. At the moment it meant a lot.

The photographers jostled for position. Ike cracked, "This is darn near an invasion, isn't it?" There were smiles and handshakes, and in the soft air of spring a tragic week began to end.

When Kennedy came to look back on the episode, he would declare, "Cuba was a hell of a time."

BOB KENNEDY

W I N D of reality blew through the White House, and it was named Robert Francis Kennedy, aged 35. Only one other man in the nation outranked him in power and influence, and that man, his older brother, had asked for his aid at a critical time. Not only was he to help Maxwell Taylor assess the Bay of Pigs wreckage, he was also to examine the White House machinery.

To those who had known Bob Kennedy from his days as chief counsel on Senator John McClellan's racket-busting committee, this news was a comfort. He was not a popular figure; he was too honest and too blunt and too hard-working and too dedicated to the Kennedy cause. But all these traits made him the man for John Kennedy to use in crucial trouble shooting.

The President never needed to fear the accuracy or the objectivity of reports from Bob. No jealousy was created in the White House staff, because Bob Kennedy's unique position was established by blood.

It was, as Bob moved into his new job, almost like the old campaign days. He wore several hats. He still was the Attorney General with the huge Department of Justice and its 32,000 employees to administer. He remained the President's closest confidant on the major issues.

Virtually every day he began his working hours at a special office in the CIA headquarters. When he left CIA, he often went to the White House, where he would meet privately with the President or sit in on policy meetings. And finally, at the end of the afternoon, he slumped, almost lost from view, in the deep rear seat of his Cadillac and sped down Pennsylvania Avenue to the Justice Department to begin his normal work.

His staff at the Justice Department stayed with him far into every night. He lined up the couches and the chairs in his office as if he were conducting classes, and long after most people were on their second martini, the staff members, who had assembled their questions and reports in precise language to save time, poured through his office on the double.

Byron (Whizzer) White, the former Rhodes scholar and all-American football player, now Deputy Attorney General and later to become a Justice of the Supreme Court, shouldered most of the load, growing thin as he juggled two jobs.

The image was familiar to all who had watched Bob Kennedy on the campaign. There had then been no limit to his effort. He used to fret that if he did not do just one little thing more, it might be the thing that would lose the election. He always had time for a bit more, he always harbored an ounce of reserve energy for that extra work. Now he sat late at night in his cavernous Justice Department office, his tie pulled down, his collar gaping. Sometimes he and White threw a football back and forth just to relieve the monotonous paper work.

In late April Bob Kennedy paused a moment toward one 8 P.M. He swung a foot up on his desk and ran his hand down over that mass of nondescript hair. The phone on his desk rang softly. His wife, Ethel, was calling. For a moment he listened. He said quickly, "I can't go. You go alone and come by afterward and pick me up."

Then he turned to the grimy business of Cuba. "All of us involved made mistakes. The President has taken the responsibility, but it was everybody's fault." Such was the general conclusion forming in those long hours with Maxwell Taylor.

His regard rose for one of the men in the tragedy. Allen Dulles, who planned to retire before the new year began, impressed Bob Kennedy with his behavior. He got the ultimate Kennedy compliment. "Dulles is a man," said Bob.

"He never complained, he took all the blame on himself." Dulles had wanted a bigger air strike in the final moments of the invasion planning, but he had been overruled by the State Department. Allen Dulles was to retire with the praise of the Kennedy brothers.

Bob Kennedy searched into the corners of the White House and listened and watched. Henceforth he would be included in National Security Council meetings and in many of the small sessions on national security.

In the immediate aftermath of the Cuban bungle, Bob Kennedy began to spot difficulties. At a National Security Council meeting on the Saturday morning following the unsuccessful invasion, he noted that awe or fear of the President sometimes interfered with honest answers, that the career men upon whom Kennedy had to rely tended to agree with him more than they would have out of his presence. They held back, waited to see how the President felt before they talked. Bob, in an inconspicuous chair in a corner behind and to the left of the President, saw how some of the officials spoke up more even in the moments the President was out of the Cabinet Room. First note: get better and more frank communication between the top people and the President.

Both Kennedys had adopted an immediate and searching skepticism of government institutions as soon as the Cuban venture had gone sour. As they looked back over the debris, they grew even more wary of the career men. They saw people who in crucial instances were more loyal to their departments than they were to the President of the United States or to the country as a whole. Worried about their futures and fearful lest they commit a blunder that would set them back in that long, unimaginative climb up the civil-service ladder, they hesitated to experiment. Their ideas and their efforts were based on the sure and safe way. It was John Kennedy's contention that in these hours the old clichés were a road to certain defeat in the cold war, that now, as many times in the past, ideas and actions had to have imagination and often risk to meet the severe challenges. "The President won't assume anything from now on," said Bob Kennedy. "Simply because a man is supposed to be an expert in his field will not qualify him to the President."

What the Kennedys sought among the government men was some of that quality that they developed in their campaign organization. It had been, in a sense, an amateur performance. In another sense it was a very professional performance.

Bob Kennedy used to talk about his early days in politics. He had watched the so-called experts. They came around to headquarters, sat behind big desks smoking cigars and telling stories. They had a few handbills printed, went out and made a few speeches and posed for newspaper pictures. "Nobody worked," remembered Bob. It was all right as long as everybody acted the same way. But the Kennedys changed the picture in Massachusetts. Everybody winked when John Kennedy in 1952 made Bob Kennedy his campaign manager for his Senate race. Bob was 26. But Bob Kennedy worked. He licked envelopes, rang doorbells, talked to people and made sure that everybody else in the organization did too. The result was that John Kennedy beat the unbeatable Henry Cabot Lodge for the U.S. Senate.

And when they went to the 1960 Democratic convention, matters had been much the same. The old-style pols had sipped their whiskey in hotel rooms and told stories and figured that was all there was to it. But for months—even years—John Kennedy's young men had been all over the country talking to the delegates. When the convention came, they had commitments on paper. They knew they would win. Such were the Kennedy amateurs. They questioned every premise. They accepted no one's word, they had to see things for themselves. They were realists. They wanted facts, not judgments. They made the judgments when they got the facts. They introduced into American politics an element of scientific procedure that changed it drastically.

Now, as the awful event of Cuba began to fade, they sought this quality in the federal government.

That's why John Kennedy called for his brother immediately, And that's why the 32-year-old Ted Sorensen moved quietly into the field of foreign policy. Their knowledge and experience was limited, but their approach was proven.

This was to be the essential change resulting from the Cuban debacle. To many it was disappointing. Wholesale firings, power realignment, job transfers are the traditional stuff of action. But none of these occurred. The important changes were to be made in the minds of the President and of those around him.

Though in the immediate hours following the Bay of Pigs the President offered his brother Allen Dulles' job, it was not a particularly serious offer. Bob felt it far too sensitive and covert a post for a Kennedy family man to accept. Should something go wrong—or, for that matter, go right—the operations were so secret that critics could accuse the Kennedys of building a secret-police organization. Bob preferred Navy Secretary John Connally or Maxwell Taylor, the retired general for whom he developed more and more regard as he worked with him and who very soon would be made a special military and intelligence adviser to the President.

There was talk of Bob leaving the Justice Department and coming in some special capacity to the White House. It was only talk, however. Bob did not want to leave the Justice Department where he was in hot pursuit of his enemy, Jimmy Hoffa, not to mention his plans for new attacks on crime.

The questioning gaze of both Kennedys turned toward the State Department. The great gray formless mass that sprawled in Foggy Bottom was a baffling element to this government. Kennedy's displeasure with the performance from State registered early. When he had asked that letters of thanks be sent to the heads of state who had sent him greetings when he took office, he had scanned some early drafts and been displeased at what he read. He ordered some of the letters rewritten, an unheard-of request in the State Department in recent years, and even on the second attempt he had not been pleased; he finally sat down in his office and dictated his own replies.

Such little items had plagued Kennedy for weeks. He had not been unprepared for troubles at State, some warnings having been given to him by his father about Roosevelt's difficulties with the State Department. No president could seem to make the department work the way he wanted it to. (At dinner one night with friends the President chuckled appreciatively when the solution was suggested of setting up an office outside the department with about thirty highly talented men who would actually handle the nation's foreign affairs, while the State Department could continue to shuffle papers and live in its civil-service world without being disturbed.)

In the hours after the Cuban failure Kennedy had asked for some new policy ideas. The minds in the State Department had been set to work drafting papers. Some ten days later the papers were ready, and it fell on the unlucky Chester Bowles, in the absence of Dean Rusk, to make the presentation at the White House. The National Security Council was summoned, and Bob Kennedy was also present, taking his place in the corner. The Bowles presentation was a disturbing collection of generalities. There were few ideas for action; it was a "soft line" proposal which added up to little more than tongue clucking.

Chin down, looking up from under bushy eyebrows, Bob Kennedy spoke. "This is worthless," he said. "What can we do about Cuba? This doesn't tell us." For five minutes Bob Kennedy continued to tear at the policy report. When he was done, it hung in tatters. Chester Bowles had tried gamely to defend it, but he was no match for the President's brother in that mood.

There was an awkward silence before the President quietly changed the subject. But before the meeting had ended, the President had assigned a task force under Assistant Secretary of Defense Paul Nitze to draw up new proposals for Cuba.

As they had discussed the idea for centralizing authority for every critical area, the Kennedy brothers had also concluded that the men in charge of these areas should be fighting men—"hard liners," in the jargon of policy politics. The men at the State Department, reasoned Kennedy, spent their lives trying to solve problems without fighting. It was against the nature of the department personnel to want to use or show force. At the head of the task force overseeing Southeast Asia he put Deputy Secretary of Defense Roswell Gilpatric. But for Berlin he did stay in the State Department and named Foy Kohler, a realistic career man.

Within the White House Bob Kennedy found the channels of communication to be haphazard. Too many people were going directly to the President, too many people did not know what other people were doing. To tidy up this situation, orders went out that all national security matters were to be channeled through McGeorge Bundy's office. He was to be the man who knew what everybody was doing and thinking.

Counterinsurgency became the password. It was given new emphasis in military training, and within the mufti ranks a special five-week course in counterinsurgency was set up for the top officers in the national security area. A part-time counterinsurgency school in Panama was expanded to give FBI training to South Americans.

The departments, particularly Defense, began to watch their own operations more closely and to tighten up wherever they could. They made such discoveries as that one fourth of the supply of torpedoes had no batteries to run them; they found stocks of guns without ammunition.

While the military and intelligence phases of the Cuban operation had failed miserably, John Kennedy's own political performance in the wake of disaster had worked rather well. Besides Ike, Kennedy had talked in private with each of the three other leading Republicans: Richard Nixon, Senator Barry Goldwater and New York's Governor Nelson Rockefeller. Kennedy had explained to each man what had happened, he had admitted his own misjudgments and he had then asked for any advice they might offer. While Kennedy did not ask them to refrain from public criticism of him, the gesture of seeking them out in confidence was enough to forestall any bitter outbursts.

Across the country the natural tendency to sympathize with their President in times of trouble caught hold of the people. Mail to the White House (8,000 letters in the first week) was generally sympathetic and understanding, only one out of every four being critical. The press still retained its liking for Kennedy, and though there was some stern criticism, through it ran tones of sympathy for a new president.

One of the ironies of that dim time was that precisely

when the Cuban venture was collapsing, the Kennedy legislative program was beginning to move through Congress. There had been in the beginning of April a gentle swell of criticism—the Congress, as usual, was dawdling in its interminable committee sessions. And the press, as usual, was writing that Congress was on dead center. Kennedy the actionist, as usual, was a victim of his own history. It was expected that Kennedy would produce action. When the Congress kept to its own timetable, the journalists blamed Kennedy.

The week before the barges began their move toward the Cuban beach, Congress had cranked out a group of favorable votes in one house or the other on new federal judges, increased social security benefits, a minimum wage of $1.25 an hour, aid for dependent children and money for depressed areas. These mild good tidings were buried in the avalanche of bitter news.

The rest of the world beyond the shores of Cuba gradually came back into focus. Kennedy summoned the congressional leadership of both parties to the White House. Seated at the huge table in the Cabinet Room, with charts to illustrate his points, the President outlined the Laotian situation, which was still in a dizzying decline. The alternatives for this country, explained Kennedy, ranged from total withdrawal to active military engagement, something that none of his military men wanted unless nothing else would work. The one hope, Kennedy explained, was to keep pushing for a cease fire and a neutral Laos. When the congressional leaders had heard the full story, none of them wanted us to plunge into a war in Laos. As they drove back to the Capitol, the best evaluation that any of them could give of the Laotian situation was that it was a "mess."

As May came, the editorial sympathy for Kennedy, which had followed so closely on the Cuban failure, began to wear thin. Everything suddenly became the President's fault. The trouble in Laos and his insistence that we neither fight nor run but try to talk was irritatingly vague and not at all like the clear-cut decisions Americans desired. He was indirectly blamed for the space flight of Russian Yuri Gagarin, because he had not yet decided what this country should do in space.

Even the small matters were thrown up to him. When Herb Klotz, a minor official in the Department of Commerce, sent a memo around his department stating that Kennedy's name ought to be mentioned more in department speeches so as to give it better play in the papers, the newsmen gleefully jumped on the hapless dispatch, they labeled it the "Klotz Botch" and Pierre Salinger was forced publicly to proclaim that the White House was not behind it, that, indeed, it was felt that the President was getting his name in the papers often enough.

In many ways these were to be the President's loneliest days. He seemed disappointed in some ways in himself, and he began to re-examine his personal working regimen, concluding that he had been trying to do too much, to see too many people. The result was that he was always "on the fringe of irritability," to use his words. He needed more rest and more calm, and he began quietly to alter his schedules.

A close family friend noted then that John Kennedy was more removed than ever before. One night he was in the White House with a group of friends, talking and joking and moving informally from room to room, when he was suddenly missed; they found him in his room going over papers. Often now, he walked impatiently out of movies and he joked less.

One evening as the sun fell into the Potomac and the great spotlights picked out the Washington Monument, John Kennedy said, "I'm going to give this damned job to Lyndon." He did not mean it, but it was a measure of his frustration.

For the time being he seemed to have lost all control of the big machine of government. Nothing he wanted seemed to be done when or how he wanted it done. His major project —Cuba—had failed. There was more talk of Berlin trouble. Laos seemed almost hopeless.

He wondered privately about the wisdom of John Foster Dulles' great pattern of alliances, seemingly made with abandon in the days when the country had no military equal and could assure complete protection to any nation, no matter where on the globe.

"When you look around the world," Kennedy said, and he gestured with his right hand in a sweeping arch, "when you look at the whole vast periphery which we alone guard day and night—we alone stand between the Russians and the free world—Cuba doesn't seem so important."

He also was a little angry. "If people knew the facts, there would be less criticism of Laos," he rasped.

That problem and the space enigma had their roots deep in the past. How could rational men expect a new administration to solve them in a hundred days?

He slipped away once to New York, and there, high in the Waldorf Towers, he met with General Douglas MacArthur. The old general, in a bit of grim humor, said about this nation's position in the world, "The chickens are coming home to roost now. You happen to be in charge of the chicken house."

One day Kennedy went to the French doors in his office and stood inhaling the air. The south lawn was a sparkling new green, the flame of azaleas adding a gaudy trim. The President dropped into the rocking chair that by now had become a national symbol. He poured himself a cup of tea, tipped in some cream and broke a piece of sugar in half, dropped it in with a plop and stirred agitatedly.

"What gets me," he said, "is that all these people seem to want me to fail. I don't understand that. If I don't succeed, there may not be another president."

Then suddenly he shrugged and admitted that criticism, whether out of ignorance or malice, was part of the burden of the job. Though the mess in Laos had developed before his administration took office and though the lag in space had begun a decade ago, they were now John Kennedy's problems just as much as if he had created them. He had asked for the chance to solve them, he had this chance now.

The need for silence and secrecy as he plotted the country's strategy was another of his frustrations. If this was to be a poker game with the Soviets, he was certainly not going to reveal his hand. He continued to caution his advisers about talking and about the need for the utmost security. Silence, however, meant that a great many questions about our intentions and our policy had to go unanswered; and unanswered questions breed criticism.

*   *   *

There came driblets of good news in these days, but nothing could change the somber hues of the headlines.

"I just want to say you have a minimum-wage bill," Larry O'Brien had reported over the phone when the Senate gave the bill a final okay. A cease-fire agreement was reached in Laos, and for the moment hopes bounded up in the White House.

Kennedy put Secretary of Defense Robert McNamara to work revising our military outlook so that we could fight the guerrilla wars we suddenly found ourselves confronted with, along with additional strengthening of our nuclear and conventional forces. The first hundred days of office had convinced him that we had to be stronger. And we would plan for civil defense, too. His idea was to give most of the civil-defense task to the Defense Department. The space challenge, which he had pushed to the back of his mind when Cuba had come along, now demanded more of his attention. All these plans would mean billions more in tax money, probably a huge deficit for his first year in office.

To present this program to Congress, Kennedy decided that he would develop a second State of the Union message either to be sent up to the Capitol or to be delivered by himself, depending on the circumstances at the time.

There was in all this planning some of the promise of the Kennedys as viewed in the campaign. But it was still promise —the action was yet to come, the enemy yet to be beaten, and in fact, the government yet to be run as John Kennedy had said.

CHAPTER ELEVEN

LIFT FROM ABOVE

THE valiant try which fails but is born of heroic intentions often wins from Americans as much admiration as does triumph. Apparently Americans so regarded the Bay of Pigs.

President John Kennedy's popularity with the voting public, as measured by George Gallup, climbed to a stunning 83 per cent in April. ("My God," said Kennedy when he was told. "It's as bad as Eisenhower.")

What was this element that appealed to people at a time when Kennedy had missed so far in Cuba and waged a formless battle of words over Laos? It was sincerity, the deep desire to do the best job as President he knew how and to spare no personal effort. The drama, as millions of Americans now watched it on their TV screens each week, was better than soap opera. Its focal point was the worried face of a young man with an amusing accent trying desperately to do a job anybody could tell you was impossible, was beyond the bounds of human capability.

The skepticism that breeds in the unhealthy political lowlands of Washington had not infected the rest of the nation. When Gallup pollsters inquired, Americans said they liked Kennedy, Cuba and all.

Yet the political experts, the pundits, the so-called thinkers, from their Georgetown dens or their office suites can nibble a man to death if he listens. And they had started. "We're going to watch him more closely now," said a high-ranking Democrat. "There's a little pause because of Cuba. We're taking a second look."

On the cocktail circuit the New Frontiersmen dipped their eyes when Cuba came up and tried halfheartedly to switch the subject.

A great many of the Democrats who had joined the Kennedy legion after victory now teetered on the edge of misgiving. One more sour act, and they would revert to "I told you so" status.

"I wonder now if I judged Ike right?" came a question from a disturbed politician.

"Give us the man of Omaha Beach—Dwight Eisenhower," exclaimed an editor.

Then, on May 5, like a gentle, cooling rain in a drought, came Alan B. Shepard.

While the whole world watched, the slender astronaut rode a great, bellowing Atlas missile into space and back again.

His flight in the nose cone of that silver beast was faultless. His recovery from the Atlantic Ocean was precise. America had put a man into space. It was only a fleeting visit, fifteen minutes as compared to Yuri Gagarin's hour and a half, but it had been done in the open, with millions of American television sets scanning every intimate detail of the preparation and the blast-off. This was how free men did things.

On that morning Kennedy had summoned his National Security Council into session for another meeting on the deepening world trouble.

As Shepard waited for the end of the countdown in the cone of that missile pointed up from the sands of Cape Canaveral, the New Frontier in Washington was frankly nervous. A disaster on the launching pad would further discredit the bruised administration. But there was no other choice. Every precaution had been taken. Project Mercury had to go ahead.

On an open line from the Cape to Pierre Salinger's office came the word that the launching was just twelve minutes away. Associate Press Secretary Andy Hatcher notified Secretary Mrs. Evelyn Lincoln, who, at five minutes before launching, broke into the NSC meeting in the Cabinet Room. The men streamed into Mrs. Lincoln's office, where a television set had been hooked up.

Kennedy stood in silence as the ominous numbers ticked off. Jackie came through the door to join her husband. And Lyndon Johnson, nervous in the stillness, opened up a direct phone line to James Webb, National Aeronautics and Space Administration head, to try to be closer to the soul of the project.

The rocket belched flame and smoke and slowly rose from its pad. In the White House there was unspoken prayer as the Atlas gained momentum. It disappeared from the probing eye of the TV camera and the men and women in Mrs. Lincoln's office shifted some.

Then came a tense wait and finally on Salinger's open line the word of rescue. Hatcher burst into the President's presence. "The astronaut is in the helicopter. The pilot says he appears normal and in good shape."

John Kennedy let a smile creep over his face that said a million pounds had just been lifted off his back, then he turned to those around him and said quietly, "It's a success."

The country had a hero, and for the moment Laos and Berlin and Kennedy and Khrushchev were all forgotten. Alan Shepard was the man who counted.

The Washington *Post's* venerable Eddie Folliard, ageless political reporter and dry-witted elder of the White House press corps, considers himself, among other things, the best living authority on Washington parades. By self-appointment he is the *Post's* parade editor. He has covered that famous mile from the iron gates of the White House up Pennsylvania Avenue to the looming dome of the Capitol as long as he can remember. There was inauguration day for Teddy Roosevelt in 1905, and in Eddie's mind there is one of those vague childhood images of the cheers and the bands and the beaming T.R. He watched the triumphal return of "Black Jack" Pershing after World War I, and to the young Folliard there was no finer day than when Washington paid tribute to this hero. He saw Taft and Wilson and Harding, Coolidge, Hoover, Roosevelt and Truman, all go that mile on a ribbon of cheers. Then came a day after World War II when another soldier had his turn. Dwight David Eisenhower, without any advance preparation, climbed into a command car and inched along the route as thousands and thousands of people cried their thanks to the general.

Eddie Folliard followed Alan Shepard, and when it was over he said there had not been anything like it along his mile of the avenue.

There was not the massive crowd of Pershing's day when a parade was planned for weeks, and was the biggest event of the year, although there were some 250,000, more than turned out to see John Kennedy inaugurated. But there welled up along those packed sidewalks a spontaneous cry of tribute to this navy commander which had not been heard on the Washington streets for many a year.

"I think these people are genuinely hungering for a hero," said Eddie as he rode behind Shepard's own car. "It's been so long."

For twenty-seven minutes the caravan crawled along the avenue—past the Treasury Building, where the employees stood between the huge columns, by the ancient Willard Hotel and the Archives Building. Five and six deep the people massed on the sidewalks, every mouth open in a cheer. Shepard and his pretty wife sat on the back of the rear seat of a cream Lincoln convertible and grinned until their jaws ached.

The crowd did not disperse when the Shepards had passed by but waited to peer at the other astronauts, who followed in the cars behind. For the first time the public knew of the courage and dedication of this hardy band of servicemen. There were homemade signs along the route and some hastily gathered confetti. But mostly there were just people, with a warm and lusty shout for a man who had triumphed at a time when the country needed a triumph.

On the steps of the Senate wing of the gleaming Capitol stood Speaker Rayburn, glowering and shouting at the horde of photographers to clear the way for the hero and his wife.

Alan Shepard had gone the mile in glory. For the moment, at least, Eddie Folliard ranked it as the best chapter in his thick book of Washington parade history.

CHAPTER TWELVE

URGE TO TALK

T H E boss has to get off in some lonely corner," grunted a hurried White House aide as he shook the Washington rain drops off his coat, grabbed a straw hat and shouldered his golf clubs.

The President headed for Palm Beach for four days of rest and contemplation. He wanted a break from the world of meetings and cables and phone calls, he wanted to view his problems from a distance; Washington is a city of stifling narrowness.

Should he go back to the Congress in person to deliver his new message at the end of the month? How much should he ask for new space projects, for new arms and training for guerrilla warfare? "It may be millions, it may be billions," said one staff member as he jammed the confidential documents into his brief case.

There were other questions, too. Should the lagging economy get a shot in the arm with a new legislative package of spending bills? Was the foreign-aid program adequate? How far should he go with civil-defense plans, a controversial program under any circumstances?

Much of the shock of Cuba had worn off now. There was anticipation around the White House. Kennedy had a gleam in his eye. "We're on the brink of a lot of things now," said Arthur Schlesinger, Jr.

"There's a feeling that the next ten days are crucial," added Fred Holborn, a White House special assistant.

Though thoughts of Cuba were pushed back more often, they were not dropped completely. Kennedy was eager to get on with whatever political and economic isolation this country could enforce. And then there was the chance that Castro might provoke us into action. If that time ever came, the Marines would be ready. There was also to be more pressure on the other Latin countries to hurry up with their internal reforms if they wanted to continue to share in American aid.

Nor were Southeast Asia's immediate problems forgotten. The President had dispatched his restless Vice President, Lyndon B. Johnson, on a colorful round-the-world trip, accompanied by Kennedy's brother-in-law Stephen Smith and his wife, to talk with the leaders in South Vietnam and Thailand and promise them more United States help and also just show himself to the leaders and the people and convince them of our sincerity.

The situation was rather frenzied. "We're just trying to keep our head above water," confessed Bob Kennedy. "It's tough."

And John Kennedy himself, viewing everything that needed to be done and the huge cost involved, and hearing that old question about whether the citizens of this country would respond to a call for sacrifice, said grimly, "We're going to give them their chance."

The fact that Kennedy had regained most of his vitality since the Cuban fiasco was evident in his irritation over news stories about his inadequacies.

"I'm going to start doing like Eisenhower and have my staff cut up the paper," he said at one point.

Indeed, life was beginning to flood back into the White House after its heart had faltered over Cuba. There was the old cheer again, there was also a new tone of humility and a new wariness.

Thus, Kennedy climbed into the scarlet-snouted Air Force jet and flew south with Jackie and their friends Mr. and Mrs. Charles Spalding of New York.

There was an element of mystery about him as he took up residence in the house of the Charles Wrightsmans, who had left their home at the close of the Florida season. Reporters sensed it but could not identify it.

In early June, Kennedy was to visit France and hold talks with Charles de Gaulle. That trip had been on the books for weeks. There was talk also of visiting other European countries, certainly normal practice for a President who would take time to fly to Europe. A stopover to see Harold Macmillan, though not announced yet, was on the schedule.

What prevented Pierre Salinger from announcing a complete itinerary? The chubby news secretary kept leaving the presidential schedule open. To NBC's Sander Vanocur the performance was singular. On all other occasions when vague statements were made he could slip into a White House staff office and get some guidance as to what was on the President's mind. But not now.

In Palm Beach Vanocur mulled the problem, and he manufactured himself quite a story. He knew that Kennedy would go somewhere else besides Paris for an important meeting. He got an atlas and went over the geography of every world trouble spot. None of them made much sense—Laos, Iran, the Congo; Kennedy certainly would not journey to these areas. Vanocur picked up the Miami *Herald* and was idly going through the news columns when an item hit his eye. Nikita Khrushchev had made another speech and had said some things about Kennedy. There was nothing unusual about that, but what he said about Kennedy was so mild— almost friendly. It was out of character for the Russian. Vanocur's mind clicked. Were Kennedy and Khrushchev going to meet some place in Europe? The supposition made sense. He thought over the problem, then got on the phone to Washington. It was Sunday and a hard time to get news sources, but he persisted, and in a few hours he had enough to convince him it was true.

Vanocur tracked Pierre Salinger down in his room. He had just come from the golf course and was relaxing with a Heineken's beer. "I hear you've been working overtime," was Salinger's greeting to Vanocur. With that, Vanocur knew his lead was hot. Already the men he had phoned had reported back to the White House.

"Unless there is some overriding reason of national security, I'm going ahead with the story," Vanocur told Salinger.

"I can't stop you," answered Salinger. That was the final

clue Vanocur needed.

As it turned out, word of the meeting had been seeping out in other places. *The New York Times'* Drew Middleton in London had gotten a tip on it a week before and had passed it on to Scotty Reston in Washington, who had hinted at it in a column of his a few days before. The French, too, had gotten a sniff from their government. But the story had not come out fully and plainly until Vanocur's flash on NBC.

It was an amazing thought. Kennedy, who had been avoiding a summit meeting with determination, now was to meet with Khrushchev while the memory of Cuba was still fresh. The idea of meeting the wily Russian leader, a veteran of such encounters, while Kennedy's own prestige as a leader was at a low point was criticized by some. Kennedy did not back away.

When the first word came out about the projected meeting, the White House kept silent. The final acceptance of the time and the place (June 4 and 5 in Vienna) had not been made official yet. Soviet Ambassador Mikhail Menshikov had called the White House only two days before to ask for an appointment to deliver the formal acceptance. He was scheduled to drop by the following Tuesday. At that time the White House would announce the plan.

Kennedy insisted that this meeting was not to be a summit meeting in any sense. He did not want to play a part in any Khrushchev act which would build world hopes for goodwill and peace out of noble-sounding phrases which the Russian would then ignore, as had been the case at Geneva in 1955 and Camp David in 1959.

Yet Kennedy wanted to look at Khrushchev. He wanted to hear him talk, listen to his words and watch him as he sat across the table. This was part of the Kennedy technique. One visit in person was sometimes worth all the diplomatic dispatches. And Kennedy wanted Khrushchev to see Kennedy, too. If the Soviet Premier had the idea that Kennedy's actions in Laos and Cuba indicated weakness, he thought that a face-to-face meeting would dispel that impression.

The meeting had been a long time aborning, and after the Cuban incident Kennedy had thought it was dead. Khrushchev had revived it. Each man wanted to see the other.

As far back as December of 1960, when Kennedy was forming his government, the first hints that Khrushchev would welcome an encounter with Kennedy were dropped by Ambassador Menshikov in a round of unusually friendly lunches with key New Frontiersmen. "Let's think about this," said Kennedy, already intrigued.

When U.S. Ambassador Llewellyn Thompson came to Washington at the start of the Kennedy administration for top-level consultation, he brought with him more feelers for some kind of meeting with Khrushchev. Kennedy talked the idea over with Lyndon Johnson, Dean Rusk and three former ambassadors to the Soviet Union: Averell Harriman, George Kennan and Charles Bohlen. The consensus was that it might be worthwhile. "I think we'll go and see Khrushchev," Kennedy said.

Thompson reasoned that a meeting would be a good thing if it could be controlled. Much of the Soviet policy, he told Kennedy, was based on Khrushchev's personal estimate of government heads. If arrangements for this session could be made in secret, followed by a quick announcement only a short time before the meeting, there would not be time enough for great waves of hope to build up around the world about the possible outcome. Results, no matter what, would thus not be disappointing. Such a meeting would take the urgency out of the cry for an honest-to-goodness summit. Further, said Thompson, it would be good to see Khrushchev before the opening of the United Nations General Assembly.

The fact that he had not talked to Khrushchev was proving to be a psychological barrier to President Kennedy. All of his big policy moves—nuclear testing, settlement in Laos, strengthening NATO—were affected by what the Soviets thought and said. A clearer idea of what to expect from the Russians might come at a meeting with the Premier. The uncommitted nations were in some instances sitting on their hands waiting for a Kennedy-Khrushchev encounter to help guide their own futures.

The reasons for such a meeting, it seemed to Kennedy and his advisers, far outnumbered the reasons against it. And as important as anything else, Kennedy had confidence in himself to perform well at the conference table.

Ambassador Thompson packed a letter from the new President in his brief case and flew back to Moscow to find Khrushchev. The Kennedy letter expressed hope for a meeting, possibly in late spring, in a neutral European city. Thompson finally caught up with the touring Khrushchev in Novosibirsk, Siberia, on March 9. The Russian leader liked the idea and told Thompson so.

In late March Gromyko came to the White House for his talk with Kennedy about Laos. Again the matter came up about a Kennedy-Khrushchev meeting. The President said he was willing, and Gromyko assured Kennedy that Khrushchev would still like it. Kennedy, too, felt the urge, because his talk with Gromyko left him feeling "off target." Kennedy liked to deal with the top people. Two weeks later, Khrushchev was walking in the garden of his Sochi villa with columnist Walter Lippmann. He told Lippmann that he and Kennedy were going to meet.

Then came Cuba. Kennedy forgot the idea of a meeting with the Soviet boss, but Khrushchev did not. On May 4 Thompson reported from Moscow that the Russians wanted to know if Kennedy was still interested in meeting. There were hints that the Russian might overlook Cuba in his talks, thus avoiding a major point of United States embarrassment. Kennedy remained willing, and the date was set.

The New Frontier began to gird itself for the conference table. It was to be a formidable line-up of meetings—first Charles de Gaulle, then Nikita Khrushchev and finally Harold Macmillan.

But before any of this, there were some other tasks. First among them was Kennedy's visit to Canada, his initial venture outside the country. It held its unpleasant surprise.

Only a short while after landing and being grandly greeted by Canada's Prime Minister John Diefenbaker and an elite corps of scarlet-coated Mounties, President Kennedy walked out onto the gently sloping lawn of Ottawa's Government House to plant a small red oak tree as a lasting memory of his visit. The tree was to go along with those planted by other presidents.

The party walked from the house, just after Kennedy had taken Diefenbaker aside to tell him of his plans for a meeting with Khrushchev. Kennedy took the silver shovel handed to him and leaned over to shovel up some of the neat pile of black earth.

Then it happened. As he bent to scoop, there was a sharp pain in his back, deep in the lower lumbar region. It was not a severe pain; the horde of photographers and reporters and visitors did not see a wince. Yet the pain was an unmistakable signal that his back was to trouble him again. A bad back had plagued him since his school days, when he ruptured a disc playing football. There had been weeks of pain after the old injury recurred when in World War II his PT boat was rammed and cut in two by a Japanese destroyer. He had almost died when infection set in, following an unsuccessful spine fusion in 1954. At last he thought he had licked the trouble. All through the campaign he had ignored his back, scrambling over cars, being pulled and shoved by crowds. He had stood on his feet for hours, played golf and swum. There had been no trouble. And now, when his government cares were the most severe, just the slight pressure of a few ounces of dirt in a shovel had done what nothing else could.

That night, as Kennedy stood in the glittering reception greeting guests, a dull and distressingly familiar ache set in. He told no one. Those at the reception found him to be as cheerful as ever. When the wife of Canada's Defense Production Minister Raymond O'Hurley told Kennedy that her relatives in Ohio and Connecticut had all voted for him, he grinned back, "Well, with a name like O'Hurley, they should."

When the two-day visit was over, Diefenbaker joked to a Kennedy aide, "I hope he doesn't come across the border and run against me."

The visit, by everybody's measure, had been a success.

But now, as Kennedy faced toward Paris and Vienna, he had one more problem. Tiny as the sore spot was, it could creep through a man's whole system.

In the final week before his departure for Europe, Kennedy laid down the law around the White House. He wanted as much time as possible for himself. He laid out an intensive amount of study on all the world issues. He asked for a series of briefings from the experts. And he wanted time to ponder how he should act, what he should say.

Appointments were cut to a minimum. Handshakers and wellwishers were whisked out of his office in seconds. Formal ceremonies were trimmed. Kennedy did find for himself long hours of solitude.

He liked the study, the diet of memorandums. "This is a game," said an aide, "this mental combat; it's a hell of a challenge, and he likes it."

Kennedy had asked the State Department days before to prepare papers on all the subjects they thought he should familiarize himself with. They poured in, inches deep. A black leather loose-leaf notebook was prepared on each of the three major personalities, so that Kennedy would know their ways.

While he was in Palm Beach, he sent an aide scurrying to find Charles de Gaulle's memoirs. He had read them once, but now he wanted to read them again, to study them and to be able to quote key phrases.

When Senator Hubert Humphrey came down to the White House on other business, he was collared by the President and questioned about his famous eight-hour conversation with Khrushchev in 1959. How had Khrushchev carried off the conversations, Kennedy wanted to know. How had he reacted to Humphrey? The President asked that the senator prepare a memo for him, a sort of personality sketch of the Soviet boss. Humphrey, delighted, went to the Hill and put his ideas on paper.

Walter Lippmann was asked to the White House for lunch, and Kennedy listened to Lippmann's account of his Russian visit. *The New York Times'* Scotty Reston weighed in with his opinions at another lunch. There were voluntary memos from a legion of staff members and self-appointed Russian experts.

Kennedy sought out the quiet and solid guidance of former Ambassador Chip Bohlen and Secretary of State Dean Rusk. Former Secretary of State Dean Acheson was asked for his views on NATO. Arthur Dean, the chubby nuclear-test-ban negotiator, flew back from Geneva. A test ban was to be a key item in the Kennedy-Khrushchev talks.

French historian and journalist Raymond Aron came to the White House at Kennedy's request and left the President with some of his writings. Henry Kissinger journeyed from Harvard to give Kennedy his latest ideas on Berlin.

This endless search for clues to the men and the issues was a spectacle that the State Department had not seen for years —if, indeed, ever. Some State Department career men said that there never had been such thorough preparation for an international meeting.

Kennedy asked and received from the files every previous conversation that American statesmen had had with Nikita Khrushchev. He read every word. He studied minutely all the give and take of the previous summit meetings. And this was not enough. He sent for a collection of Khrushchev's major speeches, and these he devoured with those restless eyes.

The fine details of conference-table strategy were also of concern to Kennedy. With Rusk and Bohlen and White House aide McGeorge Bundy, he worried over such details as what subjects should be brought up with questions by him, what subjects should be left for Khrushchev to bring up. The President wanted to know if logic worked with the Premier, how tough it was possible to be with him.

Sometimes the White House staff members who hustled the papers in and out acted as if they were training a promising heavyweight for the title bout. They wanted to have their man in the best shape possible. "An awful lot of life on this planet is one man's assessment of the other," explained Walt Rostow.

Kennedy did seem to like these hours of hard work. In a sense it was a study of history, of great personalities who shape the world. Kennedy loved no subject more.

I went to see him on the eve of this journey to Europe. He sat in his rocking chair, crossed his legs, ordered Mrs. Lincoln to fetch him a cigar, lighted it, pondered the notion of Khrushchev through the smoke.

"He's not dumb," said Kennedy at last in low tones. "He's smart. He's . . ." Kennedy's voice trailed off as if words were inadequate. He raised his left arm and clenched his fist and shook it in a gesture that was the Kennedy symbol of strength. (It was a gesture that Kennedy often had used in the campaign, when he had seen steelworkers or other construction men on the job as he had motored through cities.)

"Each crisis that I've faced so far in this job has really stemmed from Russia," Kennedy continued. "It became apparent soon after I took office that it would be foolish for Khrushchev and me to continue to battle each other through other parties. There was always the very serious chance of misunderstanding or miscalculation. That is lessened when you see one another."

Kennedy declared that he had two main considerations in these talks. He did not want to make a decision on the resumption of nuclear tests until he had gone "the last mile." That included talking with Khrushchev himself. The pressure for more nuclear tests was mounting in America. Talks with the Russians seemed hopeless, they certainly had been endless and barren of results. The suspicions mounted that the Russians might be cheating with underground testing— and it would take this nation, in its present state of nuclear lassitude, months to follow suit. The idea of abandoning all hope of agreement, of assuming a nuclear testing race, appalled Kennedy. He grimaced when he talked about it. "We test and then they test and we have to test again," he said. "And you build up until somebody uses them."

The second Kennedy consideration was to warn Khrushchev on Berlin. Week by week the threat became more real. There was no trouble to speak of yet, but there were more words from the Kremlin. The President and all his Soviet experts felt that Berlin would be the real trouble spot of the year. It was in that city that Kennedy felt Khrushchev could make a grave miscalculation. For in Berlin there was less of the vagueness that was inherent in Laos. In Berlin there were specific commitments, specific lines. This country would fight for the basic rights it retained in Berlin. War in Berlin was far more likely to bring on a world conflict than was war in Laos.

The President had an agenda of sorts for the meeting. But it was to be loose and flexible beyond the two points. He wanted nothing to bind and pinch Khrushchev. Laos, the Congo, Iran, Korea—any of those subjects could come up in any given order.

The days ticked by and the pace became frantic. Vice President Lyndon Johnson winged back from his world tour and brought bullish reports from Southeast Asia. "We never heard a hostile voice, never shook a hostile hand. We went to listen and to learn," said Lyndon, standing on the porch outside Kennedy's office.

Prince Rainier and Princess Grace (Kelly) came by for lunch. White House greeter Dave Powers was so smitten by the Kelly beauty that he took her hand, said, "Welcome to the White House, Princess," turned and started up the stairs before he remembered to whirl and stick out his hand again, "and you too, Prince."

Kennedy took quiet pride in the performance of his brother, who in an all-night vigil in his office and with tough talk over the telephone helped to prevent racial rioting in Montgomery, Alabama, as the Freedom Riders assaulted segregation in the South. Bob Kennedy had dispatched 600 U.S. marshals to Montgomery. As Martin Luther King talked to a mass meeting of Negroes in the First Baptist Church, a mob had gathered outside the church.

The Attorney General was dressed in blue denim slacks, a sports shirt, a dark blue sweater. His hair was mussed, his eyes weary. He put his feet up on his desk as the phone jangled.

"What's the situation now?" he asked. "Our first job has to be to protect those people." He got up and paced his office. "It's a bad situation. Trouble could spread all over the South."

Had Alabama's Governor John Patterson moved promptly and decisively to uphold the law, all violence might have been avoided.

"Get me Patterson," snapped Bobby. But before the call could be placed, Patterson was on the line. The conversation with Patterson was a long one. The governor's growls could be heard beyond the phone receiver. Bob broke in. "John, John, what do you mean you're being invaded? Who's invading you, John? You know better than that."

Bob explained carefully why the marshals were there, that they would cooperate fully with the National Guardsmen, whom Patterson had mobilized. Then Patterson declared that the state could protect everyone but Martin Luther King— the federal government would have to protect him.

The brother of the President exploded. Who said the National Guard couldn't protect King, asked Bob. Was it Adjutant General Henry Graham, the commander?

"Have him call me," said the Attorney General. "Have him call me. I want to hear him say it to me. I want to hear a general of the United States Army say that he can't protect Martin Luther King."

Patterson backed down, admitted it was he, not the general, who was saying it.

And then the tension drained off as Patterson went on talking.

"John, you're giving a political speech," laughed Bob.

Then he talked to King in the besieged church, explaining that the National Guard and marshals could protect the people if they stayed in the church. But King was upset and angry.

"We're there, the federal government is there, Doctor," said Bob. "You're in the church. We're talking on the telephone. We wouldn't be talking if the federal government wasn't there."

When it all ended, no blood had been shed. No regular troops had to be flown in, as had been the case in Little Rock.

There was grumbling in the Pentagon from those who had felt the administration lash over Cuba. There were leaks and counterleaks, as is the rule when the generals get unhappy. There were planted stories and hoked-up tales of sagging morale (a perpetual ailment in the Pentagon) and unhappy commanders. Kennedy gave the situation only fleeting notice at this busy time. "They're rather delicate flowers over there, aren't they?" he told one general.

He became mildly irritated over the storm that brewed on Capitol Hill because he had moved in and personally called prominent Americans and asked that they help in raising funds to buy 500 heavy tractors to exchange for the captured Cubans. This was Castro's proposition, and Kennedy felt that there was little else he could do. But the White House, without smoothing the way, proclaimed that the donations would be tax exempt. Virginia's Harry Byrd had other ideas and promptly announced that the Internal Revenue Service would answer to him as Chairman of the Senate Finance Committee if they allowed such exemptions.

The President's second State of the Union message was ready. He had made his decisions, and they were now on paper. At first he was opposed to going to the Congress in person. His congressional leaders had counseled against it, fearing that an appearance would needlessly raise partisan feelings. There was also concern that the message might raise the ire of Khrushchev at an unfortunate time.

But by May 24 Kennedy himself had labored long over the speech, and he liked it. If Khrushchev was going to be offended by the billions more asked for the defense of freedom, then that was the way it would have to be.

Kennedy went back to the Capitol himself, again waited to go down the aisle, again assessed the State of the Union. "These are extraordinary times. And we face an extraordinary challenge. Our strength as well as our convictions have imposed upon this nation the role of leader in freedom's cause."

Kennedy ticked off two billion dollars' worth of new recommendations: reorganization of the army divisional structure, beefing up of its conventional strength, more emphasis on guerrilla warfare; a redoubled space effort; a long-range nationwide civil-defense shelter program; more money for foreign aid and Voice of America.

"It is not a pleasure for any President of the United States, as I am sure it was not a pleasure for my predecessors, to come before the Congress and ask for new appropriations which place burdens on our people. I came to this conclusion with some reluctance. But in my judgment this is a most serious time in the life of our country and in the life of freedom around the globe."

The 43-year-old President became 44 on May 29th. He was toasted in Washington at an immense dinner given by the National Committee at $100 per plate. The same happened in Boston as Kennedy flew to Massachusetts for a final two days in Hyannis Port before flying to his European rendezvous. There was a quiet birthday party with his family on the Cape. Only the Secret Service and members of the family watched as the President of the United States hobbled on crutches into the weak Cape Cod spring sun and sat down on the lawn huddled in a gray Navy blanket to read some final reports for his Khrushchev meeting. The pain in his back had grown persistent and bothersome. White House physician Janet Travell had begun to treat him to ease the ache. Crutches relieved the strain, but Kennedy would not be seen on crutches in public before or during his trip to Europe. He would endure the pain. But while he could, he would try for relief. The hours were few.

He flew to New York on the first leg of the journey. There he indulged himself in one of those curious side excursions that seem to occur at the crucial moments of Kennedy's history: he went to see the Israeli Premier, Ben-Gurion.

The men around the White House like to remember the meeting as a classic example of their man in motion. The President had a suite on the thirty-first floor of the Waldorf and one hour had been set aside for the meeting. It was expected that the two men would exchange the usual clichés, shake hands and go off to await a more formal meeting in the future to discuss business.

They met in the living room of the suite and settled down in the chairs. Kennedy began telling Ben-Gurion of his own travels in Israel and of his fascination with the country. He began to ask the Israeli about his country, to listen to the answers carefully. Ben-Gurion, a crusty realist himself, was delighted. For two hours, as aides ran frantically to rearrange the presidential schedule, the two men talked. The meeting ended with a Kennedy thrust of humor. Pointing to aide Myer Feldman, the President said, "How do you think Mike Feldman would do in a kibbutz?"

"Lend him to us and we'll see," laughed Ben-Gurion.

*   *   *

Kennedy had one other duty before de Gaulle and Khrushchev and Macmillan claimed him. He stopped that night to talk briefly at a dinner for the Eleanor Roosevelt Cancer Foundation.

"It is now 1:30 in Paris and I am due there at 10:30, and I do not believe it would be a good start to keep the general waiting. So I shall be brief. . . . The Vice President and I are conscious always of the fact that we appropriate in Washington from forty-five to fifty billion dollars a year in the defense of the great Republic. And we spend a fraction of that in the fight for cancer. If in any way it will make it possible for us to make a greater effort on this cause and no longer have to build our strength constantly, then the trip which I am about to make, the trip which the Vice President made a week ago, the trip which Ambassador Stevenson will make next week are all worthwhile.

"We go to many countries but we sing the same song. And that is, this country wants peace and this country wants freedom.

"Therefore in going tonight across the sea I recognize that all of you, as citizens of the great Republic, come with me."

CHAPTER THIRTEEN

PARIS

I NTO the deep night of the New World, up over the Atlantic Ocean, its sensitized scarlet nose pointed toward a
Paris dawn, thundered Air Force One[1] on May 30.
The great wings flexed in the lower turbulence, clawing
for the cold, smooth ribbon of 35,000 feet.

Behind the cabin where Col. James B. Swindal sat in the
muted red glow of the instrument panel, his eyes as wakeful
as the radar, the President of the United States and his wife
slipped beneath the blankets in the giant planes' two bunk
beds and slept.

Some 4,600 miles away and three days earlier, the pudgy
figure of Nikita Khrushchev had settled in a private railroad
car along with his wife, Nina. From Moscow the train
chugged toward Kiev, and then it rolled on to Lvov, then to
Czechoslovakia, where it halted so the Chairman could rest,
and finally on to Vienna. At the stops the Soviet Premier
grinned and waved to the dutiful people who assembled at
the stations. It took Khrushchev and his wife a week for the
leisurely trip.

For John and Jacqueline Kennedy there were scarcely
seven hours of sleep before they were at Orly Airport, the
first stride toward Vienna.

Paris was wrapped in a sunlit tissue of spring mist as the
Kennedys' jet lowered its wheels. The President pulled up

[1] Air Force One is the code name automatically applied to the airplane in
which the President is flying.

the knot of his tie, gave his hair a last brushing and put on his coat. Press Secretary Pierre Salinger went to the forward cabin to review the plans for the arrival ceremony. Jackie settled a pale-blue pill-box hat on her head. Then the plane was on European soil.

French women in blue smocks gave the seventy-five yards of red carpeting a final sweeping to remove every speck of dirt. Grumpy American newsmen were herded into the roped-off enclosure with United States embassy personnel, servicemen and school children. Eleven members of the Garde Republicaine stood haughtily at attention, their swords point up, knee-high black boots polished like mirrors, their red plumes quivering in the breeze atop gold helmets burnished by the soft sun.

Charles de Gaulle, towering and grand, waited in a double-breasted gray suit.

The jet hiss died, the front door of the plane was thrown back, showing the seal of the President of the United States. John Kennedy ducked his head and emerged into the French morning. Jackie was a step behind, and then both of them stood at the top of the ramp as the drums rolled. Kennedy gave that short choppy wave of his, and he and Jackie walked down the ramp to the outstretched hands of the de Gaulles.

"Have you made a good aerial voyage?" asked de Gaulle in his rarely used English. When Kennedy answered yes, de Gaulle said: "Ah, that's good."

The contingents of American school children pressed to the fence and waved tiny American flags as de Gaulle and Kennedy strode toward the ornate Salon d'Honneur for the formal welcoming speeches.

Kennedy was set to pass by the color guard when de Gaulle reached out a fatherly hand and gripped his arm, pulling him back and around to face the flags and listen to the national anthems of both nations.

Jackie had been whisked around to the salon in a car, and when she entered it, two little girls in pink dresses gave her spring bouquets and she spoke her first French of the trip, *"Merci bien."*

Mrs. Joseph Kennedy was there, waiting for her daughter-in-law. "You look very nice, dear," she whispered.

Kennedy had prepared his remarks carefully, shrewdly tuning them to some of de Gaulle's own past statements.

"I come from America," he said, "the daughter of Europe, to France, which is America's oldest friend. But I come today, not because of merely past ties and past friendship, but because the present relationship between France and the United States is essential for the preservation of freedom around the globe."

De Gaulle guided his guest to a waiting Citroën for the ten-mile motorcade to the Quai d'Orsay, where the Kennedys would stay.

As Kennedy climbed into his car, a French policeman turned to American correspondents and grinned. "*Mon dieu, he's really an all-American boy.*"

Fifty epauletted motorcycle police and a mounted contingent of the Garde Republicaine formed an escort for the caravan which, in tribute to former Sorbonne student Jackie, went down the famed Boul' Mich'—the cobblestoned main street of the university district—before crossing the Seine into downtown Paris. Banners of red, white and blue waved along the streets. At first the people stood in a thin line only one and two deep at the curbs. Then their numbers began to swell as the motorcade neared the heart of Paris. Latin Quarter students hoisted a Harvard banner and others roared out a football-chant countdown of "Kenne-un, Kenne-deux, Kenne-trois . . . Kenne-dix."

The rumble from the 101-gun salute rolled down the streets as the long black caravan edged through the city. The crowd was curious and warm, but not frenetic as crowds often had been in Kennedy's campaign in America, producing the "leapers" and "jumpers" and "runners" that had been diligently catalogued by the press.

The motorcade had its Kennedy touch. Dave Powers, White House greeter and a long-time Kennedy worker, rode in one of the cars, waving and shouting "Comment-tally vous, pal," adapting his famous "Hi, pal" from the streets of his native Charlestown, Massachusetts, for the French occasion. Near the end of the line of Citroëns, Dr. Janet Travell spread her delightful smile from Orly to the Quai d'Orsay, and while she waved she took snapshots with her camera.

John Kennedy stood up in his open car to wave, de Gaulle stayed seated, occasionally gesturing to the crowd. In the car behind rode Madame de Gaulle and Jackie.

There were laughs, too, in the gay confusion of such a parade. At the statue of Joan of Arc the motorcycle escort was changed for the horse-mounted contingent of the Garde Republicaine, and in the shuffle the car of newsmen which had been allowed to ride in the parade came out staring at the massed rear ends of the horse brigade.

When the sounds of the cheers, the bands and the howitzers had died, there was no question that it had been a grand greeting. "You had more than a million out," said de Gaulle proudly to the President.

For one Kennedy staff member there was a disturbing note. Counsel Ted Sorensen, who had been with Kennedy since 1952, had gone to Paris ahead of the President. It was the first trip outside the United States for Sorensen, a Lincoln, Nebraska, native. He had savored the Parisian atmosphere for two days before rushing to the airport to be on hand for Kennedy's arrival.

Once inside the Quai d'Orsay, Kennedy had headed straight for "the King's Chamber"—a Louis XVI bedroom paneled in blue-gray silk—and had shed his clothes and gingerly lowered himself into some steaming water in the huge golden tub. Immediately Sorensen knew that once again Kennedy had back trouble; for Sorensen had lived through the long days of the first ailment. He had watched Senator Kennedy in pain, he had waited through the night when it was thought Kennedy's life was ebbing away following the spinal fusion operation. Sorenson had worked at the senator's bedside during the months of recuperation. He knew the signs too well to be mistaken. Nothing was said, however. Kennedy was due immediately at the Elysée Palace for the first of the formal talks and for lunch.

Trumpets sounded at the Elysée, the ponderous de Gaulle came forward and again gripped Kennedy's hand. The men paused impatiently for the photographers, then de Gaulle guided Kennedy toward his second-floor office to talk. They settled down in armchairs behind huge windows overlooking the superbly manicured lawn. Between the chairs was a glass table, holding French and American cigarettes. Neither man smoked them. Kennedy had brought his Upmann cigars, but knowing that de Gaulle did not like others to smoke in his office, Kennedy refrained.

They began immediately on Berlin, with Kennedy asking questions to learn de Gaulle's views. Both men said that there could be no backdown before Soviet threats and that seizure of West Berlin by the Russians would mean full nuclear retaliation against the Soviet Union. Kennedy wanted to know just how he could make this absolutely clear to Khrushchev. Kennedy was bothered by the feeling that Khrushchev was not convinced that we could not back down in Berlin. What could he say or do when he met Khrushchev in a few days?

De Gaulle told Kennedy that he was certain the Russians did not want war. He reported on his own talk with Khrushchev and how when the Soviet Premier was expounding about the horrors of war and his desires for peace, he (de Gaulle) had simply told Khrushchev that if he didn't want war, then he should not start it. It was up to him, Nikita Khrushchev.

De Gaulle pointed out that we had no force in Berlin which could stop the Russians if they really wanted to seize the city. There was only one way to defend the city and that was to be ready to unleash a nuclear attack on the Soviet Union if it used force in Berlin.

Kennedy was in full agreement, but he returned to the matter of convincing Khrushchev of this resolve. Was de Gaulle happy with the contingency plans? Kennedy said that he was not yet satisfied. His planners were considering some kind of probing action like sending reinforcements over the Autobahn from West Germany to West Berlin to make certain our rights of access were not hampered and to demonstrate to the Russians we meant business. Kennedy wondered if such a move should be made with a few companies, perhaps a division, or even several divisions. Perhaps there should be some other action?

De Gaulle thought it a good idea to reinforce Berlin and he

asked about the United States airlift capability. Kennedy told him he felt we were in pretty good shape if an airlift was needed.

There was no question, continued Kennedy, that we would fight if the communists used force against us, but what if they began nibbling away on our rights, such as signing a peace treaty with East Germany which, of course, we did not recognize. De Gaulle felt the answer to that was strength. There could be no sign of weakness. The Russians had been saying for years they were going to sign such a treaty and each time when they faced determination they put it off another six months, and another six months, and another six months.

When they ended this first meeting to go to lunch de Gaulle and Kennedy found themselves in full agreement on the need for unflinching resolve in Berlin. It had been an auspicious start to the talks that many had feared might go awry because of the unpredictable de Gaulle.

For lunch there was langouste, pâté de foie gras, noix de veau Orloff and three French wines. Kennedy's pop-eyed troop of O'Donnell, Salinger, Sorensen, Powers and Ted Reardon found themselves sprinkled among an elite selection of officials in the French government. The longest and most intense conversation was between Jackie and de Gaulle—in French. De Gaulle hardly touched his lunch, breaking off the intimacy only long enough to rise and toast Kennedy. "You saw this morning how happy Paris was to see you. I do not need to add anything to this."

Kennedy's staff members, who were used to lunching in the White House mess, began to get the feel of the visit, and they liked it. The only one on the staff who spoke French was Pierre Salinger, and he particularly delighted in the Gallic touch, which included the whispered observation from the woman beside him that Madame Hervé Alphand's dress was the exact shade of the pale orange ice cream served for dessert.

"Mrs. Kennedy and I appreciate your generosity and that of the French people," Kennedy said in his toast. "Years ago it was said that an optimist studies Russian while a pessimist studies Chinese. I prefer to believe the far-seeing are learning French and English."

Back in the Salon Doré there was more talk, this time about Laos. Again, there was agreement because neither President wanted to become engaged militarily in that remote country. France would diplomatically support any U.S. military move in Laos, de Gaulle told Kennedy, but she would not commit troops unless there was all-out war and then, of course, France would be at the side of the United States with her armies.

De Gaulle told Kennedy of France's dismal time fighting a guerrilla war in that area; he called Laos "a bad place to fight." It was de Gaulle's view that the best thing was to get some kind of coalition government under Souvanna Phouma and to reassure the other friendly countries of the area of Western support.

Kennedy asked that de Gaulle not say anything publicly about his non-intervention policy and de Gaulle readily agreed that silence was best. The Russian support of the Pathet Lao intrigued de Gaulle, who suggested the Soviets were perhaps apprehensive about the Red Chinese. Kennedy could find little comfort in the Russian presence, however. The Russian-Chinese affair reminded him, he said, of Caesar and Pompey, who did not discover their dislike for each other until after they had vanquished their common enemy.

The presidents went on to other subjects—Africa, Portugal and the need for more consultation between Britain and France and the United States, a sore point with de Gaulle. Kennedy felt that, indeed, there was a need for closer communication. And then again it was time for other things.

Slowly but surely the spectacle of France and Paris and the handsome young couple from America became almost as important as the talks.

Kennedy met the diplomatic corps. Jackie hurried off to a child-care and training center.

The President rode coatless through the cold afternoon rain up the Champs Elysée to rekindle the eternal flame beneath the Arc de Triomphe. Thousands massed along the street, not budging when dark clouds began to dump their moisture.

Kennedy was weary. The lines in his face showed. His back ached severely, though he had told no one, and he would rush back to his room for hot packs and the novocain injections which White House physician Janet Travell had used in earlier years. Yet Kennedy did not limp or slump.

Evening came, and two thousand of Paris' gilt-edged people crushed their way into the Elysée Palace for a glittering formal dinner. And then it became apparent that Jackie Kennedy just might steal the show.

Even that morning in the parade there had been hints. The cry had gone up along the caravan route, "Vive Jacqueline." She was ready for Paris, it turned out—well, not quite.

For the reality of those first hours in Paris had gone to the very soul of Jacqueline Kennedy. She had been ushered into the Quai d'Orsay and paused for a moment amid the unpacked bags and bustle and marveled to herself. She had loved Paris as a student, and she loved it now, but more. As a student she had not even dreamed of the things that had already happened to her. The Garde Republicaine had escorted her in the parade, white-stockinged footmen lined the stairs to the palace. She would sleep in the Chambre de la Reine, bathe in a silver mosaic tub and gaze at a ceiling swarming with Napoleonic cherubs.

Those who knew Mrs. Kennedy marked that day—May 31, 1961—as the day she discovered a very new and very great pleasure in being First Lady.

Much of the space of two truck loads of presidential luggage was for the array of dresses Jackie had brought with her, most of them the creations of American designer Oleg Cassini. Alexandre, the leading Parisian hairdresser, stood by to serve her, as did the top cosmetician of all Europe, Nathalie, although only once did Mrs. Kennedy avail herself of the latter's services, preferring instead her natural look.

For her first night Jackie chose a narrow pink-and-white straw-laced gown and a swooping fourteenth-century hairdo with a topknot. When she emerged from the Quai d'Orsay, there was an explosion of flash bulbs that seemed great enough to illuminate all of Paris. French praise split its seams, too. *"Charmante, ravissante,"* exclaimed the French newsmen. And even John Kennedy was impressed. "Well," he said, "I'm dazzled." For he, too, had made a discovery on May 31—his wife.

That evening, after shaking a thousand hands, Jackie's glove was stained and she was visibly weary. But her smile stayed. Her back was straight and she moved in gliding grace. This was something that America had not noticed about her. Her bearing was a vital part of her beauty. As the French women watched, they murmured among themselves, *"Elle est plus reine que toutes les reines"*—she is more queenly than all the queens.

The ultimate compliment went almost unnoticed. A sharp-eyed member of the American party who knew French spotted it in a French newspaper. It was a column of advice to teen-agers, and it said that young ladies who wanted to be beautiful should practice sitting and standing gracefully, then they should go out into the street and look at Mrs. Kennedy.

The second day in Paris Kennedy got a full preview of the trouble that was to come from Charles de Gaulle. When the subject of NATO came up on the agenda de Gaulle settled back and told the President that he wanted to talk in some detail about this matter. And, indeed, he did.

De Gaulle sketched for Kennedy the history of France after the war. In the first postwar years she was a nation of no ambition, the French President pointed out. She had had too much war and did not want power, and it was only natural that the United States should step into that vacuum in Europe. But now France had regained her health and she again had ambition, he said. There was a genuine French spirit and the country could not live under the shadow of NATO much longer; she must have her own nuclear force and she intended to develop it. De Gaulle did not say outright that NATO was the reason that he had so much trouble with his generals, but he suggested that constantly being under a "supranational" power caused discontent among them. De Gaulle declared that he would not do anything right then and that he understood the importance of Kennedy's mission to Vienna and the need not to hurt NATO, but that some time in the near future the situation would have to change.

Kennedy listened quietly as de Gaulle talked. The de Gaulle theory of an individual nuclear force was not, of course, what Kennedy wanted. The United States possessed

enough nuclear protection for the free world. It was the feeling of the United States that the cause of freedom would be
better served if the European countries built up their conventional forces to assume more of their share of the NATO
responsibilities in Europe. Further, the proliferation of nuclear capability was fraught with grave possibilities for the
future of civilization, and the United States was against it.

De Gaulle talked on. The United States could not always
be depended upon to defend Europe. And there were the
questions of where and how nuclear weapons would be used
should fighting break out in Europe. De Gaulle could visual-
ize both Russia and the United States exploding their warheads against opposing forces on European land and thus,
while destroying Europe, both the major powers would perhaps be unharmed if fighting then stopped. In de Gaulle's
vision, France had to have nuclear power of her own.

Kennedy could not agree, and he said so. America would
fight for Europe—there was no question about that, there
were no conceivable conditions under which this country
would turn away. Why would de Gaulle's national nuclear
force really solve the problem of when and how to go to war,
Kennedy wondered. Couldn't there be the same problems between France and Germany that de Gaulle suggested might
arise between the United States and France? De Gaulle's answer was that the Rhine was not as wide as the Atlantic and
there would be much concern for a neighboring country like
Germany.

De Gaulle brought in the "first strike" theory to support
his argument. The common assumption has been that the
United States would not start a war; thus Russia in a nuclear
conflict would get off the first missile strike, which might
destroy as much of Europe as of the United States.

Kennedy disagreed politely again. The United States
might very well strike the first blow in a nuclear war, he said.
If it was necessary, if our forces were in danger, if we knew
the Soviet Union was preparing to strike, if Europe were attacked, the United States would not hesitate to act first.

Kennedy repeated that Europe was, for all purposes of nuclear reaction, the United States. That was the reason we still
had troops there, the President continued. "We will go to

war if Europe is attacked," he said again.

To hear Kennedy say this, de Gaulle replied, had convinced him that Kennedy meant it, but he still wanted his own nuclear power.

Kennedy asked if there was anything that might persuade the French President to think about it again. What about a NATO nuclear submarine force totally under de Gaulle and Macmillan, asked Kennedy. Such an idea would certainly get consideration from him, de Gaulle said. The long discussion wound down, and though the tone was still cordial, the disagreement was still basic.

Disagreement or not in the business talks, the French President by the second day was calling Kennedy *mon ami* and Kennedy was smiling even more despite his backache. He broke away from security men twice and politicked along the Champs Elysée, reaching for outstretched hands and repeating his good-humored, "How are you? Good to see you," just as if he were in Pocatello or Madison.

To 500 U.S. embassy employees he joked, "I tried to be assigned to the embassy in Paris myself, and, unable to do so, I decided I would run for President." At the Hotel de Ville, Paris' gilded city hall, he brought up his ancestry. "I am the descendant on both sides of two grandparents who served in the city council of Boston, and I am sure they regarded that as a more significant service than any of their descendants have yet rendered."

But as fast as Kennedy moved around the city, as pleasing as he was to the crowds, he could not compete with Jackie's splendor.

In the tow of Madame de Gaulle, Jackie bounded through Paris. Behind her in a Citroën came Rose Kennedy, Jackie's sister Lee Radziwill, and her sister-in-law Eunice Shriver. French Minister of Culture André Malraux, who had helped plan her stay, whisked her past the collection of impressionist paintings in the Jeu de Paume Museum in forty-five minutes. "I have just seen the most beautiful paintings in the world," gasped Jackie. She received a tiny wrist watch from the president of the Paris Municipal Council. She journeyed to Malmaison, the Empress Josephine's country retreat, and ate a gourmet lunch at La Celle St. Cloud, the long-ago hideaway of Mme. de Pompadour.

Always, wherever she went, the French wanted to see her. They stood on the curbs and stared. Their reaction was two-fold; first they exclaimed over her beauty, then they turned to each other and shrugged. *"Parce qu'elle a du sang français"*—what do you expect, she's French. Indeed, it seemed at times as if she were one of them.

On the second day, late in the afternoon, she walked out of the Quai d'Orsay with only a Secret Service man. She climbed into a Citroën completely unnoticed, and for forty-five minutes she was driven through the traffic-clogged streets of Paris as evening came on. For the first time since arriving she was unrecognized. She stared out at the people and the buildings and the monuments. When she met her staff after the drive, she was bubbling with delight. "We spent forty-five minutes in a traffic jam on Place de l'Alma," she laughed. It had been a wonderful break from her official duties.

Nothing rivaled the magnificence of the second night, when in a misty Paris dusk the Kennedys and the de Gaulles drove the eleven miles to the Palace of Versailles for the most brilliant evening the Kennedys had experienced since becoming the first couple of the land. For the occasion Jackie had broken her all-American-wardrobe rule and put on a bell-skirted dress by French designer Hubert de Givenchy. It was the supreme tribute to France.

In the cavernous Hall of Mirrors, 150 guests dined by candlelight on coeur de filet de Charolais Renaissance from the gold-trimmed china given to Napoleon by the city of Paris as a coronation present.

Then the elegant party idled through the endless halls to the far wing and the gold-and-aqua Louis XV theater for a command ballet performance.

If there was a climax to this spectacular visit, it came as the young American couple stood smiling and erect with the de Gaulles in the theater and received the tribute of the select audience below and around them.

After the performance the Kennedys with their hosts slowly motored through the grounds and the gardens of Versailles. The mist still clung, giving the vast cobblestoned courtyards the mystery and romance that they had held for the

French rulers who once lived there. Huge spotlights bathed the buildings in diffused beams. The fountains glowed and sparkled, the shadows of the statues reaching into the black and conjuring up the heritage of grandeur. Twice the Kennedys stopped to gaze on this haunting scene. And the last time the President took the arm of his wife as they walked over the damp lawn, silent, deeply moved. De Gaulle joined them, and the two presidents solemnly shook hands and said good night.

While France in its own way kindled the Kennedy spirits, there was an event taking place in the Caribbean and in Washington which, though of a far grimmer nature, would also hearten Kennedy when he saw how his government handled the crisis.

In the Dominican Republic dictator Rafael Leonidas Trujillo was machine-gunned to a grotesque death.

The first unconfirmed reports were flashed to Washington and on to Paris. Press Secretary Pierre Salinger casually mentioned the news to reporters in the lobby of the Crillon Hotel, thinking it was even then spreading around the world; but it was the first break in the story. Newsmen hurried away with the Salinger fragment before Salinger suddenly realized that the story was not yet confirmed. He spent a nervous evening waiting for more reports, fearing that, if he were wrong, such a grievous mistake might cost him his job. But he was not wrong, and the confirmation of the assassination was soon cabled to the President.

In the meantime Washington had swung into motion. Only a few days before, a contingency plan for anticipated trouble in the seething Dominican Republic had been completed. It included the possibility of Trujillo's assassination.

In the seventh-floor conference room of the State Department, the meetings began under Secretary of State Dean Rusk, scheduled to depart within hours to join Kennedy in Paris. Secretary of Defense McNamara and Vice President Johnson hurried to Foggy Bottom. Allen Dulles was there, and so was Bob Kennedy. The great fear was that the communists would seize the Dominican government. There were misgivings that the contingency plan was not strong enough to deal with a revolution. But the revolution did not come. Rafael Leonidas Trujillo, Jr., the dead dictator's 32-year-old playboy son, flew home to take charge and proved more sensible than had been expected. The communists and Castroites were stalled. Cautiously the United States contingency plan was instrumented. A United States fleet of warships, loaded with battle-ready Marines, churned sixty miles off the Dominican Republic's coast. The new ruler was told bluntly that terror tactics to avenge his father's death would bring the leathernecks down the streets of Ciudad Trujillo. The pressure was so intense that Trujillo even agreed to let the Organization of American States send in a four-nation team of investigators to see how he was doing. The situation stabilized, some of the tension subsided. Dean Rusk flew off to Paris, and Bob Kennedy went back to his office in the Justice Department. It had been a win for John Kennedy, cheering news for the man who was on the final lap of Paris, readying for Vienna.

The Kennedys' last day in Paris was a gray one. But the President was feeling happy about the rapport that had been established between himself and the French leader. For two more hours he met with de Gaulle, then he faced newsmen in an impromptu conference.

In the Palais de Chaillot, he admitted total surrender to Jackie. "I do not think it altogether inappropriate to introduce myself to this audience," he began. "I am the man who accompanied Jacqueline Kennedy to Paris, and I have enjoyed it."

His statement was far more meaningful than even the newsmen who had watched the great public spectacle could imagine. For it was in the most private moments that perhaps Jackie Kennedy had been best. Often she had found herself alone between de Gaulle and her husband, and she had been the interpreter, bringing an intimacy that perhaps had never been introduced before into such high-level talk. In these moments de Gaulle often just gazed at her, obviously enjoying looking at this American woman. Sometimes Jackie found herself alone with the French President, and she took these moments to talk about what she wanted. The two of them at the Versailles theater discussed French literature and theater, subjects they both enjoy. No greater proof of de Gaulle's captivation could be had than the long-hand letter he wrote to her when she was back in America.

There was a last meeting with de Gaulle, just to firm up and seal the areas of understanding. And finally it was 4:30 in the afternoon of June 2, and the next day Kennedy was to meet with Khrushchev. Paris had been three days of high drama, beauty and deep feeling, all characteristic of France. Vienna held other promise.

De Gaulle and Kennedy stood together for the last time and de Gaulle, with true feeling, thanked Kennedy for his frankness, for the excellent spirit of the talks and for the atmosphere maintained throughout the three days. Before they parted, the young President turned to the man who had endured in the volatile French political system like a piece of marble statuary. He asked, "You've studied being head of a country for fifty years. Have you found out anything I should know?" The French President promised to speak of that another day when he had more time.

The Garde Republicaine were back on the patio of the Elysée Palace. Trumpeters stood on the lawn. Jackie drove up and hurried in to join her husband in the formal farewells. A white-gloved attendant slipped out a side door, carefully carrying the Kennedy gray fedora which the President had dutifully brought with him but had not put on his head once. The footman brushed it up a bit with his sleeve, laid it gingerly on the seat in Kennedy's waiting car.

The trumpets blared. Kennedy and de Gaulle came out and listened again in rigid silence to the national anthems of the two nations.

"Now I have more confidence in your country," said de Gaulle, wringing Kennedy's hand. The two men smiled. Charles de Gaulle strode back into the Elysée, and the short caravan of black Citroëns moved off down the gravel path.

Though formally finished with his French visit, Kennedy would spend the night in the Quai d'Orsay. But first he sped to the American embassy, where he met with his top men. Ambassador Llewellyn Thompson had flown in from Moscow. Chip Bohlen, after giving the American newsmen a background briefing on the meaning of the de Gaulle talks, turned to Russian matters. Foy Kohler, Assistant Secretary of State for European Affairs, was there as well, and Secretary of State Rusk had rushed in from the United States. White House Aides McGeorge Bundy and Ted Sorensen also were part of the skull session at the dinner table. This was the last chance Kennedy had to prepare. In Vienna the next morning he would face Khrushchev.

VIENNA

NIKITA KHRUSHCHEV arrived in Vienna the day before Kennedy. Immediately he was involved in a curious little drama that pointed up the weird ways of the communist world. Waiting at the train station in a crowd of Soviet women and children was Vyacheslav M. Molotov, who four years before had been kicked out of the Communist party by Khrushchev. "We must get together," said Khrushchev, reaching out to shake Molotov's hand. Soviet Foreign Minister Andrei Gromyko, who had once been Molotov's deputy, gave a stiff smile, said, "Nice weather we're having."

The encounter helped to underscore what American Soviet experts had been telling Kennedy: Khrushchev had his problems, too. The persistent criticism from Red China's Mao Tse-tung for being too soft on the free world continued. Albania's Enver Hoxha, a Stalinist dictator, fired off barb after barb toward Moscow. Russian agriculture was in more trouble. Pressure was mounting all across the Soviet Union for more and better consumer goods.

As in other matters, Kennedy had been well briefed on the Russian difficulties, and now the time had come to apply all this cramming.

"For Khrushchev we had sun. For Kennedy we have rain," shrugged a bus driver as early on Saturday morning, June 3, 1961, he nudged through the traffic to the Vienna airport. Light rain fell continuously, making the swarms of Austrian policemen huddle inside their gray slickers.

Reporters, who had been billeted in army barracks and routed out with a bugle call followed by a brass band in the courtyard of the army post, now massed damply on the landing apron.

The Vienna-American contingent was there in force. In American style, they had hoisted placards above the fence. "Give 'em Hell, Jack," read one. Another said, "Help Berlin." Others: "Lift the Iron Curtain"; "Innocents Abroad Say Howdy."

Aboard his jet plane John Kennedy nibbled at a roll and sipped orange juice as he huddled with his advisers on the Soviet during the brief flight from Paris to Vienna. He was out of the plane door with a wave. Jackie one step behind him. She was stunning in one of Cassini's creations, this one a brilliant aqua. But the interest here was not in fashion. The glowering clouds over the city only tended to heighten the tension that had been building since the day before, when Khrushchev had arrived.

Kennedy was gratified at the sight of the Austrians who lined the fifteen-mile motorcade route from Schwechat to Alte Hofburg, the residence of Austrian President Dr. Adolf Scharf. Police estimated that there were 70,000 along the way, standing and waving despite the rain. In the sunny weather of the day before, Khrushchev had drawn but 50,000.

Kennedy and his contingent disappeared behind the high barbed-wire fence surrounding the residence of Ambassador H. Freeman Matthews.

The President paced the halls restlessly, talking with aides as he waited for the first encounter with Khrushchev.

Even the surroundings had a somber look. The boxy gray stucco residence with an ugly tan stone trim was a totally unappealing building. Around the barbed wire paced Austrian guards with huge police dogs that wore wire-mesh muzzles. The clouds persisted and a chill wind rushed through the pines. Now and then rain splattered the gravel drive.

Precisely at 12:45 a four-door black Chaika crunched up to the steps. Khrushchev thrust his stubby legs out of the car, took a couple of short strides. Kennedy, at last face to face with his adversary, bounded out of the hall and rushed down the few steps. He smiled, leaned over and thrust his hand out. "How are you?" he asked. "I'm glad to see you."

Khrushchev looked up only for a second, smiled and then tried to move up the steps. He looked fit and was dressed in a neat gray suit that was only a shade lighter than the gray Kennedy wore. On his left chest were two star-shaped medals, Lenin Peace Medals. Like Kennedy, he was hatless.

The two men struggled up the stairs. Photographers scrambled desperately for pictures. They shouted, cursed and pleaded. "Another handshake," they cried. Kennedy turned to the interpreter. "Say to the Chairman that it is all right to shake hands if it is all right with him." Khrushchev beamed and stuck out a pudgy hand for the pose. Kennedy fixed a slight smile on his face, but instead of turning toward the cameras, he stepped back a pace and turned toward Khrushchev. Then for a few seconds Kennedy bluntly surveyed the Russian from head to toe. He thrust his hands into his coat pockets and continued to stare. Soviet Ambassador Mikhail Menshikov stepped on Dean Rusk's foot in the scramble on the small concrete porch and blurted out his apology.

Then they turned and went inside, the reporters noting that Khrushchev came about nose high on Kennedy.

As they walked toward the residence's red-and-gray music room where the talks were to start, Kennedy presented U.S. Ambassador Llewlyn Thompson as "our ambassador to Moscow."

Khrushchev shot Kennedy a mischievous glance and replied about Thompson, whom he had come to like during Thompson's long service: "He's our ambassador."

In the music room they settled in a circle of chairs, Kennedy on Khrushchev's left, and opened their talks with some pleasantries of past association. Kennedy recalled that he had met the Russian leader back in 1959 when, during his tour of the United States, Khrushchev had stopped by the Senate Foreign Relations Committee. "I'm glad to see you again," said Kennedy.

Indeed, Khrushchev said, he remembered that meeting. Further, he had some time ago taken note of the up-and-coming politician named John Kennedy. He was a young man, continued Khrushchev, applying a little flattery, to have such great burdens of office.

Then they began their long, sometimes bitter, verbal struggle that was to last through eleven hours, two lunches and a lonely walk by the two men and their interpreters through blooming mock-orange in a spring-freshened woods.

Reporters and the curious Viennese crowded outside the gates of both the U.S. embassy residence and the Soviet embassy as the talks changed locale.

There was a break on Saturday night for a huge state dinner in the Schönbrunn Palace. Khrushchev edged his chair closer to Jackie, seemed smitten with her as de Gaulle had been as, with eyes twinkling, he told her funny stories.

On Sunday morning the Kennedys listened to the Vienna Boys' Choir in the huge St. Stephen's Cathedral; at the same time Khrushchev solemnly laid a wreath of red carnations at the base of the Russian war memorial in Schwarzenbergplatz.

But the interludes were only fleeting. The grim business of discussing the future of the world held the focus of the two men who could alter it in seconds.

Kennedy sized up the man beside him in the first minutes. He was no buffoon. There would be none of the shoe-waving antics remembered from the incredible Khrushchev visit to the United Nations in 1960. Though the truncated frame of the Premier was roly-poly, it seemed to move with animal agility. The eyes darted and pierced, pride was worn on his sleeve, and Kennedy made certain not to offend by any careless remarks about trivialities. His adversary was immensely well informed.

Khrushchev was quick to quote back to Kennedy excerpts from the speech he had made the week before to Congress in which he cited the Soviet threat and asked for more money to improve United States ability in guerrilla fighting.

"I've read all your speeches," he admitted. He declared that Kennedy had reversed an order to send U.S. Marines into Laos. And when the President responded that he had done no such thing, Khrushchev shot him an unbelieving look and said he had read it in the American press.

Khrushchev's knowledge of history was broad and deep. At one point, as they talked about letting peoples of the world have the right of self-determination, Khrushchev noted that

Western powers had interfered in Russia's revolution and also that Tsarist Russia had considered the United States a dangerous and revolutionary nation, much as the United States now viewed Russia.

Within the stilted philosophy of communism, Khrushchev could advance telling points, present logical arguments. After sixteen years, did it not make sense to have a German peace treaty? Was not Formosa really a part of the Chinese mainland? And after all, the United States was supporting a good many undemocratic governments around the world— what about Franco? These were the Khrushchev thrusts. Never was the Premier completely cowed or backed into a corner. When he was caught, he simply did not answer.

"We admit our mistakes," said Kennedy once. "Do you ever admit you are wrong?"

"Oh, yes," said Khrushchev. "In the speech before the Twentieth Party Congress I admitted Stalin's mistakes."

"Those weren't your mistakes," shot back Kennedy. The Russian changed the subject.

It was rarely, however, that the Premier trailed off into silence. He usually had a last crack.

As the talks went on, Kennedy brought up two Chinese sayings. First, he quoted Red Chinese boss Mao Tse-tung as saying that "political power grows out of the barrel of a gun." Khrushchev remonstrated. He had never heard Mao utter this saying, and he did not think Kennedy had heard it either. In fact, he could not believe that the peace-loving communist had used those words.

A little later, in talking about the nuclear-test meeting as a first and needed step toward peace, Kennedy said, "The journey of a thousand miles begins with one step."

Khrushchev gave Kennedy a quizzical look, then he grinned. "You seem to know the Chinese very well," he said.

"We may both get to know them better," answered Kennedy.

"I know them well enough now," concluded Khrushchev.

Sometimes they bantered good-naturedly about their systems of government, telling political jokes on themselves.

Khrushchev often talked in fables. When Kennedy drove up to the Russian embassy on the second day, Khrushchev said to his guest, "I greet you on a small piece of our Soviet territory. Sometimes we drink out of a small glass, but we speak with great feeling."

Answered Kennedy, "I'm glad to hear this."

The Kennedy wit was in evidence. Touching one of the two star-shaped medals on Khrushchev's chest, Kennedy asked what they were for. Khrushchev replied that they were Lenin Peace Medals. "I hope you keep them," said Kennedy with a chuckle.

Kennedy noted that Khrushchev's knowledge of agriculture was particularly deep. But there were times when he had to ask about the technical details of nuclear testing. At all times the Soviet leader wore that brittle veneer of superiority. Kennedy sensed that Khrushchev liked the talk, liked the challenge of argument. He was agreeable much of the time. Only toward the end and only when the talk turned to the grim issue of the moment—Berlin—did Khrushchev raise his voice. When the arguments had run their course and capitalism and communism ended in head-on opposition, Khrushchev became hard. At other times he liked to leaven his converation with humor.

Once as the President lighted a cigar, he waved the match to put out the flame and it slipped from his grip to land behind Khrushchev's chair. Spotting the burning match, Khrushchev asked, "Are you trying to set me on fire?" Kennedy assured him he was not. "Ah," laughed the Soviet Premier, "a capitalist, not an incendiary."

These talks were not dominated by Khrushchev, as so often had been the case in the past with Americans. The time was divided. And Kennedy was in good form, blunt and frank and as well informed on each issue as was the Russian.

When Khrushchev complained that he had not been invited to sign the Japanese peace treaty in 1951, Kennedy was ready. He had read the same complaints in the transcripts of the earlier Khrushchev-Eisenhower talks, and Kennedy reminded him that this was an old issue which had been brought up before. The subject was dropped.

Khrushchev told Kennedy that Franklin Roosevelt back in 1944 had planned to withdraw forces from Germany in three or four years. The President remembered the old documents and rattled off the fact that Roosevelt had based that statement on the assumption of a united Germany. Again Khrushchev had no answer.

"You're an old country, we're a young country," jibed the Premier.

"If you'll look across the table, you'll see that we're not so old," came back Kennedy.

When the former Georgia farm boy Dean Rusk mentioned that this country had developed a dwarf corn that could mature in a short time, Khrushchev shook his head in disbelief and declared that no less an authority than his old friend, Iowa's Roswell (Bob) Garst, had assured him it could not be grown in great amounts. Rusk persisted, offering to send Khrushchev some of the dwarf corn. But Khrushchev was not really interested in whether or not we had developed better corn. He insisted that our great amounts of fertilizer and machines had put us ahead. Once Russia got these aids, she would bury us in corn, too.

Kennedy did not forget the corn conversation. When at lunch Khrushchev downed an American martini (Kennedy sipped Dubonnet), he said that Russia had developed a way to make vodka from natural gas. Hearing this, Kennedy laughed. "That sounds like more of Dean Rusk's corn to me."

Each man played a central theme. Kennedy's was that the destruction of civilization as we know it could stem from miscalculation and that it would be total folly for the two massive nations who hold most of the world's power to become involved in a dangerous wrangle over such tiny pieces of land as Laos and Berlin. He cited the history of miscalculation and misunderstanding that had led up to the last three wars, showed how countries had carelessly wandered down a pathway that they never dreamed could open into swift and bloody conflict.

Khrushchev did not disagree. In fact, he endorsed the belief that nuclear war would destroy that which both nations sought and that it would not vindicate either system of government. But, he insisted, the tide of history was on the side of the communists. It was inevitable that communism would sweep over the face of the globe. There were three kinds of war, he said—nuclear war, conventional war and war of revolution. The first two kinds of war were unlikely in the years ahead; but the internal wars of revolution—"holy wars," he called them—would go on. For the United States to oppose them was to oppose the will of the people.

Kennedy wryly noted that what Khrushchev had said represented a turn in communist philosophy which nuclear weapons had brought about. Khrushchev did not dissent.

When the first day's meetings were over, Press Secretary Pierre Salinger and his Russian counterpart, Mikhail Kharlamov, hurried back to the Hofburg Palace to brief the press. It turned into one of the biggest briefings in history, with 1,500 correspondents and photographers jammed into the huge marble ballroom of the palace. So vast was this arena that each man was furnished with his own tiny transistor radio with ear plugs, through which the press secretaries broadcast. There was a brief flurry when Kharlamov described the day's talks as "fruitful." The official joint release had used the words "frank and courteous." Was there disagreement, Salinger was asked. Wary and cautious, Salinger held firm. "I think I will stand with the statement I made at the outset." This was the hint that the newsmen sought. It meant there had been no concessions, no agreements, no deals.

For Kennedy it was the "hardest work in the world." Every energy was focused on listening and talking. Khrushchev took little interest in the issues of Cuba and Laos. He did not throw up the Cuban invasion fiasco to the President, but he declared that the United States had made Fidel Castro a good communist. The neutrality of Laos was what the Russians desired too, said Khrushchev.

Kennedy sometimes saw that Khrushchev's understanding of the United States was sorely limited. Khrushchev mentioned the group of fifty top industrialists whom Averell Harriman had rounded up for Khrushchev to see when he was in the United States. These men, the monopolists, said Khrushchev, controlled Kennedy. When the President insisted that none of them had supported him in the election, Khrushchev was unbelieving and confused. "They are clever fellows," he said, and changed the subject.

Once, as Khrushchev pressed Kennedy about our support

of undemocratic governments, Kennedy reminded the Premier of his satellite nations. What about Poland, he asked. He was not at all sure that the people would choose communism if given an honest chance to express their will. The Soviet leader bristled, declared that Kennedy had his nerve.

"Poland has a fine government, more democratic than the United States," he charged. "Its election laws are more honest than those in the United States. You recognize Poland."

As hour after hour and point after point passed, Kennedy began to get a great unsettled feeling. Never before when he had sat down to talk with men who disagreed with him had he found, when human suffering or great tragedy might result from the differences, that they would be totally unbending. Always under such circumstances there had been some admission that needless injury to others should be avoided, that both should give in somewhat. But now Kennedy could find no "area of accommodation." When Kennedy talked with Khrushchev of the tragedy of killing millions of people in both countries in a matter of minutes should either nation misjudge the other, and that therefore perhaps both men should soften a little in their positions, he found the Russian to be unmoved. Khrushchev would admit the disaster of nuclear war but would not admit that concessions, no matter how slight, were a way to avoid it.

Kennedy had learned what he hoped that he would not learn, that the enemy was more unbending than he had imagined, even after the lessons of Laos and Cuba. Item by item Kennedy had been shown the steely constitution of communism since the day he took office. This was the latest. His delicate desire for establishing some communications in hopes that there was some area of compromise that the two nations might find to ease the world tension was suffering another and almost shattering blow.

The Soviet premier explained that he intended to sign a peace treaty with East Germany; after that, the West could deal with East Germany on access to Berlin and the right to station troops there. Kennedy answered that the West was in Berlin legally and would use force to maintain its rights there "at any risk."

Khrushchev admitted that he was under pressure to resume

nuclear testing. He said that he had heard that Kennedy was being urged to test also. He bragged that the Soviet Union would wait for the United States to resume testing, as it probably would do soon. Then, when the United States tested, the Russians would follow.

As the meetings drew to a close over lunch at the Soviet embassy, the somber feeling had spread through the ranks of the staffs. The subject was Berlin, and the talk was dark.

Khrushchev stood up and, in a champagne toast, left no doubts in anybody's mind about his intent to press on with the Soviet cause in the same manner as he had been doing.

Kennedy stood to respond. He had brought to Khrushchev a gift of a model of the famous old fighting ship the "Constitution." The model now sat in the middle of the table. He had come to Vienna, Kennedy said, to make every effort to prevent a war that would destroy both Russia and the United States. He noted that western Europe had been the previous battle ground and had always managed to recover from the conflicts. Then he gestured toward the model of "Old Ironsides" on the table. Its guns had carried only half a mile, he said. In those days it had been possible for nations to recover from wars in a matter of months or years—as, indeed, western Europe had done after World War II. But now, in the age of nuclear weapons, a war would leave its effects on generations of men. Such a war should not be allowed to happen.

Kennedy was scheduled to leave then, but he did not want to go. He wanted one more chance to talk to Khrushchev. "No," he barked to his staff. "We're not going on time. I'm not going to leave until I know more."

The words between Khrushchev and Kennedy grew stronger. Khrushchev growled that his decision to sign a peace treaty with East Germany by December was "firm," was absolutely "irrevocable."

Kennedy looked at the Russian, both men unsmiling. "If that is true," he said, "it is going to be a cold winter."

The meetings had ended. At 4:35 P.M. on June 4, John Kennedy and Nikita Khrushchev came down the stairs and out the front door of the Russian embassy. They had not spoken as they walked. The frigid effect of their final words clung to them. Kennedy thrust his hands into his pockets. On the steps the two men paused for photographs. They forced a final smile and handshake. The President hurried into his bubble-top Lincoln. Dean Rusk slid in beside him. Khrushchev, now on the steps, was grinning, his old self. Kennedy's smile was strained. As the car moved slowly out into the street, Kennedy and Rusk stared ahead and did not speak. The President threw his left arm up along the back of his seat, the fingers of his left hand drummed frantically on the ledge beneath the rear window. Then he was gone.

CHAPTER FIFTEEN

LONDON AND HOME

THE world still waited for the deeper meaning of the Kennedy-Khrushchev talks. The language of the official statement following the meetings was as obscure as it was meant to be. "President Kennedy and Premier Khrushchev have concluded two days of useful meetings, during which they have reviewed the relationships between the U.S. and the USSR, as well as other questions that are of interest to the two States. . . ."

Chip Bohlen, sitting on the edge of a desk swinging his leg nervously, had briefed American correspondents and had been more frank, cautioning the newsmen to refrain from any optimistic speculation over what might result.

Yet the air of uncertainty was not cleared. What had been said, what had been felt by John Kennedy in those long hours with Khrushchev?

The first hint of the discouragement came as Kennedy's jet sped toward London. The President talked briefly with the pool of newsmen who were flying with him, and the dim presidential mood was immediately detectable.

Kennedy was tired and unusually silent. He sat down with the reporters and muttered, "It's been a tough four days. Seeing Macmillan will be easy after this." Twice he stared down at his shoes and shook his head and said how unbending Khrushchev had been.

From White House staffers came other hints. "He [Khrushchev] was a tough S.O.B.," said one. "He wouldn't give on anything." "Don't build any castles," warned another. The stories filed that night said that the Soviet Premier had cast a spell of gloom over the Americans.

Kennedy's stop in London was brief. He reported to Prime Minister Harold Macmillan, dined with the Queen and again was airborne over the Atlantic, this time headed for Labrador, where he would rest before flying on to Washington.

As he came up the ramp to his plane in London, he was the same smiling young man that he had been when he had left America. He was in his tuxedo from the Buckingham Palace dinner. His men—Rusk, Bundy, Sorensen, Nitze, Kohler—had hurried onto the plane before him.

"Are you comparing castles?" Kennedy had kidded these officials as he walked by them to his cabin. The grin was there, the old bounce seemed intact.

But this appearance was misleading. His back throbbed. Inside he carried the cold weight of Khrushchev's gloom, and he could not sleep, even though it was near midnight when he had boarded.

He sat surrounded by staff and with his sister Eunice Shriver. Jackie had stayed in London with her sister, to go from there to Greece for a vacation.

Dean Rusk clung loosely to the baggage rack beside Kennedy as the two weighed the talks. The President had some hot soup and thumbed through the latest newspapers.

Then he wanted to know from friends what America would think about it all, what was going to be written during the week, the week after Vienna.

Sometimes the figure of the President of the United States can seem lost in the vastness of his job. Sometimes the trappings of the position—the huge airplanes, the big cars, the army of staff—seem to overwhelm the single man. To those who watch, the reality of such moments is disturbing. The President becomes human. He becomes a man as other men, with a body that suffers pain and fatigue and with a mind that grows weary of the hopeless and complex problems of the nuclear age. Fortunately these are fleeting moments. This nation cannot afford to have a mere human in a superhuman job.

But the early hours of June 6 represented one of those

times of disquieting realism. The presidential aura had thinned. I talked to him.

The persistent whine of jet power pierced the cabin walls as Air Force One plunged on through the blue-black night of the Atlantic Ocean.

John Kennedy sat in his shorts in the dim plane light. The litter of newspapers was around him. His eyes were red and watery, dark pockets beneath them. He shifted stiffly in his seat to ease the back pain, occasionally reached to touch the spot that ached, as if such action might dispel it.

For a few seconds he turned to me. How had I been, was the trip good, had I gotten to see some of Europe? Human questions. Then he wanted to know what had been written, what would be written, did the trip seem a success to the journalists?

He was pleased that the account of the meetings with Khrushchev had not once gotten out of hand. There was no euphoria from this voyage to lie later in fragments, as had the spirit of Geneva and the spirit of Camp David.

He would talk to the American people in a special report in the coming week, said Kennedy. And he would be honest about it all.

He wondered out loud what would follow in Berlin. The President clutched his bare knees and in silence looked out the plane's window. His mind snapped back to his confrontation with Nikita Khrushchev. He frowned. "It was invaluable, it was invaluable," he said, half to himself.

Ahead lay some serious days for the United States. About this there could be no question. But Kennedy could now work in that cool atmosphere of reality that he preferred. He had heard with his own ears, seen with his own eyes. Yes, the future was grim, he thought, but not hopeless. The news would, indeed, continue to get worse for some time more before it would get better. Yet the President could see a clearer way ahead.

Though the warnings of Khrushchev were still ringing in their ears, though the memory of Cuba had not faded, though the mystery of Laos still persisted and though the President of the United States was now hampered by pain, the confidence of the New Frontier in itself was rekindling.

If there came a single time when it could be said that the line graph of the Kennedy administration effectiveness in foreign affairs broke from the nadir of Cuba and began to climb, these hours of June 6, 1961, were that time. The line representing public confidence on this imaginary chart lagged behind, as it always does. In fact, it may have continued to plunge as the Russian threats in Berlin materialized later. But it, too, would have its moments of upturn.

Back in the United States, Kennedy moved quickly. That evening he reported to the people from his office. "I went to Vienna to meet the leader of the Soviet Union, Mr. Khrushchev. . . . I will tell you now that it was a very sober two days. . . . But I found this meeting with Chairman Khrushchev, as somber as it was, to be immensely useful. . . . We have wholly different views of right and wrong, of what is an internal affair and what is aggression, and, above all, we have wholly different concepts of where the world is going . . . The one area which afforded some immediate prospect of accord was Laos. Both sides recognized the need to reduce the dangers in that situation. Both sides endorsed the concept of a neutral and independent Laos. . . . No such hope emerged, however, with respect to the other deadlocked Geneva conference, seeking a treaty to ban nuclear tests. . . . This battle goes on, and we have to play our part in it. . . . We must be patient. We must be determined. We must be courageous. We must accept both risks and burdens, but with the will and the work, freedom will prevail."

Kennedy had to confess his back trouble to the nation. He had to admit that he had been on crutches and would be on crutches, that he was undergoing treatment for the new strain. White House reporters, remembering Eisenhower's heart attack and his stroke, rushed to the phones when Salinger made the announcement. They clamored to see White House physician Janet Travell, but Salinger would not produce her for an interview and she would not talk to the press. Her reports, issued through the press secretary, were all that was available, and they were skimpy.

Then John Kennedy wanted a rest and time to think about

what he had learned. He flew to Palm Beach with only his friend Charles Spalding. He stayed in the home of the Wrightsmans, a ghost mansion now as the muggy summer heat came on Florida. Its furniture was swathed in dust covers which Kennedy did not bother to remove. He stayed on the patio, totally out of sight of the public. He slept late and lounged in his pajamas. When he moved about, he went on crutches, and he received more treatment for his back.

In the evenings he sipped daiquiris and pushed Frank Sinatra records into a small portable player, but he only half listened to the tuned-down voice in the background. His mind was still half a world away.

He felt better about his encounter with Khrushchev as his health improved in the sun. It had become clear that his precautions had paid off and that the country had an honest and sober reckoning of the meetings. By anybody's scorebook, there was no winner. Neither Khrushchev nor Kennedy had bested the other in the talks. But Kennedy had done well, and he felt it.

One morning he squinted into a fine rain that drifted through the open Spanish columns. "To me," he said, "having spent the time with Khrushchev gives a clearer idea of the intensity of the struggle we are in. The next ten years are going to be difficult. I came away feeling that in view of the Russian commitment to their system in certain areas and our commitment to our system in the same areas, it was going to be a close thing to prevent war. There is heightened danger for both countries."

He had concluded, continued the President to a friend, that he was not going to get any agreement with the Soviets on nuclear testing—that was out. He must decide this country's action on its own merits. There would be no immediate United States resumption of tests, he said. For the moment the political disadvantages outweighed the military gains.

Kennedy saw how total the deadlock over Berlin now was. Already he had ordered a step-up on the contingency planning for that city. His belief that this country must prepare to fight guerrilla wars was strengthened, and he planned to give even more attention to that phase of defense.

His thoughts of the weeks ahead were sober, but knowing

Khrushchev better gave Kennedy more confidence.

The trip to Europe gave him something else—the official credentials as leader of the free world. By the right of inheritance he actually received the title when he took over from Eisenhower. But it really was not his by virtue of his own actions. Now he had gone to see de Gaulle. He had journeyed on to see Khrushchev. And he had stopped to report to Macmillan. He had gathered in the strings of the alliance.

When he talked with the Soviet Premier, he did not dwell on the necessity of clearing decisions with his allies. When he stated the position of the free world, he stated it as the leader—"This is where we stand." And afterward he gave his own evaluation of the talks with Khrushchev before false hopes could arise and circulate.

John Kennedy was working better, and things were working better for John Kennedy.

CHAPTER SIXTEEN

MIDSUMMER AND WORRY

ENNEDY turned to the task of strengthening the free world. Khrushchev tried to shake it apart.

The Russian leader went on TV before his people, as Kennedy had done. In a bare floodlighted studio, speaking slowly, peering intently at his manuscript, pausing often to gulp mineral water, Khrushchev edged his voice with steel and declared, "We cannot delay a peace treaty with Germany any longer. A peaceful settlement in Europe must be achieved this year."

One day he donned the dark green uniform of a Soviet lieutenant general and, with a chestful of medals, waddled up to the rostrum in the Kremlin's Great Hall. It was the twentieth anniversary of Hitler's invasion of Russia, and he had a few more bitter things to say to the West, including an answer to Kennedy's warning that the United States might have to begin nuclear testing again if no agreement was reached in Geneva. "Such threats will frighten no one. We must warn these gentlemen: the moment the United States resumes nuclear explosions, the Soviet Union will promptly start testing its nuclear weapons. The Soviet Union has quite a few devices that have been worked out and need practical testing."

Then Khrushchev announced a 30 per cent increase in Soviet defense spending.

The reaction to his words in Khrushchev's own East Germany and East Berlin was immediate. Not since the 1953

East German uprising had the tide of refugees from communism reached such proportions. The somber procession of escapees leaped from the normal 500 a day to nearly 1,500.

The 12,000 allied troops in West Berlin began to sharpen their alert. In the gray dawn hours of late June the 5,000 American combat soldiers fled their warm beds and rushed to their defense positions in a practice alert. Troop carriers and tanks rumbled over the misty streets, machine-gun positions were set up along the curbs. Thus began a time of waiting.

On the floor of the House of Representatives, California's Chet Holifield clamored for a resumption of nuclear testing.

Uneasiness crept through the country as on TV the people saw Kennedy hobble on crutches to his plane in Palm Beach, to be lifted in a cherry-picker crane up to his cabin door, returned to the ground in another hydraulic lift when he arrived at Washington's Andrews Air Force Base.

A virus caught the President, and for a day and a half, as Dr. Janet Travell and Dr. Preston Wade, called from New York to make sure the presidential temperature was unconnected with the back ailment, uneasiness hovered around the White House. The newsmen were willing to believe anything.

As always, they craved details. Kennedy had taken a swim the night before. Dr. Travell had seen him in the evening, and he had been feeling well, no hint of a virus. Then, around 1:30 A.M., he awoke and felt ill. His throat hurt, his head ached, his stomach was just a little upset. Kennedy took his own temperature and found he had a fever. He called Dr. Travell, who sped over shortly after 2 A.M., after alerting her assistant, Dr. George Burkley. Worried, Jackie had gotten out of bed to help her husband. Dr. Travell gave the President an intramuscular shot of penicillin (1.2 million units) and then some tetracycline by mouth. She also increased the amount of corticosteroids that he normally took for an adrenal insufficiency, this to help combat the infection. Dr. Travell and her patient stayed awake all night; at about 7 A.M. the temperature reached 101.6, then broke. By 11 A.M. it was normal, and John Kennedy was asleep. The details flashed out over the wires.

"Now we've got an invalid for President," snorted one Republican on the Hill.

"How much longer do I have to hang around here?" grumbled Kennedy from his bed.

Hour after hour, while the virus died, the President summoned his Berlin advisers. He met with them in the mornings in his office, sometimes he invited them to lunch and sometimes they gathered around his bed in the early afternoon as he rested and had hot packs on his back.

Over scrambled eggs and coffee in the family dining room, the President told his congressional leaders that the United States and Russia seemed on a "collision course."

In his private moments the President worried about the state of preparedness of the country. Were the people ready for a showdown? Most persons did not realize the seriousness of the situation, thought Kennedy. And appeals over TV, stories in the magazines and newspapers, his warnings in the news conferences were not enough. There had to be some sense of participation.

Kennedy mulled over a plan for partial mobilization. He ordered McNamara to take another new and searching look at our state of preparedness. He talked about getting ships out of mothballs, of putting the Strategic Air Command bombers on a more intensive alert.

Kennedy sought advice from everyone. Former Secretary of State Dean Acheson, preparing a basic paper on the threatened city, asked the help of former Soviet Ambassador Averell Harriman. The two of them, both veterans of the Truman era, met one morning walking to a National Security Council meeting.

"It seems like old times," said Harriman.

Acheson grinned, and the two strode into the familiar Cabinet Room.

Summer settled fully on the Potomac. The temperatures climbed into the eighties, and the tourists descended like locusts. On one day 13,595 sightseers went through the White House, a new record, but a record that was soon shattered by another vacation-time onslaught. Kennedy sought Hyannis Port on the week ends, and on workday evenings he sometimes boarded one of his two yachts, the "Honey Fitz" or the

"Patrick J.," for a cool cruise on the Potomac.

He turned to improving his own staff. He announced that Maxwell Taylor would become his military adviser. This was his answer to the Pentagon for the Bay of Pigs. Kennedy would have at his elbow an expert and questioning mind to review the military proposals that poured from the Joint Chiefs of Staff. Taylor had finished his secret evaluation of the Cuban failure. Bob Kennedy had grown to have more respect for Taylor each week as he met his select review committee. The President, too, had watched with growing appreciation. Having looked over the national security problems looming ahead—Berlin, Vietnam, Laos—he decided he needed the wiry general who had once commanded the "Battered Bastards of Bastogne," the famed 101st Airborne Division.

Back to writing and his New York law practice went Adolf Berle, special Latin American adviser. Of all the areas that could not get going, Latin America was the worst. The irascible Berle gallivanted all over the State Department, irritating the career men. He swept into Latin America itself with his sandpaper personality, and the protests followed his trail. He was a man of brilliant ideas but abrasive application. For five months the job of Assistant Secretary of State for Inter-American Affairs had been vacant. Kennedy desperately wished to get his Alliance for Progress moving, and he wanted the best man he could find to head his Latin section. But the policy area was populated not only by Berle but also by White House staffers Richard Goodwin and Arthur Schlesinger, Jr., not to mention self-anointed experts by the legion. Twenty-one persons were sounded out for the job, but all refused when they peered at the spider web. Someone had to go, and it was Berle. Then Kennedy recalled Ambassador to Chile Robert F. Woodward, naming him Assistant Secretary of State for Inter-American Affairs.

One former Roosevelt man looked over the sprawling New Frontier at this point and was horrified. He offered a three-point formula for smoothing the path: (1) Have the President stop talking to two out of every three newspapermen he was seeing. ("Sooner or later John Kennedy is going to have to learn that he can't deal with reporters now the same way he did as a politician.") (2) Fire every other New Frontiersman. ("Most of the trouble now stems from the eggheads, the professors Kennedy brought in. The old Kennedy staff members who have been around don't cause trouble, but the professors not only meddle but talk about it.") (3) Eliminate the dinner party. ("They ought to make all the staff eat in a common room all the time with guards at the doors. There is too much talk at Washington dinner tables, you can hear anything you want to hear from responsible men if you get invited to enough dinners.") The man who had spoken was only half joking.

Kennedy felt stung by some of the criticism of his method of operation. One publication declared flatly that his White House system simply was not working, had become bogged down in a maze of overlapping special advisers and task forces.

A reporter for this same publication had reached home wearily one night about 8:30 and was mixing himself a martini when the phone rang. "I hear you bastards have done it to me again," came the unmistakable voice of John Fitzgerald Kennedy. "I haven't read it yet—everybody says not to, that it would just make me all the madder, but I hear it's the worst you've done." There followed between bites of the President's own dinner (the phone apparently being cradled between the Kennedy shoulder and cheek) some pointed observations on contemporary journalism and its practice.

But while the outward view was more ragged than ever before, Kennedy felt better about the shape of things inside. He had adjusted his own time, so that he felt better. He did not try to do everything and see everybody himself. Maxwell Taylor swung immediately into his new chores. At last the State Department began to assume the direction of Latin affairs. Kennedy rested after lunch, made sure that he swam once or twice a day in the White House pool, which had its water warmed to 87 degrees. His back was making satisfactory progress until a string of unlucky accidents set it back. He once leaned from his desk chair to pick up a paper he had dropped, and the unruly chair dumped him out on his side, wrenching his back. Another time he leaned over some letters and gave the sore muscles another tug. And one morn-

President-elect Kennedy and President Eisenhower leave the White House front door on the way to Kennedy's inauguration.

Joseph P. Kennedy and his son, now 34th President of the United States, watch the inaugural parade in front of the White House.

Kennedy delivers his first State of the Union message, a somber assessment of our position in the world. Behind him, Vice President Johnson and Speaker Rayburn.

The famous Kennedy forefinger picks out a questioner at one of his televised press conferences.

With the Eiffel Tower in the background and with Secretary of State Dean
Rusk following, Kennedy strides to a meeting in Paris during his 1961 visit.

Madame
de Gaulle,
Mrs. Kennedy,
the President and
General de Gaulle
form the
receiving line
during a
glittering
moment in Paris.

The chilling end of the Kennedy-Khrushchev meeting in Vienna in 1961. Khrushchev offers his hand on the steps of the Russian Embassy as Kennedy prepares to fly to England and then home.

With lessons learned from the Bay of Pigs, Kennedy's high command functioned smoothly in the 1962 Cuban missile crisis. The President conferred often with the key men (ABOVE, right to left: JFK, Gilpatric, Rusk, McNamara, Bundy, Robert Kennedy; lower: Harriman and Ball). After a week's deep secrecy, the President went on the air (LEFT) to tell the nation.

The President in one of his many rocking chairs, prescribed for a sore back, but swiftly a symbol.

A two-cigar man after lunch, John Kennedy puffs away on the lawn outside his Hyannis Port home.

Kennedy almost always went to the crowd to shake a few hands as he is doing here in Wheeling, West Virginia in 1962.

The President and his brother Edward rib each other at a Boston fund-raising dinner in 1963.

The first family watches the famed "Black Watch" regiment of the Royal Highlanders perform on the south lawn of the White House, two weeks before the President was killed.

ing when he came to breakfast with his congressional leaders, he teetered back on the rear legs of an antique chair in the family dining room. There was a minor explosion and the chair split into pieces, depositing the frightened President on the floor.[1] Again, his back suffered. But these were temporary setbacks. Steadily the pain eased.

Kennedy accepted a chance to send another direct warning to Khrushchev. The Soviet Premier's son-in-law Alexei Adzhubei, editor of *Izvestia,* and Mikhail Kharlamov, chief of the press section of the Soviet Foreign Ministry, had appeared on a TV debate in New York with Press Secretary Salinger and *The New York Times'* Harrison Salisbury. Salinger invited them to a hasty meeting with Kennedy.

Khrushchev had just made another of his speeches, this one predicting that the Soviet Union would outstrip this country economically by 1970. Kennedy had read the speech with interest, ordered some of his own figures for his forthcoming press conference. They showed that at the current rates of growth (United States, 3½ per cent; Soviet Union, 6 per cent) the Russians would not reach two thirds of our output by 1970.

Would Adzhubei be seeing his father-in-law soon? asked Kennedy.

Yes, answered the Russian. He would see him on Wednesday morning, two days hence.

"Your father-in-law has his view, but I want to tell you ours. Here's what is really going to happen," said Kennedy, reciting the growth figures.

"But those aren't our figures," protested Adzhubei.

"You people have been spouting your figures," said the President. "How about us giving ours out?"

"It is like the story of a high jumper," continued the President. "Between zero and six feet he can go up a foot at a time. But above six feet he can go up only an inch at a time."

Then Kennedy looked at the two Soviet men levelly.

He again addressed himself to Adzhubei. "I just want to make sure that you and your father-in-law have no doubts about our position in Berlin."

1 After this incident, he sought out the White House curator and said that he appreciated antiques but wondered if he could have just a plain old chair that would hold him up, never mind its heritage.

Get tougher, be hard. This was the Kennedy dogma at midsummer, 1961.

"The State Department is a bowl of jelly," he growled privately. "It's got all those people over there who are constantly smiling. I think we need to smile less and be tougher."

For hard times, continued the President, we needed more hard people. The greatest gratification had come to him when in Vienna he had introduced his aide Kenny O'Donnell to Premier Khrushchev.

"Kenny gave him the coldest look he got on the trip," laughed the President with great relish.

Everybody else in Vienna, said Kennedy, had run around making sure not to do anything to offend the Russians, always to smile. "I'm beginning to think," he said, "that when we go around like that all the time, those people just think we're soft."

As if taking his own advice to heart, Kennedy named bigbomber man Curt LeMay to head the Air Force. It was a surprise to many that this old warrior would get the job at a time when the younger, smoother, more flexible generation of missile men was in vogue. But LeMay had the toughness Kennedy felt the country needed most.

Kennedy brooded more about his State Department. Though it was not functioning the way he wanted it to function, he did not blame Dean Rusk, whom he found to be an increasingly skillful diplomat and valuable adviser. Yet, if Rusk was to perform these functions and not run the shop, somebody else should run it. It seemed, at the time, anyway, that nobody had hold of the wheel.

Kennedy was disappointed in the ideas produced for the Berlin crisis by the State Department. "It's a disgrace what the State Department comes up with sometimes," said one high-ranking New Frontiersman. "A high school kid could do as good. The first draft of the *aide memoire* on Berlin was awful. You wouldn't have submitted it in Government I-A at Harvard. The stuff they did on Cuba was bad. They didn't do anything on Southeast Asia. One of the best papers that's been done on Southeast Asia came from the Defense Department."

What had been building for some weeks came to a head. Kennedy decided to try to move Chester Bowles, the State Department's number-two man, into a job that better suited his temperament. As Under Secretary, it was Bowles' responsibility to get the department running correctly while Dean Rusk followed the more glamorous path of high policy. But the mechanics of a vast government bureaucracy were not to Bowles' liking. The former advertising man preferred to think big thoughts about the world. On desks throughout the State Department the small problems that make the big problems went unsolved. Unanswered routine requests backed up in folders as Bowles persued the questions of what to do with continents. White House aides began to gripe openly about him. Whenever he was involved in a matter with the White House, it seemed to turn fuzzy.

He had been quick to make it known after Cuba that he had been against the operation, thus undercutting Kennedy. He had come to the National Security Council meeting in the Cuban aftermath with the soft paper which Bob Kennedy had chewed to bits. As a one-time proponent of the two-China policy, he had irritated a great many administration people by his insistence that there should be a full-scale debate on the question. Bit by bit he had worn out his friends.

Kennedy asked him over for lunch. The President was jovial as always. After they had a swim in the White House pool, a new Kennedy softening technique, they went up to the private quarters to eat and talk. Gently the President suggested that Bowles might like to move into something different, away from the tiresome details of running a department—perhaps into an ambassadorship, such as the very desirable spot in Chile; or some special adviser's post, where he could roam and think. The President talked in generalities. If Bowles did not become alarmed as he sipped Kennedy's excellent French wine, he did when he left the office. The conversation added up to one thing: he was being moved aside. He alerted his liberal friends, and immediately they leaked a raft of stories about the injustice of trying to dump the one man who had opposed the Cuban fiasco. Over a July week end it blew into a full-scale newspaper flap. Kennedy came back to Washington and invited Bowles to a second meal to smooth matters out, since the President for that moment wanted no more trouble. Bowles had delayed his own execution; but he had also made certain it would come in the next few weeks. He had performed masterfully just that kind of an operation which the Kennedys detest. "He'll go," said Kennedy in private, then turned to the business of Berlin.

The country was getting the feel of crisis, whether John Kennedy thought so or not. Vacationing America romped along the beaches and hiked into the mountains, but an edge of uncertainty made people turn on their transistor radios more frequently and scan headlines with more regularity than a vacation schedule usually demanded.

John Kennedy adopted some of the double life himself. He summoned his advisers to the fantail of his father's yacht, the "Marlin," in Hyannis Port. Clutching a big black loose-leaf notebook stuffed with the top-secret Berlin papers (his staff called it the "Berlin Book"), Kennedy lounged in sport clothes, soaking up the welcome sun. The boat might run the eight miles to Dead Neck or it might hover off Egg Island in Nantucket Sound. Perhaps Dean Rusk and Kennedy would keep the conversation going as Robert McNamara and Maxwell Taylor swam, to come back cooled and refreshed to join again in the urgent policy discussion.

Separating the business and personal lives of John Kennedy is, in the journalistic world, as difficult as splitting the atom in the realm of physics. In the course of a normal day it is virtually impossible. It is as accurate to say that he plays golf (or did, until his back injury stopped that) while he works as it is to say that he works while he plays golf. He may grant an interview while he swims, and the number of sun-lighted conferences on his patio or on one of his boats are so many they have gone uncalculated. Yet they have been as vital as any other conferences. He recharges himself at the same time that he expends energy. He has not in recent years had a pure moment of rest or escape as defined by the mass of Americans. He comes close to being a perpetual-motion machine of flesh and blood. Many marvel at this energy. The answer is not complex: since he is extremely wealthy, every concern, every menial service, which consume half or more of a less affluent citizen's time, is not even a thought in Kennedy's mind. His clothes, his cars, his phones, his airplanes— these come naturally, they always are there. The wants of his wife and children are no worry. If it is a swim or a boat ride or sunshine he wants, he has it in a moment, or at least in a swift airplane ride. Staff, press and a gasping public scramble to even imagine the pace they must set to keep up. Exhausted themselves, they spread the myth that the Kennedy glands must be superhuman. But the answer once again lies in the mystique of the dollar, which, when gathered in sufficient quantities, can bathe a man in the human services that free his mind for total concentration on his work. The tribute to John Kennedy and his entire family is that this concentration has turned on public service. Others with equal wealth have found their "work" in the perfumed chambers of café society, somewhat remote from the country roads of Wisconsin and deserted mines of West Virginia, where John Kennedy won the right to run for the presidency.

In such times as the summer of 1961, the value of perpetual refurbishment in the war of wills that was developing was immense. For the Kennedy fight was now showing in virtually everything the President did. He became immersed in Berlin. It claimed some part of every minute, whether in his conscious world or in the subconscious.

He lashed out in his press conferences. "The crisis over Berlin is Soviet-manufactured," he stormed. "The obvious purpose here is not to have peace but to make permanent the partition of Germany. . . . No one can fail to appreciate the gravity of the threat. . . . It involves the peace and the security of the peoples of West Berlin. It involves the direct responsibilities and commitments of the United States, the United Kingdom and France. It involves the peace and the security of the world. . . ."

If Khrushchev cared to listen, there was still some Yankee humor, too. "Chairman Khrushchev has compared the United States to a worn-out runner living on its past performance and stated that the Soviet Union would outproduce the United States by 1970. Without wishing to trade hyperbole with the Chairman, I do suggest that he reminds me of the tiger hunter who has picked a place on the wall to hang the tiger's skin long before he has caught the tiger. This tiger[2] has other ideas. . . . We invite the USSR to engage in this competition which is peaceful and which could only result in a better living standard for both of our people. In short, the United States is not such an aged runner and, to paraphrase Mr. Coolidge, 'We do choose to run.' "

The President withdrew even more from the outside world as threats from Berlin grew. A staff member found that now and then as he talked to Kennedy, the President was not listening, his mind had wandered on to other things. "He is more serious for far greater lengths of time," said an old Harvard friend. "I've spent a lot of time with him when he's been relaxing. In the old days he was more bantering. He tosses off fewer wisecracks now."

Sometimes those closest to the President could see it the least. "It's like osmosis," said Dave Powers, the White House receptionist and crony. "He just kind of absorbs it without realizing it."

The Kennedy Cabinet officers often became frustrated by the consuming international matters. Secretary of the Interior Stewart Udall, who had worked fiercely to develop a far-seeing conservation and development program, could hardly get the presidential ear. "He's imprisoned by Berlin," fretted Udall. "He has a restless mind that likes to roam over all subjects, but ever since Europe, Berlin has occupied him totally."

Kennedy looked a little different, too. His sedentary life (his back ruled out golf), as well as French Chef René Verdon, shot his weight back up to 180.

His isolation was a cerebral one, because never before had he been so surrounded by family and close friends. He could, and did, with a phone call summon such intimates as K. Lemoyne Billings from New York for a movie—it was only an hour's plane flight. He actually worked at home; lunched there, played there. Jackie and Caroline were nearer than

---

2 This reference was particularly amusing to reporters and members of the White House staff who had, with some regularity, come to call the President "the Tiger."

when he was in the Senate, and he saw much more of them. His brothers and sisters were all, with the exception of the Lawfords and the Teddy Kennedys, in Washington on federal jobs. Friends from his college days, his Navy days and the campaign swarmed in to take federal posts. But Berlin blanked them out.

The words of Joe Kennedy came back: "The family can be there. But there is not much they can do sometimes for the President of the United States."

There was another subtle change: John Kennedy became the head of the Kennedy clan; he was the focus of the family. All the energies of its energetic members were being applied to help him succeed. His decisions were the family's decisions.

The presence of the enigmatic Joe Kennedy faded even further from public view. His desire was to see that he did whatever he could for the President of the United States. When the President was in Palm Beach or in Hyannis Port, the elder Kennedy devoted himself to seeing that his son was comfortable, was not bothered, did and had what he wanted. A new boat pier went up off Joe Kennedy's section of Hyannis Port beach, to make it easier for John Kennedy to go cruising aboard Joe Kennedy's yacht, the "Marlin." The playing field below "the big house," Joe Kennedy's residence in the three-house compound, which the father had so carefully selected for his athletic boys when he bought the property, became a helicopter pad, and when John Kennedy whirled in for a week end, his father was standing on the edge with his wide reassuring smile. For the Kennedy back, there was the light-blue electric golf cart that would whisk him anywhere on the premises. Joe Kennedy's own masseur was at the President's disposal; he had the use of any of the rooms of the big house for visiting dignitaries and government conferences.[3]

When John Kennedy was in Washington, he sometimes talked to his father daily by phone. But these were not calls of intrigue; they were calls of encouragement and reassur-

[3] Joe Kennedy, using his old Hollywood contacts, helped negotiate the movie rights for Bob Donovan's book *PT 109*, the story of the President's war experiences. The deal came to a tidy $150,000, some $2,500 for each of the crew members or their widows and the remaining $120,000 for Donovan.

ance for the President of the United States and also the most important man in the Kennedy clan.

The rantings of Khrushchev were totally forgotten on the evening that Pakistan's visiting President Mohammed Ayub Khan and his wife were feted on the lawn of Mount Vernon, George Washington's magnificent prominence that commanded a sweeping view of the Potomac. Delighted by the use of the beautiful old palaces for official entertaining during her trip with the President to Europe, Jackie had returned to Washington with the idea that the same thing could be done here.

On a warm July night four freshly scrubbed white Navy ships lay quietly tied at Pier Number One in the naval weapons plant on the Anacostia River. There was the metal-hulled "Guardian," one of four remaining PT boats, the two Presidential yachts—the "Honey Fitz" and the "Patrick J."—and Navy Secretary John Connally's own boat, the "Sequoia."

Along the wharf, the white-coated Navy and Army escort officers bustled back and forth, making sure that the 138 guests boarded the right ship, each guest to be piped aboard in the finest Navy manner.

Inside the yachts everything was astir. There were strolling musicians on each, white-coated Filipino waiters hurrying cocktails. Beyond the western bank of the Potomac a huge orange sun was setting in a cloudless sky. With such lighting, even the silty river became a golden ribbon.

The presidential limousines rolled up to the pier, and the convoy churned out into the river. First went the big PT boat, followed by the "Patrick J." The President's favorite, the "Honey Fitz," with Kennedy and Ayub on board, followed in their wakes. Last came the "Sequoia," with Jackie and Ayub's daughter on the polished fantail.

The western sky flamed as the sun set and Lester Lanin's trio on the "Sequoia" swung into "Mack the Knife," one of the First Lady's favorites.

Jackie drifted in and out among her guests, chatting a little with each. Lanin's trio (bass fiddle, accordion, guitar) whanged out "The Eyes of Texas Are upon You," and the guests made Speaker Sam Rayburn stand up.

Franklin Roosevelt, Jr., a destroyer skipper from World War II, stuck an inquisitive nose in the pilot's cabin to see how the Navy crew navigated. Oklahoma's famous football coach Bud Wilkinson, in Washington for Kennedy's physical-fitness program, climbed to the upper deck, thrust his lean jaw into the wind and decided it wasn't quite as good as a prairie breeze—but almost. Allen Dulles reminisced about some of his sailing days with his brother, the late John Foster Dulles, and in this way, making a creditable eleven knots, the flotilla of party-goers slid down the river to Mount Vernon. On the boats were the Dillons, the McNamaras, the Robert Kennedys; Senators Mansfield, Dirksen and Symington and their wives; Vice President and Mrs. Johnson; Mrs. Nicholas Longworth; ambassadors, congressmen and assorted others.

As the boats came to Mount Vernon, each paid its honors, as is the Navy custom. The bells tolled and the crew and guests stood reverently on the side facing the big mansion.

From the boats the guests were transferred to a string of black Cadillacs for the trip up the steep hill. Marines in full dress lined the road at present arms. On the lawn, while mint juleps were served, a short pageant on the fighting techniques of Washington's own Revolutionary War regulars was performed.

Mount Vernon shone brilliantly under spotlights, the first time in history it had been equipped with electric lights. The ladies in short skirts, the men in white dinner jackets (all except the President and his brother, who wore black tuxedos) wandered fearlessly over the grass. The Army engineers had for three days running sprayed four square miles of the area, and not a mosquito, chigger, tick or ant had survived this military might.

Under a huge tent the guests were seated at small tables, and they ate by candlelight. White House chef Verdon presided proudly over a culinary innovation. His avocado and crabmeat mimosa, poulet chasseur avec couronne de riz clamart, frambroises à la crème Chantilly and petits fours secs had been rushed from his basement domain at 1600 Pennsylvania Avenue aboard mobile Army field kitchens, kept hot and delicious until a legion of waiters offered them to the guests.

After dinner the party left the pavilion and strolled across the lawn to rows of camp chairs set up for a concert by the National Symphony. The orchestra played beneath the stars, and a huge ash tree, its top lighted, made a natural stage setting. As the orchestra played Mozart's "allegro con spirito" from the *Symphony No. 35 in D Major,* and Gershwin's *An American in Paris,* waiters passed champagne and Corona Coronas.

Back on board the boats, the guests danced as the music echoed out over the water, which now reflected the starlit blackness. Jackie's staff members had thoughtfully rounded up sweaters and jackets to protect the ladies from the unfamiliar cool of the river valley.

When the party was over in the first hours of the next day, the stodgy old capital on the Potomac admitted there had been nothing like it in this century, maybe not even since Mount Vernon's original owner had grandly welcomed his own guests on that magnificent hill above the river.

CHAPTER SEVENTEEN

THE WALL

I N T H E west, great thunderheads piled up over the Potomac valley, bringing premature darkness but breathing coolness on a Washington which had smothered in 93-degree heat all day.

Faint light filtered through the tall arched window on the west side of the White House's second floor. In this muted tone of a day's end two figures sat in a vast silence. One was the President of the United States, the other was his trusted friend Dave Powers. The date was July 25, 1961. The Berlin crisis—indeed, the world crisis—had grown to such proportions that John Kennedy had decided once again to talk to the American people. That night he was to go on television to explain his latest proposals for strengthening the free world against the communist threat.

In his hand was a copy of the speech he would give to the United States and the world. It was, perhaps, as tough a speech as any president has ever had to give in peacetime. It was a call to America for partial mobilization, for psychological preparation for the Berlin showdown. It was a ringing warning to Russia that the free world would not abandon its obligations.

Kennedy read and reread the paragraphs, now and then glancing out the window at the gray hulk of the Executive Office Building, which had once housed the Departments of State and War in a lusty young nation. Beyond, the clouds, still darkening, tumbled and whirled as a front of cooler air fought to sweep away the heavy heat.

The speech was not yet completed. Kennedy had changed and added and cut. In the west wing of the White House secretaries typed furiously to produce a reading copy of the talk by the deadline of 10 P.M.

For the moment the President sat in the West Hall, which Jackie had turned into an informal living area. On the walls around the President hung paintings by great American artists—Sargent, Homer and Prendergast. They loomed dimly through the thin light, reminders of the American heritage of which Kennedy was the guardian.

He still labored over the ending of the speech. He did not like the words that were written. He took a yellow legal tablet, cradled it in his lap and began to scribble. "We must look to long days ahead which if we are courageous and persevering can bring us what we all desire. . . . In meeting my responsibilities in these coming months as President, I need your goodwill and your support and, above all, your prayers. . . ."

As a summer bachelor, with his family away on Cape Cod, Kennedy often dined with Powers. Now the two men moved to the dining room. Page by page the final speech arrived. As each fresh page was delivered by messenger, Kennedy read it as if he were before the TV cameras. Powers timed his delivery, keeping track of the total minutes. There was a minimum of banter between the two. Generally when he was with Powers the President relaxed. Powers swam with him in the pool, accompanied him on trips, ate with him when the family was gone. At such moments they would talk of baseball, football, politics and people. But there were times when Kennedy did not want to talk, and this was one of them.

It was a serious hour, but it was not a grim one. Kennedy had reached the end of long hours of deliberation. He had listened to endless advice from his officials. He had read thousands of words of memorandums and he had pondered Nikita Khrushchev's threats. Then he had made his decisions, and now he was ready to talk about them.

Kennedy had sat on the fantail of the "Marlin" or in the

low wicker chairs on the patio behind his house, fringed with petunias, weighing world events. Slowly a Kennedy philosophy had emerged.

To react blindly and with panic to each world crisis by sending troops, mobilizing National Guard units or supplying new arms and ammunition to the local armies was not an answer to Khrushchev, it seemed to Kennedy as he studied the globe. Thus, to ship or fly fresh armies into West Berlin and to make it a bristling arsenal would be foolish, went his reasoning. Khrushchev could simply ignore Berlin—for as yet there was no real trouble there—and start a brush fire someplace else in the world; this country would be confronted again with the job of moving troops, running with its tongue out to catch the enemy, and all, of course, at huge expense.

What had to be done, Kennedy concluded, was to revamp and strengthen our armed forces so that this extra muscle could be applied around the globe with ease. More flexibility was needed—more airlift capacity, more guerrilla training, just more men. But it all had to fit in with some kind of civil-defense program.

Dave Powers in his total devotion to his boss liked to say that Knute Rockne must have coined the phrase "When the going gets tough, the tough get going" for John Kennedy. As Dave watched Kennedy perform from his first election in 1946 through all the other campaigns into the White House, he found that Kennedy went better as an underdog.

It seemed to be true in the month of July, as the crisis grew. Kennedy's own sense seemed sharper. He was brusque, more to the point. He enjoyed finding solutions to the problems as they came along, and he showed more confidence in himself and in his conclusions.

"Here's a picture for you of a couple of old soldiers," chortled Kennedy one noon to me. He held up a color photograph taken the day before of Douglas MacArthur and himself. MacArthur had been a luncheon guest in the White House. "How about that for a magazine cover? You know what MacArthur said at lunch? He said that we shouldn't put one American soldier on the continent of Asia—we couldn't win a fight in Asia. I thought some of the Republicans were going to choke when he said that. Come on, how about a swim?"

But before he went out the door, he circled Mrs. Lincoln's office, scanning the letters she thrust at him. She held the phone. "Chester Bowles is on the line." Kennedy reached for the receiver, settled behind his secretary's desk and at the same time picked up another batch of letters.

"Hello, Chet, how are you? . . . You're leaving for Asia? . . . Have a good trip. . . . I'll see you when you get back, all right?"

"Let's go swim."

The President walked out along the porch, glancing down the south lawn.

"I tried to do too much at first. I've got things better organized now so I can do this."

I suggested timidly that I hadn't come equipped with a bathing suit.

"That's okay," said Kennedy. "In this pool you don't need one. It's a little hot, but I need it for my back. I've decided that the real trouble is sitting in that office all day. When I was out on the campaign, I got exercise and my back didn't bother me."

The pool, built in 1933 by Franklin Roosevelt, lies in the connecting link of the house between the main mansion and west wing executive offices. It is fifty by fifteen feet, and off one end is a small exercise room.

Its deep blue-green water was perfectly still. At one end near a low diving board a blue plastic boat drifted, left over from a romp by Caroline. A Secret Service agent stationed himself at the pool door.

The President, stiff-backed and slow, went down the chrome ladder into the water.

Now his mind turned to Berlin and Khrushchev. He stood in the shallow water, hands on his back, and stretched the muscles.

The enigma of the Soviet Premier still nagged at him. Khrushchev provided one of the most baffling and disappointing of his experiences in office. As he looked back over the talks, it was evident that there had been no region of "philosophical agreement" about the tragedy that a nuclear war might bring. "That was what was so discouraging about Vienna," said Kennedy.

He backstroked down the pool, showing some of the old Harvard style that had put him on the swimming team. He clung to the side and kicked gently, tread water and then just walked about in the warmth.

He talked of the Berlin decisions he had made. There would be no declaration of a national emergency. Such a move would be too extreme. There would be no wholesale call-up of the National Guard or reserves; select units and skilled men only would be called. The draft would be increased to get more men. But the situation did not demand an all-out effort yet, he said. Further, he feared a severe round of inflation if he moved too fast. He had decided that we needed an extensive fallout-shelter program, some food storage and a vast home-shelter education plan. The whole program would cost the taxpayers between $3 and $4 billion more. He had just about decided that he should ask for a tax increase to pay this extra bill—that would give the nation a feeling of participation in the emergency.

Other matters were on his mind, too.

"Maxwell Taylor's damned good," he mused about the man whom he had recently named military adviser. "I can't even remember who suggested him. But he's going to be fine. I thought that at first there might be a problem between him and some of the others. But there doesn't seem to be so far. I don't anticipate any difficulty at the Pentagon. Taylor doesn't have that kind of personality."

As he swam more, Kennedy seemed to loosen up. "I wonder who leaked those stories about Chester Bowles. They must have come from the State Department. I don't think any of the White House people did it."

He chuckled about a story in *Time* magazine's "Press" section which reported on some troubles that the New York *Herald Tribune* was having.

"I love to see Republicans giving it to each other. The *Herald Trib* has given me plenty. I wonder how they like it for a change."

His mind leaped from subject to subject, roaming, summing up. He swam the length of the pool in a strong crawl.

"I was ready to go into Laos. Yes, we were going to do it. Then because of Cuba I thought we'd better take another look at the military planning for Laos. What I found wasn't good—only two airstrips and all that. We'd have really been in bad shape if we'd done that. So I did what I could. It's good to have men like Curt LeMay and Arleigh Burke commanding troops once you decide to go in. But these men aren't the only ones you should listen to when you decide whether to go in or not. I like having LeMay head the Air Force. Everybody knows how he feels. That's a good thing right now."

The new Central Intelligence Agency head had been chosen—John McCone. But there would be no announcement right now, said Kennedy. Any premature leak would make it seem that Allen Dulles was being forced out. Dulles was to stay and serve out the term which he had set for himself. He had done a great deal for this country, was an honorable and able man. The last thing John Kennedy wanted to do was slight him.

As he walked toward the ladder after fifty minutes, Kennedy reflected on Dean Rusk, his Secretary of State. He was a good man, and he was getting better by the day. Maybe at first Rusk had not been tough enough, said Kennedy. But he had learned quickly. The State Department still was not functioning just as he wanted it to function. There would be some more changes, but perhaps not right then.

On his crutches Kennedy hobbled off for the elevator and lunch. In his bedroom he propped himself up in his huge canopied bed, sipped a bloody Mary. His food was brought to him on a tray. He ate with gusto: onion soup, fish, spinach.

He fretted about the publishing world, which at the moment was not treating him in the kindest way. "I figure that the publishers have the most high-powered lobby in the country," he said. "They killed that postal bill nicely. The information industry is controlled by such a small group of men. No other industry is so narrowly held—there's Luce, Cowles, Roy Howard, Dryfoos, Sarnoff, Paley and a few others. They account for most of it."

His old adversary Richard Nixon did not escape the day's notice. Nixon had written an article on foreign aid which had appeared in papers across the country that morning. "The same Nixon," Kennedy declared. "He started out saying that everybody should be for long-term foreign aid and then he said he was for the Judd proposal, which is just the opposite. He's trying to win both the liberals and the conservatives. He's too clever. People see through it."

The President even had a moment to worry about the little white Russian dog Pushinka, which Chairman Khrushchev had given to the Kennedys. At first the dog had been terribly nervous, but now he seemed to be happy, reported Kennedy.

Then it was time for his rest. There still was much to be done on the big speech.

The speech had taken shape much as Kennedy felt it would—all except the reference to a tax boost. On the day before the talk he had summoned his Cabinet to go over the idea. The political men, such as Abe Ribicoff and Arthur Goldberg, had argued for it. But the fiscal experts had opposed it. Douglas Dillon, with aid from Budget Director David Bell and economist Walter Heller, maintained that the economy was strong enough to stand the extra burden. Kennedy accepted the view of his experts.

Kennedy himself had labored hard on the speech in Hyannis Port. Sometimes he was alone in his second-floor bedroom at the Cape, sometimes he sat in a living-room chair beside his special White House phone, one foot up on a footstool, the yellow legal pad in his lap. At such times the house was purposefully hushed, so that he could concentrate. His scribblings were sent on to Sorensen, who worked in Washington. Four major drafts were completed before the speech read as the President wanted it to. In the last hours Kennedy drafted personal letters to Macmillan and de Gaulle, explaining his talk to them.

Ten P.M. of July 25 approached, and Kennedy walked from his living quarters to his office. It was a jungle of cables and microphones and arms and legs of reporters and technicians.

The air conditioning was turned low, so that the microphones would not pick up the hum. The big kliegs blazed and the cameramen sweated and cursed.

"Gimme a light reading, will ya, Dave? . . . Damnit, who turned off that light, clumsy? . . . Hey, Pierre, which door will he come through? . . . Move that light to the right a little, Cleve. . . . I'm gettin' nothing. Hurry, hurry, what's wrong? He's almost here. There, there it goes, whew. . . . Can I stand here? . . . No, that's for the stills. . . . Where do the reels go? . . . What about us reporters, Pierre? Goddamned television anyway. . . ."

The figure of the President slipped in through the French doors. The room quieted, and then John Kennedy looked into millions of living rooms. In the heat he began immediately to perspire.

"Good evening. Seven weeks ago tonight I returned from Europe to report on my meeting with Premier Khrushchev and the others. His grim warnings about the future of the world, his *aide memoire* on Berlin, his subsequent speeches and threats which he and his agents have launched, and the increase in the Soviet military budget that he has announced, have all prompted a series of decisions by the administration after a series of consultations with the members of the NATO organization. . . . We are clear about what must be done—and we intend to do it. . . .

"I hear it said that West Berlin is militarily untenable. And so was Bastogne. And so, in fact, was Stalingrad. Any dangerous spot is tenable if men—brave men—will make it so.

"We do not want to fight—but we have fought before. And others in earlier times have made the same dangerous mistake of assuming that the West was too selfish and too soft and too divided to resist invasions of freedom in other lands. . . .

"(1) I am tomorrow requesting the Congress for the current fiscal year an additional $3,247,000,000 of appropriations for the Armed Forces. (2) To fill out our present Army divisions, and to make more men available for prompt deployment, I am requesting an increase in the Army's total authorized strength from 875,000 to approximately one million men. (3) I am requesting an increase of 29,000 and 63,000 men, respectively, in the active duty strength of the

Navy and Air Force. (4) To fulfill these manpower needs, I am ordering that our draft calls be doubled and tripled in the coming months: I am asking the Congress for authority to order to active duty certain ready reserve units and individual reservists, and to extend tours of duty. . . . (5) Many ships and planes once headed for retirement are to be retained or reactivated, increasing our airpower tactically and our sealift, airlift and antisubmarine warfare capability. In addition, our strategic air power will be increased by delaying the deactivation of B-47 bombers. (6) Finally, some 1.8 billion—about half the total sum—is needed for the procurement of nonnuclear weapons, ammunition and equipment. . . . We have another sober responsibility. . . . In May, I pledged a new start on civil defense. . . . Tomorrow I am requesting of the Congress new funds for the following immediate objectives: to identify and mark space in existing structures—public and private—that could be used for fallout shelters in case of attack; to stock those shelters with food, water, first-aid kits and other minimum essentials for survival; to increase their capacity; to improve our air-raid warning and fallout-detection systems, including a new household warning system which is now under development. . . . The addition of $207 million in civil-defense appropriations brings our total new defense budget requests to $3.454 billion, and a total of $47.5 billion for the year."

Such was the program, and it brought back memories of other voices from the early 1940's. The talk was war talk.

Kennedy had some more words for Khrushchev before he walked back to his room in the deserted White House. "We have previously indicated our readiness to remove any actual irritants in West Berlin, but the freedom of that city is not negotiable. We cannot negotiate with those who say, 'What's mine is mine and what's yours is negotiable.' . . . The world is not deceived by the communist attempt to label Berlin as a hotbed of war. There is peace in Berlin today. The source of world trouble and tension is Moscow, not Berlin. . . . The steps I have indicated tonight are aimed at avoiding that war. To sum it all up: We seek peace—but we shall not surrender. . . ."

*   *   *

The country had listened well. It responded.

The Congress—Republicans and Democrats alike—fell into line and passed the legislation for which the President had asked.

Approval came from allied leaders and even from a number of neutral nations. Mail to the White House ran 100 to 1 for the President. Men volunteered for the Army or recall with the reserves and the local civil-defense headquarters, which for years had been forgotten, suddenly were besieged for information. In Chicago, Leo Hoegh, Eisenhower's old civil-defense head, who now had charge of selling shelters for Wonder Building Corporation, found that orders spurted. A normal month's quota was 400, but in two days the firm sold 137. Nobel Prize-winning chemist Willard Libby, former member of the AEC, dug himself a fallout shelter in the side of a hill, protected it with railroad ties and sandbags and proudly posed for photographers, reciting the total cost of $30.

John Kennedy's spirit lifted with the nation's.

Talking to a friend over the phone, he flared at some criticism. "Be tough?" he asked. "Everybody says, 'Be tough.' What do they mean? Invade Cuba now, go into Laos? What else are you supposed to do?" Maybe, joked the friend, they mean bomb Moscow. "That," shot back the President, "is the coward's way out."

Noting a paragraph in a national magazine which pointed out the fact that the "clothes-conscious" Kennedy brothers had appeared in black tuxedos for the Mount Vernon party while the rest of the male guests were in white coats, the President phoned his objections. "What do you mean, the 'clothes-conscious' Kennedy brothers?" he asked. "I may be, but I don't think Bobby is."

The correspondent, not believing that he heard correctly, said simply, "What?"

"I don't think Bobby is very well dressed, do you?" came back the answer. "Why, he still wears those button-down shirts. They went out five years ago. The only people I know who still wear them are Chester and Adlai."

Another time, as a visitor sat across the desk from the President, the phone rang and he was told his brother was calling. Only a few days before Bob Kennedy had been rated by a news magazine as the man with the greatest influence at the White House. Picking up the phone, Kennedy paused, put his hand over the speaker. Turning to his guest, he said with a trace of mock sarcasm, "This is the second most powerful man in the nation calling." [1]

But there was scarcely time for such banter.

East Germans fled—1,500 of them a day—across the border, out of fear of the future. Another 1,000 were turned back every day as the communist police began to drag its victims off the commuter trains, to invalidate identification cards, to clap them in jail.

Kennedy's disarmament adviser, John McCloy, flew back to the United States and reported to Kennedy on a conference with Khrushchev at the Soviet leader's Black Sea dacha. The Russian had been in a totally belligerent mood, McCloy told the President. Khrushchev had seemed absolutely intent on extracting what he called the "rotten tooth" of Berlin.

Up from a Soviet launching pad went Gherman Titov for an incredible seventeen earth orbits—the second Russian astronaut. And the Russian Premier began to shout about a Soviet nuclear bomb equivalent to 100 million tons of TNT. "Gentlemen," he cried to the West, "your arms are too short."

The fear that the East Germans would close the Berlin border mounted, sending the count of escapees to new heights. As the East German officials made threatening noises, the near panic became worse, not better.

On August 13 it happened: Walter Ulbricht built the Berlin Wall. It happened swiftly, in about four hours. The grim work started at 2 A.M., and by dawn much of the ugly wall seared the heart of the city.

First came the scream of sirens, then the rumble of tanks

[1] A few days prior to this conversation, the story goes, the two brothers had met in the White House. In the old competitive family spirit, John Kennedy reminded his brother of the same article. "Well," he said to Bob. "There's only one way you can go now—down."

on the cobblestones. There were motorcycle outriders, buses jammed with the steel-helmeted East German troops that stretched for block after dark block. Cargo trucks hurriedly dumped out their rolls of barbed wire, concrete pillars, stone blocks, picks and shovels. Millions of misery-ridden people were in a huge communist pen. They would stay no other way.

The response from the West was silence. In the first hours no one had any advice. John Kennedy and his government had no plan of action for such an event, despite the sheaves of emergency measures dreamed up for every other crisis. There were not even any meetings about the wall in the White House. Kennedy questioned his top advisers by phone, because he was in Hyannis Port. No one suggested an immediate move; not even West Berlin Mayor Willy Brandt had an idea right then. And our military commanders on the spot never seriously considered knocking down the wall which stood in East Berlin, beyond their rightful territory.[2] The city had been divided for fifteen years, the communists had maintained an invisible wall until the morning of August 13. As belated cries demanded that we tear down the wall, Kennedy pondered the suggestion briefly. Tear it down to have the communists build it up fifty yards farther back? Practically speaking, the communists had long ago established their right to seal off their part of the city. Free movement was a myth: free movement was only possible through designated checkpoints. Kennedy decided that this nation should do nothing about the wall, leaving it to stand as a momument to the failure of East Germany's communist system.

There were other things to do. The President summoned

---

2 General Bruce C. Clarke, Commander in Chief, U.S. Army, Europe, later wrote of that time: "I have heard it discussed in the press that we should have immediately knocked down the Berlin Wall. I would point out that the wall was not built overnight. It was a long time in forming and completing. It was built on East Berlin territory. Could we have knocked it down without a military reaction on the part of the Soviets that the Allied Garrison in Berlin could not have coped with? History will have to decide this one in the light of future developments. But, I can say that I know of no one in a position of responsibility that recommended that we knock down the Berlin Wall at the time it was being built. Neither General Watson [Major General Albert Watson II, Berlin commander] nor I ever made such a recommendation or seriously considered it."

his lanky Vice President, Lyndon Johnson, and asked him to fly to Berlin to give the people American assurances that though the wall would not be torn down, the rights that Kennedy considered basic to West Berlin—access from West Germany, the freedom of the city's peoples, the right to station our troops there—would not be withdrawn.

Then he announced that 1,500 troops of the 8th Division would cross East Germany along the Helmstedt-Berlin Autobahn in armored trucks, in an out-and-out test of the crucial right of access.

CHAPTER EIGHTEEN

TROOPS TO BERLIN

W HO is Colonel Johns?" asked the President of the United States.

It turned out he was a tall, sandy-haired Texan with a distinguished combat record and a flair for the dramatic. He became an important figure in some of the most intense moments of John Kennedy's first year.

Col. Glover S. Johns, Jr., was chosen August 18 by General Bruce C. Clarke, U.S. Army commander in Europe, to lead the American battle group across the 110 miles of communist land between West Germany and West Berlin.

This was to be the test of communist threats: if our troops were halted or interferred with to any great degree, it meant that the sacred right of access was being tampered with; it could have meant shooting.

Kennedy called for a biography of Colonel Johns. He studied it closely, then asked, "He isn't a West Pointer. How come?"

The military planners said that Johns had a fine record as a field commander in World War II. (Indeed, he authored a book about his experiences called *The Clay Pigeons of St. Lo.*)

Since General Clarke did not want to pull troops out of the line on the border facing the communists, he turned to Johns' 1,500 men, the 1st Battle Group, 8th Infantry, stationed in Mannheim. They were nearly 400 miles away from the entry point at Helmstedt, but they were on the

Autobahn and could move almost immediately.

Back in the White House, tension hung in the corridors like a ground mist before sunup. It had been building since Kennedy and Khrushchev met in Vienna, and if a single day can be pointed to when the President felt the nation was entering the danger zone, it is August 20, when the troops raced those 110 miles into West Berlin.

This symbolic reinforcement had been talked about for weeks. When the wall went up it was given new impetus— and new danger. The President was apprehensive. Kennedy's strategy in the chess game with Khrushchev was never to trap the Russian, always to give him a way out, never to provoke him beyond legitimate political bounds. To send a military mission through the communist hinterland at that time had some minor overtones of provocation. We were within our rights, but there was the question of whether the deliberate mission was an unnecessary irritant. The President was concerned about the time it would take to get the battle group up to the jumping-off point. Would this delay be too much of a challenge to the Russians? Could they sit and wait and be expected to do nothing as the battle group marched from Mannheim to Helmstedt, then across their land to Berlin? Access had not yet been interferred with. Kennedy wondered if he was going too far. He reviewed the plans again and considered the possibility of airlifting the men to Berlin. But by this time the plan was too far developed with word of pending troop movement already out, it would be worse to back down.

The operation had been planned in detail. The trucks were to go in serials, so as to move more easily and avoid the "accordion" action that can snarl a long string of vehicles. Also, if trouble developed not all of them would be caught inside communist territory.

General Clarke had been warned of the coming mission by phone from Washington, but the Pentagon became so involved in itself that the official orders were slow in getting to Heidelberg, Clarke's headquarters. Lieut. Gen. Earle G. Wheeler, director of the Joint Staff in Washington, called and told Clarke that it was vital that the troops arrive in Berlin in daylight on Sunday afternoon, August 20. Vice President Johnson, accompanied by former Berlin Commander General Lucius Clay, was to be there to greet them. The afternoon was to be a spectacle of American force, determination and spirit. It was designed to build the sinking German morale in Berlin. It was Friday afternoon when Wheeler talked to Clarke, and Clarke hastily calculated that the battle group would have to move out around 6 A.M. on the next morning, get to Helmstedt by that night, cross the communist land on Sunday morning.

General Clarke pulled Colonel Johns away from a social evening on Friday; he called him into his office about midnight for verbal orders. Clarke had had to bypass the normal chain of command—Seventh Army, V Corps, 8th Infantry Division—because of the shortness of time. With the mission sketched out for him, Johns hurried back to his unit after midnight. About 2:00 A.M. the official orders came in via Paris. Events were already beyond them.

Johns alerted his troops, fed them breakfast and assembled them in the post theater for orientation about the movement. They were to be the symbol of the free world, Johns said. They were to pass in review before the West German people, Vice President Johnson and General Clay and, really, the world. They might even get into some fighting, he added. But neither he nor any of the other military men, including General Clarke, really believed that.

These men, who had been dealing with the Russians for years, knew them well. When confronted with determination and force, the Russians always backed down, Clarke felt.[1] But to the young administration in Washington, the enemy was not that well known yet.

By 5:30 A.M. on Saturday, General Clarke was at Mannheim, looking over the battle group, which was ready to move out. A group of West Point cadets, attached to the group for training, suddenly became a problem. Clarke, remembering his own cadet days and what such an adventure

---

[1] Writing after his retirement, General Clarke even refused to call these hours a time of "crisis." "What we have had in the Berlin situation have been various forms of 'harassment,' he said. "They have not come to the 'crisis' state as I would define a crisis." The farther away from Berlin a person got and the nearer he came to Washington, the graver the situations seemed, he declared.

would have meant, took a moment out to make sure that the boys could accompany the convoy. At 6 A.M. the battle group moved onto the Autobahn.

Clarke sent Lieut. Gen. Frederic J. Brown, the V Corps Commander, along to Helmstedt in his two-car diesel command train, which had all the latest communications equipment. Clarke received hourly reports from Brown and from the moving column; these he relayed to Washington and to General Lauris Norstad, U.S. Commander in Chief in Europe, who was in Paris. On Saturday, Clarke's entire command was alerted.

By Saturday the communications channels from the Pentagon had smoothed out and now a flood of instructions came to Heidelberg—so many, in fact, that Clarke could not possibly heed them all. Every detail for the movement was contained in the orders; instructions, for instance, to the men in the convoy on how to dismount and what to say if they were challenged at the checkpoints. Clarke stacked them on his desk and indexed them for ready reference. There was one order, however, that did not come; he waited for it all Saturday and never did receive it. The missing order was on the question of ammunition for the troops. The battle group normally carried its ammunition in trucks and did not issue it to the men. Clarke felt that to ask Washington for instructions on this matter would be to invite confusion and delay for an operation already timed to the minute. He ordered the ammunition issued in boxes to all vehicles in the convoy, in each case the ammunition to be under the control of a noncommissioned officer. It was to be broken out only upon order of each march-group commander.[2]

On Saturday afternoon General Clarke heard from Bonn that Lyndon Johnson and his party were en route to Berlin, but that they planned to stay in the city only until 2 P.M. Clarke was upset, since he could not be absolutely certain that his troops would get to Berlin by that time; certainly not all of them would arrive that soon. The climax of this maneuver, it seemed to Clarke, was to be the review of the

2 When the battle group arrived safely in Berlin, the ammunition was dutifully gathered up again and put back into the ammunition trucks, and nobody said a word.

troops by Johnson. He called Maj. Gen. Watson in Berlin and asked that his feelings be made known to Ambassador Walter Dowling and to Johnson.

About 7 P.M. Saturday, Clarke picked up his phone, and the cool voice of McGeorge Bundy in the White House came through. "I've gotten word you're dissatisfied with the Vice President's program for tomorrow," said Bundy. Clarke said that he was, indeed. "It would be the greatest mistake you could make after all this," he added. The movement of the troops had now captured the attention of all Europe and much of the world. Clarke felt that Johnson should greet all 1,500 men.

"I'll see what I can do," said the laconic Bundy. Clarke turned back to keeping tabs on the convoy now gathering at Helmstedt, where they would bivouac at an airfield for the night, pushing off at 6 A.M. Sunday.

Everything was now on hair-trigger alert. Clarke could communicate with general Norstad in an instant should his or Kennedy's word be needed. Instructions for the other forces in Europe were fresh. Norstad had plans for air and ground support in case of fighting, no matter how limited or unlimited.

In the White House concern deepened. One White House staff member later declared, "It was a much greater crisis than people know. Talking to Kennedy then was like talking to a statue. There was the feeling that this mission could very well escalate into shooting before morning."

As the fateful Sunday morning approached in Germany, Saturday night approached in Washington. Normally Kennedy climbed aboard Air Force One and flew off to Cape Cod and a week end of sun and water. Not so this night.

"I'll never forget that General Marshall couldn't explain where he was on Pearl Harbor Day," one of the President's aides told Kennedy. "We shouldn't declare war from Hyannis Port."

Military Aide Ted Clifton was given the assignment to stay up all night at the White House to notify the President if anything should happen. Clifton scurried to double and triple check all channels of communication.

Since the restless Kennedy had decided that he wanted to

see a movie that night, his aides scoured the town but could only produce a mediocre western, the title of which has now been forgotten. Kennedy lasted through about half of it; then, bored and still filled with unrelieved worry, he got up and left.

About 10:30 P.M. Kennedy called Clifton for a rundown. No trouble had developed so far. The President went to bed near midnight. He was up at 8 on Sunday morning and demanded news. There was news, and it was good. The first contingent of the armored column had entered the Autobahn leading to the Berlin gate and had passed through Helmstedt without trouble; the rest of the troops followed unhampered. Slowly the tension eased and Kennedy flew to Hyannis Port.

In Berlin, Lyndon Johnson and General Clay not only greeted Colonel Johns and his troops, but they stayed until every man had passed unharmed from the communist corridor into West Berlin. It was near 8 P.M. when the final group went by the checkpoint. For Johnson and his party it had been an extremely moving day. Hundreds of thousands of West Berliners had come out to greet him and the battle group. To Berlin's House of Representatives the Vice President had cried, "This is the time for confidence, for poise, and for faith—for faith in ourselves. It is also a time for faith in your allies, everywhere throughout the world. This island does not stand alone." This was the tonic Berlin needed.

It was not, by far, the end of the grim days which sometimes across the country brought a tinge of real fear to the people as they tried to understand events. But it was another clear showing of commitment to freedom, something that Khrushchev understood.

There were still more surprises from the Kremlin, however. On August 30, as the Soviet radio was droning out a long government communiqué, the message suddenly became clear: it held the shattering news that the Russians planned to renew nuclear testing. "The United States," went the gray voice, "and its allies are fanning up the arms race . . . preparing a new world holocaust while the Soviet government strives for peace. The Soviet Union considers it its duty to take all necessary measures. . . ."

Just forty-nine hours later a great fireball rose over the central plains of Asia. Khrushchev's cocky predictions that the United States would first resume testing, his vows that the Soviet Union would not resume unilateral testing, lay in shambles.

Khrushchev characteristically could not have cared less about his word. He began immediately to bully. "The Soviet government has been compelled to take this step under the pressure of the policy of leading NATO powers," he shouted. "This aggressive bloc leaves the Soviet Union no other choice."

To make certain that the world understood what was afoot, more talk came out of Moscow about the 100-megaton bomb, 5,000 times the size of the A-bomb that destroyed Hiroshima. No one anywhere was safe from this monster. "No superdeep shelter can save them from an all-shattering blow from this weapon," said the Russian.

Tass's first announcement of the intention to resume testing had been picked up by the United States' huge and sensitive ears that surround the Soviet Union. An alert operator in the Middle East had heard it and flashed it to the United States.

When it clattered in over the supersecret teletypes in the White House, John Kennedy was speeding to a press conference in the New State Department Auditorium. Back in his office at 4:50 that afternoon, he was talking to his staff when McGeorge Bundy walked through the door with yellow paper that bore the message, by then verified by the Central Intelligence Agency.

It was still two hours before the Soviet Union officially announced that it would resume testing. But Kennedy began to plan. He met with Dean Rusk, Allen Dulles and Bundy. He was puzzled, as were the others, about why the Soviet Union had taken the step. It was a vast propaganda defeat for the Russians.

But one thing was clear to Kennedy, as he related to me later: the United States would also have to resume nuclear testing. For the time being, in answer to Russia, Kennedy decided to resume only underground testing, but it was almost as certain as he sent out the orders for the underground tests that before many months we would have to test in the atmosphere. He reached these conclusions instantly when the news came. Details and timing remained to be worked out, but there was only the slightest doubt about the eventuality.

In all his decisions John Kennedy is governed by logic. And the logic which pointed out the inevitability of the resumption of our test program on a major scale was quite clear. We could not afford, despite our commanding nuclear lead, to let the Russians test and test without taking our own steps. Sooner or later the Soviets would overtake us. Kennedy's own dealings with the Soviets had conditioned him to the very real fact that a test agreement was remote. There was in reality only one conclusion, and Kennedy's mind raced to it—the nuclear-testing race was on again.

There was no immediate announcement of his conclusions. Kennedy quietly ordered the Atomic Energy Commission and the Pentagon to get ready for underground tests at the Nevada test side. But he did not even plan to make that announcement then. Instead, he planned to wait until the Russians had begun their own tests, so that in the next few days the Soviet Union would have a chance to reap all the unfavorable world opinion.

His first statement on August 30 about the Russian intentions said: "The Soviet government's decision to resume nuclear-weapons testing presents a threat to the entire world by increasing the dangers of a thermonuclear holocaust. . . . The termination of the moratorium on nuclear testing by the Soviet unilateral decision leaves the United States under the necessity of deciding what its own national interests require. Under these circumstances, Ambassador Arthur Dean is being recalled immediately from Geneva."

On the following morning Kennedy summoned his National Security Council, key aides and the congressional leaders for a thorough briefing. At noon the White House issued another statement calling the Russian announcement "atomic blackmail."

The Senate howled for the resumption of our own testing, but Kennedy kept quiet so that the world fury would all be directed at the Russians.

On Friday there were meetings at the White House with test-ban negotiator Arthur Dean, who had arrived back in this country. Dean charged that the Soviet Union rested its policy on "the terrorization of humanity. But the Soviet government," he continued, "underestimates the people of the world if it thinks they will capitulate to a strategy of blackmail and terror."

There were more briefings for the congressional leaders. This was a delicate matter. Kennedy wanted to keep any panic from developing; the leaders were assured again and again of our commanding nuclear strength.

On Friday afternoon the predicted message came in: the Russians had set off their first bomb. Kennedy accepted the news calmly, and the White House made the announcement to the world. Fifty minutes later John Kennedy was on board his jet headed for another Cape Cod week end. There was nothing more that could be done just then. At the Cape he leisurely loaded eighteen of the clan's children on his electric golf cart and bumped off to the candy store.

Already in Moscow was another appeal to Khrushchev. Kennedy had wanted to make a final plea to halt the tests. He had sought and received British Prime Minister Harold Macmillan's endorsement. "The President of the United States and the Prime Minister of the United Kingdom propose to Chairman Khrushchev that their three governments agree, effective immediately, not to conduct nuclear tests which take place in the atmosphere and produce radioactive fallout. . . ."

There came a second Russian explosion. Kennedy was cruising in his father's yacht "Marlin" when the news was radioed to him. The "Marlin" curved toward shore through the choppy blue waters of Nantucket Sound. In his house Kennedy said to a waiting aide, "Get Dean Rusk on the phone. Get my brother."

Again the feeling predominated that Kennedy should wait a little more before making an announcement about his plans for resuming underground tests.

Back in Washington the following day he called in the AEC's Glenn Seaborg and Deputy Secretary of Defense Roswell Gilpatric to talk over the preparations for the American underground tests. Only a few minutes after they had left Kennedy's office, McGeorge Bundy was at the door with word that a third Russian blast had been detected by the United States monitoring system.

Kennedy decided instantly to make his own intentions known. He picked up the phone and called Dean Rusk to tell him so. He summoned legislative liaison man Larry O'Brien and asked him to be sure to brief the congressional leaders of both parties. In an hour the statement was ready: "In view of the continued testing by the Soviet government, I have today ordered the resumption of nuclear tests, in the laboratory and underground, with no fallout."

"I had no choice," said Kennedy privately later. "I had waited two days for an answer to the message that Macmillan and I sent to Khrushchev. That was plenty of time. All they did was shoot off two more bombs."

The New Frontier's steps appeared to have been wise and firm and the country began to feel better. The tension still existed, but the leader of the free world seemed to have a better idea of what he was about.

Probably only Nikita Khrushchev knows how close we were to war, since this nation would never have initiated a critical action. But looking back months later, Bob Kennedy could say sincerely, "We felt war was very possible then."

It had been Bob who had sat one night late in the White House with his brother and talked about Berlin. The two Kennedys had discussed all the details, all the possibilities. John Kennedy had been more somber than ever. All his days had been spent planning the steps up to and into a nuclear war, should it be required of this country. On that night as they talked, there was the eerie realization that war could be the product of a whim, a misunderstanding, a human mistake. The President looked at his brother. "It really doesn't matter as far as you and I are concerned," he said. "What really matters are all the children."

But this kind of reflection at that time or at any time, was rare. The Kennedys did not brood. And seconds after making the above statement, the President began to plan what civil-defense steps should be taken. Distress simply was not a condition allowed to exist long in the Kennedy household. He had learned to live normally in the midst of crisis. In an instant he could shift his thoughts from nuclear war to the latest home-talent production of the twenty or so children who inhabited the Kennedy compound at Hyannis Port during the summer.

He lounged late in his Hyannis Port bedroom one morning and told a visitor, "It all depends now on the Russians."

While he talked, Jackie sat next to him and John, Jr., climbed across his feet; then the President suddenly forgot about the communists and talked with relish about antiques for the White House.

In Washington he glanced over his two poached eggs at his weekly breakfast for the Democratic congressional leaders and said matter-of-factly, "We had no alternative but to go forward with nuclear testing."

He took pride in the fact that he had trimmed off ten pounds. Swimming in the pool with Dave Powers, he would dig in hard to strengthen his back muscles. He set his mind adrift, too. "I wonder," he asked Powers one day, "if Maris or Mantle will break Babe Ruth's home-run record?"

With a foot propped in his chair, he looked a reporter straight in the eye and said, "There is no question about Berlin—we'll fight."

When he was told that the millionth tourist of his regime was due to go through the White House, he joked, "Will he be a Cuban or a freedom rider or a woman in shorts?" (It was none of these. It was the very attractive Mrs. Edith Sprayberry, a schoolteacher from Rome, Georgia, selected, of course, with more thought to appearance and background than to precise numerical order.)

In Berlin, on order of the President, General Lucius Clay poked and prodded the communist wall. A war of credentials flared. Busloads of touring GI's were sent into East Berlin to make sure the gate stayed open. American helicopters watched the wall. Armed troops leered across at each other and tanks roamed the intersections to prevent trouble from starting.

John Kennedy ordered up the movies *Tiger Bay* and *Expresso Bongo*. He reread Alfred Duff Cooper's *Talleyrand* and told friends, "It's a great book."

Early one afternoon a small puff of sand appeared over Rainer Mesa and Kennedy, in Washington, announced that the United States had reluctantly completed its first nuclear-weapons test in nearly three years.

He stood up one night at a family dinner on the Cape and sang as if he were still a Harvard undergraduate, a simple sincere strain of "September Song." It came out in reedy tones that brought a tear or two from his sisters.

He flew off to Fort Bragg to review the Army's fire power and its new training program for guerrilla warfare, his special project. He personally ordered the Special Forces to resume wearing their green berets, which had been taken away by Pentagon brass. "I like those berets," he said. "The Special Forces need something to make them distinctive. My father even wears one now."

"I had plenty of problems when I came into office," he told his family once in a light mood. "But wait until the fellow who follows me sees what he will inherit."

Just twelve minutes after the first United States plane was buzzed by a Red fighter in the Berlin air corridors, Kennedy had received the news. "What are the instructions given to the Pan Am pilots?" he asked, nodded his approval when he heard. "Was it deliberate? Were the Russian planes lost? What do we do next time?"

On the Hyannis Port golf course it was the seventeenth hole, and he watched Jackie flail away in a sandtrap until he could not watch another time while the ball fell back at her feet. "Open the face of the club, follow through," he called from his golf cart. "Let me show you," he said finally, taking the club. He gave a couple of professional-looking practice swings, raised the club in a graceful arc, then brought it down smoothly and powerfully. The ball rose two feet, dribbled back into the sand. Kennedy looked down calmly, handed the club back to Jackie, said, "See, that's how you do it."

He pondered the action of the neutral-nations meeting in Belgrade, which poured more criticism on the United States than it did on Russia over the breach of the nuclear-testing moratorium. It was incomprehensible to Kennedy that these nations could have watched Russia resume tests, for which she secretly prepared for months while professing a desire for a test ban, and still find the United States equally guilty for the new round in the nuclear race. He was irritated by a visit from Indonesia's President Sukarno and Mali's President Keita, who hurried to Washington from Belgrade with a message urging the United States not to take any stand which might provoke war.

One close aide to Kennedy watched him and declared that he had broken through the "sound barrier" of his job. In the early days of his administration he had often seemed almost afraid to discuss the thought of nuclear war. Now he had come to live with it, minute by minute.

But trouble that found its way back to Kennedy was not limited to Berlin or to Laos or to the high reaches of the atmosphere, where new accumulations of fallout were drifting.

On the night of September 17, a Sunday, in the loneliness of the White House's international-situation room, a map-lined chamber in the basement of the west wing, Walt Rostow, deputy special assistant to the President, kept a sharp eye on the German election reports coming in from the State Department. Kennedy had a keen interest in them, and he had asked to be kept up to date. He had flown to Hyannis Port as usual for the week end, and Rostow was the duty officer assigned to scan the reports as they came in and send the vital ones on to the communications room in the basement of Hyannis' Yachtsman Hotel.

Rostow was also watching, but with somewhat less immediate interest, the progress of Dag Hammarskjold, who had kept in close cable contact with the United States concerning his moves in the Congo, where bloody fighting again had flared up in the continuing war between Katanga, which had seceded from the Congo Central government, and the UN troops, which, through Hammarskjold's insistence, were attempting to force Katanga back into the Central government.

Over the wire came the brief message that Hammarskjold's plane was overdue in Ndola. There was no cause for alarm, and Rostow did not worry. Yet just a bit of uneasiness crept into the night. Rostow decided to call this information to Hyannis along with some other intelligence.

Air Force Aide Col. Godfrey McHugh was the briefing officer for this week end. It was after 9 P.M. on Sunday when he got the short message from Rostow. Being an Air Force officer, McHugh worried more than Rostow. For many an Air Force man such short notices had been the start of an obituary. McHugh decided to drive the two miles to the President's home and give him a short briefing, including the late returns on the German election. The Air Force officer sped through the clear, cool night, was waved on at the white police pillboxes that guarded the Hyannis Port neighborhood and crunched to a halt in the Kennedy drive. The President was alone with his family. McHugh told Kennedy immediately about the Hammarskjold item. The presidential eyes shot McHugh a quick, piercing look. The same uneasiness that had first pervaded the White House basement minutes before had been transferred to the brightly lighted Kennedy living room.

In Washington more messages began to trickle in on Hammarskjold, and they were all negative. His plane had not landed, it was long overdue. Three more times that evening McHugh scurried out to Kennedy's home with scraps of intelligence, though nothing was conclusive. But all the men now had the gnawing sensation that here was more trouble for the world.

"Keep me advised," said the President as McHugh left his home for the last time that night.

In Washington, Rostow gave up the vigil in the early morning, went home for a few hours of needed sleep, then hurried back at 7 A.M. What he had feared stood all but confirmed. Hammarskjold was now more than twenty hours overdue. Searches were being organized to look for his plane. Rostow ate his breakfast in the situation room as he worked over the cables.

In Hyannis, McHugh gathered the cables from Rostow and drove back down the misty Cape roads to the compound.

He arrived before the President was up. At 7:30 A.M. the President awoke and called to McHugh to come to his bedroom, and McHugh gave him the glum news.

"It couldn't have happened at a worse time," said the President as he hurried back to Washington on his jet. The word had not yet come that Hammarskjold was dead, but there was only a slim hope that he was alive.

News Secretary Pierre Salinger first spotted the flash over the Reuters wire that Hammarskjold's plane had been found and that the UN General Secretary was dead. He tore the bulletin off, rushed into the President's office, handed the ragged piece of paper to Kennedy. The President read it in a glance and stood for a silent moment, shook his head, then turned back to his desk.

Again the Soviet Union had an advantage. The Russian tirade against the United Nations had reached fever pitch during the summer. They had not only demanded a three-headed directorate (Troika), but had also wanted to fire Hammarskjold and had hinted that they might walk out of the United Nations entirely. In short, they wanted to wreck the United Nations which, under Hammarskjold, was wrecking some of their plans.

The sixteenth General Assembly was due to open the following week. Kennedy had debated whether he should address the assembly, which was so sorely beset. Hammarskjold's death decided him. He would go to New York.

Kennedy stood before the General Assembly and, with warmth, restraint and eloquence, paid tribute to Dag Hammarskjold.

"We meet in an hour of grief and challenge. Dag Hammarskjold is dead. But the United Nations lives. His tragedy is deep in our hearts but the task for which he died is at the top of our agenda. A noble servant of peace is gone. But the quest for peace lies before us.

"So let us here resolve that Dag Hammarskjold did not live, or die, in vain. Let us call a truce to terror. Let us invoke the blessings of peace. And, as we build an international capacity to keep peace, let us join in dismantling the national capacity to wage war."

Once again he sketched the United States position on the

problems of the world, ending with a moving plea. "Ladies and gentlemen of this Assembly, the decision is ours. Never have the nations of the world had so much to lose, or so much to gain. Together we shall save our planet, or together we shall perish in its flames. Save it we can—and save it we must —and then shall we earn the eternal thanks of mankind and, as peacemakers, the eternal blessing of God."

In the meantime, backstage in the United Nations, Dean Rusk and Andrei Gromyko played diplomatic cat and mouse as they sought out each other without appearing to do just that, in an effort to talk about Berlin, to see if some compromise could not be reached. The evident desire of the Russians to talk hinted at one deep and satisfying development: The tension over Berlin was beginning to dissolve—slowly, ever so slowly, but it was going.

CHAPTER NINETEEN

REST IN NEWPORT

THE President of the United States can never genuinely take a vacation. The White House and its camp followers tag along with him. He must remain always at the end of those insistent cables from around the world. The Secret Service men must always prowl nearby.

But the President can at least leave Washington. He can hide himself away from the public and see other people besides politicians. This, however, it not as easy as it seems, even on vacation.

Towards the end of September, Kennedy bid Congress good-bye in a series of White House coffee hours. He was perhaps too easy with his praise for a Congress which passed 172 of his 355 requests. But they had come through with thirty-three important pieces of legislation (by New Frontier count)—not a bad showing for a President who won his election by two tenths of one per cent.

Then he headed for Newport, Rhode Island, for some uninterrupted time off. Naturally, before he could stretch out on the vast lawn of Jackie's parents' home, Hammersmith Farm, which looks out over Narragansett Bay, he had to wade through the remaining business.

On his jet flight from New York to Newport, following his United Nations speech, he signed ninety bills, part of those which the Congress had passed in its last gasp. He also appointed William Foster director of the new disarmament agency.

If Kennedy had ideas of sneaking into the gray mansion of Hammersmith Farm and starting his vacation in a low key, he forgot them as he landed at Quonset Point, Rhode Island. It is not possible for a President to arrive unnoticed. Tied up at the Navy pier was the aircraft carrier Lake Champlain, its entire crew in blues, manning the rail in silent tribute to their Commander in Chief. Kennedy was an hour and a half late, but the sailors stayed at their posts in the 90-degree heat.

A twenty-one-gun salute greeted the presidential plane, which blew out a tire on landing, thus causing the wires to hum with an exciting little story. Kennedy was unaware of the blowout until he was told of it after he left the plane, although five crash trucks had streaked down the runway after the plane, which pilot James Swindal wisely let coast to a stop so as not to endanger the other tire on the left landing gear.

There were 2,500 people to greet the Kennedys at the air station. A Navy band blared "Hail to the Chief" as the President shook endless hands, including those of Rhode Island Governor John A. Notte and his wife, not to mention Mrs. Claiborne Pell, wife of the Rhode Island senator, plus assorted lesser politicians. Nor did Kennedy escape the ceremonial function of trooping the line, this line consisting of a thirty-five-man Marine honor guard.

Finally the presidential couple boarded a helicopter and lifted up over the bay for Hammersmith. But ceremony was not over yet.

Newport Mayor James L. Maher, his wife, Newport Police Chief Joseph A. Radice and Police Capt. Arthur S. Maloney lined up on the grounds of Hammersmith in wait for the helicopter.

Caroline raced down into her father's arms, and he picked her up and carried her to the house. It looked for a moment as if there would be ease at last. Just then the local delegation of greeters moved in.

Mayor Maher pressed honorary-citizenship certificates onto both Kennedys. He also brought them a couple of souvenir plaques. Not stopping at that, Maher produced a guest book which, he slyly suggested, he would leave for the President and Mrs. Kennedy to sign, "when they wanted to." This is an old dodge, an excuse for another interview. Kennedy grabbed the book and signed on the spot, giving Newport one of his usually unidentifiable signatures. ("The only reason I know it is his was I saw him do it," said Maher later.)

The good mayor was not finished, however. He asked if the President might not make some kind of public appearance or at least allow the city-council boys to come around and say hello.

Kennedy smiled, reminded the mayor that he had come to rest, then quickly said to Maher, "You say hello to the council for me." With that he took Caroline by the hand and went into the house.

The logistics of a presidential vacation can be compared somewhat to those of a minor military invasion. Vast quantities of men and machines must be moved by land, air and sea. As Kennedy was parrying the thrusts of Mayor Maher, three Navy boats with the hundred or so assorted White House newsmen, broadcasters, Secret Service men, communications technicians, stenographers and other staff members were plowing through the rolling waters of the bay for the Naval War College, which would be the functioning White House headquarters.

The Navy had spiffed everything up, but as usual had overlooked one tiny detail: Dwight Eisenhower's big, smiling portrait still hung in the hall right outside the temporary staff offices. Overnight Eisenhower came down and Kennedy went up.

All the town's facilities were lined up for the President in case he wanted them. He could play golf at the Newport Country Club for free. The course was just across the road from the green pastures of Hammersmith. (The Auchinclosses were in Europe at the time.) The heated swimming pool of Mrs. Robert R. Young at her mansion, Fairholme, on the other side of the exclusive island, was ready for the presidential exercise period, should the President want it. He could use the swank private Bailey's Beach, and he could invade the sacred premises of the Reading Club and the Clambake Club.

The Secret Service had been over the farmhouse and staked out its guards. A direct White House phone line was put in the den. Marine helicopters had dutifully flown in Kennedy's special mattress and backboard from Hyannis Port, so that the presidential back would have its customary support.

At the naval base the huge network of teletypes and Western Union wires for the press and for the White House staff were working again. The President's yacht, the "Honey Fitz," had plowed up the coast from Annapolis and now lay at anchor awaiting Kennedy's pleasure.

Newport Police Captain Maloney had done handsomely. "No Parking" signs lined Ocean Drive along the borders of Hammersmith. A cop with a loud-speaker in his car shooed gawkers along their way if they decided to loiter.

In the windows of Newport stores hundreds of blue-and-white stickers proclaimed, "Welcome, President Kennedy." United States flags hung from staffs in further tribute to the Chief Executive.

Thus the President of the United States started a vacation.

The President put on slacks and sports shirt, sat in the marvelous Newport sun and little by little was forgotten. Only a dutiful trio in the press launch with a handsome new "White House Press" flag flying from amidships and a few curious pleasure boats trailed the "Honey Fitz" on his luncheon cruises.

Only twice in a week did Kennedy have to break stride. Once he came out of hiding to name John McCone the new Central Intelligence head and to pay tribute to the retiring Allen Dulles. Another time, for reasons that only a Massachusetts politician could fathom, Kennedy swore in Peter W. Princi (Winthrop, Massachusetts) as collector of customs for Massachusetts. The ceremony was on Hammersmith grounds, and for a moment it looked as if it might get out of hand. Princi brought with him his wife, five children, seventeen other relatives and three selectmen from Winthrop. Kennedy performed his duty and then, with the help of the Secret Service, cleared the grounds again.

The "Honey Fitz" slid out into the blue water of the bay, soothing strains of semiclassical music coming from the loudspeakers. Caroline romped over the decks of the ninety-two-foot yacht as Jackie snapped pictures. Caroline liked the sailors, and she engaged them in earnest conversation. Lieutenant Commander Walter Slye, a former riverboat captain, was the ship's genial commander.

Beside the "Honey Fitz," two black-and-white water-jet speedboats cruised with Secret Service guards. The small boats could go forty-five miles per hour and they were used to warn off insistent sight-seers, to take Caroline and her friends to the beaches to play while the adults ate lunch and, of course, to tow Jackie on water skis.

The "Honey Fitz" moved up the bay, its blue-and-white presidential standard, which denotes the presence of the Chief Executive, snapping in the breeze. Jackie put on a blue bathing suit, tugged on a blue swim cap and the top part of a black rubber skin-diving outfit. She called to one of the Secret Service boats, clambered down the ladder on the side of "Honey Fitz" into the little boat. A short way from the yacht she slid into the water, and then she was up on a single water ski, gracefully slaloming. After a few minutes she dropped the towline, swam to the "Honey Fitz" and changed for lunch.

The press boat lolled about 100 yards away while reporters watched with binoculars, an established ritual that every President had to endure. Once when Jackie was seen looking back through her own powerful glasses, the correspondents framed a facetious note and sent it to Salinger, protesting the first family's invasion of their privacy.

One day as the "Honey Fitz" lay at anchor in the bay, the big gray hulk of the frigate "Willis A. Lee" came slowly by after exercises at sea. Through the "Honey Fitz" radio the President asked if she could stop to allow him to look her over. Within ten minutes of getting the request, the frigate's commander, A. W. Cox, had turned out his 225 men on the rail.

The "Honey Fitz" poured on all of its eleven knots and passed by the towering ship, which is twice the size of a normal destroyer. Jackie held Caroline and pointed out the spectacle. The President of the United States stood on the fantail and gave the crew a big wave.

According to Navy tradition, when two ships meet, the junior commander must ask permission to "proceed on assigned duty." Cox dutifully radioed and got, not only permission to proceed, but also a special Kennedy thanks.

Even the world seemed to co-operate for Kennedy that week. It stayed in apprehensive but sustained calm. Dag Hammarskjold was buried in Uppsala, Sweden, the city in which he grew up. Dean Rusk caught up with Gromyko, invited him to lunch to talk about solving the Berlin crisis. And Richard Nixon announced that he would be a candidate for the governorship of California.

Kennedy pursued his newspapers as diligently as ever, either at Hammersmith Farm or on the fantail of the "Honey Fitz." And every day he was given a briefing on the supersecret intelligence reports that are prepared for him no matter where he is or what he is going.

There was more sun for the President, more water skiing for Jackie, and one day the crew of the "Honey Fitz" affixed an array of colorful balloons to the railing of the boat as a special tribute to Caroline and her little cousin, Ivan Steers, who was also staying at Hammersmith and who had become a regular passenger.

As the week went by, the White House correspondents studied the characters in the daily drama of the "Honey Fitz."

John Kennedy, as the head of the floating court, sat in his deep brown leather chair which is bolted to the boat's deck and talked, listened and read the newspapers.

Jackie was the persistent athlete, off on the waves on her water skis despite the chilly water.

Washington artist and friend Bill Walton seemed to be a budding Cecil B. deMille, appearing constantly with a movie camera and grinding out endless footage on the President.

Franklin Roosevelt, Jr., stood on deck like an old sea dog, surveying the water.

And Caroline continued to flirt with the sailors, often sitting with her legs dangling over the side, eating an apple and peering up at the young men in spotless whites.

Then the week was over. It was time for Kennedy to hurry

back to Washington to find out what Dean Rusk had learned about Berlin from Andrei Gromyko.

Despite all the hazards of being President, Kennedy found as he departed that it had been a restful week. "It's the best vacation I've had in two years," he told his staff.

CHAPTER TWENTY

GROWING

CONFIDENCE

THE rising spirits of John Kennedy were reflected in his mood and manner as midautumn came and faded. When he drove to the Statler-Hilton Hotel for a luncheon to observe the publication of the first four volumes of the papers of President John Adams and his descendants, he turned to Adams' great-great-great-grandson, Thomas Adams, and said, "It is a pleasure to live in your family's old house, and we hope that you will come by and see us."

Walking from his helicopter to his office on the White House's south lawn, he noted the abundance of crab grass and demanded that it be done away with.

To aides he declared in loud firm tones, "The budget has to be balanced." And with that challenge he dove into a careful review of budget requests.

One noon he slipped away from the White House totally unnoticed and drove to St. Matthews Church. It was National Prayer Day and Kennedy, undetected, sat in a dark rear pew. To many who had watched him through nine months of crisis, it seemed that his church attendance and the reference in his talks to prayer had become less mechanical and more meaningful.

While the world series was being played, Kennedy did what most other Americans did: he flopped in front of a TV set and watched. He became so engrossed in the opening game that he called his staff to come to his room for a meeting, so that he could see the final innings.

Mrs. Woodrow Wilson came by the White House to watch
the President sign the bill which would create a commission
to study plans for a memorial for her husband. "I want you to
move closer," said Kennedy when the photographers appeared. He helped the frail lady slide over. He handed her
the first pen he used, and she beamed, "Thank you. I didn't
dare ask for it."

"I hope," said Kennedy, turning to his visitor and those of
her family, "that the commission will plan a memorial that
expresses the faith in democracy and President Wilson's
vision of peace and a dedication to international understanding that President Wilson himself did so much to
advance. . . ."

The presidential temper was working, too. Spying a New
York *Herald Tribune* story about his short talk at the Adams
papers luncheon, the President erupted. He did not like the
lead of the story, which had picked up a remark the President had made that both he and Adams had spent a good
many days away from the White House. Kennedy's displeasure was relayed to Salinger, who called in the offending reporter, David Wise, who had just returned from a month's
vacation in Europe. "This is a hatchet job," said Salinger.
"As far as we are concerned, we'll send you back to Europe
for another month."

For visiting Sudan head General Ferik Ibrahim Abboud
there were Shakespeare excerpts in the East Room, the first
time the bard had invaded the White House. Two representatives from the Winchester Company measured Abboud for
a new high-powered hunting rifle, a gift from the President,
who chuckled appreciatively when Abboud asked, "Do you
know what the most dangerous wild animal is? The buffalo;
he thinks."

Sadness entered official life with the news that Speaker
Sam Rayburn lay dying of cancer in Texas. "I have learned
with deep sorrow of the serious illness of my friend, Speaker
Sam Rayburn . . ." began the statement the President issued.

Though Rusk and Gromyko had not come to any settlement in their New York talk, the Russians had at least shown

a willingness to talk. From Moscow the rumblings of Khrushchev had stilled somewhat, and gentle feelers came, seeking to find out what the United States wanted to do about Berlin.

Kennedy decided to talk it over with Andrei Gromyko, and once again the Soviet Foreign Minister flew down from New York.

On a Friday evening Gromyko was led into the Oval Room in the second-floor living quarters of the White House. The autumn sun cast its gold on the turning leaves that could be seen through the huge windows which frame the Washington Monument and the Jefferson Memorial in the distance.

The President, in his rocking chair, gestured to a lounge chair to his right for Gromyko.

"I'm sorry Mrs. Kennedy isn't here," said the President. "She's up in Rhode Island with the babies."

"Give her my best," said Gromyko, who was then engulfed by still photographers.

When they trooped away, the Russian sighed, "The invasion's over." Kennedy fumbled for a cigar, took the paper off and was preparing to light it, when the wave of movie photographers came at them. "Oh, no," cried Gromyko. Kennedy put his cigar away and waited.

For the first part of the two-hour, seven-minute meeting Gromyko droned out a tedious memorandum giving the familiar Russian position on Berlin.

Then John Kennedy got a chance to talk. He and his aides had sensed that the Russian position was softening and, in fact, the Soviets seemed to want to talk about Berlin more than the United States did. It was the Kennedy strategy to back away from the idea. So far, Kennedy told the Russian, the Soviet Union had made no acceptable proposals for any possible bargain; until it did, the United States was not interested in negotiations.

On the subject of the Russian plan to internationalize Berlin, in exchange for undefined guarantees of access, Kennedy looked his visitor in the eye. "You have offered to trade us an apple for an orchard. We do not do that in this country."

Kennedy had prepared well for this second encounter with Gromyko. As the meeting ended with a fruitless discussion on Russia's impossible Troika concept for the United Nations, the President casually picked up a book from a nearby table, thumbed through it until he found the place he wanted. Then he silently handed it to Gromyko to read.

It was a poem by Ivan Andrevich Krylov, taken from a collection of the Russian's fables published in Moscow. It was called "The Swan, The Pike and The Crayfish." Gromyko shifted in his chair and read as Kennedy watched him.

> When among partners concord there is not,
>   Successful issues scarce are got
> And the result is loss, disaster and repining.
>
> A crayfish, swan and pike, combining,
> Resolve to draw a cart and freight;
> In harness soon, their efforts ne'er abate.
>   However much they work, the load to stir refuses.
>
> It seems to be perverse with selfwill vast endowed;
>   The swan makes upward for a cloud,
> The crayfish falls behind, the pike the river uses;
> To judge of each one's merits lies beyond my will;
>   I know the cart remains there, still.

Gromyko threw back his head and laughed when he had finished. "Yes," said the Russian, acknowledging that this had been a good stroke, "but those are animals. We are talking about people."

Light had faded and the stars sprinkled a clear fall night as Gromyko hurried to his car to take Kennedy's message back to Khrushchev.

"We touched on several important matters," Gromyko blurted to newsmen. "Of course, as far as the position of the Soviet Union is concerned, we stressed first of all the importance of a peace treaty with Germany. I think that this conversation is useful."

As Gromyko was caught in the TV lights, Dean Rusk shouldered through the reporters, unnoticed. In the shadows he summed it up more accurately. "It was interesting, but that is about all you can say about it."

*   *   *

Kennedy began to look around his country.

It was an encouraging sight. Across the United States, 82,000 reservists and National Guardsmen prepared to answer a call to active duty. Old memories, old fighting names were back on people's lips. Bands played for Main Street parades. There were farewell parties, homes broken up in some cases, and jobs quit in others. There was grumbling, but not much. The people were answering Kennedy's call of the hour. And the people were like those 10,000 officers and men who made up Wisconsin's 32nd Division which had fought in the Meuse-Argonne during World War I and in the Pacific in World War II: the men of the Red Arrow Division were as good as ever.

The President flew to the bedside of Sam Rayburn. When he left the room of Mr. Sam at Baylor University Hospital, he walked down the corridor, head lowered, jaw grimly set. "They don't make them like that any more," said the President, breaking the silence. "He has the courage of ten men."

Back in Washington, he sat down with his defense chiefs to talk over the military budget. On one manpower figure he looked up, puzzled. It was an adequate strength when the world had peace, his men told him. "We don't have world peace," snapped Kennedy. "Let's be realistic."

Deciding that he needed a fresh hard look at the growing trouble in South Vietnam, he dispatched Maxwell Taylor to that country for a realistic report.

"We went out on one mission and found another," wired the general. Sent to study primarily the military problems of the threatened small nation which was being plagued by communist infiltration, Taylor reported that the political corruption and the civil disaster were of such proportions that something should be done about these problems before turning to military matters. Six months of hard work were needed in the country to straighten it out internally before the major question of whether this nation should send troops or not should even be considered, Taylor cabled.

Disagreeing with other more pessimistic reports from the area, Taylor felt that we had time in South Vietnam. For President Ngo Dinh Diem's army there was desperate need for radios, helicopters, boats. More training, reorganization of troops in the field and better logistical support were other needs. It was not a happy picture which Taylor drew, but it was not hopeless either, as some journalists wrote.

The men of Kennedy's administration began to speak more of this country's great strength.

No better words were spoken than those of Roswell Gilpatric, who talked to the Business Council in Hot Springs, Virginia. "Our confidence in our ability to deter communist action, or resist communist blackmail, is based upon a sober appreciation of the relative military power of the two sides. The fact is that this nation has a nuclear retaliatory force of such lethal power that an enemy move which brought it into play would be an act of self-destruction on his part. The United States has today hundreds of intercontinental bombers capable of reaching the Soviet Union, including 600 heavy bombers and many more medium bombers equally capable of intercontinental operations because of our highly developed in-flight refueling techniques. Our carrier strike forces and land-based theater forces could deliver additional hundreds of megatons. The number of our nuclear delivery vehicles, tactical as well as strategic, is in the tens of thousands: and, of course, we have more than one warhead for each vehicle."

This was the nourishment that the country needed at that time.

An old man in a baggy gray suit dropped by the White House as October came to an end. Carl Sandburg, poet, Lincoln scholar, and expert on anything and everything, sat in the Cabinet Room waiting to see the President. "The way he is doing is almost too good to be true," said Sandburg about Kennedy. "There has never been a more formidable set of historical conditions for a president to face since Lincoln."

One of the new conditions was Russia's monster bomb. It exploded in the Soviet Arctic with a force of fifty-eight megatons, the largest man-made explosive in history.

The White House had been prepared for the blast. Kennedy wanted the news immediately. When at last it came over the wires, White House aides ran to tell the President.

They could not find him in or around his office. It was Dave Powers who located him: Kennedy was reading a bedtime story to Caroline.

The hints from the New Frontiersmen that our own atmospheric nuclear tests might take place before long came with frequency. Adlai Stevenson first sounded off in the United Nations that this nation, in self-protection, might have to test in the air. Then McGeorge Bundy, in a little-noted speech, had this to say: "It is obvious that massive atmospheric testing by the Soviet Union creates a new situation. While very large explosions like the one last week are senseless and irresponsible acts of international outrage, the Soviet series as a whole must be assumed to have military importance."

Kennedy left no doubt on November 2. He locked himself in a morning meeting of his National Security Council, which gave final approval to a statement on nuclear testing that he was about to make. The White House brimmed with officials, who rushed in and out. Even former President Harry Truman was invited to the meeting. "Get out of my way," Truman cheerily shouted to reporters. "The President wants to see me. I don't know what this is—all I know is the President said he wanted to see me and here I am."

At 12:37 Kennedy entered his office to give the statement before TV cameras. He was as grim at this moment as at any time during his presidency. Without a word he walked to his desk. He sat down and the cameras started to grind, but Kennedy did not like the small reading platform in front of him.

"Just a moment," he said. "Just stop taking pictures for a minute."

He lifted the platform off and laid his paper down on his desk.

"The United States is carefully assessing the current series of nuclear tests being conducted by the Soviet Union. . . . In view of the Soviet action, it will be the policy of the United States to proceed in developing nuclear weapons to maintain this superior capability. . . ." No tests, said Kennedy, would be undertaken just to frighten the world, as the Russians had done, but only to maintain our edge in nuclear technology. "In the meantime, as a matter of prudence, we shall make necessary preparations for such tests so as to be ready in case it becomes necessary to conduct them."

From then on until April 25, when the first United States shot exploded in the air over the Pacific, Kennedy did not change his course. He did not announce his decision, for he still clung to a thread of hope that some test ban might be worked out with the Russians. Also, there was no need to harvest world criticism for testing during the months the United States would need to prepare its tests.

Kennedy was gruffer with guests, more abrupt with staff. In a late-evening meeting with French Ambassador Hervé Alphand he said bluntly that he was growing weary of French objections to his efforts to solve the Berlin problem without any French offers of help. Much the same tone he used with West Germany's Ambassador Wilhelm Grewe. He was tired of the rumors that we would abandon West Berlin; we would make no concessions to the Russians at West Germany's expense, nor would we let West Berlin slip away. Yet he told the German that there was little hope for German reunification as long as Russian troops and the communists controlled East Germany.

One night he rocked furiously and slapped his thighs, pulled up his socks, obviously feeling in top form physically and mentally. "It's going better," he told me. "We're making a little headway here and there."

Why did he not speak out, as Roswell Gilpatric had done about our own power? Kennedy shook his head. "I don't want to get up against Khrushchev like we were last year." He took both fists and brought them together as if they were two heads smashing against each other. "I want him to be able to get off the hook in this thing. I don't want to force him into anything. When I get up and say those things it sounds too belligerent."

He turned to journalism, always a favorite subject. "You know, editorial writers should all come to Washington for a while, and Washington reporters should all get out of Washington for a while. That would do more good than anything I can think of. They just don't understand what is going on in the other place. There was an editorial about reciprocal trade and it said that we might put it off a year because we were afraid it was too tough politically. Now they just don't know the facts. The politicians are the ones who want to go ahead, and the diplomats are the ones who want to postpone it a year. George Ball over in the State Department says that the effects of the Common Market won't be known for a year and it would be better to work out a trade act after we see what that all means. But Larry O'Brien says we'd better go ahead next year because otherwise it might look like we are afraid. How can you win?"

He leaped out of his rocker, walked out of his office and grabbed the Washington evening *Star*. "Look at this," he cried, thumping a picture of Eisenhower and Truman making friendly eyes at each other. "Isn't that something?"

With an eye on his legislative hopes for the coming year, Kennedy flew off to Poteau, Oklahoma, to visit Senator Bob Kerr, emerging as the most powerful single figure in the Senate. There, city boy Kennedy sat in the feed lot of Kerr's ranch and watched prize black Angus cattle parade by. Beside him sat the ranch manager, Dr. Paul Keesee. During the short cattle show Kennedy plied Keesee with questions about the cattle business.

Though always beyond his years in politics, the art of making a living was something which multimillionaire Kennedy did not fully understand. Having lived in the protection and comfort of his father's vast fortune, he never experienced the anxieties of a wage earner. Once when asked if he remembered anything about the depression, he admitted frankly that it had not interfered in his life. He learned about the depression only in history books in school. The "big experience" in Kennedy's life had been the war.

Sitting on the low platform that had been especially constructed for his visit, Kennedy became fascinated by the cowboys who herded Kerr's cattle before him. He leaned over to Dr. Keesee and pointed to Arthur Gee, a tanned man with sloping shoulders, thin as a reed and with the look of the range about him. "I'd like to meet him," he said.

"What are the salaries of cowboys?" asked Kennedy. He was told that they amounted to about $200 per month, but

that cowboys got a home and free milk and other side benefits. Kennedy mulled over the information.

"Now, tell me about how cattle are mated," he said to
Keesee. "When do they have calves? How many cows can you
breed to a bull each year?"

The questions kept coming. Kennedy was in a strange
world. Not only were the economics foreign, but he was not
one who understood farmers or ranchers. Often during his
campaign days he remarked about the melancholy appearance of the people he met in the farm states. He found them
colder than the miners and factory workers. He wondered if
the lonely country life was as good as it was sometimes adver-
tised to be.

With Congress recessed, with winter coming, it was a time
for reflection in the White House. And it was a time to assemble some of these thoughts and to talk about them.

In the University of North Carolina's stadium he spoke
about living in the gray times of the cold war, when neither
total victory nor total defeat was possible. "It is a dangerous
illusion to believe that the policies of the United States can
be encompassed, stretching as they do worldwide, under
varying and different conditions—can be encompassed in
one slogan or one adjective, hard or soft or otherwise, or to
believe that we shall soon meet victory or total defeat. . . .
Peace and freedom do not come cheap, and we are destined,
all of us here today, to live out most—if not all—of our lives
in uncertainty and challenge and peril. . . ."

He went to Arlington National Cemetery on Veterans
Day. The sun that morning hung in its low fall orbit, sending
its light into the hills above the Potomac River, flooding the
white sepulcher of the unknown soldier from World War I,
glancing off the marble slabs that mark the graves of the unknowns from World War II and the Korean War. The people from Washington, in bright fall clothes, streamed up
through the rows of small white stones. Across the river the
dome of the Capitol and the Washington Monument stood
up boldly. The strains of "America, the Beautiful," played
on the cemetery carillon, aptly described the scene.

Each of us who follows the President year in and year out has his own moments of special significance. Sometimes they are the big events—the war threats, the meetings of heads of state. But sometimes they are little-remembered occasions that do not get headlines, that are forgotten by most people minutes after they happen.

For me, November 11, 1961, in Arlington Cemetery was one of those occasions. Perhaps it was the beauty of the day. Perhaps it was the President's words. Perhaps it was just the feeling of strength and peace that I got standing amid our nation's great memories and looking at Washington, the feeling that once again we had lived in a year of danger and we had emerged wiser and stronger.

As John Kennedy entered the cemetery grounds, a gun began to boom its melancholy salute. Cars glinted far away on the Potomac bridges, and even the murky water of the river reflected the blue sky.

In silence the President placed a wreath on the tombs of the unknowns, and then he stepped back to listen to taps, the haunting tones gliding over the valley and echoing faintly back.

He turned and strode into the amphitheater.

"Today we are here to celebrate and to honor and to commemorate the dead and the living, the young men who in every war since this country began have given testimony to their loyalty to their country and their own great courage. . . . Bruce Catton, after totaling the casualties which took place in the battle of Antietam, not so very far from this cemetery, when he looked at the statistics which showed that in the short space of a few minutes whole regiments lost 50 to 75 per cent of their numbers, then wrote that life perhaps is not the most precious gift of all, that men died for the possession of a few feet of a cornfield or a rocky hill or for almost nothing at all. But in a very larger sense, they died that this country might be permitted to go on, and that it might permit it to be fulfilled, the great hopes of its founders. . . . There is no way to maintain the frontiers of freedom without cost and commitment and risk. There is no swift and easy path to peace in our generation. . . ."

*　　*　　*

Mr. Sam died, and a saddened John Kennedy flew west to say farewell to the Speaker: Sam Taliaferro Rayburn who had been born and reared on the dusty plains of Texas, the son of a Confederate cavalry officer who had ridden to Appomattox with Robert E. Lee; Sam Rayburn, who had served in the House of Representatives longer than any man in its history—forty-nine years—a man who had been speaker for 17 years, more than twice as long as Henry Clay, his nearest competitor, a man who had served with eight presidents. An age was passing away.

The young President paid his tribute on a gray, chilly day in Bonham, Texas, but not before he had taken a firmer hold as freedom's leader.

In the University of Washington's Edmundson Pavilion in Seattle, the President had spoken more optimistically than at any time since assuming office. He had talked back to the critics of the far right who had called Kennedy "soft" and demanded more military bluster in world affairs. And he had answered those pundits who constantly criticized him for not having a grand plan for the direction of the world. In the crimson academic robe of a Harvard LL.B. he had said: "We cannot, a free nation, compete with our adversaries in tactics of terror, assassination, false promises, counterfeit mobs and crises. . . . We cannot abandon the slow processes of consulting with our allies to match the swift expediencies of those who merely dictate to their satellites. . . . In short, we must face problems which do not lend themselves to easy or quick or permanent solutions. And we must face the fact that the United States is neither omnipotent nor omniscient— that we are only 6 per cent of the world's population—that we cannot impose our will upon the other 94 per cent of mankind—that we cannot right every wrong or reverse each adversity—and that, therefore, there cannot be an American solution to every world problem. These burdens and frustrations are accepted by most Americans with maturity and understanding. . . . But there are others who cannot bear the burden of a long twilight struggle. They lack confidence in our long-run capacity to survive and succeed. Hating communism, yet they see communism in the long run, perhaps, as the wave of the future. And they want some quick and easy and final and cheap solution—now. There are two groups of those frustrated citizens, far apart in their views. . . . On the one hand are those who urge upon us what I regard to be the pathway of surrender—appeasing our enemies, compromising our commitments, purchasing peace at any price. . . . On the other hand are those who urge upon us what I regard to be the pathway of war, equating negotiations with appeasement and substituting rigidity for firmness. . . . Each side sees only 'hard' and 'soft' nations, hard and soft policies, hard and soft men. The essential fact that both of these groups fail to grasp is that diplomacy and defense are not substitutes for one another. Either alone would fail. . . ."

CHAPTER TWENTY-ONE

A WAY OF LIFE

H E New Frontier grew to be more than government. It became a way of life, it became Washington's new society, it became sensitivity to the arts, no better illustrated than through Jackie's broad program of restoration for the White House. It was a vigorous outdoor life of riding, swimming, golf, tennis, boating and touch football, not to mention skiing and hiking and softball. And, in fact, it all became so vigorous sometimes that it was overdone, a step beyond good fun. Bob Kennedy's Hickory Hill estate became headquarters of the cult because of the confining atmosphere of the White House.

Walt Rostow found himself striding over the dewy ten acres in Virginia as he talked about guerrilla warfare before breakfast. Max Taylor took to the new Hickory Hill tennis court.

Pierre Salinger was unceremoniously tossed in the Kennedy swimming pool as a fitting end to a huge lawn party. Teddy Kennedy dived in on his own accord, just out of sheer exuberance.

A journalist interviewing Bob Kennedy found himself striding up and down the side of the swimming pool, shouting his questions as Bob swam. When one question offended Bob, he simply submerged, swam under water to the other side of the pool, crawled out and stalked off up the hill, leaving the perplexed newsman standing.

A Secret Service agent found himself singing nursery

rhymes on board the Kennedy sailing sloop in Hyannis Port as it headed, brimming with children, for a picnic on a beach.

Don Wilson, the United States Information Agency's deputy director, met a Kennedy tennis challenge in his bare feet. Many a brave man plunged headlong into the rose bushes on the Hyannis Port lawn to catch a touch football pass. Guests of the Kennedys at Stowe, Vermont, could only win endorsement if they hurtled down near-vertical ski slopes. And those intimate friends who vacationed with Bob and Ethel found that 5 A.M. was a reasonable time at which to expect the first athletics—and there was no curfew.

The President did his back exercises, carefully prescribed by New York University's Dr. Hans Kraus, on the floor of his jet plane, in his bedroom and occasionally in the pocket-sized White House gym. He frequently challenged his chubby Press Secretary to do pushups. He asked his entire staff at one point to lose five pounds each. After seeing some tough paratroopers at Fort Bragg, he prodded his own desk-bound military advisers into a fitness course.

White House staffers Ted Sorensen and Mike Feldman hurried downtown in the mornings for a tennis game before work. And Under Secretary of the Navy Paul Fay, a personal friend of the President's, became so fitness-conscious that, as he flew around the country for speaking engagements and inspection tours, he took to challenging the young gobs to pushup contests.

It was not athletics alone that demanded such verve. Every activity was to be engaged in at full throttle. When the word spread that John Kennedy read 1,200 words a minute and read everything in sight, White House staffers enrolled in speed reading courses, even set up a special class in the White House. Ian Fleming's mystery books were devoured, as were such other Kennedy favorites as *Melbourne* and vast quantities of history. One White House aide tried to assemble a shelf of all the books written by New Frontiersmen, no small task.

Loud and sloppy dress disappeared among and around the Kennedys. Pierre Salinger, after a struggle, gave up his California-type shirts with their pink, yellow, orange and green hues. Only in the most casual moments did he feel safe wearing them. On some occasions he was noted wearing a vest. The pendulum had swung.

The button-down shirt, which the President declared out of style, disappeared as well.

Naturalness became the rule. Bob and Ethel Kennedy came to Hyannis airport to pick up Central Intelligence Agency Director Allen Dulles and loaded him, to his delight, in a convertible full of children. When the stiff White House protocol made no sense, Kennedy simply ignored it. He lingered by the door at night to bid his party guests good night when the rule book said that he should have gone upstairs and let the guests find their way out. He grabbed people and shoved them in the receiving lines when he thought they should be there, and rank and order meant nothing.

He could kid his famous guests, as he did the day he greeted India's Prime Minister Nehru in Newport. On the "Honey Fitz," gliding by the great mansions of a past era, Kennedy casually waved to the huge homes and said, "I wanted you to see how the average American family lives."

Harry Truman and Bess were invited to stay overnight at the White House for the very simple reason that the Kennedys thought they might enjoy it. They did—immensely. Margaret and her husband came too.

The gaudy expense-account restaurants became less chic as the Kennedys established the smartness of dining at home. Night-clubbing was not on their agenda much, either. Nor was heavy drinking. The gentle sipping of a daiquiri or a bloody Mary was about as far as liquor went.

It was not what people were, it was what they could do. Under this rule a new official society was born. Those who had talent, not money alone, were asked to the White House. They included a vast spectrum, from workaday newsmen to titled foreigners.

By right of office the first couple can control official society. But sometimes in the past, as with Bess Truman and Mamie Eisenhower, they simply did not want to. As the luster of Jackie's entertaining became known, it became obvious that the Kennedys were now society.

The newspapers which arbitrate found little space for other events. A White House whing-ding swept all else off the pages. Caroline's birthday parties, Jackie's Virginia horseback riding, the President's cruises on the "Honey Fitz," the first couple's house guests—these were the headline materials. The huge stiff embassy receptions, which had been forever and probably will continue forever, dwindled to mere paragraphs buried on the inside pages with the grocery ads.

The successful hostesses were those who got the President and his wife to their homes (such as Mrs. John Sherman Cooper, wife of the Republican senator from Kentucky) or, next in line, the Robert Kennedys (the Don Wilsons). Next important were the other members of the family, then came close friends, and then the frighteningly intelligent members of the New Frontier, such as Arthur Schlesinger, Jr., Walt Rostow and McGeorge Bundy.

Gone, or at least out of sight for the time being, were the mastodons who had ruled in previous eras simply by the heft of their bankbooks. Perle Mesta had taken flight after endorsing Nixon loudly and publicly, and she stayed in New York making plans to return to Washington after a decent interval. But when she finally did come back to the capital, she did not make the splash she had predicted. Something funny had happened to her on the way to the New Frontier.

Gwen Cafritz looked in every mail, but there was no invitation to any of the White House soirees. She threw her annual "Supreme Court" party in October and carelessly let it conflict with a White House affair. Not a single Supreme Court Justice showed up.

A gay party giver of lesser years, Scottie Lanahan, F. Scott Fitzgerald's daughter, also made the fatal miscalculation and gave a party on the same night the Kennedys were having one of their intimate gatherings for the people they liked. Mrs. Lanahan got the third team, those not invited to the White House—hardly a smashing success.

Another of Mrs. Cafritz's affairs which managed to lure only a thin sprinkling of New Frontier talent was described by one of those who attended as "the most uninteresting collection of people that anybody could find anywhere."

The Kennedy group was described by one Washington society writer as "the richest, prettiest, most interesting" young people in the country. As a matter of fact, the praise was so lavish that it grew a little heavy.

Government was the code name. The Kennedys described what they were doing as the most interesting thing in the world. Public service was the challenge. Those who answered the call and who did well and who got to know the Kennedys and whom the Kennedys liked were apt to be society.

Some of the rich young men around the nation heard the call. Paul (Red) Fay took a biting cut in salary when he left the family's lucrative construction firm in San Francisco and came back to be Under Secretary of the Navy at $20,000 per annum. So did Don Wilson when he gave up heading *Life* magazine's Washington bureau to work for the United States Information Agency.

There was another side to the picture, however. Kennedy's friend Bill Walton found that the demand and hence the price of his paintings went up as his association with the White House became known. Chuck Spalding, who had joined with another young man to start an obscure investment office, suddenly became a noted New York investment banker in the newspaper columns. K. LeMoyne Billings, a New York advertising executive, found that his stature in the trade rose in direct proportion to the degree he became known as a close friend of the President's. Correspondent Charles Bartlett found increased interest in his column "News Focus" when his old friend John Kennedy was elected and took office.

Money still helped around Washington, but it did not rule. An eager young couple with imagination and wit could lure the cream of the New Frontier into a tiny Georgetown garden for an evening of folk singing when the Cafritzes and the Mestas could not entice them to come out.

Almost forgotten in their stone mausoleums were the old, old Washington society. "We don't even cover those old ladies with canes any more," acknowledged one society reporter.

Jackie's entertaining deserved its reputation, because she worked at it. Each affair was a new creation. She crawled on the floor among diagrams as she arranged the complex seating. She went over the menus minutely. She made sure to know what food each guest could and could not have.

There used to be an embarrassingly silent time at official functions as the guests were pushed into line to shake hands with the President and his wife. Jackie added the soothing music of the President's own red-coated Marine band to coax her guests through that half hour.

When Finland's President Urho Kaleva Kekkonen and his wife came to visit in October, they were ushered into the State Dining Room for lunch. It was decorated in blue and white flowers, the colors of the Finnish flag. The Marine band played *Finlandia,* and in the private quarters on a table Jackie had arranged the dolls which Mrs. Kekkonen had sent earlier as a present to Caroline. Aware from her study that Mrs. Kekkonen liked art and antiques, Jackie gave her a set of books on American art, antiques, homes and literature. And when the men went off to talk business, Jackie arranged for the Finnish lady to visit Mount Vernon and the National Gallery of Art.

In mid-November the Kennedys scored another first: Pablo Casals played in the East Room. The 84-year-old cellist had refused since his self-banishment from his native Spain in 1939 to play publicly in any country that recognized Franco. But as a special tribute to Kennedy, he had come back to the White House after fifty-seven years—the first time since he had played as a youth for Teddy Roosevelt.

American composers from across the land were invited to the white-tie affair. So were the leading patrons and critics of music. There were other noted guests, such as New York Mayor Robert Wagner and labor leader George Meany.

Casals was superb, and so were the praises that echoed for days. (Months later, still being complimented on the fact that her husband had done so much for music through the Casals performance, the story goes that Jackie kidded, "The only music he really appreciates is 'Hail to the Chief.' ")

Not only was this a new kind of society, it was a new tribute to culture.

The Kennedys both felt that American artists and performers should be honored by being invited to the White House, that American arts and skills should be displayed for the world to see in this manner. Culture was not only to be enjoyed in this country, but to be spread abroad as a peaceful tool in the cold war.

And then, of course, if John Kennedy was allowed to slip in a couple of reporters, some key congressmen, a labor bigwig or two, it did not really offend anyone and it certainly helped in the old grubby political war.

Adding to the new Washington life was the new grace and charm of the White House itself.

Jackie had set out with determination to restore the interior that Thomas Jefferson had originally planned for the building. For all its majestic proportions, which came from Architect James Hoban in 1792, the inside was a hodgepodge. There was no unifying theme to its furnishings, and in most cases no authenticity. The old building had been through a violent and diverse history. Abigail Adams had hung her wet laundry in the unfinished East Room back in 1800. Dolly Madison had added a green bathtub and, fleeing before the advancing British Army in 1814, had ordered her servants to smash the frame of the famous Stuart painting of George Washington so that she could save the picture. Jackson hauled a 1,400-pound cheese into his quarters for a final reception before he retired from office, smelling the place up for months. Martin Van Buren sold $6,000 worth of furniture, some of which James Monroe had purchased in France and smuggled into this country to avoid criticism from local craftsmen. Abe Lincoln's Union soldiers slept on the White House couches with muddy boots, cut up the drapes for souvenirs. And Chester Arthur, sniffing that the White House looked like a "badly kept barracks," auctioned off twenty-four wagonloads of furniture and hired Louis Comfort Tiffany to redecorate the place to look like a steamboat gambling parlor.

Jackie Kennedy cared. She felt that the time had come when the White House should cease to be just living quarters for a President, when it should become a "national object," to be cared for like a museum. "I don't know why I feel that way," she said. "How can you help it? When you read Proust or listen to Jack talk about history or go to Mount Vernon, you understand."

When she had first moved into the White House on that cold inaugural day, she was overwhelmed with it all. "Everything we had came in little boxes," she recalled. "I was so confused. They were painting the second story and they had moved us way down to the other end. The smell of paint was overpowering, and we tried to open the windows in the rooms and we couldn't. They hadn't been opened for years. When we tried the fireplaces they smoked because they hadn't been used."

But there was one room in the mansion that had survived the waves of gilt and plush. It was Lincoln's old Cabinet Room, now known as Lincoln's bedroom. And there still was the massive bed, the furniture that Lincoln had used, the atmosphere of Old Abe.

"Sometimes," said Jackie, still recalling the first days of her White House tenure, "I used to stop and think about it all. I wondered 'What are we doing here?' and 'What are we going to be doing in a year or so?' I would go and sit in the Lincoln Room. It was the one room in the White House with a link to the past. It gave me great comfort. I love the Lincoln Room the most, even though it isn't really Lincoln's bedroom. But it has his things in it. When you see that great bed, it looks like a cathedral. To touch something I knew he had touched was a real link with him. The kind of peace I felt in that room was what you feel when going into a church. I used to sit in the Lincoln Room and I could really feel his strength. I'd sort of be talking with him."

Jackie Kennedy glowed when she talked of her project. This was a world she loved.

She appointed a Fine Arts Committee to oversee the undertaking. She hired a curator. She formed a scouting party of herself, the curator and a secretary, and she led them through the fifty-four White House rooms and sixteen baths looking for forgotten or hidden treasures.

"I had a backache every day for three months," she said.

In a ground-floor men's room she and her troop found the stained and chipped busts of Andy Jackson, George Washington, Christopher Columbus, Amerigo Vespucci and John Bright. All of them were nose to nose in a stony and dust-laden conference that must have been going on for years. All were priceless sculpture, more than 100 years old.

In a carpenter shop, propped up for a handy workbench,

was a massive Bellange pier table from the days of James Monroe. It was rescued.

A butler gestured toward some age-blackened knives and spoons in the cluttered storage shelves deep in the White House basement and said, "There's some old junk in there." Jackie and Lorraine Pearce, her curator, gently picked out the pieces, put them in a soap-pad box, then back in the temporary curator's office they dropped on their knees and studied them: this was some of the gold and silver flatware which President Monroe had ordered from France in 1817.

In the huge White House storage sheds in Fort Washington, Virginia, she found some chairs that had been Rutherford Hayes'. At first she hung the portrait of Andy Jackson in the Red Room. But then she noted an old photograph of Lincoln's Cabinet, and the picture had been hanging on the wall in Lincoln's second-floor offices. Jackie moved Jackson to where Lincoln had placed him.

Word of the project spread, and money and antiques came in. "I approve of what you are doing to the White House as much as I disapprove of your husband's policies," wrote one woman. There were no partisan lines to this undertaking.

In the first flood of gifts and purchases, Jackie received furniture which had belonged to George Washington, Abraham Lincoln, the Madisons, James Monroe, Martin Van Buren, Nellie Custis and Daniel Webster. Secretary of the Treasury and Mrs. C. Douglas Dillon gave a room full of Empire furniture including Dolly Madison's own sofa. Miss Catherine Bohlen, of Villanova, Pennsylvania, donated a chair from the original set of furniture James Monroe had ordered for the Blue Room. So it went.

One morning Jackie tied her hair with a lavender ribbon and launched another expedition in the house. I followed her this time. In low-heeled shoes she walked through the corridors and the rooms. She had poked into them all and she knew them well. She waved at the new dining room which she had made out of Margaret Truman's old bedroom. "You had to wait an hour for a pat of butter or else go down the elevator yourself," she explained. The kitchen had been in the basement, but under her direction a small family kitchen had been installed next to the new dining room, in the space that used to be Miss Truman's dressing room.

She worried about the West Hall, which had become the first family's sitting room. "There is no central fireplace," she fretted. In New England fashion, she liked a hearth in the center of a room.

On she went. She paused in the second-story Oval Office. Beyond the windows was Harry Truman's famous balcony and the spectacular view of the Washington Monument and the Jefferson Memorial.

"This is a beautiful room," she said. "I love it most." Then she looked up and out the windows. "There's this magnificent view. It means something to the man who stands here and sees it—after all he's done to get here.

"I've added paintings here to help out," she said with a look at the West Hall. "Six Sargents, two Winslow Homers, some Prendergasts, all from the National Gallery."

Jackie tapped an elegant round table with a marble top in the center of the room. "We found out from an old bill of sale, where the dimensions are listed, that this was an original Monroe piece."

Out in the big hall she walked on. She motioned to the walls, now partially covered with paintings of American Indian scenes and landscapes of the Far West. "All the art here is going to be American," she said. "This comes from the Smithsonian. There is wonderful American art and I want to display it."

At the far end of the second floor Jackie went to the door of the Monroe Room and looked in. "This had been the furniture dump of the White House," she laughed.

In the State Dining Room, she paused and looked. "It is rather pure," she said. "All 1902. We're making it lighter, however, by repainting."

"Everything is reproduction," she frowned in the Red Room. "The red damask is Renaissance and that isn't right. I've tried to relieve some of the redness by putting pictures high up on the walls."

In the Blue Room she grew excited. "Teddy Roosevelt went over everything in this room and they made it a wonderful plain blue. Then in 1948 they added a basket pattern to the design and that doesn't belong. The room is so formal and useless. It needs a round table and it could be one of the best rooms. It is a very hard room to do because it has four doors and none of them are lined up. You can't center things in it."

In the China Room, where the great collections of famous china and silver are kept, mostly behind lock and key, the First Lady commented, "It is such a shame to lock it all up and never use it. We're going to use some of it now."

On down into the basement she charged, through the cement corridors with their bare light bulbs, on through the screened-off storage areas with shelves of glassware and china and knickknacks that had belonged to presidents.

She rummaged through the dusty shelves. A black smudge appeared on her neck.

"Look, look," she cried. "Look at that Lincoln cake plate." She reached in and lifted out the fragile piece. "I wonder if there is enough china here to set nine places for tonight. Senator Gore would love to eat off Lincoln's plates."

In the map room, which had become the curator's head-quarters, cluttered with donated objects, Jackie stopped and stared about her, the wonderful feeling of the past soaking in. Then she turned. "My mother brought me to Washington one Easter when I was eleven. That was the first time I saw the White House. From the outside I remember the feeling of the place. But inside all I remember was shuffling through. They didn't point anything out. They didn't even give you a booklet telling about it. I didn't remember anything specific. Mount Vernon, the National Gallery and the FBI made a far greater impression. I remember the FBI because they fingerprinted me."

Just to get the feel, she sat in a refinished and reupholstered Monroe chair that was to go in the Blue Room. She hefted other chairs and busied herself in a box of vermeil, black with age but promising to yield more White House secrets.

There was no end to what might be uncovered. Curator Lorraine Pearce paused to contemplate a passage from a history book which quoted a letter of Dolly Madison's written to her sister in haste on August 23, 1814, only hours before she fled from the British. "At this late hour," Dolly wrote, "a wagon has been procured: I have had it filled with the plates and most valuable portable articles belonging to the house. . . ." After reading this, Mrs. Pearce asked aloud, "I wonder if there are not more things which Dolly Madison took out before the fire that no one knows about?"

"Before everything slips away," said Jackie, "before every link with the past is gone, I want to do this. When the last Civil War veteran died a year or so ago, that was a break with the past. I want to find and go to all these people who are still here, who know about the White House—the nephews of the sons, the great-grandchildren, the people who are still living who remember things about the White House."

Then again she became reflective. "I want every little boy who goes through this White House to get some sense of history, to be shown things and have them explained. But I also want it aesthetic. Girls must go out and make homes, and I want it not only to seem significant but to give them a sense of beauty so they will be inspired in their jobs."

CHAPTER TWENTY - TWO

A NEW YEAR

THE old year had to be tidied up and a new one begun. Though the world had stilled, it was still a dangerous place. Though Kennedy felt more confidence in himself and his government, he had just barely made a start on his mission.

Stern tests lay ahead, this he knew fully. But everyone had learned a lot in the first year—even the country. Its faith in itself seemed more solid, and that was the bedrock of everything.

To the Cabinet Room John Kennedy summoned his National Security Council and a roster of other top administration aides in late November. On the coffin-shaped table lay a thin book, bound in light-blue paper and stamped with a red TOP SECRET. It was a scientific and intelligence estimate of the results of the Soviet nuclear-test series.

Until then the New Frontier had been inclined to believe that the Russians had not learned anything startling from their explosions.

The core of the report was a cold analysis by a group of scientists headed by physicist Hans Bethe. It amounted to the fact that the Soviet Union had made immense progress in strategic thermonuclear weaponry and that they were coming up fast in tactical atomic abilities. If the United States sat still, there was real danger that the Russians would soon surpass this country.

They clearly had made progress on an antimissile missile. They showed a capability for developing atomic weapons with vastly more explosive yield per pound of weight than American scientists had thought them capable of doing before. There was evidence that they had improved on the triggering device for the hydrogen bombs.

The men around the table glumly weighed in with warnings about the future.

"All right," said Kennedy. "Just what did you gentlemen expect after all of the Soviet shots?"

If there was much doubt that the United States would resume atmospheric testing in the coming April, it diminished now as word of the report leaked out.

But as the grim weapons race went on, so did the race for the minds of the people of both countries. Kennedy again shattered precedent. He granted an interview to Alexei Adzhubei, editor of *Izvestia* and Khrushchev's son-in-law. For two hours in the living room of his Hyannis Port home, Kennedy answered Adzhubei's questions. True to the agreement, the full text of the interview was published in the Russian paper, a notable breakthrough in communications.

And one week Kennedy fixed up his State Department the way he wanted to. The change came with such swiftness that it caused few ripples. Dean Rusk called Chester Bowles back from a Harvard-Yale football week end, and on a Sunday when the gray State Building was quiet he told Bowles that he was not to be Under Secretary any longer. Waiting outside Rusk's office was White House Counsel Ted Sorensen, who then talked soothingly with Bowles for two hours to convince him that the President still wanted him, but in a different post. The following day Kennedy flew to Washington, called Bowles to the White House and made him Special Representative and Adviser to the President for African, Asian and Latin American Affairs. To replace Bowles, Kennedy named George Ball, Under Secretary for Economic Affairs. He moved George McGhee, then head of policy planning, into the job as Under Secretary for Political Affairs. And from the White House went Walt Rostow to take McGhee's old post.

Other minor shifts finished the job, and Kennedy flew off to the Army-Navy football game as calm as could be.

Kennedy, the former Navy lieutenant, lectured to fifteen of his Army commanders, who had come back to this country from their posts around the globe for some Pentagon updating. They stood somewhat self-consciously in a semicircle around the President in his office. "Mr. President, these are your commanders around the world," said Secretary of the Army Elvis Stahr. "I realize that this is entirely a coincidence that this meeting occurred at the time of the Army-Navy game," began the President. When the laughter died down, he stuffed his hands in his pockets and became serious.

Certainly, he told the generals, they were skilled in their work and he was unskilled, but there were two or three things he would like to say.

They were experts in conventional war, he said. But that was not enough. Now they would have to learn about the internal wars—insurgents, guerrillas, counterguerrillas, police activity. This was the war Khrushchev had sketched so plainly in his speech of January 6 that year.

"And just military competence is not enough," Kennedy declared. The new leaders would have to know politics, economics, government administration and intelligence techniques. It was vital, he added, that they went out to find and train this new breed. There would be no letup in his insistence that we master guerrilla warfare.

Not long before, he had listened to his military experts discussing what small arms to send to Vietnam. Kennedy asked to see what we had to offer. The brass hastily rounded up an old M-1 rifle, a new M-14, the World War II carbine and a new Armalite weapon developed by the Air Force. Sitting in his chair, the President hefted them all, sighted out the window to get the feel of the guns. "You know," he said finally, "I like the old carbine." He turned to his experts and asked them if the gun was satisfactory for the Vietnamese. He was assured that it was. "You aren't going to see a guy 500 yards in the jungle," he mused, half to himself. Why not send them carbines, since this nation had thousands of them in surplus piles? A problem was solved.

* * *

As the first year faded, he was sometimes shorter with critics. Listening to the words of a disapproving university professor, Kennedy snapped, "Where does he sit? At that university, not here where decisions have to be made."

Yet humor certainly had not left him. In New York, talking at a luncheon for the National Association of Manufacturers, he wryly noted that most of them had supported his opponent in the election "except for a very few who were under the impression that I was my father's son."

In Miami the very next day he spoke to the Young Democrats and brought a merry shout when he said, "For all I have been reading for the last three, four or five months about the great conservative revival that is sweeping the United States, I thought that perhaps no one was going to show up. Artemus Ward once said, about fifty years ago, 'I am not a politician and my other habits are good also.' " Just down the street in Bal Harbour, Fla., Kennedy greeted the annual CIO-AFL convention with, "It's warmer here than it was yesterday."

As Christmas neared, the first couple stood in a Venezuelan farmyard and looked down at life-weary peasants. Jackie wore a dress and coat of apricot-colored linen and silk. And the President, slender and tanned, was everything that New World wealth had wrought. Yet they were not resented; their dignity and sincerity came through. "We will be more than good neighbors," said the President. "We will be partners in building a better life for our peoples." Speaking in Spanish, Jackie added, "No fathers or mothers can be happy until they have the possibility of jobs and education for their children. This must be for all and not just a few."

There was personal sadness. When the President returned to Washington from his highly successful South American visit, Joe Kennedy, the family patriarch, was struck down with a stroke on a Palm Beach golf course. In his office John Kennedy broke off a conversation with Pierre Salinger, picked up his phone and after a tense conversation replaced the phone on the hook, looking stunned. "Dad's gotten sick," he told Salinger. Then he flew off for Palm Beach to be at his father's bedside.

The press began its summing up of the first year of the New Frontier and the new President. It was for the most part cautiously favorable, noting the punishing times that he had been through, noting also that he had seemed to learn and learn fast. The view of the second year was one of hope.

A thoughtful Eunice Shriver, who had watched her brother closely during these hard months, commented, "I never heard him say once during the year, 'What a fool I was.' "

Kennedy himself was laconic. "There's this fantastic responsibility. . . . But it's an interesting job."

The Oval Office with its awesome quiet remained. The white shaft of the Washington Monument could still be seen in the early December night. John Kennedy sat again in this atmosphere and talked.

"It's been a tough first year, but then they're all going to be tough. We're in better shape now, but there are so many chances for trouble because the world is full of trouble."

The President turned from his visitors for a moment, strode out to the adjoining office and picked up the evening paper. He beckoned to a barber to come in. The man spread a white barber's cloth in the center of the thick green rug with the great eagle of the United States woven into it. He placed a chair in the center of the cloth. Mechanically the President of the United States sat on the chair, tilted back on its hind legs. The guests glided quietly out a side door. There came the clip, clip, clip of the barber's shears. But the President for the moment did not hear or see around him. His eyes squinted at the fine print. His mind, his soul were engaging themselves in the new problems.

For the New Frontier, 1962 began auspiciously enough. Kennedy's second State of the Union message did not have the deep verbal knells of the year before. It was a skillful hedge between pessimism and optimism.

On a February morning the New York society band of Lester Lanin still was going strong when the White House party given by Jackie Kennedy for her in-laws the Stephen Smiths suddenly began to buzz as if a giant electric shock had been sent through it. Guests hurried down the halls for phones. The President departed and went to his room but did not undress and go to bed. Pierre Salinger, whose affinity for parties is famous, rushed off to his office, never having taken a drink all evening. It was near 3 A.M. when all became clear. A call from Berlin reported that Francis Gary Powers, the pilot of the high-flying U-2 reconnaissance plane which had been brought down over Russia on May 1, 1960, had been exchanged for the Russian master spy Rudolf Abel, who had been captured in this country in June, 1957. Reporters tumbled out of bed and rushed, first to hear Salinger tell the news, then off to a darkened Justice Department, where Edwin O. Guthman, assistant to Bob Kennedy, related the mysterious story of New York attorney James B. Donovan's negotiation of the exchange in East Germany in a sequence of events that did justice to any mystery book.

Later the same month, on a sunny afternoon, the President's Naval Aide Tazewell Shepard rushed into his office. "Mr. President, Colonel Glenn is on the line."

Kennedy walked to his desk, stood behind it and picked up the receiver.

"Hello," said the President. Hearing no answer he boomed into the phone, "Colonel?"

"This is Colonel Glenn," came the faraway voice. Indeed it was Col. John H. Glenn, Jr., 40, the American astronaut who had just made three successful orbits in space around the earth and had been plucked out of the Atlantic Ocean and was standing safely on shipboard.

"Listen, Colonel, we are really proud of you, and I must say you did a wonderful job," Kennedy yelled into the phone. "We are glad you got down in very good shape. I have just been watching your father and mother on television, and they seemed very happy. . . . Well, I am coming down to Canaveral on Friday and hope you will come up to Washington on Monday or Tuesday, and we will be looking forward to seeing you there."

"Fine," said Glenn. "I will certainly look forward to it."

Kennedy had a last thought. "How was the trip?" he

asked, not realizing the circuit was already cut. He put the phone down and smiled. It was a time for the whole country to smile, because the United States was definitely in the space race.

And in early March Kennedy went before the people to announce that we would soon be entering another race: ". . . I have today authorized the Atomic Energy Commission and the Department of Defense to conduct a series of nuclear tests—beginning when our preparations are completed, in the latter part of April. . . ."

The President kept a watchful eye on Berlin, still a sore spot. His intelligence reports told of tension in the air corridor. An exchange between a Soviet flyer and his base went something like this: "I'm flying two meters above him [transport plane]. . . . I can see his expression and he can see mine. . . . I am waving him down. . . . He is waving back. . . . He did not move. . . . Can I have permission to shoot him down. [No answer.] . . . Can I get permission to shoot. [Still no answer.] . . . I'm breaking off and returning. . . ."

However, the next crisis was not in Berlin. It occurred in Kennedy's office.

CHAPTER TWENTY-THREE

CRISIS WITH STEEL

APRIL seemed to be a fateful month for John Kennedy. In 1961 it brought the Bay of Pigs. In 1962 it brought Roger Blough, chairman of United States Steel Corporation.

Tuesday, April 10, was a sunny day, full of spring. Caroline's pony Macaroni had grazed leisurely in the tender shoots of grass behind the mansion before taking his young mistress for a ride as Jacqueline Kennedy watched.

Blough called first about 3 P.M. from his New York headquarters. The call was taken by one of Kenny O'Donnell's secretaries who reside in the office outside the President's. It was a normal call. "I would like to see the President this afternoon on a very important matter concerning steel," he told the girl. Would it be possible to arrange an appointment for later in the afternoon? Blough was leaving his office in a few minutes to fly to Washington. He would check for confirmation when he arrived.

His request was not particularly surprising to O'Donnell, who took it to Kennedy. Blough had gained rather easy access to the Oval Office over the preceding months. He was chairman of the Business Advisory Council, which Kennedy treated very tenderly in an effort to keep matters smooth with the business community. And since the preceding fall Kennedy and Labor Secretary Arthur Goldberg had become deeply involved in the negotiations between the steel workers and the giant steel companies.

Kennedy had come into office with the firm belief that the

key to a successful administration was more stability in the national economy. He was convinced by considerable argument from the men around him that he must somehow solve the riddle of our current stagnation and send the nation into a period of sustained expansion. Without it our own strength would suffer and the strength of the free world would be in peril. But economic growth need not be accompanied by rounds of inflation that rob the productive increases of their rewards for the people, reasoned Kennedy. There could, with a diligent government and conscientious labor and business leaders, be boom times without inflation.

Essential to this end was the price of steel. It had not been raised since 1958, and in June of 1962 a new contract with the United Steel Workers was due.

As Kennedy saw it, an increase in the price of steel would not only bring new wage demands from the steel workers, but would send its ripples throughout industry, causing price increases in virtually all other fields because steel was such a basic commodity. Likewise, harsh labor demands if won by the United Steel Workers would cause steel to boost its prices, starting the cycle.

Kennedy and Arthur Goldberg had launched their campaign for a "noninflationary" steel settlement early in July of 1961. When Blough brought his Business Advisory Council to a White House meeting with Kennedy, there was time before the council meeting for Blough, the President, Goldberg and David McDonald, President of the Steel Workers, to sit down and talk about the coming contract negotiations.

Three more times before this April would these four men get together to go over the problem. Two of the meetings, in September and January, were so secret that no news accounts were written about them until months later.

Out of this came a contract between big steel and the steel workers that called for no wage increase and only a ten-cent-an-hour boost in fringe benefits. It was hailed by Kennedy and labor as "noninflationary." Now steel prices would not need to be raised. This had been the reason why the President had brought management and labor together and had argued for the national interest. He congratulated both sides.

On April 10 Kennedy was still basking in the glow. It

seemed that price and wage stability could be achieved.

But as Kennedy reflected on Blough's request for a meeting, he became a little disturbed. There had been a rumor over the week end that one of the big steel companies might actually be ready to hike its prices, despite the favorable labor agreement. Kennedy called Goldberg to see what he knew. Goldberg gave the President a totally negative answer, declaring that he had just the opposite reading—as far as he knew, no steel price increases were anticipated by anyone.

Arriving in Washington, Blough phoned the White House again and was told that he could see the President at 5:45. He was prompt and was taken to the Cabinet Room to wait for the President. For a change the President was almost on time and Blough had to linger only a couple of minutes. He seemed no different than usual to the staff members who had grown used to seeing him come in. ("He was in a jolly mood," said Kenny O'Donnell later. "He bounced in like a man who was about to cut steel prices.")

There was the friendly Kennedy handshake and smile, the gesture to the couch while Kennedy took his rocking chair. The goodwill soon terminated, however.

Roger Blough had come to tell Kennedy that United States Steel Corporation was raising steel prices $6 a ton.

The news was in a four-page news release which Blough handed to the President and which Kennedy hastily read. "I think you're making a mistake," said Kennedy.

He looked at the release again. Then he quickly went to his office door and asked Mrs. Lincoln to get Goldberg in a hurry. The Secretary of Labor arrived in less than five minutes. And his first reflex was to start to argue with Blough against a price increase.

"Wait a minute, Arthur," said the anguished President. "Read the statement. They've raised the price. It's already done."

Kennedy's initial shock began to wear off and he got angry. But it was controlled anger. Goldberg was not so restrained. He declared the price rise to be a mistake. He sharply criticized Blough for sitting in the meetings whose whole purpose had been to prevent a price rise and never hinting that a price increase was intended, indeed, on the contrary, accepting all along the offices of the President to help get a favorable labor contract and, having achieved that, announcing the price increase. This deception as much as anything was incomprehensible to Goldberg and Kennedy.

They asked Blough to reconsider, but he would not. Goldberg told Blough that he had defrauded the American people, flouted the national interest, and that not only the steel industry but all industry would now suffer. Goldberg said that his own credibility as a man who could bring management and labor together had been destroyed by this act, that labor's demands in the wake of Blough's performance would be harsher than ever after this faithless performance by management. Blough was unbending, patiently repeating the need for the price increase. For fifty minutes the meeting went on. Kenny O'Donnell wondered what was happening because of the unusual length of such a session with the President. The news by then was coming over the wires from coast to coast.

Blough left and Kennedy paced furiously, flopping now and then into his rocker. Staff members Bundy and Sorensen, waiting on another matter, came through the door. When they saw the President so agitated, they did not take chairs but just stood in the office, watching Kennedy. Goldberg remained, and Associate Press Secretary Andy Hatcher entered. O'Donnell was there also.

And then came the fateful phrase about the big steel men.

"My father always told me they were sons of bitches, but I never really believed him until now." [1]

[1] In his May 9th press conference Kennedy was asked about the reports of this. "The statement which I have seen repeated as it was repeated in one daily paper is inaccurate," he explained. "It quotes my father as having expressed himself strongly to me, and in this I quoted what he said, and indicated that he had not been on many other occasions wholly wrong.

"Now, what was wrong with the statement was that as it appeared in the daily paper it indicated that he was critical of the business community and the phrase was 'all businessmen.' That is obviously in error, because he was a businessman himself. He was critical of the steel men; he worked for a steel company himself, and he was involved when he was a member of the Roosevelt administration in the 1937 strike, and he formed an opinion which he imparted to me, and which I found appropriate that evening. But he confined it, and I would confine it. Obviously these generalizations are inaccurate and unfair, and he has been a businessman, and the business system has been very generous to him. But I felt at that time that we had not been treated altogether with frankness, and, therefore, I thought that his view had merit. But that is past. Now we are working together, I hope."

Kennedy sent for Walter Heller. Goldberg put in a call to David McDonald. There was immediate concern for McDonald's position, since he had led his steel workers into the new contract. McDonald's position was considered none too solid anyway; this new move might injure him badly. But in his conversation with the President and Goldberg McDonald was quite calm about it, suggested that the White House should give the union some public support for its good faith.

For nearly two hours Kennedy roamed his office, discussing what to do. It was plain to the President that he had to fight back. The first thing involved was his manhood. Nobody, not even enemies, had respect for somebody who would lie down and take such a beating. Goldberg said flatly that if nothing was done he would resign as Secretary of Labor.

Further, there was still a chance that the steel price might be rolled back. Five steel firms followed U.S. Steel's lead immediately and raised prices. They represented some 85 per cent of production capacity, but the front was not solid yet. Perhaps Kennedy could hold the crack in the door open and by other pressures force the giants back into line.

Kennedy was on the phone. He called Robert McNamara, who was in a strategic position for this fight because of all the defense orders for steel and also because of McNamara's lingering friendships from the world of business, including many steel executives. Kennedy phoned Douglas Dillon, then in Florida, who, like McNamara, could help in contacting crucial people. Kennedy talked to his brother and he called Clark Clifford back into service.

What could be done? There was the possibility of antitrust action, based on the unusual circumstances of all the major companies announcing their price increases at once. There was the thought of trying to divert some defense procurement to the companies who held the price line. There was even the suggestion of price and wage controls. And, as always, in Congress there were a handful of proposed bills— Tennessee's Albert Gore had one suggesting regulation of steel prices, and Estes Kefauver, the other Tennessee senator, had a bill calling for advance notice of such price increases.

But at that moment, as the sun began to fade in Washington, none of these plans seemed promising. The one great weapon immediately available was an appeal to public opinion. Kennedy had a press conference scheduled for the next afternoon. He could, and he would, lay his outrage before the people.

Now and then as the staff members watched Kennedy, they made attempts to find something good in the situation. The steel companies had only hurt themselves, the people would rally around the President more than ever before, they suggested. Kennedy would have none of it. "This is a setback," he snapped. It hurt everything he was working for —price stability, a balanced budget, ease in the trade barriers, reduction of the gold flow, unemployment.

As a year before, when the Cuban invasion was beginning to crumble, Kennedy had to leave his office around 8:30 to dress for the annual congressional reception. Thinking of the coincidence of timing as he went out, Kennedy managed some humor: "I'll never have another congressional reception."

But unlike the reception of a year ago, where Kennedy could not share his misery, this one proved to be a working session. Lyndon Johnson was at the President's elbow, offering his help in the offense against big steel. Albert Gore was there, ready for battle. Kefauver ambled by and said, "I think the steel price increase is awful." Arthur Goldberg turned up in the Red Room, and there he and the President held a lengthy council of war.

In the meantime the office lights burned in the west wing of the White House and in the Executive Office Building. Walter Heller's staff was busy amassing economic figures. Ted Sorensen was toying with ideas for the press-conference statement. Goldberg left the reception and went back to his office, where he put down his thoughts in a memorandum.

A final and bitter touch was added during the night. About 10, a messenger delivered a letter to Walter Heller's home, but Heller was still in his office, working. It was a handwritten message on a small piece of blue note paper from the Sheraton-Carlton Hotel.

"Dear Walter," it read. "I discussed the enclosure with the President briefly late today and thought you would like a

copy. Hope to discuss it with you sometime soon—Roger."
The note was clipped to a copy of the U.S. Steel price statement. It naturally became known as the "Dear Walter"
document and was placed among other exhibits in the White
House file, which was growing by the hour.

On the following morning, when Kennedy had breakfast
with his aides, they brought their ideas and figures with
them. Normally such breakfasts break up at 9:30, but this one
lasted until 10:30 as the men worked over the points Kennedy should make in his TV appearance in the afternoon.

Back in his office, Sorensen fitted and refitted the phrases,
and Kennedy himself added and subtracted words. The statement, which would open the conference to be carried on live
TV, was actually not finished until 3:22, just eight minutes
before air time. Then Kennedy got up from his desk and
walked to his limousine. On the short drive to the New State
Department Auditorium he still mulled the sentences over.
He barked questions at Sorensen and Hatcher, who rode
with him. When had the last big company signed its contract
with the Steel Workers? When did the contracts go into
effect? When had Blough put out the public statement about
the price increase? Be sure about it.

After his first outburst Kennedy's anger had subsided into
determination. But for the press conference a controlled fury
was a necessary act. Kennedy was a superb performer.

I recall lounging in a front-row seat in the well of the auditorium waiting for the press conference to begin and specu-
lating with *The New York Times'* E. W. (Ned) Kenworthy
on just how tough Kennedy would be. We all knew he would
be critical. But I had never seen Kennedy in my years of
covering him sustain more than a few seconds of public anger,
a luxury that men hungering for high public office can rarely
afford. My hunch was that by now his energy was all focused
in his secretive effort to pressure the steel companies to
rescind their action, that his public statement would be rather
a moderate and logical appeal to reason, thus riling no more
people than necessary while he hunted for the jugular in
the back rooms. New Englander Kenworthy was of a different mind. "I think he's really going to give it to steel," he
said. We made a bet.

Kennedy came out the side door, and I first noticed that the slight, wry smile that he usually gave to the correspondents who knew him was missing. He did not even look at them. He strode across the carpeting, teeth set, jaw a bit out. Two assistants, Hatcher and Jay Gildner, followed in a cloud of gloom. He placed his papers on the rostrum, stiffened both arms and gripped the stand. I sensed that I had lost my bet with Kenworthy.

"Simultaneous and identical actions of United States Steel and other leading steel corporations increasing steel prices by some $6 a ton constitute a wholly unjustifiable and irresponsible defiance of the public interest. In this serious hour in our nation's history, when we are confronted with grave crises in Berlin and Southeast Asia, when we are devoting our energies to economic recovery and stability, when we are asking reservists to leave their homes and families for months on end and servicemen to risk their lives—and four were killed in the last two days in Vietnam—and asking union members to hold down their wage increases, at a time when restraint and sacrifice are being asked of every citizen, the American people will find it hard, as I do, to accept a situation in which a tiny handful of steel executives, whose pursuit of power and profit exceeds their sense of public responsibility, can show such utter contempt for the interests of 185 million Americans. . . ."

It was Kennedy's most withering public fire. Roger Blough watched the show in silence in his New York conference room.

The mood pervaded the rest of the press conference. Rarely did Kennedy smile. Once, pointing to a questioner, he growled, "Yeah?"—something that he had never done before in a news conference. In answering other questions he would return to the steel issue just to make sure that everyone knew his concern.

Kennedy walked out of the auditorium as unsmiling as he had come in, and he went straight to a small anteroom, where he sat down for a few seconds. He did not speak. And when aides came to him to congratulate him on the manner in which he had presented the steel statement, he just stared at them in silence. He was not at all happy.

Kennedy's offensive began to pick up steam. When Bethlehem Steel Corporation's President Edmund Martin began to deny a statement attributed to him by newsmen that there should be no price increase in steel if American firms were to remain competitive, Bob Kennedy sent the FBI out to establish the facts. The zealous agents routed reporters out before dawn, and immediately the Kennedys were accused of gestapo tactics. Other FBI agents, armed with subpoenas, swarmed into the steel-firm offices to hunt for incriminating evidence. The Justice Department announced it would start a grand-jury investigation to see if the steel industry had violated antitrust laws through collusive pricing. Bob Kennedy said that his department was going to consider whether U.S. Steel ought to be broken up on the grounds that it had monopoly power to set the industry prices. From the White House came the facts and figures to "prove" that U.S. Steel did not need a price increase. Government attorneys went to work on emergency legislation that called for a rollback of the increases for ninety days. In Congress Kennedy won support from the liberals. Estes Kefauver declared that his Antitrust and Monopoly Subcommittee would probe the industry.

Kennedy had assembled an informal task force to plan the steel offensive. It first met at 8:50 A.M. on April 12. Ted Sorensen was the leader of the group when the President was not there. There were Lee Loevinger, head of the Justice Department's Anti-Trust Division; Arthur Goldberg; Robert McNamara; Walter Heller; Larry O'Brien; Bob Kennedy; Paul R. Dixon, head of the Federal Trade Commission; Henry Fowler, Under Secretary of the Treasury; Nicholas Katzenbach, deputy Attorney General; and James Tobin, a member of the Council of Economic Advisers.

Only a few minutes after the meeting started Kennedy came in with a fistful of telegrams. He pushed them across the table. "We're way ahead," he said. The first tally of the public response to his press conference was 2.5 commending him to 1 criticizing. The White House kept a close eye on these returns because the public attitude was a huge factor in the struggle. (There was an uneasy moment when the first telegrams were placed on one aide's desk. He picked up the top one and read: "Mr. President, why are you picking on the steel industry?")

Kennedy complained to the men around him about the morning column of Scotty Reston, which had pointed out in good humor that it was just a year ago that Kennedy had been in the midst of the Bay of Pigs misadventure. Good humor or not, the President did not want the notion spreading that he was involved in another Bay of Pigs. Before he rushed off to meet with the Shah of Iran, who was visiting Washington at the time, he asked that public opinion be kept aroused. Cabinet officers McNamara and Hodges and Dillon were to hold press conferences. These men were to detail just what the increase would mean for farmers, white-collar workers, laborers.

As the task force worked at the problem, the men began to eliminate the impractical suggestions. Price and wage controls were out of the question—too drastic an action. The suggestion that tariffs be reduced to allow foreign steel into this country, thereby forcing American prices back, was also abandoned. The influx of foreign steel would damage the steel workers as much as the industry management.

McNamara was not very optimistic about the pressure which could be applied by selective procurement of steel for defense needs. In only a few instances, he pointed out, could orders be shifted without hurting the national interest.

Roger Blough took to television in New York to answer Kennedy, but his sincere, fact-studded appeal was smothered by the din from Washington.

Kennedy did not bother to watch. "I don't need to listen to him," he snapped. But the White House took notice, just to be certain. The Army Signal Corps, which handles the President's communications, recorded Blough's performance on tape to hold at the ready should the facts be needed. (Kennedy was much less reluctant to listen to himself. Back in the White House after his own press conference, he had dialed in a replay of the press conference and listened intently. At one point, anticipating the next day's journalistic opposition, he had turned to his aides: "I can tell you what the New York *Herald Tribune* editorial will say tomorrow.")

The phone lines from the White House and from all the major departments of the government grew hot from the calls to steel executives around the country.

Goldberg and Clark Clifford kept the communications open between Washington and U.S. Steel, arguing that the company should roll back prices. Bethlehem was another target, particularly since President Martin was in such an uncomfortable spot for having made his statement before the price increase was announced.

But Roger Blough's Achilles' heel was Inland Steel, Chicago. With its central location, this firm, the eighth biggest, had a snug market and was in a position to cut into the markets of the eastern giants. Inland had not joined the other six companies in the price hike but waited cautiously in the wings. Inland's chairman was Joseph L. Block, a member of Kennedy's Labor-Management Advisory Committee, but he was in Japan. However, Goldberg and Under Secretary of Commerce Edward Gudeman called their friends Philip D. Block, Vice Chairman of Inland, and Leigh B. Block, an Inland vice president. Philip Block told Kennedy that he was not at all certain his firm could hold prices down. But for the time being, he said, perhaps ten days or two weeks, Inland would not boost prices. The news, announced on Thursday, was a strong gain for John Kennedy. "Good, good, very good," he said.

McNamara, in examining his procurement orders, found that he could add some persuasion. The Navy's Bureau of Ships promptly announced that a $5,500,000 order for steel-plate for Polaris submarines, which normally would have been split between U.S. Steel and Lukens Steel Company, the only two producers of this type of steel, would go entirely to Lukens, a firm which had not raised prices.

Friday morning Walter Heller had some interesting calculations. He had figured that the companies which were holding prices down comprised about 16 per cent of the production capacity of the nation. He estimated that with the business the government could swing to these companies and the extra business they would get from the natural play of competition, they might gain some 9 per cent of the market, bringing their capacity to 25 per cent. McNamara pointed out to Sorensen's war council that this might not seem like much change in the picture, but it should be remembered that not a single steel company would want to lose 9 per cent of its business. Heller could have gone further. Steel executives were acutely aware of the fact that to gain or lose a fraction of 1 per cent of the market in a year was highly significant in terms of the huge gross sums of steel's annual business.

Meantime there had come the first hint that Kennedy's offensive might be making headway. Thursday night Clifford had met secretly with U.S. Steel officials in Washington. He had urged a price rollback. The steel men had been firmly against it, but they did want to continue talking about the developing situation. About midnight Thursday, Clifford phoned the President in the White House to tell him of this slight crack in the door and to report that if steel wanted to talk more, Roger Blough would phone him the next morning.

Blough did phone early and asked that they continue to discuss the matter. Kennedy sent Clifford and Goldberg hurrying to New York.

While Ted Sorensen's battle group kept up its fire, Kennedy had to turn to other things. On Friday he flew off to Oceana, Virginia, to join the Navy for a week-end review at sea.

His big jet roared into the Naval Air Station, and Kennedy climbed out into a chill, 30-knot wind. He received military honors, gave a wave to the crowd and turned to board his helicopter.

It was then that the flash came from Washington: Bethlehem Steel had rescinded its price increase. And about an hour and a half later, as Kennedy finished inspecting the nuclear submarine "Thomas A. Edison" and stepped back on land there were calls from the White House and New York reporting total victory: U.S. Steel had taken the same action as Bethlehem. As he boarded the command cruiser U.S.S. "Northampton" for his night at sea, Kennedy, though still somewhat amazed at his swift conquest, was thoroughly pleased. "I think the other companies will all follow now," he said. "They can't afford not to." He drafted a statement commending the steel companies for their action.

Saturday, as Kennedy stood on the foredeck of the

"Northampton" steaming down a double row of ships nine miles long, steel prices were back to where they had been at the start of the week.

As soon as price rollback came, arrangements were made for a reconciliation between Blough and Kennedy, to take place the following week at Blough's convenience. And so on Tuesday morning, just seven days after he had phoned and started the steel drama, Blough was on the line again, this time to Mrs. Lincoln.

"This is Roger Blough," he said. "The man you've been reading about." As before, he had no trouble getting an appointment, this one for 6 P.M.

On Tuesday noon before Blough was due, Kennedy stared out of his office into a soft, spring day and reflected on the whole steel episode. The magnolias near his windows were blooming, so was a fringe of red tulips. Workmen were unrolling sod in the new Rose Garden. He walked out along the porch and headed for the mansion and lunch. He was still mulling over the steel matter.

"Roger Blough is coming to see me this afternoon," he said abruptly to a companion. "I suppose he wants to re-establish communication. I'm sympathetic to him."

What would be the President's attitude now toward business, he was asked. Was it war in the old F.D.R. style?

At the ground-floor elevator Kennedy punched the button; when the door slid open he entered silently. Then he suddenly turned to his questioner. "No, no, we're not going to do that. They're our partners—unwilling partners. But we're in this together. I want business to do well. If they don't, we don't."

The living quarters of the White House were quiet, and the President walked across the hall to his room for lunch. On the stand beside his bed where he stretched out was a book—*On Moral Courage* by Sir Compton Mackenzie.

He was concerned deep down about the aftermath of the steel episode, it was plain. He had won the price battle. But had he lost the business community? So far there was no indication that such was the case. There had been the expected outcries from the Republican industrial strongholds. Editorial reaction was split. Blough's timing of the announcement and, indeed, even the need for a price rise had been questioned by some leaders of industry as well as by the New Frontier. Congress had remained calm and the public had not stirred much and, if anything, seemed to like to see a tycoon assaulted with such skill. Yet, it was still pretty early, and any earth tremors down in the bedrock would not have had time to come to the surface.

Reflecting some of this apprehension, Kennedy talked on. "No, no. There's no war. I'm not against business—I want to help them if I can. But look at the record. I spent a whole year trying to encourage business. And look what I get for it. . . . What do they mean by all this 'antibusiness' stuff anyway? I don't get it. Point out to me a single instance in the last year when I've said anything that's antibusiness. Show me a single thing I've done that is antibusiness. You can't point to a statement or an action that is antibusiness. Ike could have tried to give business a tax break. But he didn't do it. I'm at least trying. We're going to give them better depreciation credit. Ike had the power to do that and he didn't do a thing. We recommended that the government get out of the railroads. I spoke to the National Association of Manufacturers, no Democrat or Republican has done that recently. We're trying to do something about trade with our bill this year."

His interest in the price of steel was an extension of his concern about business, about trade, about the economy. It was basic to the country. "I don't see how the price increase would have solved United States Steel's problem anyway," he went on. "All the steel companies have different problems. Get a copy of the statement we put out. We were trying to look at it the best way. See how many stock splits they had in recent years. See their profits. They've been trying to modernize their plants out of profits. Then they got caught in politics. They made a deal with Nixon in 1960 not to raise prices until after the election. Then they got caught in the recession and couldn't raise prices, so now they think they'll do it. How could they possibly justify an increase this time when the new labor contract didn't cost them anything and when they didn't raise them the last time when wages really were increased. But whether we look at it right or not, they can't expect to play the game the way Roger Blough did. If, last fall, he'd have said they had to have a price increase, all this wouldn't have happened. I'd have talked to them. We would have tried to work something out. But it's the way they did it. When we talked with Roger Blough he always said he had problems and that it was difficult for the company, that's true. He never promised he wouldn't raise prices. I never asked him. But he sat right down with us and never said a word about his intentions to raise the price of steel. That was my whole purpose in having those talks—to keep the price down. He knew that. I didn't want to have a fight. Nobody noticed that on the same day I did the steel thing I invoked Taft-Hartley to settle the shipping strike. I'm sympathetic to Blough's problem. But I think I ought to get a little more response from business."

The President was by now resting on his bed against two huge pillows. He sawed away on a piece of chicken. He was testing ideas. "I think maybe I ought to get a little tougher with business. I think that may be the way to treat them. They understand it. When I'm nice to them they just kick me. I think I'll just treat them rougher. Maybe it will do some good."

The President said that he regretted the FBI agents having routed out the newsmen in the dead of night. It had not been intended for them to act in this way. He was not totally regretful, however. "Maybe it didn't hurt," he mused.

The lawsuit on price fixing, which was already in the court, would have to go forward, he explained. But the idea of breaking up U.S. Steel would be dropped.

"This couldn't happen again," said the President, taking a long look back at the previous week. "No other set of conditions in industry are like those in steel. It is so basic. What steel does is vital to the national interest. Nothing else can be compared with it."

Then he thought ahead to the afternoon meeting. "I'll talk to Roger Blough and we'll be friends again. . . . What if he wants to raise the price of steel again?" The President let out his dry, quiet chuckle, then he lay down for a quick nap.

*   *   *

Roger Blough was on time again. He walked in at the southwest gate, unnoticed except for one photographer. The light was fading as he went up the drive, a guard with him to guide him to the correct door. Again Blough was shown to the Cabinet Room, and again he waited only a few minutes. Kennedy came out of his office. The two men shook hands and Kennedy asked, "How are you?"

He led the steel man to a chair beside his desk for this visit. The rocking-chair intimacy was gone. Blough was first concerned about the photographer who had spotted him, but Kennedy did not worry—in fact, he intended to announce the meeting when it was over.

For forty minutes they talked about the problems of steel, of industry, of the United States. Kennedy told Blough that he realized U.S. Steel had problems, as did all the business community. He did not want to fight them, he wanted to help them, but he needed some help from them in return. Again he ran over the record of his efforts that he considered friendly to business. It was not a warm meeting, understandably. Blough had not come to apologize or ask forgiveness for trespasses. They talked somewhat as unwilling partners, to use Kennedy's words. But they were together again.

"We are aware of the disadvantages of victory," said Walter Heller as he and the other New Frontiersmen waited and watched to see what would happen to public and business opinion.

In the first week to ten days they had nothing much to worry about. Larry O'Brien tuned in on the Congress and found mostly support from the Democrats. Mail to the White House on this issue was split, half supporting Kennedy, half denouncing him. But this was not considered abnormal—the situation had occurred before.

The President took what precautions he could. He hurried over to a Chamber of Commerce meeting in Constitution Hall and spelled out his feelings about the need for business to do well if the country was going to do well. When a report from his twenty-one-member Labor-Management Advisory Committee came in, he took special pains to see that it got proper public notice, since that report recommended some curtailment in labor's power. Kennedy sent a wire congratulating Yale University and Roger Blough, who was being honored by the school. It would have been a strange performance at any other time.

The high Democratic politicians during the first post-steel week actually began to think that, if anything, Kennedy had strengthened his political base. He had, indeed, alienated some businessmen, but they had voted for Nixon anyway. Kennedy's basic political strength was with labor, and certainly labor had not found his action against steel objectionable.

"Not one of those bastards who is making the noise now voted for us in 1960," said one party leader. "And not one of them is going to vote for us. Who are they trying to kid? We never had them and we aren't going to get them. Let me tell you something, to win elections you've got to have someone to be against. You've got to have the right enemies. If I were running for office I'd want to have the Chamber of Commerce oppose me, to have big business oppose me and if you threw in the AMA, I'd be sure to win."

Kennedy during these days repeated whenever he could the uniqueness of the steel action. "The steel situation won't happen again. That was a personal thing."

Walter Heller and Douglas Dillon toured the business-banquet circuit. Whenever and wherever the New Frontier could place a speaker to talk about its hope for business, the man was dispatched with presidential blessings. Kennedy hand-picked a blue-ribbon delegation to go to Hot Springs for a meeting of the Business Council (formerly the Business Advisory Council).

Walter Heller was the chief theologian for the Kennedy business message. A new business-government relationship had been evolving nicely under Kennedy, he pointed out. Suddenly there came a revolutionary interlude. But that interlude did not destroy the real basis for this new relationship. The real basis was what Kennedy was actually doing to help business—tax reduction, new trade bill, new depreciation schedule. It was easy when trouble broke out between the President and business for business to slip back to all the old clichés about bureaucracy, Heller noted. He went to a Chamber of Commerce banquet, and when he sat elbow to elbow and talked with the men, he found that the areas of agreement were vast. There was more common ground, he said, than other. But Washington is a strangely insulated and isolated city. It feeds on itself. The correspondents talk to each other, its bureaucrats talk to each other, its legislators talk to each other, and the President talks to those around him. These groups exchange views, and thus the talk first rotates in the little circles, then is flung into the larger orbit, but rarely is tested beyond the Potomac. And not much can penetrate from the outside. The dust of a prairie is soon washed off in Washington and often forgotten. The luxurious interors of Washington salons also soon blot out memories of smoke-stained factory towns.

Beyond the District of Columbia there were some perceptible shivers. The denunciations of John Kennedy which had been contained within the walls of New York's Union League Club, Pittsburgh's Duquesne Club, the Omaha Club and the other bastions of businessmen throughout this land, began to filter out to the street.

On April 23 *The New York Times* published a recapitulation of the steel drama. For the first time in the *Times'* 111-year history they used the words "sons of bitches"—and they put it in the mouth of the President of the United States. The steel incident now became an intimate battle beween businessmen and a hostile President.

Actually Kennedy's pungent description of big steel men had been printed a few days before the *Times* carried it, but it had been largely passed over. The *Times* gave it awesome authenticity.

There are few words more devastating. Yet there are few profane exchanges among males in which the words are not used. It is a full-blooded American epithet. And each of the last three presidents has been a practitioner. Harry Truman called Columnist Drew Pearson an s.o.b. within earshot of reporters, and the incident caromed through the newspapers for weeks. Eisenhower, it appeared, had lived through eight years without getting caught, though he was a splendid cusser in private. But in May of 1962 labor writer John Herling published his book *The Great Price Conspiracy,* the story of the antitrust violations in the electrical industry. He wrote that at a Cabinet meeting Attorney General William Rogers had brought along a copy of an electrical executive's notes on the private rules of price conspiracy. It was such a singular document that it was passed around the Cabinet table. "The only thing those sons of bitches forgot to warn them about was: 'Don't take notes,' " Ike was reported to have told his Cabinet.[1] Kennedy, of course, got caught at the start. And, indeed, there seemed to be considerable relief among the populace that his Harvard vocabulary was suitably buttressed with basic expressions.

Nevertheless, this was the opening that businessmen needed. The fight became very personal. Their initial peace with the New Frontier had been unnatural. Many had been uneasy in it. Almost with glee they joined the battle.

They did not deify Roger Blough. In fact, many a steel executive was more harsh on him than Kennedy had been. But they attacked Kennedy's involvement with the free-enterprise system. They questioned his wisdom and his authority in saying anything about steel prices. In the United States, went the argument, U.S. Steel and anybody else had a right to go broke if they wanted to. It was, in short, none of Kennedy's damned business.

May 28 was blue Monday. The stock market plummeted. Visions of 1929 filled Wall Street. The sincere testimony from John Kennedy's economic experts that the message of price-wage stability and Kennedy's intention to enforce it had gotten through, causing bloated stocks to deflate to a realistic level, was swept away in the anguished cries against Kennedy. They were not only from the brokers and industrialists this time. The fifteen million Americans who held stocks were jolted. Disillusionment crept into every part of the land. Small-town merchants, farmers and white-collar workers who had put money in stocks for their old age suddenly found their paper profits wiped out. It was a grim experience for many who had ridden the spirals of the market to astounding heights.

[1] After his brush with steel, Kennedy learned about the Herling reference, called Herling to confirm the fact. Herling then took a copy of his book to the White House.

Yet beneath all the concern there was a layer of confidence in the economy that was not shattered. The figures showed that 1962 would be an excellent business year. Indicators for 1963 were good. On the following day Kennedy called in his top economic brains, and in the Cabinet Room they reaffirmed their belief that the plunge was a needed shake-out. The President decided to do nothing but to talk confidence. Douglas Dillon walked from the Cabinet Room to face reporters: "The general economy is very sound. . . . Stock prices had been too high. They dropped to an area where they bear usual relation to reasonable profits. . . . I see no reason for panicky selling. I don't see anything particular the government can do."

The market rallied, then slipped again. It wavered, fell more. But over the weeks it began to steady. Apparently the diagnosis of bloat had been correct.

That made little difference in the attack on Kennedy. Businessmen sported SOB buttons. Jokes spread with the speed of sound. Joe Kennedy, went one, had awakened the morning after the stock-market drop, seen the headlines and said, "I never should have voted for that son of a bitch." There was the one about John Kennedy, Bob Kennedy and Lyndon Johnson in a sinking boat. Who would be saved? Answer: the country.[2]

[2] Months later the White House press would make up a song about the incident as is the custom with notable days of every administration. This one, sung to the tune of "Side by Side" went:

> Roger Blough wanted to make money,
> Jack didn't think it was funny,
> So he went on TV and said publicly,
> SSSSSS—OOOOOO—BBBBBB.
>
> Bobby said I'm a tooth for an eye man.
> So he called up the Federal BI men.
> They jerked reporters from bed.
> But Jack only said,
> Don't blame me.
>
> He said we're just fighting inflation.
> What if your profits do fall.
> And if no steel leaves the station.
> It really doesn't matter at all.
>
> I know what I learned from my daddy.
> On his knee he said, my laddy,
> In big business you'll find only one kind,
> SSSSSS—OOOOOO—BBBBBB.

Circumstance did not co-operate with the New Frontier in its efforts to steady the economic nerves of the nation. May 29, the day after Blue Monday, was Kennedy's 45th birthday. It was noted with a touch of bitterness by some that multi-millionaire John Kennedy received another $5 million under the terms of the trust his father had set up for him. How could a man of his vast and secure holdings understand a normal person's anxieties?

Trucks drove up to the White House with flowers for Kennedy, and among them was a rocking chair covered with yellow chrysanthemums and white carnations, a present from Frank Sinatra. The White House hastily sent it out to Children's Hospital, the President not even taking a look. White House Chef René Verdon whipped up a chocolate cake, a Kennedy favorite, and sent it out to Glen Ora, where the family was gathered for the President's birthday party. And then the story broke that Kennedy had become so angry over the treatment of the news by the stanchly Republican New York *Herald Tribune* that he refused to read it any more, ordered the White House's twenty-two subscriptions stopped and replaced by the St. Louis *Post Dispatch,* a stanchly Democratic paper.

The national atmosphere was unhealthy as June approached, and Kennedy knew it. He was still convinced that his economic reasoning was sound, but he feared that the business community's bitterness toward him might actually affect its confidence in the future, and such a loss of confidence could seriously affect the economy.

He asked New York banker Robert Lovett down for a long searching talk. Should the margin requirements for the stock market be lowered? Should he go on the air to reassure the American people about the basic stability of the economy? Should there be a tax cut now to unfetter the economy? He sought out similar advice from McNamara, Hodges, and Dillon, from Roger Blough, Senator Robert Kerr, John McCone, Federal Reserve's William McChesney Martin and Clark Clifford—those he knew with business background and connections. But the men Kennedy talked to were a special group. They had either deserted business for government service or they belonged to the community of New York financiers, all of whom sympathized with the President's problems more than the men directly in industry in Detroit or Chicago. There were no men near Kennedy who ran a steel mill or were responsible for a production line. Though Kennedy might not have learned economics from such men, he might have learned their mood, what made them think as they did.

Sensing his slumping popularity, Kennedy decided to make a major business speech in mid-June at Yale University, where he was to receive an honorary degree. He and his economic advisers labored for days on the speech, and Kennedy even penciled in paragraphs as he flew to New Haven.

The second company of the Connecticut governor's foot guards greeted him at the airport. The band played "Beautiful Ohio," and Kennedy, clutching his speech, sped off for the campus in the muggy June weather. For thirty-two minutes Kennedy talked to some 10,000 students, parents and visitors on Old Campus. His was the first speech allowed during the graduation ceremony since 1903.

From the standpoint of his economists, his speech was superb; it championed their doctrine. From the standpoint of his relations with business, it was a failure.

"It might be said now that I have the best of both worlds," began Kennedy. "A Harvard education and a Yale degree. . . . I am particularly glad to become a Yale man because as I think about my troubles, I find that a lot of them have come from other Yale men. . . . Now that I, too, am a Yale man, it is time for peace. . . ."

But Kennedy's offer of peace was strictly on his terms. "As every past generation has had to disenthrall itself from an inheritance of truism and a stereotype, so in our own time we must move on from reassuring repetition of stale phrases to a new, difficult but essential confrontation with reality. For the great enemy of the truth is very often not the lie—deliberate, contrived and dishonest—but the myth—persistent, persuasive and unrealistic—today I want to particularly consider the myth and reality in our national economy. . . .

"There are three great areas of our domestic affairs in which, today, there is a danger that illusion may prevent effective action. . . . If a contest in angry argument were forced upon it, no administration could shrink from response, and history does not suggest that American presidents are totally without resources in an engagement forced upon them because of hostility in one sector of society. . . .

"Let us take first the question of the size and shape of government. The myth here is that government is big and bad —and steadily getting bigger and worse. . . .

"Next, let us turn to the problem of fiscal policy. . . . We persist in measuring our federal fiscal integrity today by the conventional or administrative budget—with results which would be regarded as absurd in any business firm—in any country of Europe—or in any careful assessment of the reality of our national finances. . . . It omits our special trust funds; it neglects changes in assets or inventories. It cannot tell a loan from a straight expenditure—worst of all, it cannot distinguish between operating expenditures and long-term investments . . . it can be actively misleading. . . .

"It is true—and of high importance—that the prosperity of this country depends on assurance that all major elements within it will live up to their responsibilities. . . . But there is also the false issue—and its simplest form is the assertion that any and all unfavorable turns of the speculative wheel —however temporary and however plainly speculative in character—are the result of, and I quote, 'lack of confidence in the national administration.' This I must tell you, while comforting, is not wholly true. . . . Business had full confidence in the administrations in power in 1929, 1954, 1958 and 1960—but this was not enough to prevent recession when business lacked full confidence in the economy. . . .

"Some conversations I have heard in our country sound like old records, long-playing, left over from the middle Thirties. . . ."

On its way to the airport for Kennedy's return flight to Washington, the President's motorcade roared through the factory district of New Haven. In windows were the workers, waving and cheering to Kennedy. It was a welcome sight and sound because his Yale audience had not responded with much enthusiasm, and many of the country's businessmen would consider the talk an outright insult. As he flew back to Washington, Kennedy wondered if an open war with business was not inevitable, in the F.D.R. tradition, and if his efforts to re-establish a "dialogue with business" was not foolish. But this was only a thought, and Kennedy soon dismissed it. Business had to do well for him to succeed.

Perhaps one of the most perceptive observations of this time came from the Washington Evening *Star*'s Mary McGrory, who watches government people with a rare insight. No economist, no financial writer was she, but one of her half-humorous, half-serious columns hit home.

"Obviously," she wrote, "President Kennedy is not succeeding with business. But is he really trying? Has he instituted, for instance, at the great clubs frequented by his officials, a policy of 'Bring a Businessman to Lunch'? Has he bidden U.S. Steel Chairman Roger Blough to Glen Ora? . . .

"Politicians and businessmen proceed in somewhat the same manner, even if the profit motive is different, with the first wanting power and the second merely money. Both classes must be good salesmen, ruthless competitors and big gamblers. . . .

"But President Kennedy never talks to them [businessmen] about what they have in common. He doesn't even speak their language. At Yale, he explored 'myths and clichés,' not the usual coin of exchange at the Rotary Club. . . . Incurably intellectual, he told them that it was necessary to move from the reassuring repetition of stale phrases to a new, difficult but essential confrontation with reality. . . .

"The President also spoke of the need for ending the 'angry argument,' but it appears he cannot resist pointing out that it exists, perhaps a reflex action in a Democratic President. . . . As a partisan, he may even be relishing it. At the Chamber of Commerce building yesterday, when he spoke to the Peace Corps, he remarked cheerfully that he 'Never expected to get such a warm reception in this building.' At his press conference later, he went out of his way to say he could not believe he was where the businessmen would like him to be and that they would be happier if there were a Republican in the White House. These are things he has never said about his Republican political opponents. . . .

"In his dialogue with the sulking tycoons, he says seriously that no matter what they do, he will have the last word. . . . This gambit recalls an earlier Kennedy, the campaigning senator, who used to tell stubborn leaders in his own party that they had better go along because he was going to win anyway."

CHAPTER TWENTY-FOUR

OXFORD, MISSISSIPPI

THE moment of decision came near 11 P.M. on Sunday night, October 2, 1962.

John Kennedy sat in his black chair at the center of the coffin-shaped Cabinet table, its vast expanse of dark mahogany sullen in the glow of the overhead neon grill.

He was neatly dressed: dark blue suit, blue tie, white shirt. He had just come from addressing the nation on television, and his face was as somber as his clothes.

He and his brother Bob were in the Cabinet Room with a handful of aides, and they were following Negro James H. Meredith's enrollment at the University of Mississippi.

Bob sat on the President's left, holding the phone which connected him with Nick Katzenbach, his Justice Department deputy, who, in Oxford, Mississippi, held the other end of an open line that burned through the night. The tiny brass name plate on the arched leather back of Bob's chair read, "Secretary of the Treasury," but on this night the economy was not in crisis and Douglas Dillon was not there.

In the room there was only the sound of Bob's low voice, repeating the news as relayed by Katzenbach from his command post inside Ole Miss's Lyceum Building.

Behind the President and his brother, seated along the wall, were the men who always seem to gather in moments of great triumph or despair: Ken O'Donnell, Larry O'Brien, Ted Sorensen. Burke Marshall, Bob's civil-rights assistant, was a newcomer to the inner circle.

These were the vital minutes. Around Katzenbach in Oxford violence swirled. Over the phone Bob could hear a ragged background of riot.

It was a discouraging and stunning hour after weeks of the most careful effort to conduct a faultless, sympathetic campaign to register Meredith, to win for a United States citizen the rights that the Constitution guaranteed him.

Meredith, 29, was slight and shy; he was one of ten children, the grandson of a slave, a nine-year veteran of the Air Force. He took correspondence courses while in the service and later attended the Negro Jackson State College but decided that he wanted "something more." Had "something more" been only education, he could have found it peaceably in literally hundreds of northern schools, most of them far more creditable academically than Ole Miss. But Meredith's "something more" was the cause of his people.

There came to the White House the news that French reporter Paul Guihard, Agence France-Presse, had been shot and killed. It was almost as if there had been the rattle of small-arms fire across the White House lawn. Then there followed a rumor that a Mississippi state trooper had been killed and another frantic story that a United States marshal had died.

Katzenbach passed each desperate report along as it came in, trying to give the President and his brother the feel of the moment.

There was a warning of a shortage of tear gas, and for several minutes the men in the Cabinet Room ached with anxiety, as if they had been on the scene. Then the gas arrived and over the phone the silent men could almost hear the marshals pry open the wooden crates and rush back to the dark night and the mob harangued by former Maj. Gen. Edwin A. Walker, who had resigned from the Army after being admonished for wild right-wing talk and who ironically had been the commander of troops in Little Rock in 1957.

Earlier there had been Mississippi Governor Ross Barnett on the phone from his Jackson headquarters, pleading, weaseling, almost wild, afraid, deceitful, crying out: "They're saying I sold out down here. . . . Can't you get him [Meredith] out of here? . . . Get Meredith off the campus. . . . I can't protect him."

John Kennedy had talked on the phone, angry that he had learned that the Mississippi state troopers had left the scene —the scene of the sullen mob on a southern campus and a lone Negro in his room on that same campus, waiting for daybreak so that he might enroll and break the color barrier in the deepest southland, hate growing.

"Listen, Governor," shouted the President of the United States into the phone. "We're not moving anybody anywhere until order is restored. . . . You are not discharging your responsibility, Governor. . . ."

Barnett whimpered again that he was trying.

"You're just not," said Kennedy, "because the state police can't be found on the campus. . . . There is no sense in talking any more until you do your duty. . . . There are lives in jeopardy. . . . You fulfill your function. . . . I'm not in a position to do anything, to make any deals, to discuss anything until law and order is restored and the lives of the people are protected. Good-bye."

The President had slammed the phone down. There was little more that could be said to such a man. Through two days the Kennedy brothers had tried to come to terms with him. He had proposed deal after deal, only to back down and change his mind. He wanted Meredith to get on the campus, to be registered, but he did not want to be blamed for it. He wanted the federal forces to overwhelm him, but he did not want trouble.

The plan to bring Meredith on the campus the Sunday before he was to register had been worked out by Bob Kennedy and Barnett. It seemed good. The campus was quiet on the week end. The mob would probably swell on Monday, since it had been widely publicized that Meredith was to register then.

Meredith had been flown to Oxford, escorted onto the campus by state troopers and federal marshals (some 500 marshals had been flown in to help 200 troopers maintain order; 200 of the marshals were on the campus). Then the mob had formed, and suddenly the troopers had left. Barnett blamed his officers on the scene, claiming a mix-up in orders.

The troopers came back but left again at a critical moment. Alone, the federal marshals could not quite handle the riot, which had begun to flare just as Kennedy had gone on TV to explain his position and appeal for peace in the South.

There came a fateful fifteen minutes. The marshals, with their new supply of tear gas, held. It seemed to Nick Katzenbach that the worst was over, but there were nine hours until morning, and everybody was near exhaustion. Nobody in the Lyceum Building knew what other outbreaks might come out of the blackness of the campus.

Katzenbach thought help should come from federal troops, who had been staging for the emergency since Saturday.

Kennedy rose from his chair in the Cabinet Room without saying a word. He walked across the green carpeting through secretary Evelyn Lincoln's office and into his own deserted office. It was clear now of all the TV gear from his talk. There he sat down and put in a call to Secretary of the Army Cyrus Vance. Send the federal troops in, Kennedy ordered. Vance was ready; the word went out instantly. A company of federalized National Guardsmen who lived in Oxford began to move. The bulk of the troops were still off in Memphis, and it would take three hours for them to get to the scene. But the marshals held and the campus began to quiet. Kennedy stayed in his office, listening to Katzenbach's reports. The report of two deaths was confirmed, the other rumors of more loss of life were proved untrue. At 5:30 A.M. Kennedy decided to go to bed. The federal troops were arriving, the situation totally in hand now. "I want to be called if anything happens," Kennedy told his staff. And he walked out into the dawn to get some sleep before he began a busy White House day of routine business.

There was some disappointment in the White House because there had been loss of life and damage to the university campus and because once again the world could point to the fact that the United States government had to bring in fixed bayonets to give a Negro the same rights as all its other citizens possessed.

And there was criticism that Kennedy had again overintellectualized the problem and had waited too long before ap-

plying the federal force that would have prevented an outbreak of violence. Who really knew?

Before the riot occurred, there was genuine concern that
the sight of federal troops on the campus would have incited
even more violence. But there was also evidence on the day
before that violence was almost inevitable. Burke Marshall,
who had been in Oxford, flew back to Washington and reported on Saturday afternoon that the United States marshals
might not be able to handle the job if a mob of 20,000
formed, as the local authorities predicted.

Early on Sunday afternoon, with Meredith on the campus,
the mounting tension could be detected. Katzenbach warned
the White House about it. Yet everyone felt that the marshals with the state troopers could maintain order. Why had
Kennedy trusted Ross Barnett at all? The President had
been warned even by southern legislators that the man could
not be relied upon in such a hazardous undertaking. Actually, Kennedy did not trust him. But he was a governor of a
state of the Union. Kennedy's whole strategy was based on a
legal, patient approach through the local and state authorities. And up until Sunday there had been no violence.

The thought of Little Rock and Eisenhower's precipitous
dispatch of federal troops haunted the Kennedys. They felt
that not enough attention had been paid to the Little Rock
situation before it became necessary to send in the Army.
The suddenness of the action had not only embittered the
South but it had also shocked the rest of the United States
and the world.

The year before, in Montgomery, Alabama, Bob Kennedy
in an all-night vigil had slowly applied pressure through
United States marshals in a highly successful operation. Violence had been prevented, no troops had been needed. Oxford was a more difficult case, but the preparations were even
more painstaking, even more deliberate. Every legal means
was explored and tried, and every appeal was made to the
state and school. In the first attempts to bring Meredith on
the campus when the gate had been blocked, the federal
authorities had turned back. Until every other means had
been exhausted, there was to be no force. For a week the
game went on until the federal judges, who had ruled that

Meredith must be allowed to attend the university, grew impatient with the federal delay.

As the exhaustive search for a peaceful solution was reported to the nation, as Ross Barnett's tragic performance became clear to those who watched, the southern racists suffered an overwhelming setback. And this, in the long run, overshadowed every other aspect of the Oxford incident.

Southern leaders, many of whom opposed integration, admitted the fairness of Kennedy's approach. Some harshly criticized Barnett. Others turned away in disgust as they saw his crude tactics injure their cause.

To some, Oxford promised to be the last serious convulsion of determined southern resistance to integration. At least when it had been accomplished, when Meredith was registered and attending classes, under guard, there was relatively little bitterness across the South.

The final result of the struggle had never been in doubt from the moment the federal court had ordered Meredith's admission. The full weight of the national government would sooner or later be brought to bear on the problem. That was inevitable.

The Kennedys never worried about the fact they might have to bring in troops. This was a possibility from the start. What they sought to avoid was to enroll Meredith by bayonets directly. Even if paratroopers had to line the streets to keep order, civil authorities were going to take the Negro up to the admission desk.

In the final hours of the drama Barnett seemed to want to allow Meredith on the campus and then to have him forced off by the angry mob. Such a result would benefit Barnett twofold: it would purge him of the contempt-of-court charge he faced for not allowing Meredith on the campus; it would leave Ole Miss still a totally white school, and Barnett might persuade Kennedy it was too dangerous to try again then. Matters never worked out that way.

The plan that was finally used appealed to the Kennedys for these reasons: Barnett could purge himself of the contempt charge by allowing Meredith on the campus, and thus the federal authorities would not have to arrest Barnett, an action which might have triggered a violent struggle, inflaming the whole South and setting back the cause of real integration by years; Meredith could be registered by civil authorities; and Barnett could be calmed by being allowed to claim that he was forced to the wall by the overwhelming buildup of marshals and troops, thus salvaging some face in his red-neck league.

Plans for such crises, however, like wars, rarely go off as devised. This one was no exception. But when the tragedy of the moment had faded, there was no question that it had been a striking victory for the cause of integration, for the dignity of the law and for the cause of understanding and decency.

CHAPTER TWENTY-FIVE

BLOCKADE

D O G days set in on the New Frontier in August and September. Kennedy's popularity as measured by George Gallup slumped to 61, the lowest rating he had received.

Though the nation's military strength had continued to grow and the world had stayed relatively calm through the first three-fourths of 1962, there was a lingering displeasure from the President's steel action. It had, by New Frontier admission, spread further than anyone had anticipated.

There seemed to be too many Kennedys in too many places doing too many wrong things at the wrong times. A huge formal party on the lawn of Bob Kennedy's Hickory Hill turned into a public-relations disaster when Ethel Kennedy fell in the swimming pool and Presidential Assistant Arthur Schlesinger, Jr., leaped in to help her while the guests— nearly everybody of any importance on the New Frontier except the President and his wife—laughed. So this was how Washington showed its concern over the stock market?

Teddy Kennedy's campaign in Massachusetts for his brother's old Senate seat smacked of an unconscionable power grab to many. Would the Kennedy family ever be satisfied?

Jackie extended her vacation in Ravello, Italy, from two weeks to four weeks and stories of her happy nighttime and daytime ventures in the tiny town flooded American papers. To many in this country, caught in the late summer heat and dust, her vacation seemed not austere enough to fit the glum national feeling.

The talk for a quickie tax cut to spur the economy became more than talk. Kennedy was wary, but his economists were for it and the pressure mounted. But then there was Wilbur Mills, from Kensett, Arkansas. As Chairman of the House Ways and Means Committee, which must originate all tax measures, he held the yes or no power. He said no, and kindling hopes for a tax cut faded out to promises for a tax reduction and reform effort in 1963.

Up on the Hill, New York Senator Kenneth Keating kept insisting that the Soviets were building Cuba into a military camp. Russian technicians and Russian equipment, including missiles, were pouring into the island, said Keating. Kennedy was forced to act. First he summoned congressional leaders. "I wanted to acquaint you with what is taking place in Cuba—which is not my favorite subject. We have a new CIA report." The men were told of the presence of 5,000 Russian technicians, antiaircraft missiles, PT boats with ship-to-ship missiles. But the buildup was strictly defensive, said Kennedy. As long as it remained that way, this country planned no action against Cuba. Some of the men did not like the news. Congressman Charles Halleck, GOP Minority Leader, could not understand how we could be so positive that the weapons were only defensive. House Republican Whip Leslie Arends wondered about the Monroe Doctrine; the Soviet presence seemed like a clear violation of it.

The White House issued a statement with the new Cuban facts and the same assurances: the buildup was defensive, it would be watched.

But for many the approach was too casual, Kennedy too certain that the Russians would not try something. The Soviet experts in the State Department kept pointing out that the communists had never extended a nuclear capability beyond their own lands. Other top officials worried about what Russia might do in Berlin if we acted against Cuba. Kennedy noted that we had missiles in Turkey pointed at Moscow, that we had thousands of military technicians in Vietnam. These facts were true enough, but they seemed a little like excuses for lack of courage.

Charlie Halleck, the gut fighter, sniffed the air. "Things

just aren't right," he said. "They Goddamned well need to do something and they aren't doing it."

Kennedy tried again at his press conference. "If at any time the communist buildup in Cuba were to endanger or interfere with our security in any way . . . or if Cuba should ever attempt to export its aggressive purposes by force or the threat of force against any nation in this hemisphere, or become an offensive military base of significant capacity for the Soviet Union, then this country will do whatever must be done to protect its own security and that of its allies."

Washington became oppressive for the President, and he welcomed the approach of the political season, the chance to get out around the land again. This was his source of strength. He felt that if he could talk to the people directly, he could get his points across. And he always got a lift from just looking at the country, watching and listening to the crowds.

He flew west to help California's Governor Pat Brown in his fight against Richard Nixon. He invaded West Virginia, the Monongahela Valley, New York, Pittsburgh, New Jersey and Michigan. He was trying to reverse tradition which produced off-year losses in Congress for the party in power. He could not, he knew, transfer any of his own popularity. But he could stir up interest in the election, and if there was enough interest he felt that the Democratic party—the majority party—would benefit.

Then came the dawn of October 14. In the high thin air over western Cuba the cameras in a U-2 reconnaissance plane whirred and the tiny clusters of Russian military equipment below that were an embryonic medium-range ballistic missile site were recorded on film. There had been suspicious signs earlier, and Kennedy had ordered close surveillance, but in the days before October 14 bad weather had interfered with high-level photography. And, the White House would confess to itself later, American intelligence was just a bit drowsy. It had been lulled into that state by the constant assurances of the Soviet affairs experts in the State Department that it was highly unlikely that the Russians would take missiles outside communist land. There was no precedent for such action and no indication they would change their habits at this time.

But the experts were wrong and now there was proof. The following day an alarmed team of photo interpreters hunched over a single picture that in the next weeks would become famous, not for its beauty, because the light of early morning made it gray, but for its detail.

The Pentagon experts found eight large missile transporters in a Cuban field. They discovered four missile erector-launchers already deployed in tentative firing positions. Missile-fuel vehicles were lined up nearby. Other pictures were checked, and the beginning of another missile site was found. Even a Russian convoy just arriving at a site was captured on the high-resolution film.

By that night McGeorge Bundy had been told the shattering findings. By now he knew Kennedy well, and he knew that the President would demand uncontrovertible confirmation before he acted on such dismaying news. Bundy decided not to tell the President that Monday night. He asked the Central Intelligence Agency and Pentagon experts to keep at their work, to be as certain as they possibly could be of their facts by the next morning.

The call from Lieut. Gen. Marshall Sylvester Carter, Deputy Director of CIA, came early. Bundy was waiting at his desk in the basement of the White House's west wing. The evidence was clear, Carter told him. There was no mistake.

Bundy got up quickly, walked through the quiet White House corridors, for it was still before 9 A.M., and took the tiny elevator up to the President's private quarters. He strode into the bedroom where the President was finishing breakfast. The President looked up from his newspaper. There was no noticeable change in his expression. There never is at such times. But the President would acknowledge later that in addition to the gravest concern there had been great surprise—he had not thought the Russians would make such a move.

Kennedy's first question was about the authenticity of the information. Could they be sure? He wanted to see the pictures himself. He wanted the surveillance flights over Cuba stepped up and he wanted the pictures checked and rechecked. And he asked Bundy to round up the top security men in the administration for later in the morning. The whole thing, he cautioned, would have to be closely held.

For a few minutes before Bundy left, the two of them considered what the United States should do if the evidence was irreversibly confirmed, and deep down both men knew that it would be.

From this moment Kennedy was convinced there would have to be strong action from this country. His and Bundy's initial reaction was that the United States probably would have to bomb the missile sites and the bombers to destroy them and wipe out the military threat to this country. The two men talked quietly in one of those vital moments of history; there was more of the scholar than the soldier in both of them. The scene was a symbol of the times—two men, one forty-five the other forty-three, setting in motion and shaping in a few calm minutes a chain of events that might alter civilization. Fortunately, the full weight of such times is not felt by the men, because they are too engaged in the immediate problem.

Though the reality of finding missiles in Cuba produced a profound shock in Kennedy, he was not fully without blueprints for action against the island. Following the discovery of the defensive arsenal, the New Frontier thinkers had begun to consider the various forms of responses open to them should more profound trouble arise. In the Pentagon was a plan for invading Cuba prepared after the Bay of Pigs and kept current since then.

Kennedy and Bundy both knew that this would be a critical test of the country, of the administration, of themselves —the one they had been preparing for in two crisis-ridden years. Memories of the Bay of Pigs had not faded fully. Would the government work smoothly this time? In those first minutes of Kennedy's involvement in the Cuban crisis he resolved that this time it would work properly. This time the challenge was real.

At 10:30 he was at his desk, and General Carter, a photo analyst and Bundy were hovering at his elbows as he pored over the sheaf of pictures. Carter filled in the President briefly on his conclusions drawn from the detailed study of the pictures that had gone on all night. The technician carefully pointed out the telltale pieces of evidence that could be fitted together like a puzzle.

At 11:45 the men the President had summoned began to gather in the Cabinet Room. One by one they hurried through the door, walked silently across the thick carpet and took seats. At the far end of the table were the pictures. General Carter was there with two photo experts, and again he went through the explanation.

The collection of men in the room was notable. They had been hand-picked by Kennedy, and they represented the men in whom he put his reliance for conducting this country's security affairs. Over the next two weeks they were to be in almost constant session, either as a full group or as splinter units. These were the men who would form the backbone of Kennedy's team: Lyndon Johnson, McNamara and his deputy Gilpatric; Dean Rusk and Under Secretary Ball and Assistant Secretary of State for Latin America Ed Martin; Douglas Dillon; Bob Kennedy; General Maxwell Taylor, now chairman of the Joint Chiefs of Staff; Sorensen and Bundy. Those who joined later were UN Ambassador Adlai Stevenson; another McNamara assistant, Paul Nitze; CIA Director John McCone, who was represented at first by Carter; Under Secretary of State Alexis Johnson; Llewellyn Thompson, former ambassador to Moscow; and Admiral George Anderson, Chief of Naval Operations.

As Carter spoke, the room was quiet. There were no smiles. When the photo briefing was done, Kennedy told the men that quick and decisive action was necessary. He turned to Rusk and McNamara and asked that they prepare specific recommendations. He poured out questions about United States military preparedness and he repeated his desire for the closest possible surveillance. Kennedy asked for the deepest secrecy. Whenever possible, normalcy should be feigned. Kennedy would go on with his White House appointments, and his plans to campaign that very week end, and a spectacular jet-plane trip from coast to coast would go forward, at least for the time being. Those who watched John Kennedy during the Bay of Pigs and again on October 16, 1962, found him a far different President on the second occasion.

He knew the men around him—they were all his choices. Taylor and Anderson, the two top military minds, had been appointed by him just that year. The top rung of CIA which had planned the Bay of Pigs were all gone. McCone and Carter were Kennedy men. Bob Kennedy was in this crisis from the beginning. So was Sorensen. The deputies of Rusk and McNamara were there so that in each department there would be some knowledge in depth of the details of the plan.

The failure to coordinate, the lack of inner communication, had helped doom the Bay of Pigs. This time the President was determined to prevent it. "On that very first morning," said one aide intimately connected with the crisis, "the President gathered all the threads together in his hands and he held them."

Kennedy kept in touch with each man and made certain that each man kept in touch with him. This was generally taken care of by assembling the crisis task force and letting every man say what he wanted to say before the whole group.

Then began a frantic and clandestine week in the back corridors of the White House, in the Pentagon, in the State Department. There were hushed phone conversations between Kennedy and Rusk, Kennedy and McNamara. There were the constant comings and goings in the White House. Bob Kennedy was there almost as much as the President.

To avoid detection, the men had to adapt Indian tricks. Abnormal collections of big, black cars were to be avoided. (On one evening ten of the top officers of the United States piled in a single car to ride from the State Department to the White House, the scene being much like a Marx Brothers movie.) Back doors were used. Beards were shaved despite all-night work. Normal greetings were given and normal clothes worn and, when possible, normal schedules kept.

There were some breaks going for Kennedy. For one thing, the White House press corps was in total disarray because of the political campaign. They were dispatched on Fridays with duffel bags packed, and then through Saturday and Sunday there ensued a dusty race across America to listen to Kennedy on stump, to look in the faces of the voters and to write it all down and send it out before they enplaned for the next stop. It was a job which drained all physical and mental energy. They struggled back to Washington on Monday and collapsed for two days at home, returned to the

White House in time to get their new marching orders. What few hours they had between planes were spent in talking to politicians about the candidates and the districts that they would encounter during the coming week end. Not only was the regular White House group so employed, but they were joined by virtually every other reporter of stature around the capital as the focus of national interest shifted to November 6. Other newsmen preceded Kennedy to the crucial political areas or came after him to sample his effect on the populace. Politics, the natural love of journalists and statesmen, was the consuming interest. The men simply could not cover the world and the campaign together. The normal White House staff members and State Department and Pentagon sources who were consulted regularly on Berlin or on Vietnam or Cuba were forgotten at this season. Thus, the men deeply involved in the Cuban crisis had a rare freedom from the prying press.

Early in the Cuban planning the list of possibilities was established.

1. The United States could launch a full-scale invasion and conquer the island, destroying the missile sites. But what of those Russians and their equipment? What would the Soviet response be? What would it have to be?

2. There could be an attack from the air. No nation on earth was more proficient at pinpoint bombing. The missiles and their launching complexes could be destroyed. But again, what of the Russians who would inevitably be killed in such an operation?

3. A blockade was technically an act of war, but it offered the opportunity of showing force without taking lives and it did not prevent one of the more drastic acts later if it failed to persuade the Soviet Union that we meant business. After the first day of deliberation, this alternative became the most attractive.

4. We could deliver an ultimatum to the Russians to get their missiles and bombers out, put a time limit on it and prayerfully wait for their response. But why would Nikita Khrushchev believe us now more than he had believed our determination in the weeks before? He had, after all, been saying that the western powers would not fight, that they had

become weak and too much enthralled with their easy life to risk it over such a minor irritation.

5. We could do nothing.

There were endless combinations of the above suggestions. Almost from the start the question of negotiation was raised. Suppose the Russians wanted to talk the problem over? What was our negotiating position? Could we offer anything? We were already planning to dismantle our soft missile sites in Turkey when our undersea Polaris forces were of such strength as to allow it. This was a possibility. For the time being, however, that was left in the background. Our first action had to be decided, and more and more the blockade appealed to Kennedy and the men around him. We could poise our forces for an invasion, throw a cordon of ships into the Caribbean to halt any new shipments of offensive weapons and demand the dismantling of the missiles and their removal along with the bombers. Our Navy was the mightiest afloat, and the Caribbean was our water. If the Russians chose to challenge us on the seas, victory in a limited battle was assured. No one who talked to Kennedy in these hours thought the Russians wanted to go beyond that and risk nuclear war.

On Tuesday and Wednesday the planning was concentrated in the Pentagon and the State Department. Kennedy, on center stage, flew off for half a day's campaigning in Connecticut.

Near 9 P.M. he returned and was met at the airport by Ted Sorensen and his brother, who rode with him back to the White House. In the meantime another meeting of his task force was in progress in the State Department.

U-2's continued to prowl the upper atmosphere. As the pictures piled up by the hundreds, so did the evidence of the size, audacity and speed of the Soviet move.

Frantically the Russians were rushing to complete six sites for MRBM's, four missiles to a site. The photo technicians positively identified the missiles when they spotted tailfins sticking out from under tarpaulins. They were identical to the fins of the MRBM's photographed in Moscow in the May Day parade that year. The MRBM missiles were capable of reaching 1,200 miles—to Houston, St. Louis or

Washington—with their one-megaton warheads.

On October 17 the faint scars in the Cuban earth revealed launch construction for intermediate-range missiles. These monsters could fire 2,500 miles and reach and destroy any American city. The intelligence men found three IRBM sites (four missiles each) under construction and another undoubtedly planned.

In late September huge crates coming into Cuba on Soviet ships had been photographed, and the intelligence experts thought they might contain IL-28 (Beagle) jet bombers. Now that hunch was confirmed when the crates were broken open and assembly of some of the bombers begun. Forty-two unassembled bombers had been delivered to the island, the meticulous photo analysts concluded.

All Russian equipment was catalogued in the greatest detail, some of it having been photographed in early fall. There were new MIG-21's, called Fishbeds. These fighter-interceptors were equipped with air-to-air missiles. There were older MIG-15's also, which the Soviet Union had given to Cuba earlier. The torpedo boats with their ship-to-ship missiles that had been detected before October 14 were rephotographed. Coast defensive missiles were found emplaced along key beach areas. The existence of Soviet ground battle groups was discovered, each fully equipped with assault guns, tanks, tactical rockets, antitank weapons and motorized infantry carriers. The estimates of Russian troops and technicians would climb before the crisis subsided from 5,000 to 22,000 on the basis of the unerring camera lenses. In Russian camp sites the photographs even showed delicate stone and flower mosaics of the unit insignia.

And though they never got an actual picture of a nuclear warhead, the Pentagon analyzers felt certain that they had photographs of the trucks which brought the warheads to the missile sites.

The pace of emplacement of the MRBM's was staggering. By the day, by the hour, the emplacements grew, more of the missiles became ready to fire. The bigger, more complex IRBM's were believed to be, not on the island, but in the holds of some of the eighteen dry-cargo ships then steaming for Cuba. But the construction of their sites leaped ahead.

The mobility of the entire operation was dazzling.

What did it all mean? Kennedy pondered the bigger questions when he had time between the details. Why had the Soviet Chairman attempted such deception? He had assured the world when the antiaircraft missiles were found that he was intent only in providing Cuba with a defensive complex. Other Russians had brought the same word. Twice within little more than a year Khrushchev had attempted to deceive Kennedy. At Vienna he had declared piously that the Soviet Union would not resume nuclear testing until the United States did so. All the time his technicians had been busy in preparing the greatest series of explosions that the world had seen. Now he was still mouthing his hopes for peace, still declaring his innocent intentions in Cuba.

Was this a test probe for pressure on Berlin? The suggestion was made to Kennedy by his Kremlinologists. Perhaps Khrushchev planned to see if he could get away with emplacement of the missiles. If the United States did nothing but voice its anger, then maybe the screws could be turned on Berlin? But that did not seem quite on target to Kennedy.

His experts calculated that the cost to Russia for such a tremendous operation was near a billion dollars. The Russian economy could hardly stand such an expenditure unless the purpose was even greater.

Gradually Kennedy became convinced that Khrushchev had gambled heavily to tilt the balance of power in his favor, or at least to make it seem so to the world.

The old myth that the Soviets had a missile gap over us had disappeared long ago. The United States had 150 intercontinental missiles ready and aimed at the heart of Russia, which had at best 75 ICBM's ready to fire toward America. By the end of the year the United States would have 200 ICBM's and, of course, there were more than 100 Polaris missiles in submarines and they were, in effect, ICBM's. The Russian MRBM's and the IRBM's planned for Cuba would be a factor in the nuclear struggle. Khrushchev obviously had hoped to get the missiles in place without United States detection, then to confront Kennedy—and the world—with the accomplished fact. He might even have done it casually in the United Nations General Assembly, which he had hinted he might attend.

Ironically, a meeting had been arranged between Kennedy and Andrei Gromyko for late on Thursday afternoon. Gromyko was to fly back to Moscow on October 21, and he wanted a final talk with Kennedy so that he could relay Kennedy's thoughts to Khrushchev.

The President planned to say nothing to Gromyko about Cuba. Secrecy was still vital until the United States was ready to act. Kennedy would let Cuba come up naturally in the discussions, but the main subject would be Berlin, which seemed to be more on the minds of the international politicians than any other subject. Since calls on Kennedy by Gromyko were getting almost routine, this one caused little stir despite its rather unusual length of two hours and fifteen minutes.

The two men and their aides met in the Oval Room and, indeed, Berlin was the immediate topic. Gromyko was tough and even threatening. He shrugged Cuba off, told Kennedy that the buildup there was defensive. This conversation supported Kennedy's growing conviction that there would be no connection between Soviet action in Berlin and in Cuba. The Russians would apply the pressure in Berlin no matter what we did in the Caribbean. Kennedy read portions of his September 13 statement on Cuba to be sure Gromyko was aware of his pledge to act against an offensive threat.

Gromyko left. After dinner Kennedy's men trooped in for a long and important meeting. Kennedy sat in his rocking chair and the others took the seats around him. By now the focus was coming to rest on the blockade. There were no serious advocates of an invasion. The surprise air strike was labeled a "Pearl Harbor" and rejected. The blockade provided the flexibility that Kennedy wanted. From it he could move to another response, depending on the Russian reaction. It also gave the Russians a chance to back out, a leeway that Kennedy always tried to allow when dealing with them. He never wanted to force them into a corner where their only actions could be to fight or surrender.

McNamara led the Thursday night meeting because a blockade would be primarily his responsibility. He reviewed the military preparation that would be needed and the readiness of the forces, some of which had been alerted since Tuesday. When McNamara finished, there seemed little doubt that the blockade would be the best move. Since Kennedy, however, did not want to decide finally on Thursday night, he left the decision hanging. But everything was drawing together and everyone was working on the blockade plan.

The President was scheduled to begin his week-end political marathon the next day, and he thought briefly about the whole campaign. His decision was quick and simple. After this trip, there would be no more politics. "The campaign is over," he told his aides. "This blows it—we've lost anyway. They [the critics] were right about Cuba."

Cuba had become an issue in many areas. Democrats who hitched their campaigns to Kennedy were hard put to explain away his inaction. They could only turn away from the issue and say that in such matters the President knew best. The opposition could wave the flag and demand some action against the communists ninety miles from our shore—much as Kennedy had done against Nixon in 1960. Now, Kennedy felt, with the worst about Cuba being confirmed, many of the Democratic candidates were apt to be defeated. There was no better example than the Senate race in Indiana, where the incumbent Republican, Homer Capehart, was crying for an invasion of Cuba. The young Democratic hopeful, Birch Bayh, had stayed with Kennedy, accused Capehart, with some effort, of warmongering. What would happen now that Capehart had been proved right? It seemed, at the White House at least, that Bayh was doomed.

Kennedy took only the briefest time to consider such things. He had become totally immersed in the Cuban crisis. "I've never seen a man so fully engaged," McGeorge Bundy was to comment weeks later.

Kennedy walked through his routine appearances physically, but his mind was never there. There were still moments of rather grim humor, but there was never anger. "You can't afford anger with your enemies," said one White House man.

The President became like a defense attorney. Every witness who came before him was questioned exhaustively to see if there was a weakness in his testimony. This would not be a

Bay of Pigs if the human mentality in the White House could prevent it.

Security remained tight, much to Kennedy's amazement. The circle of men who knew what was about to happen was widening now and would soon get bigger. Yet no one suspected. Some of the men involved, keeping luncheon dates with reporters so as not to arouse suspicions, talked through the meals about matters which had now become trivial.

When the crisis had passed, Bundy, to satisfy his own curiosity, asked some of the men involved how many of them had told their wives at the beginning. Most of the group had told their wives, including John Kennedy. The women behaved magnificently, not one of them breaking security, and all of them who knew what was happening tried to keep their family life normal so that children and friends would suspect nothing. In fact, Bundy learned from his postcrisis sampling that those men who had not told their wives had made a mistake. The women, sensing the enormousness of the problem by the all-night absences of their husbands, became far more upset than those who did know.

Before Kennedy flew off to campaign on Friday, he met with the Joint Chiefs of Staff. Monday night was chosen as the time to spring the trap. Kennedy would go on TV and reveal the whole story. Sorensen was ordered to start work on his speech. In case information leaked out before, there was a contingency plan to make the announcement on Sunday night. But the extra day was needed if security could be kept over the week end.

Kennedy was only fifteen minutes late starting on his campaign week end, hardly anything to raise the eyebrows of the traveling press who had waited hours on other occasions for the habitually tardy President.

Hundreds of thousands of Cleveland's unsuspecting people lined the motorcade route which took Kennedy from the airport to Public Square in the heart of Cleveland. "So these are the issues of this campaign," Kennedy shouted. "Housing, jobs, the kind of tax program we write in the coming session, the kind of assistance we provide for education. . . ."

Behind every speaker's stand there was a phone linked to the White House. There were phones in the cars and in his jet. He was never more than seconds out of touch. Each chance he got he talked with his men who now were nearing the action phase of the Cuban plan.

The land lay calm and beautiful in Springfield, Illinois. It was the kind of prairie day that Abraham Lincoln would have liked. There was the warmth of Indian summer, a pale-blue sky with wispy clouds that filtered the sun. The pastures were turning brown and the oaks and maples dropped their leaves in the stillness.

Kennedy went to Lincoln's tomb, which broods on a prairie hill. Perhaps he gained some strength from that pause to honor Lincoln. He squinted up at the bronze face on the stringy figure sitting above the doorway. Inside, he placed a wreath on the tomb and stood a moment in silence as taps sounded.

Mid-America, weathered and solid, filled the Springfield State Fair Grounds livestock pavilion. The roar they gave Kennedy when he arrived was a tonic, whether he had his heart in his work or not. "In the last twenty-one months we have not, by any means, solved the farm problem," Kennedy said. "But we have achieved the best two-year advance in farm income of any two years since the depression. . . ."

He flew on to Chicago, and then it became clear that he would have to cut his campaign short. The President's counsel was needed too often now to handle the crisis by phone. It was the only time during the thirteen-day crisis period that Kennedy's aides felt he had become "unplugged." He decided to fly back to Washington on the following morning, but first he would need an excuse. He could say he had developed a cold. It was a rainy, cold night in Chicago, more of the same weather was promised for the next day, which was to be a day of outdoor campaigning. Perhaps the story would be believed by the harassed press corps.

That night he spoke to the faithful at McCormick Place, and afterward, when he went down in the basement to talk to 3,500 precinct workers, he even managed some humor. Harking back to his eyelash victory in Illinois, he said: "I just want to see who did it last November, 1960, and there they are. They said terrible things about you, but I never believed it. I hope that you will do the same for Congressman

Sid Yates. . . . I understand that Mayor Daley plans to keep you locked up here until November 6, then turn you loose."

Next morning the correspondents were hastily summoned, and the bulletin about the President's "cold" and plans to return to Washington were given out.

Reporters in Washington were far more suspicious than those traveling with the President. The weather was miserable in Chicago and, as a matter of fact, the week before Kennedy had canceled an appearance in Red Cloud, Minnesota, because of similar weather. It was true that he had a hard day of outdoor campaigning ahead of him, and he had always had trouble with his throat. Weary correspondents, not relishing the remainder of this trip, easily persuaded themselves that Kennedy did have a cold and that he should go back to the capital.

They looked closely as he came out of the Sheraton-Blackstone Hotel. He wore a raincoat and a hat, both unusual even in such cold, wet weather. But reporters who watched confessed they could not detect the signs of a cold.

Kennedy's staff became jumpy about security. On the jet back to Washington Larry O'Brien glanced out at the press contingent in the back of the President's plane and wondered to Kenny O'Donnell, "Will they swallow that cold story?" They did—at least long enough to matter.

The national security task force came back to the Oval Office in the mansion as the sun settled across the Potomac. Kennedy made the almost-final decision on the blockade, which was to be called a "quarantine." It could still be changed, but the chances of a change were slim. It now had everyone's approval. A blockade would put our prestige on the line, backed with force. We would not alienate our allies, both in Europe and Latin America, by an abrupt military action, and we might even win their endorsement. The blockade also gave Khrushchev time to consider his own course of action.

Kennedy looked up at the men around him then, the fateful step now taken. "The worst course of all would be to do nothing," he said.

The phrase caught the ear of Sorensen. Already he had the first draft of the TV speech done and the President now took some time to go over it, making suggested changes as he went. Sorensen went back to his desk and worked through the night. The next draft of the speech contained a new sentence—"The worst course of all would be to do nothing."

Now the ripples of crisis began to be detected. Military alerts became known. Leaves were canceled, units prepared to move and maneuvers called off. The Washington press corps got the scent.

Washington *Post* reporters and executives were called away from Saturday night social engagements, and a frantic telephone campaign began to try to unlock the mystery. *The New York Times'* Kenworthy, just back from vacation, went to Bureau Chief Reston's home and the two spent the night on the phone searching for clues.

Still, security held. Friends told friends, "I'd like to help you, but this time I just can't."

On Sunday morning the Washington *Post* bannered the story of crisis. But the paper did not tell what the crisis was and said it did not know.

There lingered in Kennedy's mind even at this time some thoughts about an air strike against the missile sites. Should there be something more than a quarantine? Sunday morning Kennedy summoned his top military men, and this time General Walter C. Sweeney, Jr., head of the Tactical Air Command, came along. Kennedy wanted to know how quickly and how accurately our planes could knock out the Soviet missiles. Was there a danger that some of the missiles might be fired before we could destroy them all? The precise estimates of the military men remain secret, but Kennedy was told that there was the possibility the Russians could and would launch some of the MRBM's at this country in the few minutes between the time our planes attacked and the end of their mission. With this information, Kennedy abandoned any idea of an air attack as an initial move against Cuba.

In the afternoon Kennedy called his men back into session in the mansion. The final approval of the quarantine, outlined in detail by Admiral George Anderson, was given by the President. The speech that the President would give was studied word by word. The complex and lengthy chain of political and diplomatic moves preceding the public statement was worked out. Congressional leaders, now scattered across the country, were to be flown back to be briefed. The President's Cabinet was to be called in. Our allies were to be told; a special briefing was to be held for members of the Organization of American States. Kennedy planned to call Macmillan, Eisenhower, Truman and Hoover. Embassies had to be alerted, heads of state written to.

Monday was a mild fall day. Gardeners raked the falling leaves into big piles on the White House lawn. Tourists loitered along the streets, peering in at the mansion. But there was a sense of foreboding. By now all the newspapers were aware of a crisis, but it was still formless. Some had penetrated the first layer of security and were aware that missiles had been detected in Cuba. This story was not printed, however, when the White House appealed to the press corps. But what Kennedy planned to do remained in doubt until near the time he announced his intention.

On Pennsylvania Avenue pickets hoisted conflicting placards in a strange side drama. "Cuba Can Be Negotiated," read one. "More Courage and Less Profile," read another.

More than a hundred newsmen filled Salinger's office when he announced that the President had asked the TV networks for time at 6 P.M.

Military jets flashed across the country, bringing the congressional leaders. Louisiana's Congressman Hale Boggs was found in the Gulf of Mexico fishing and was hoisted ashore in a helicopter and put on a plane for Washington. California's Senator Thomas Kuchel put on crash helmet and flying suit and sped 2,300 miles in four hours in the cockpit of a Navy jet.

There was an uneasy moment when a rumor arose that Andrei Gromyko was going to say something about Cuba. Had the Russians found out? Gromyko was to leave Idlewild for Moscow, and before stepping on the plane he met reporters. The White House sent a man to listen to the Russian. He said good-bye and flew back home. The White House contact man hurried to a phone to call in his calming report.

France's Charles de Gaulle and Germany's Konrad Adenauer received advance notice from former Secretary of State

Dean Acheson, who was sent by Kennedy as a courtesy. The Latin diplomats were summoned to the State Department. At 3 P.M. Kennedy's task force met for a final review of the plan. At 4 the complete Cabinet heard from Dean Rusk and the President of the national crisis and the action to come. Kennedy had to attend to a ceremonial duty: greeting Prime Minister Milton Obote of Uganda. At 5 P.M. Kennedy looked around him at the congressional leaders. "I think you ought to know what we are going to do here," said the President. CIA's McCone unraveled the facts which, at first, shocked the men into silence. There was dissent, however, when the plan for the quarantine was revealed. Georgia's Senator Richard Russell, chairman of the Senate Armed Services Committee, felt that we should invade Cuba and clean out the mess once and for all. There could be no solution to Castro and communism in this hemisphere until that was done, he said. He was supported by William Fulbright, chairman of the Senate Foreign Relations Committee. Kennedy listened, but there was to be no change in plans. His mind was made up.

At 5:30 both in the Kremlin and in Washington the Russians were told. Then it was nearly time for Kennedy to tell the American people.

He gave his hair a swipe or two with a brush, walked to his desk, straightened the sheets of his speech.

"Good evening, my fellow citizens. This government, as promised, has maintained the closest surveillance of the Soviet military build-up on the island of Cuba. Within the past week, unmistakable evidence has established the fact that a series of offensive missile sites is now in preparation on that imprisoned island . . . this secret, swift and extraordinary build-up of communist missiles—in an area well known to have a special and historical relationship to the United States and the nations of the western hemisphere, in violation of Soviet assurances, and in defiance of American and hemispheric policy—this sudden, clandestine decision to station strategic weapons for the first time outside of Soviet soil—is a deliberately provocative and unjustified change in the status quo which cannot be accepted by this country, if our courage and our commitments are ever to be trusted again by either friend or foe. . . . To halt this offensive build-up, a strict quarantine on all offensive military equipment under shipment to Cuba is being initiated. . . . I call upon Chairman Khrushchev to halt and eliminate this clandestine, reckless and provocative threat to world peace and to stable relations between our two nations."

The sights and sounds and feelings of wartime were in the nation. The First Armored Division, "Old Ironsides" which had won fame at Anzio, moved stealthily 1,300 miles from its Camp Hood, Texas, base to Fort Stewart, Georgia, where it groomed itself for an amphibious assault. Florida beaches bristled with missile launchers. Flight after flight of jets streaked into Homestead Air Force Base from their California and Colorado bases. The families of the men who man Guantanamo, our naval base on the eastern tip of Cuba, were put on a ship and brought back to the United States. Some of the men, busy preparing the base defenses, learned about the evacuation when they returned to their quarters to find their families leaving. If Khrushchev had any doubts now, all he had to do was look at the assembling arsenal in the southeastern United States. An amphibious and airborne army of five divisions, 12,000 Marines and 1,000 airplanes was ready, just in case. The Navy sent twenty-six ships to form a picket fence around Cuba, kept 150 ships in reserve.

The White House now took a few breaths and waited. Kennedy's security task force was given a formal name (Executive Committee of the National Security Council) and a formal meeting time (10 A.M. every day). Salinger issued his voluntary code of discretion and caution in handling news, so as not to injure the national cause.

Twice a day now Air Force 101's and Navy F8U's roared over Cuba below a thousand feet. And the news from their pictures was that construction was going forward. So detailed were the low-level photographs that Russian soldiers were caught on the run trying to reach antiaircraft guns. But our planes were too fast and too low to be detected in time.

The Organization of American States, after meeting all day Tuesday, approved by 19 to 0 a resolution authorizing the use of force, individually or collectively, to enforce the quarantine. The United States cited the Rio Pact of 1947 for its legal authority, and Kennedy waited for the OAS action before signing the quarantine proclamation. The endorsement, and that of our other allies, firmer than we had dared hope for, was a solid jolt to the Soviets, who were hoping for diplomatic confusion.

At 7:06 P.M. on October 23 Kennedy signed the proclamation for the quarantine to go into effect at 10 A.M. the next day. The unsmiling President three times asked a lighting technician what date it was. He quickly scrawled "John Fitzgerald Kennedy"; then he got up and walked away without a word.

From the Black Sea to the Atlantic fringes of the western hemisphere the prying eyes of American reconnaissance planes watched the oncoming ships with their suspected missile cargoes.

The ships held their courses Tuesday night, and tension now began to build in the White House. For a few hours Kennedy and his strategists thought that they would have to sink a ship or two to prove to the Russians that they meant business.

Whenever he could, Kennedy broke from the endless conferences and paced up and down on the open porch outside his office, inhaling the clear fall air. On the south lawn Pushinka, the Russian space pup, a present from Khrushchev, romped with Charlie, Caroline's terrier. At least there was pleasant coexistence on one level.

The security officers became more concerned about the protection of the President. Patrol cars lurked at the corners of the grounds after dark. Motorcycle officers cruised continuously around the eighteen acres. A news photographer set up a long telephoto lens for a view of the rear White House lawn, and a policeman came up to him and asked to look. "I just wanted to be sure there were no cross-hairs," said the officer.

Before tourists were admitted to the White House, they were asked to check packages and cameras. Large women's handbags were investigated and the checked packages were run through a fluoroscope which was hastily set up in a trailer outside the White House's east wing.

Evacuation plans for the President and a skeleton government were reviewed and updated. Salinger called in a select number of newsmen and told them they had been picked to go with the President in case of attack. They were to keep the White House switchboard informed of their whereabouts. Plans for running the government from underground were discussed. In one of the back halls a door opened and a man's voice drifted into the corridor: "The area is beneath several hundred feet of rock, there is plenty of room and a cafeteria. . . ."

Kennedy had time for some routine business which had been forgotten during the previous week. The paper pipeline with its never-ending current had been, for the first time in two years, almost totally plugged. It had backed up into a sizable reservoir. The stream began to flow again with postmaster appointments, disaster relief money, proclamations and all the other trivia of government.

There was even time for the President to attend a small dinner which Jackie gave for the Maharajah and Maharani of Jaipur, who had entertained the First Lady on her Indian trip.

Some 48,000 telegrams poured into the White House in the first days following Kennedy's TV speech. They supported him in the ratio of 10 to 1, a gratifying endorsement.

But more than telegrams from sympathetic Americans was needed. The crisis remained. The Soviet ships bore on.

Then the first break came. One by one the ships suspected of carrying more missiles and bombers swung in wide arcs and headed back toward Asia.

The dialogue began between Moscow and Washington. It first came in response to a proposal by U Thant, Secretary General of the United Nations, who proposed that there should be a two- or three-week suspension of the arms shipments and the blockade while negotiations were held. Khrushchev was quick to accept, but the United States, fearful of losing the initiative she had gained, turned the suggestion down.

In the meantime our UN Ambassador Adlai Stevenson took the incriminating photographs of the Soviet missile sites to the UN Security Council and confronted Russia's Valerian Zorin with them.

On Friday morning two destroyers, ironically one of them the USS "Joseph P. Kennedy, Jr.," named for the President's older brother killed in World War II, the other the USS "John R. Pierce," halted the Russian-chartered Lebanese freighter "Marucla," boarded her and found sulphur, paper and trucks. After coffee with her Greek skipper, the boarding party cleared her to proceed through the cordon of U.S. Navy vessels.

There came a new appeal from U Thant. He urged the United States to avoid confrontation of Soviet ships and he asked Khrushchev to keep his ships out of the quarantine zone. Both agreed, but Kennedy drew attention to the Soviet presence in Cuba and said that the withdrawal of the weapons was of "great urgency."

There was more talk now about new action against Cuba because the Russians were still working feverishly on the missile sites. Newspapers began to print stories about the possibilities of an invasion or an air strike.

On Friday night the teletypes in the State Department clattered out a secret letter from Khrushchev to Kennedy; it was to open an amazingly frank and free-flowing exchange between the Kremlin and Washington, a new and highly encouraging development in cold-war diplomacy.

Beyond that, the tone of the letter was important. "It was a plea for peace—almost eloquent," said one White House aide. The Chairman had written of the vast progress his people had made and of the tragedy to his land, the United States and the world that nuclear war would bring. He asked Kennedy for coolness and reason, for he feared events were getting out of control. Though it was not stated specifically, the letter offered to withdraw the offensive weapons under United Nations supervision in return for an end to the blockade and assurances that Cuba would not be invaded.

The men in the White House were first amazed, then guardedly jubilant. There was hope, they felt, when the Russian leader could write a letter so drastically contrasting with his previous style. At last Kennedy seemed to have found in Khrushchev the feeling that he had sought at Vienna but had not discovered—a feeling of the horror of nuclear war.

The euphoria was soon dispelled. Saturday morning, as the men gathered to draft a reply to the Khrushchev letter, the news flashed from Moscow that Khrushchev had just sent another letter, the text of which was broadcast there. It had not yet been transmitted to the State Department over the government wires. Now, as had been expected, Khrushchev wanted to trade the Cuban missile bases for our missile bases in Turkey. The suggestion was unacceptable. That had been decided earlier. But the Kennedy strategists were baffled for a short while about what to do. They now had to answer two letters with conflicting offers. The solution was to issue immediately a short statement indirectly but plainly turning down the missile swap and go on drafting a reply to Khrushchev's private letter almost as if his second letter had not been written.

The Russian maneuver was disturbing and unfathomable. Did the switch in terms indicate a Kremlin power struggle? No one knew for the moment just what Khrushchev had in mind.

Real tension began to mount in the White House when the news came that one of our U-2's was missing. "It looked as if it might be slipping out of our control," said one White House man. "We were not then on the edge of nuclear war, but we couldn't be sure. There was the feeling we were moving toward it."

In these hours Kennedy began seriously to consider an invasion of Cuba. Though the troops had been assembled and poised earlier and the rumors of an imminent assault had circulated freely, an invasion had never been foremost in Kennedy's thinking. Saturday, however, the possibility loomed larger.

The strident voice of Fidel Castro from Havana early Sunday gave the first hint. He did not really care about the missiles, he said, he only cared about peace. At 9 A.M. (EST) the Moscow Radio began to broadcast another letter from Khrushchev to Kennedy, and this was the word that Washington had so fervently awaited. Khrushchev stated that he had ordered work on the missile sites halted, the missiles crated and returned to Russia, the action to be verified by the

United Nations. In return he asked for the blockade to be lifted, the United States and other nations of the western hemisphere to pledge not to attack or invade Cuba. The deal was made.

An enormous peace settled on the White House. Weary staff members came out in the open again and smiled. Reporters clustered on the porch beside the President's office to watch him board a helicopter to join his family in Glen Ora for the rest of the day. McGeorge Bundy, surrounded by his four children and his wife who had come to lunch with him in his office, watched too. Then, one by one, the offices and the phone booths began to empty. It was just another Sunday afternoon in Washington, a dead town on the week ends.

This time Khrushchev lived up to his word. The forty-two missiles were taken down and shipped home while our Navy counted them. The sites were destroyed. The IL-28's were recrated and sent back to Russia. We were not granted on-site inspection and we therefore did not give the Soviets the "no-invasion" commitment they wanted.

It was true that Castro still resided in Cuba, the communists in full control. He was in many ways just as irksome and as perplexing a problem as he had been before.

But the crisis had never been an American-Cuban affair. Its genesis was much broader and more important. It was a basic cold-war confrontation, a struggle between Russia and the United States. Therefore its solution was of much deeper meaning than Castro.

There was the unassailable fact that Khrushchev had gambled and lost. There were none of his offensive missiles in Cuba and none of his IL-28 bombers. Whatever his plan had been, it had failed and failed rather grandly.

If, indeed, Khrushchev had not held much respect for Kennedy's determination up until then, he did now. The message had been unmistakable.

The United States, as the backbone of the free world, found itself held in rare esteem, and the stature of John Kennedy grew with it. The Organization of American States was more united than ever, and for the time being the allies had drawn closer than they had been before.

There was the fervid hope among the top policy planners that the cold war would enter a new phase, that the free world had seized a thin edge of initiative which, with skillful and diligent pressure, could be expanded so that communism could be inexorably rolled back.

It was still too early to judge for certain, but there were encouraging signs. The fissure in the communist monolith grew as Red China criticized the Kremlin's Cuban backdown. The appeals for peace from Moscow increased in intensity and frequency, and abruptly talk of a new Berlin crisis vanished. There were seemingly sincere overtures to halt nuclear testing.

Kennedy faced cautiously into this new wind. Though deeply gratified by the turn of events, he was also disturbed by the complete untrustworthiness of Khrushchev. Many were quick to suggest that now with Khrushchev at last aware of the American will, relations between the United States and the Soviet Union would warm. But Kennedy wondered how you could do business with a man who had deliberately tried to perpetrate the most monumental deception of recent history.

Nor was Kennedy deceived about the nature of the world problems that lay ahead. Britain's entry into the Common Market was in question. De Gaulle's insistence on France's becoming an independent nuclear force ran against the wishes of the United States, which wanted an integrated European force. Social and economic problems in Latin America were as onerous as ever. Though we were not losing the war in Vietnam, we were not clearly winning it. Red China and India were in a mountain war that threatened to spread.

Yet there was a new feeling of confidence in the White House. It was a confidence of the President in his government, a confidence of the men in themselves. They had performed superbly in the thirteen critical days. The effort had succeeded—the New Frontier had worked well in its toughest test.

"The President," said an aide, "now has a sense that his own government can work, that he can mobilize his own resources, that he can judge people correctly. There is a conviction of the correctness of the direction he is going."

"It was an enormous human experience," said one member of the special committee. "There was a deep sense of the sharing of danger."

Kennedy's team had drawn closer to one another, had relied more on one another. The President was moved, too, by this feeling of comradeship. How it affected him became clear when, without any warning, at the end of one of the meetings of his crisis group, he handed to each man a small silver calendar of October mounted on walnut. The days 16 through 28 were etched deeply so they stood out from the others. In one corner were his initials, in another corner the initials of the recipient. Kennedy had conceived the idea himself, ordered the calendars made at Tiffany's, then had carefully gone over the list of men he wanted to honor. He also gave one to Jackie.

There had been no question, of course, of how his staff felt about him. The public was the fickle one. And, suddenly, it was in love again. George Gallup soon found that 74 per cent of the voters liked the way John Kennedy was doing his job.

On November 6 their endorsement showed in a way that would gladden the heart of any politician, particularly one who was President.

CHAPTER TWENTY-SIX

THE PEOPLE
APPROVE

THE 87th Congress was a mild ache to John Kennedy. It was true enough that it turned out far more important legislation than it was credited with passing, but that did not seem to matter. It balked on Kennedy's big social programs. And what it did accomplish was done in such a prosaic manner that it seemed downright dull. Even some of its hairbreadth failures couldn't arouse much interest. Part of the trouble was the contrast with the old days. Those memories of a Democratic congress under Eisenhower were splashed with color.

Gone were the flamboyant productions of the Texans, Lyndon Baines Johnson and Sam Taliaferro Rayburn, who ran the Congress up until 1961. Lyndon had been the magnificent general who could organize Senate affairs backstage like an infantry division and march in the votes at the dramatic moment. He could produce cliff hangers or landslides, whatever the occasion demanded. But most of all he could produce legislation, and it always came in Vista-Vision. When things got a little too gaudy over in the Senate Chamber, you could turn to Mr. Sam, who was American heritage. He was all heart, all true, all care, all wisdom and all else that the Texas prairie and the United States House of Representatives could impart to a man—and that was plenty.

Kennedy could be blamed somewhat for the miserly appraisals of the old 87th. He moved the stage down Pennsylvania Avenue and would have it no other way. The senators and congressmen languished in the White House shadow. They craved the spotlight, but they got only a flicker now and then.

When the 87th finally went home on October 13 after having at last created a distinction of sorts for itself—meeting longer in one session than any other Congress since 1951—it was calculated that Kennedy had received 304 requests out of a total of 653. It was about an average score quantitatively, and there were even some notable achievements qualitatively. The great problem in rating the Kennedy program arose because his highly publicized legislation fared dismally.

Among the wins, Kennedy could point to the boldest trade legislation in history, giving him power to slash tariffs by at least 50 per cent and remove some entirely. In any other era, that bill alone would have marked the 87th for history. But these times demanded more. Kennedy won his proposal to help out the United Nations indebtedness by buying up to $100 million in bonds. A three-year program to retrain unemployed workers got by, and a proposal to set up a private corporation to operate a communications satellite was approved. The 87th okayed a Constitutional amendment to outlaw poll taxes in federal elections, all of Kennedy's beefed up defense-money requests, a farm bill with tougher production controls to help curb surplus crops, a housing bill, aid to depressed areas, an increase in the minimum wage from $1 per hour to $1.25 per hour, a tax revision measure to give a 7 per cent income tax credit to business for new equipment, a postal rate increase and a public works bill. Some of the bills were compromises with what Kennedy really wanted and asked for, but compromise is part of the Kennedy system.

Kennedy failed to get his bill for medical care for the aged under social security, and this was a major blow. Medicare had been a lynch-pin of his whole New Frontier image; he just could not budge it. The 87th refused to give him a new Department of Urban Affairs, it chopped away with glee at foreign aid, it turned him down when he asked for long-term aid financing. Kennedy had rated an aid to education bill as important as any of his new proposals, but in the first session of the 87th it became enmeshed in a fight over whether it should include both public and parochial schools, and it died. There was nobody brave enough to revive it in the second session.

The agonizing thing was that the Democratic majorities in both houses of Congress failed to function like majorities. One or two votes in a committee sometimes stalled legislation, or powerful and obstinate committee chairmen simply refused to act. Kennedy was resigned to the traditions of Congress which gave the committee chairmanships to the senior members. He was equally resigned to the clumsy congressional system, which routed legislation through subcommittees, committees, and more committees, each stop being full of traps. The system could be tampered with a bit, as when in 1961 and 1963 the House Rules Committee was enlarged to give it a more liberal cast and thus make it a more freely flowing legislative avenue. The Rules Committee had to assign each bill (except appropriation measures) a time and form for debate, and thus by simply refusing to grant a "rule," the committee could strangle legislation. But beyond this there was very little that Kennedy felt he could do to remove the anchor that dragged at his legislative efforts. The very nature of the men themselves, each representing a tiny section of land which might reflect but a single economic or social view, could affect the outcome of a program for the nation. Through longevity one congressman could rule a powerful committee molding all the legislation which passed through him to suit his conservative or liberal tastes. John Kennedy, who was responsible for the national good, often felt that legislation which had run through this Rube Goldberg route was far wide of the majority will. The President also felt that the huge wealthy lobbies, such as the Chamber of Commerce, the Farm Bureau and the American Medical Association, had become bureaucracies themselves, no longer genuinely attuned to their memberships. Policy was made in the headquarters and handed down to those who paid the dues, rather than being a reflection of the membership. Their power was great, primarily due to their increasing wealth, and they used it in massive attacks on Congress.

About the only way that he felt he might alter the legislative complexion of the House was to try to win a handful of congressmen who would vote with him. Inevitably on his pet pieces of legislation conservative southern Democrats would join with Republicans, and often they would defeat him if, indeed, the legislation was not sunk before by the same process in committee. The votes were so close that Kennedy had some hope that four or five new congressmen might tilt the balance in his favor.

But he faced that nasty political habit that the electorate had of cutting down the congressional forces of the party in power. Only Roosevelt in 1934 had broken it, and then the country had been on its knees begging for help. The prospects in prosperous 1962 were not good for a Democratic victory at the polls.

Kennedy decided that he would campaign harder than any President in history to try to win more leverage in Congress. There were those who suggested he was foolish. A President did not have to commit his prestige for a bunch of congressmen, particularly when international peril was as rampant as now. Under this theory, if Kennedy failed to beat tradition, his loss of prestige on the Hill would be even greater and his program would suffer more. Why not, then, make some token political speeches but remain above the battle? When the returns came in, if they were not too bad, claim a great victory for his policies; if they were bad—well, shrug and point out that it happened to everybody in the off-year.

Kennedy was of a different mind. He believed that his prestige was fully committed anyway. No matter what happened to his party in the election, the President would be blamed or praised. He was party leader, he cast the image. Kennedy would not be above the battle, he would do all he could to elect a Congress that would look with more favor on his big bills.

There also, in long range, was the national interest. Kennedy wanted taxes cut to strike at the roots of many of the ills plaguing the country—sluggish growth, idle plants, unemployment, depressed areas, narrow profits, the gold outflow. Correcting these evils was necessary not only for internal national health, but also for our international strength. We could not sustain, indefinitely, our relative superiority in arms, both nuclear and conventional, with a stagnant economy. In Kennedy's mind, the economy had become the key to the future; his tax bill had become the key to the economy; and Congress was the key to the tax bill.

The President did not begin the political season under auspicious signs. In the early fall his own popularity had fallen. And a Gallup poll had shown that among the voters, some 43 per cent of the Republicans said they had a reason to vote, while only 30 per cent of the Democrats said they had a reason. This was unmistakable evidence of that political disease called apathy.

Kennedy put his staff to work finding out what happened in the off-year elections all the way back to 1930. He wanted the ground properly pessimistic before he started. The technique was called "underdoggery." If one started low enough, any gain was cheering news.

The diligent researchers soon had the answers, and they showed that since 1930 the average off-year congressional loss for the party in power was thirty-nine House seats and five Senate seats. If the 1934 election is eliminated from these figures, the average is forty-six House seats and seven Senate seats. In 1950, after Truman's close 1948 victory, the Democrats lost twenty-nine House seats and five Senate seats. Viewed from almost any angle, the figures were not encouraging.

Yet there was the generally unrecognized fact that the 87th Congress had very little Democratic fat on it. Most of the 263 Democratic members of the House came from solid Democratic districts. Often in presidential elections the winning presidential candidate will pull along with him a goodly number of Democratic congressional candidates who normally would not win and many of whom are then eliminated in the off-year election. But Kennedy, in his squeaking 1960 victory, lost twenty-one House seats. Thus in 1962 there was little for the electorate to "normalize."

The President from the start made ambitious plans. When November 6 rolled around, his aides calculated that he would have traveled a record-shattering 19,000 miles (more in one year than Eisenhower's 14,500 accumulated in 1954 and 1958 combined).

At first the White House strategists were preoccupied with the idea that the President could wing his way through the hustings on "nonpolitical" trips, dedicating dams, inspecting national forests and military installations and just, incidentally, have the area's candidates up on the stage with him. This plan not only lent a statesmanlike quality to his campaigning, but made that huge jet, which cost $2,350 per hour to run, a legitimate government expense item. Otherwise the National Committee—already nearly a million dollars in the hole—would have to pay for the trips.

Kennedy tried it out in a natural-resource-oriented swing to the West Coast and again in a loop through the South, where he inspected the nation's space research and launching complexes. But these were not satisfactory. They were a little phony, and Kennedy sensed it. He could not take off his gloves and join the row—he had to watch what he said and what he did too closely. He loved politics and all the dazzle that went with it—the motorcades, the crowds, the brass bands and, best of all, shouting hoarsely for the people to vote Democratic and get rid of the Republicans. He abandoned his "nonpolitical" role and joined the fight.

Kennedy had to grope a while to find his old form and to decide what his line of attack would be. He began his genuine 1962 electioneering in the grandest manner known to mankind—from the depths of the State Farm Arena in Harrisburg, Pennsylvania, still pungent from a 4-H parade of Jersey milch cows that had passed through only six hours earlier. It was a monster rally, with all the bunting and the bellowing and the electric organ that make a politician's hair stand out straight. This was the country of the $100-a-plate fund-raising dinner, conceived and nurtured by Matt McClosky, a dumpy Philadelphia millionaire who for years as national treasurer had stoked the party's coffers and now had gone on to his reward: Ambassador to Ireland. Mat would have been proud that night in September. It may have been the biggest political dinner in all history. It was claimed that more than 12,000 were fed on the fourteen-acres of floor in the State Farm Show Building, netting nearly a million dollars.

Oliver B. Rotzell, a Philadelphia caterer, mounted a twenty-five-truck gastronomic convoy in the afternoon that rolled into Harrisburg with 12,000 pounds of precooked beef,

1,680 pounds of peas, 120 gallons of Russian dressing for 1,425 heads of lettuce and 12,000 tomatoes, and a two-ton truck filled with watermelons. The food was consumed in a blue cigar fog, and then the diners moved into the arena for the main event.

The audience roared and whistled, and the organ nearly caused the building to cave in. Kennedy stood there, hands in his pockets, and let the sound roll over him like a soothing ocean swell. "I will introduce myself," he began. "I am Teddy Kennedy's brother. . . ." Once again the great chorus of approval welled up but Kennedy silenced it. And then he began to hammer, forging his theme for 1962. "It was a cold day in January when this Democratic administration took office. The nation's engine was idling. . . . All of this was twenty months ago tonight, and were I to tell you tonight that all was well, or were I to say that the 87th Congress had done all the things which we feel must be done, I would be setting my sights too low. But the facts of the matter are that progress has been made on every single one of these problems, that the decline in our position has been reversed, and that this country is moving again."

Kennedy often had said that beyond the confines of Washington things always looked different. But nobody had really known how much until they heard Kennedy. "At home the gross national product, which is the measuring stick for the productivity of the United States, has risen by more than 10 per cent since that day, by nearly $50 billion above its previous peak. . . .

"The wages and salaries of our working men and women have risen $27 million, or 10 per cent. . . .

"Although unemployment is still high, and is still much too high, it is 40 per cent less in this state than it was twenty months ago. . . .

"The profits enjoyed by our businessmen have risen over 10 billion, or 26 per cent. . . .

"Seven hundred depressed areas are finally receiving redevelopment aid. . . .

"We have passed the most comprehensive housing bill in the history of this country. . . .

"A $900 million public works program . . .

"No other Congress in recent years has made a record of progress and compassion to match this. . . ."

All the thunder was there and all the trappings, but something was wrong in Harrisburg.

The claims by Kennedy were too extravagant. He had never before been that much of a demagogue and seemed ill at ease in the role. At that, he had dropped out a paragraph from the prepared text, a paragraph that was even more laudatory: "We have seized the initiative in trade and aid and diplomacy—stemmed the tide in Vietnam—and stopped the conquest of Laos. Mr. Castro has not taken over Latin America, Mr. Gizenga has not taken over the Congo and Mr. Khrushchev has not taken over West Berlin. . . ." One reporter folded up his portable typewriter and shook his head. "I'm amazed," he said as he trudged out of the deserted arena, "that he didn't mention the fact that the Indians have not yet recaptured Manhattan Island."

A week later in Wheeling, West Virginia, Kennedy began to find his form. Along the highways in this state, which in the 1960 primary election had launched him toward the White House, the people showed some of the old frenzied adulation of two years ago.

Kennedy had come to help out Cleveland Bailey, a 78-year-old congressman who had been redistricted and now was fighting another incumbent, Republican Arch Moore, Jr. Bailey was a stooped, bald little man who had once taken a swing at Harlem's Congressman Adam Clayton Powell, but he did not connect solidly enough to do damage.

It was raining when Kennedy got up on the platform. But one by one he named the congressmen around him, letting his audience savor each endorsement. He slipped when he turned to Bailey and called him by his opponent's name, Congressman Moore. He hurried over the error, but not before the local press caught it.

He did some bragging about what he had done for West Virginia, but it was subdued. And besides, it was true. He had made certain that the state got a lot of attention in his two years. Then he settled into the routine that he would use in one form or another in most of his coming stops.

"Two years ago I said that it was time to get this country

moving again. In the last two years, we have made a start, but just a start. But we have begun to act, for no Congress in a generation has passed as much affirmative and constructive legislation as the present Congress. . . . Last year 84 per cent of the Republicans voted in the Senate against nation-wide financing of unemployment compensation . . . 81 per cent of the Republicans in the House voted against the area redevelopment bill; 95 per cent of the Republicans in the House voted against the Housing Act; 80 per cent voted against the minimum wage of $1.25—80 per cent of the Republican members of the House of Representatives voted against giving a man $1.25 for a forty-hour-week, an hour."

Kennedy scowled, he waved a clenched fist into the rain, and then cried: "This is the issue in this campaign. We want to finish the job that we have started here in West Virginia and in Ohio and Pennsylvania. . . ."

Before he left, he went down to the crowd. He was still coatless and hatless, and the rain pounded down. He reached out for the damp hands. "How are you. . . . Good to see you. . . . Better get out of the rain. . . . Nice of you to come out." Now he felt it, now he was moving the right way.

In Cincinnati, Ohio, Republican heartland, he met the political enemy. The signs read, "Where Are Those Fighting Irish"; "OK, We Licked Mississippi. Now How About Cuba?"; "Russian Rockets 90 Miles Away. Blockade."

Kennedy answered them. ". . . this administration has added five combat divisions. We have increased our Army from eleven to sixteen divisions in the last twenty months. . . ." Then he turned to the real enemy of the day, the Republicans. "Now you have a chance to decide here in Ohio and in this district whether this is the kind of Congress and country you want—one that sits still, one that lies at anchor, one that drifts, one that says 'No.' They [Republicans] have made the word 'No' a political program. . . ."

He went on to Detroit: "Every off-year in this century with the exception of once, the party in power has lost votes, and I can tell you after the razor-thin majorities by which we have won or lost, that we need every vote we can get. Otherwise this country will stand still. The decision is yours and we ask your help in Michigan." In Hamtramck, the Poles lined the streets and sidewalks to watch him go by slowly on the back of a top-down convertible.

He was in full flight then. He rushed on to Flint and Muskegon and hopped over to Minneapolis.

The following week in Baltimore he took aim again at the social issues. "I am proud to come back to this city and state and ask your support in electing Democrats—those members of the House and Senate who support the minimum wage and medical care for the aged, and urban renewal, and cleaning our rivers, and giving security to our older people, and educating our children, and giving jobs to our workers. That is the issue of this campaign."

In Newark on Columbus Day he added a personal touch. "My grandfather always used to claim that the Fitzgeralds were descended from the Geraldinis, who came from Venice. I have never had the courage to make that claim, but I will make it on Columbus Day in this State of New Jersey."

Next was New York, Pennsylvania's Monongahela Valley where steel mills stood idle, Indianapolis, Louisville, Buffalo, and back home, weary but gratified that the line was beginning to catch hold.

"He just keeps putting more in his schedule," said one White House staff member. "He's going to kill us all."

When Eisenhower took to the stump with some biting criticism of Kennedy and his New Frontier, the politicians were delighted, not at what he said, but at the fact that he was moving around, that there would be a lively fight.

"We'll pay Ike's fare any day he wants to go out and make those speeches," said Pierre Salinger.

"The lack of political enthusiasm is still our big fear," added another aide.

It was a foregone conclusion that the President would help rouse the people. Wherever he goes in that glistening jet, the people are smitten. With him come the White House press corps, the Secret Service, a flotilla of gleaming limousines—the presidential aura. The newspapers carry the story by the literal foot, and pictures of the Kennedy smile fill page after page. TV follows him as he comes into town in a motorcade that is certain to wind through the heavy

Democratic districts so the streets will be filled. The candidate with a President on his side is rarely hurt.

As Kennedy rested for the next onslaught, he learned about the Russian missiles in Cuba. In his heart the campaign died as he shifted the focus of his energy to the crisis.

It was a shame to have to abandon such an experiment as the one begun October 19. It was to have been one of the most horrendous political week ends on record, with 5,500 miles of flying from one end of the country to the other. On this journey Kennedy would have talked to 900,-000 people in the flesh, another five million on television, shaken 2,700 hands and heard "Anchors Aweigh" another fifteen times. It might even have had some effect on the election.

On October 28, when Khrushchev announced that he would remove the missiles and bombers from Cuba, politics was back in style, and Kennedy was again vitally interested. But good politics, right then, was to stay in Washington and keep a wakeful eye on the Russians in Cuba—and hope.

On election night Kennedy sat with Larry O'Brien. It was not the happiest of evenings at the start. O'Brien's most secret estimate was that the Democrats would lose nine House seats. He figured that they would gain in the Senate, but that was not the vital issue in this election. The Senate was not the legislative bottleneck that the House had proved to be.

O'Brien's public estimate had a fat safety margin. He put in on the record for reporters that Democrats might lose ten to fifteen House seats.

The secret nine-seat estimate was about the President's own calculation that evening as the polls closed and the first meaningful tallies began to come in. There was a shocker right off which sent their chart plunging more. Down in Kentucky, Frank Burke was roundly defeated. For a few minutes the flash was demoralizing. Burke had been picked by O'Brien as a solid winner. No man had given Kennedy more support in Congress, and now he was sunk by a Goldwater conservative, Gene Snyder. O'Brien and Kennedy groaned together. They upped their estimates of House losses on the basis of Burke's defeat and thought that they would be lucky to keep them down to twenty-five seats.

The sun swept toward the west and the tide of returns washed east. The Burke pattern did not hold and hope began to build. Surprising names were added to the Democratic rolls. The young Birch Bayh became the senator-elect from Indiana, beating fourteen-year veteran Homer Capehart. The 38-year-old Don Fraser from Minneapolis was in possession of the House seat of Walter Judd, former medical missionary to China and lecture-circuit rider. Gaylord Nelson, Wisconsin governor, removed Alex Wiley from the Senate after twenty-four years. The President went to bed near midnight feeling that he might have shattered tradition.

Not all the news was good, however. The big-four governorships fell with a jarring (to the White House) crash into the Republican column. Nelson Rockefeller smothered Robert Morgenthau in New York with a margin of half a million votes. Humpty-dumpty Mike DiSalle was tumbled by James A. Rhodes in Ohio. Even the young and vigorous suffered. Michigan's one-termer John Swainson, 37, articulate and energetic, lost to George Romney, 55, also articulate and energetic. Out in Pennsylvania, Philadelphia's ex-Mayor Richardson Dilworth was defeated by Congressman William Scranton.

For John Kennedy this lineup would be of particular interest because it was likely that his opponent in 1964 would be one of those governors.

The Democrats could point to Hawaii, Iowa, Massachusetts, New Hampshire, New Mexico, Vermont, in which they won governorships, but somehow these states did not have the high political voltage of the big four and Colorado, Rhode Island, Oklahoma and Wyoming, which the GOP also won.

In the South there were the vestiges of a two-party system, with new Republican sproutings in Florida, North Carolina, Tennessee, Oklahoma and Texas.

The Democrats were quick to point out that it could be bad news for the Republicans if their southern members were no more loyal to the party program than southern Democrats were loyal to Kennedy.

*   *   *

Kennedy was awake at 7 A.M. on November 7, and his TV set was blaring the good news as the first timid rays of the morning sun melted the frost off the White House lawn.

As he heard more returns from across the nation, the President's smile became as persistent as the daylight. That political habit had been broken.

The Democrats added four Senate seats, making their total forces 68 out of the 100. In the House they lost four seats, which was only a fraction of the usual off-year loss. And because the House, which had temporarily been increased to 437 members when Alaska and Hawaii became states, reverted to its normal 435 members, the Republicans gained only two seats in the totals. The lineup would be 259 Democrats to 176 Republicans. There were 67 new congressmen in all, most of them having replaced members of their own parties, thus altering the numerical balance only slightly. But the Democratic dopesters calculated that among the new men there were more Kennedy supporters —they might supply as many as twelve new votes for some Kennedy bills.

Kennedy was soon on the phone, his goodwill flooding the town. He talked to staff members, successful candidates, unsuccessful candidates, the party faithful. And, of course, he talked with Senator-elect Edward (Teddy) Kennedy of Massachusetts.

For the outside world his reaction was subdued. "I am heartened by the results of yesterday's election," read his official statement. "This country and the Congress face major responsibilities in the coming two years, and I am certain that the Congress will meet its responsibilities in a progressive and vigorous manner."

But inside the Oval Office things were not so strait-laced. The remarks about loser Richard Nixon, who had exited from yet another political platform after ungracefully accusing the press of being unfair to him, were, according to witnesses, pungent and satisfying to New Frontiersmen.

Counsel Ted Sorensen went joyfully to work calculating the proportions of victory for inquiring newsmen and politicians. And up in his second-story walnut-paneled den, Larry

O'Brien sat with a foot on his desk and yellow ticker copy curling across his lap. The phone calls were coming in now from all districts and O'Brien cradled the receiver between his shoulder and his ear as he smoked Pall Malls.

"Ya did a great job out there, Jesse. . . . Now keep moving ahead. . . . Yeah, the President feels pretty good about it. . . ."

Between calls he sent out congratulatory wires and letters, made frantic arrangements to be sure that his emissaries were riding herd on the very close contests such as Endicott (Chub) Peabody's thin lead over John A. Volpe for the governorship of Massachusetts.

Democrats wondered why they had won—what they did. Naturally everybody felt that Kennedy's handling of the Cuban crisis was a major factor ("We were 'Cubanized,' " cried Republicans). But it wasn't quite as simple as that. There were indications that the younger, more attractive men fared well in both parties—the Democrats seemed to come up with more of them year after year. The extremists, both left and right, lost. The Democratic victories in the Midwest (George McGovern for the Senate in South Dakota; Hughes for governor in Iowa) could, in a roundabout way, be linked to the final death of the Catholic issue, which had hurt in 1960. There were strong indicators that Congress' failure to act favorably on Kennedy's plan of health insurance for the aged had cut deeply into some districts and states.

Of course the men in the engine room of the Democratic party listened to all the lofty talk and then turned and suggested that maybe there ought to be some notice given to grass-roots organization when they were looking for reasons of victory.

For the first time in history California was organized somewhat like an eastern state. "By our standards back here," said one party worker, "it was only a fair job, but by their standards it was excellent." In Los Angeles County alone, they reckoned, there were some 13,000 paid workers out getting people to the polls in cars, in buses, on foot. Mountainous Jesse Unrah, speaker of the California Assembly, was the man who did it under the tutelage of the

White House experts. Larry O'Brien's tracks were detected in the state just four days before the polls opened. "He didn't go there for the sunshine," said one Washington politician.

Birch Bayh's win in Indiana could be attributed to just about any cause and every cause—Cuba, young candidate versus old candidate, emphasis on medicare. The boys back in Washington gave a sly smile. "Indiana just happened to have the best-organized and best-financed campaign of any state in the union," said one. Indiana's Governor Matt Welsh, holding the party reigns, had sweated his party into top condition. A half-million-dollar war fund didn't hurt. Where had the money come from? "Why," said one party functionary, "from the flower fund, of course."

For a moment in the first hours of November 7, the White House experts looked ahead and Kennedy's likely opponent got first consideration.

"Rocky is the boy," said one.

He already seemed far ahead in presidential positioning, and nobody knows like the Kennedys what it means to begin early and run hard. They reasoned that George Romney would have a tussle with the obstinate Michigan legislature and would lose a good deal of his Bryl Cream look in two years. Scranton was too much of a novice yet. They even, for the moment, found chinks in Rocky's armor plate. (Chinks that would grow when Rockefeller married "Happy" Murphy.)

"Rocky won with less margin than last time and he was up against a nobody," said one national-committee power. "And I do mean a nobody. Nice, smart guy, Morgenthau. But zero as a candidate."

All this was fun, but the most important consideration was the nature of the 88th Congress, and that nobody could really fathom until it had assembled, organized itself and deliberated for months on the Kennedy program.

CHAPTER TWENTY-SEVEN

EDUCATION IN
ECONOMICS

I N T W O years John Kennedy went through economic metamorphosis. In the embryonic stage he was a budget balancer (at least he talked it, though he never actually achieved it). With his wings fully developed, he proposed not only a budget with a $11.9 billion debt for the fiscal year 1964, but he coupled it with a tax cut, which was more than enough to make any old politician choke on his cigar.

It was political heresy. Tax cuts were supposed to come when surpluses developed. Mounting debt was supposed to be countered with an increase in taxes. Every fiscal folktale seemed to have been violated. Kennedy appeared to be dignifying debt, which everyone knew was evil.

But in the Kennedy back shop it was simply another manifestation of the pragmatist, of a decision based on the best and most current economic facts, an innovation encouraged and endorsed by some of the country's top economists, a bold and sophisticated (Kennedy's enchanted word) step into the future for a nation whose fiscal woes were bewilderingly complex.

At least that was the way they explained it. There were others, however, who found the whole idea shocking, and they questioned not only Kennedy's judgment but that of his advisers and the very validity of his economic facts. These doubters, many with impeccable credentials in the financial world, wanted a tax cut but felt that the huge debt was wrong, that Kennedy should cut government spending along with cutting taxes.

Reduced to its simplest terms, the Kennedy plan was to unleash the economy by removing burdensome taxes and letting the fresh money flow into industry for plant modernization and into consumer hands for spending on new products. If the economy responded to the transfusion properly, it would mean such boom times that tax collections would swell and erase the temporary deficits.

But on paper the program and the reasoning behind it became a forbidding forest of figures and charts.

It was irony that John Kennedy as he entered 1963 dwelled deep in that forest and seemed quite at ease.

It was Joe Kennedy back in 1960 who had wailed with mock seriousness that none of his sons cared about business and that he was the only one who would bother with the family fortune.

John Kennedy himself in private confessed that making money and the business community had never stirred him in the slightest.

And Bob Kennedy said outright that the Kennedy boys had sought public service because it beat "following the dollar."

Yet it was John Kennedy at midterm who was more intricately and importantly involved with the dollar than any man in the United States.

The fact that the country had not begun to move again as Kennedy had so harshly demanded as a candidate, the fact that the economy was not soaring, was the deepest disappointment and the greatest challenge to the New Frontier as it began its third year.

Wealth was the base of our national security and our foreign policy. A nation "moving again" could help heal some of its own sores—unemployment, depressed areas, inadequate schools, bad roads. In short, following the dollar, tending to its health and proliferation, had become Kennedy's main business.

Ironically, too, there were few men with less direct experience in the anxieties and difficulties of managing the dollar. When he took office, it was roughly estimated that Kennedy's personal holdings, those that he came into possession of under the terms of his father's trust and those still in the trust, amounted to nearly $10 million, yielding him an income after taxes of $100,000 a year. As President his salary was another $100,000 (taxable) plus $50,000 expense money and another $40,000 for travel. (There were other driblets, such as book royalties.) It all added up to the fact that he went from being incredibly rich to being even richer.

As a senator he had had only remote contacts with the grubby world of the dollar. He had been responsible for his automobiles and airplanes and homes, but that was about all. Every month the Kennedy central accounting office in New York, which handled the family's vast affairs, toted up his outgo and his income and sent the figures down to Washington for his perusal. As a senator he had looked them over with some regularity, though there are no recorded incidents when he ever had those soul-quenching sensations which come occasionally to men as they ponder the bills and reach the inescapable conclusion that it is impossible to rear a family in the twentieth century. Kennedy's senatorial salary of $22,500 was sent to New York and dumped in the big pot with his other earnings. He gave more than his salary to charity every year, a practice he continued in the White House. He and Jackie both had checking accounts. Yet he never held a credit card, and many times he had no money with him. He once gave a friend good-natured hell for not tipping a waitress enough at the Milwaukee airport after the friend had paid the tab. He was incessantly asking how much people earned, as if he had never really considered wages and salaries as more than statistics in economic reports. Occasionally he would ask a staff member with a large family how he was making out, but this was the exception. Dollars just did not interest him.

When Kennedy moved to the White House, his isolation from everyday economics became even greater. He dropped his regular review of the Kennedy accounts sent down from New York. There was no longer a house to worry about, or servants to hire, or cars to buy, or airplanes to charter. This was all done by the White House staff, and it kept the books. There was no necessity for him ever to see a bill come through the mail.

As President, he grew a little more careful about carrying money with him. But it was not because he was more interested, but because the national gaze was on him at all times. And even then there were lapses. When he was called upon to open the National Heart Fund drive, he discovered that he did not have any change and had to bum a quarter from a Secret Service agent to drop in the can. He has had to borrow money for church offerings from his companion, Dave Powers. On balance, however, he does pretty well. He usually takes out his wallet in church and, holding it extremely low and close to him, fishes out a bill which he folds tightly and puts in the plate. Try as hard as he can to obscure the amount of money he gives, somebody usually finds out. When he dropped a $100 bill in the plate in Los Angeles, the news quickly passed from the church usher out onto the news wires and across the nation. In Washington once he deposited a brown envelope in St. Stephen's collection, thinking this would be the complete camouflage, but churchmen are as curious as others, and when the final organ strains had died, the envelope was isolated and torn open, and another presidential $100 bill became an historical footnote.

His formal education in the mystic science of economics was considered minimal. He took just enough economics to get through Harvard, and his grades were not exciting. When he went west to enroll at the Stanford Business School, most of his interest centered on a Buick convertible which he bought with his earnings from the book *Why England Slept*. And his stay at the London School of Economics earlier and his exposure to Socialist professor Harold J. Laski had been more in the nature of atmosphere than academic endeavor.

What Kennedy knew when he came to Congress about economics was learned, said one friend, in his "father's little red school of economics." Courses there were colorful but nontechnical.

In his Senate days he learned something about labor economics from his position on the Labor and Education Committee. He rubbed up against many of the big names in economics—Sumner Slichter, James Tobin, Seymour Harris,

Paul Samuelson, Walt Rostow and John Kenneth Galbraith. He asked advice from these men, read their memos diligently. Kennedy sought a seat on the Joint Economic Committee, but when he finally got it in 1960, he was in the heat of his presidential drive and only managed to attend a few meetings. However, to prepare himself for the campaign he read many heavy reports from the Joint Committee. He sensed the importance of the issue and used the slogan "Let's get this country moving again" in the campaign. But foreign policy remained his real interest.

The primary campaigns in Wisconsin and West Virginia which assured his nomination by the Democrats in Los Angeles in 1960 brought home to him some of the economics of poverty. He saw some of the battered houses of the dairy farmers, visited the rundown mining towns and looked into hundreds of discouraged eyes. One aide remembers his sitting in his car in Wisconsin mulling over some newly acquired facts about the price of milk and what it all meant in terms of the people.

Once in the office, he was faced immediately with the problem of dwindling gold reserves. The economy was shakily emerging from a recession, and the related problems of unemployment and automation nagged at him. Our relationship to Europe's Common Market was unsolved and there were pressures from foreign products. There simply was no escape—he had to learn more about economics.

He took pains in selecting his Council of Economic Advisers: Walter Heller of the University of Minnesota; James Tobin of Yale University; and Kermit Gordon of Williams College. He increased the council's budget, strengthened the systems of economic information gathering.

From the start he developed a close association with Douglas Dillon, who played a vital role in all the major economic decisions. Robert Roosa, a vice president of the Federal Reserve Bank of New York, joined Dillon's staff to give it extra luster.

Kennedy himself set out on his own improvement program. In the old days he used to hurry by the heavy fiscal news in his papers but once in the Oval Office he began to linger longer with the financial pages.

He demanded the Labor Department's statistics on unemployment and economic growth rate just as soon as they were available. Memos or letters from economists such as Samuelson were given top priority and sent straight to the President. Heller, as Chairman of the CEA, was granted as easy access to the President as any staff member.

Special articles on the economic problems of the country and the world were sought out by Kennedy, and he became an avid reader of Edwin Dale, *The New York Times'* economic correspondent for Europe who wrote frequently and knowledgeably about the Common Market. *The Economist,* the British weekly heavily oriented toward economic developments, received more presidential attention than before.

While the President always commented to reporters about political pieces, he started doing the same thing about the more prosaic stories and articles on budgets and taxes. He urged his friends in journalism to write more about the national economy, and in the final months of 1962 there was a mysterious outbreak of stories about balance of payments, new ideas for reporting the budget and the need for tax reduction and reform, and many were traceable back to the President.

Walter Heller proudly proclaimed Kennedy "the best student I ever had." Indeed, the economists never had had a president so willing to listen to them. Kennedy trusted hard facts, not hunches, and though the science of economics was to a degree based on hunches, it could marshal an impressive array of figures and charts to support the hunches. The politicians could not match that, and so the pragmatic Kennedy naturally turned more to the economists.

Heller found Kennedy's mind to be open. It was not necessary to knock down preconceived ideas. Teachers, like Heller, usually must spend a large part of their time countering the folklore about money and taxes which has been deeply embedded in our industrial society.

The openness was to some degree traceable to Joe Kennedy's influence on the President. Joe Kennedy was a skeptic, a loner, an unholy one along Wall Street, a disbeliever. Joe Kennedy was a great one to suspect the common sayings in financial circles, to find out for himself what was going on rather than taking somebody else's word. Often the President mentioned the fact that his father had frequently rejected the popular view of things in his own business career.

Some of the experts found Kennedy a little too ready to accept the figures presented to him. Tabulated neatly, such figures can be powerful evidence in a case. Economists who work with them so much know their vulnerability better than laymen. One of the President's advisers was sometimes reluctant to present too many calculations to the President, for fear he would attach too much importance to them.

Kennedy's fast reading rate was an asset in his development as an economist. He could race through the heavy memos and retain most of what he read. The President's ability to focus his concentration helped him, and his unemotional nature was another characteristic ready-made for a budding economist, who never can afford to confuse what he wants to be with what actually exists.

Kennedy liked the economists, was intrigued by their art. When he decided he wanted Tobin in Washington to work for him, he called Tobin at Yale and asked him. Tobin protested, "I'm just an ivory-tower economist."

"That's the best kind," said the President, then added, "As a matter of fact, I'm an ivory-tower President."

Answered Tobin, "That's the best kind." He accepted.

As in other policy matters, it was virtually impossible to trace the origins of Kennedy's decisions about the economy to specific persons. The question often was asked of just who had the most influence over Kennedy. It was never really answered. The hysterical critics shouted the names of Schlesinger, Bowles and Galbraith as the ones who tried to lead Kennedy toward socialism. Of course Bowles no longer dwelled in the high policy ranks, having been moved out by Kennedy himself. Schlesinger tended to United Nations and Latin American affairs. Galbraith was off in India as the United States ambassador. However, he did still comment through letter on the state of the economy. But Galbraith preferred public spending to cutting taxes as a spur to the economy. In the first two years his theories were rejected by Kennedy, who turned to the idea of a tax cut.

"Kennedy is an economic conservative," said one of the nation's top economists in attempting to describe the President's position.

Kennedy would dwell somewhere in the center of a triangle of ideas formed by joining the policy positions of Walter Heller, Douglas Dillon and Ted Sorensen, he said. The elements of business, theory and politics were all represented.

But to many it was hard to reconcile conservatism with the twin proposals of a tax cut and $11.9 billion deficit. And this doubt brought anguish to the White House. The President's conviction was that without this rather drastic step the tax structure would continue to weigh down our free-enterprise system. He felt so strongly about it that, as opposition developed against his tax program, he began to warn that without it we might have a fifth postwar recession.

"Kennedy really believes," pleaded an aide, "that business should prosper, that profits should be adequate, that people should be rewarded for initiative and achievement."

Though the Kennedy tutors after two years claimed that he fully understood the complex problems facing him, such as balance of payments, taxation, economic growth, gold flow and the federal budget, there were times at first when he was as baffled as any freshman.

He could not fully remember, for instance, just when to apply the terms fiscal and monetary, although he understood these economic functions when talking about them.

He devised his own system, remembering that M for monetary also stood for Martin (William McChesney Martin, Chairman of the Federal Reserve Board) and that everything else was fiscal.

Kennedy once joked with Walter Heller about this identity device. "If Martin leaves," he said, "we will have to get somebody with a name beginning with 'M'."

"That's easy," said Heller. "We have Mitchell [George W. Mitchell, member of the Federal Reserve Board]."

Actually, in all the sophisticated thinking, the inherent virtue in a balanced budget remained unscathed. It was to Kennedy and all those around him a desirable thing in stable times. He discovered that the times were far more unstable than he had thought. His doctrine at first was that only national security matters or domestic emergencies should be grounds for producing a budget deficit. He had accused the Eisenhower administration of imperiling this country's defenses by trimming them to fit the budget. In national security matters he vowed to fit the budget to the needs, and in his first year, as the crises mounted deficit spending could not be avoided as he beefed up the armed services.

But the harder he studied the problems of the economy, the more dimensions he saw, and one of those new dimensions was the intricate relationship of the federal budget to the national economy.

To Kennedy, the budget was not just something to be balanced, it was an instrument to be used in the pursuit of his administration's policy objectives. Since getting the economy moving was a major objective, the effect of the federal budget on the economy was important to him. In oversimplified terms, it was easy to see that if the government through taxes drew off too much of the money from the private sector of the economy there was danger of curtailing activity in that area, by far the most important sector. And turned around, if the government plunged into debt too much, there was danger of inflation. But how could one accurately measure such a complicated thing?

After World War II there had been disquiet with the way the budget was calculated. It was a stark listing of estimated tax receipts pasted up against estimated expenses. It failed to differentiate between cash outlays and loans. It did not take into consideration any of the money that went into the huge trust funds, such as social security and the highway fund. It made no distinction between capital and operating expenses. In short, it did not measure the impact of federal activities on the over-all economy.

In the mid-1950's the Commerce Department developed what it called the National Income Accounts. This was a way of measuring the impact of federal spending on the national economy. It included transactions in the trust funds. Loans and their repayments were excluded. Taxes were counted when the money was set aside, not when it was paid. Expenditures were treated similarly. For example, the construction of a missile base affects the economy when a contractor pays his workers and buys his materials, not just when he finally gets the check from the government.

The first full use of this new view of the budget came in the fall of 1961. The heat of the Berlin crisis was searing the New Frontier and Kennedy proposed a $3.4 billion increase in defense spending to meet the mounting pressure from communism. Coupled with the proposal was Kennedy's concern that the people of the country were not responding enough to the emergency. The politicians in his Cabinet, such as his brother Bob and Abe Ribicoff, argued for a tax hike, not only to cover the defense expenses, but more, really, to give the nation a sense of participating in the crisis. The economists opposed it. Secretary Dillon, Heller and Bell, who became known as the economic "Troika," pointed to the national income accounts figures.

They showed that the economy was basically strong and was still pulling out of the 1960 recession. If, indeed, a tax increase were imposed on the economy, it would heavily load the receipt side of the budget, drain off billions of dollars that should be left in the private sector of the economy. Kennedy's own political nature leaned toward a tax increase. But the figures from the national income accounts were too compelling and he sided with his "Troika" and rejected a tax increase.

Since the symptoms of economic lethargy had not shown fully in his first year, Kennedy still talked hopefully of balancing the budget. When he increased defense spending, he pledged a balanced budget for the coming year (fiscal 1963). In his second State of the Union message he promised it again. And he submitted a budget calling for a $500 million surplus, though it was based on so many "ifs" that it could not be taken seriously. Yet, so strong was the virtue of a balanced budget, Kennedy felt he had to at least make it appear his goal.

His education went on. He considered details as well as broad principles. He sorted through the minutiae of the budget with David Bell as few presidents have done. He was sincere in trying to cut fat out of the requests, although his success was not great. He found that he could curtail requests for the Forest Service and trim back the plans to build federal office buildings. When he noticed a request for more White House gardeners, he asked how many gardeners the White House had. He was told six. "Six," he exploded. "What do they need six gardeners for? I've got one man up in Hyannis Port who could do it all alone." The request was denied.

Kennedy wedged in his budget work whenever he could. Bell found that he was called into conference with Kennedy in automobiles, in airplanes, in the presidential bedrooms, in the Hyannis Port back yard, at Palm Beach, in the Oval Office, in the mansion, in the Rose Garden and along numerous White House corridors. The most notable meeting in the early months took place the day after Thanksgiving, 1961, when Kennedy presided over a six-hour session at Hyannis Port, and budget talk was woven into high policy matters.

One of his staff members suggested that Kennedy had easily learned in his intensive training the equivalent of a postgraduate course in political economics at Princeton. Another aide "awarded" him a doctor's degree from Harvard.

He won his best marks from his instructors the day he flew to Yale to talk about his relationship with the business community. He left Washington without reinforcements. Neither Walter Heller, the man with the facts, nor Ted Sorensen, the speechwriter, went along. Kennedy was solo.

As he flew to New Haven he noted a story in the *Wall Street Journal* suggesting that a budget deficit would bring inflation and encourage the flow of gold. Kennedy searched his mind and decided that this viewpoint did not jibe with the facts he had learned. It was true that in 1960 when there was a deficit the gold flow reached $5 billion annually. But there had been no inflation. And in 1958, another year of budget debt, there had been no gold flow nor any inflation.

Kennedy decided that this was a case with which he might illustrate the theme of his Yale talk that many of the old economic clichés and myths needed to be abandoned.

The President thought about the matter and then, taking one of the ever-present yellow legal pads, he began to write an insert for his speech. He wrote out the example from the *Journal* and then he thought of another. The week before,

Wisconsin's Senator William Proxmire, a Yale graduate, had suggested that the United States should follow a stiff fiscal policy (budget balance) and an easy monetary policy (low interest). The same week the International Bank in Basel, Switzerland, a highly conservative and knowledgeable organization representing the central bankers of Europe, suggested just the opposite. The point was that oversimplified labels and clichés could not be used to explain such a problem.

Kennedy had still another idea which he added. Many bankers in the previous fall had suggested that the debt for fiscal 1962 would create strong inflationary pressures. Yet there had been no inflation. Once again the old ideas, the pat answers had been wrong.

In all, Kennedy wrote out eight new large paragraphs, a seventh of the total speech.

Kennedy's audience was not overwhelmed with them, but back in Washington Walter Heller was thoroughly delighted. From an economist's viewpoint, the new passage in the speech was not only sound but eloquent.

Early in 1962 there was evidence that the economy was not yet regaining full health. Not only did the government economic experts begin to talk about further action, but outside economists fretted too. The Ford Motor Company's Vice President for Finance, Ted Yntema, wondered before the Joint Economic Committee if Kennedy's precariously balanced budget for fiscal 1963 was not too restrictive. He cited the national income accounts figures which showed a sizable surplus. Kennedy, he suggested, was running a risk that the high receipts would have a depressive effect on the economy.

In the next few months there began to be some talk about a cut in taxes. It spread from Washington across the country as people became aware that the economy had a fever and was in danger of real sickness if something was not done.

The idea for a tax cut took solid root among the experts. But it was not accepted by others as easily as might be thought. The nation's debt was $300 billion, a scary figure in the minds of most citizens, who could not find comfort in Kennedy's explanations that while large, it diminished in proportion to our economic capacity every year. (Since the war, corporate indebtedness went up 200 per cent while federal debt mounted only 15 per cent.) Eisenhower's stern pronouncements about balancing the budget and cutting spending had penetrated farther than many thought.

"Not one American in a hundred can accept the fact that a budget deficit need not be bad," said Paul Samuelson.

There were other complicating factors in this Kennedy dilemma. For a President to change his policy from the simple and appealing slogan of a balanced budget to the complicated economic jargon of a tax cut plus a huge deficit presents a political problem of monstrous size.

While the economists could say, as one did, "A rational approach is never in one direction—you have to zig and zag in a world [economics] of incomplete information," Kennedy knew full well that zigging and zagging in politics hardly inspired confidence. Even so, pressure for a tax cut became so great on the New Frontier that its leaders considered asking Congress for a cut in the fall of 1962. Weeks before, Kennedy had launched a public education campaign to try to win better public understanding of this "sophisticated" business. His Yale speech had been the first round. Heller, Dillon, Bell and others took to the lecture circuit to win back business confidence, and there was headway.

There was no headway, however, with the one man who counted most—Wilbur Mills, Chairman of the House Ways and Means Committee, which must originate all tax measures.

Mills found no strong sentiment for the tax cut among the people or among congressmen. Further, his dream was to overhaul the tax laws completely to close loopholes and cut off special concessions. Though he was not fully against a tax cut he was not for it, either. And he certainly was not for a tax-rate reduction without tax reform.

Faced with this immovable object, Kennedy became a resistible force. He contented himself with announcing that he would seek a tax reduction in 1963. He set about preparing for what he knew would be the most difficult legislative problem he had yet faced. He could confidently predict that virtually everybody would find something in new tax proposals to criticize and criticize harshly. Every man would have his special interest; the poor would accuse the rich of getting all the benefits, the rich would charge that low-income groups had preferred treatment, the middle groups would claim that they were ignored, business interests would complain that corporate taxes should be reduced more than proposed. Beyond that was his absolute irreverence for the fiscal shibboleths. A tax cut plus a huge debt was a terrifying thing to try to explain.

Kennedy went ahead. He possessed a cautious confidence founded on his own hard study of the nation's economic problems and the vast array of expert advice with which he surrounded himself. Whatever one thought of his program, there was no denying by anyone that it represented a bold venture into the political unknown. Almost immediately when he announced his program there was controversy. Businessmen claimed there should be more of a cut in corporate taxes, labor leaders shouted that there was not enough of a break for the low-income man.

Fortunately, Kennedy faced it with his humor intact.

One day in January 1963 as the President worked at his economic message for Congress in which he spelled out answers to the critics of his economic program, he looked up at Walter Heller, red-eyed and weary from his long nights of work on the message. "Walter," said the President, "I want to make it perfectly clear that I resent these attacks on you."

CHAPTER TWENTY-EIGHT

THE LAST YEAR

As THE NEW FRONTIER entered 1963—its third year in office—it basked in the glow from the successful blockade of Cuba. John Kennedy was the one who had to counsel against too much optimism.

In his office, his arms folded as he looked through the high windows, he acknowledged that once again he seemed to be popular with the people. But such adoration was fragile, he said. "These things go up and down so fast," he added, and he took his hand out of his coat pocket and traced his thought in the air.

He was prophetic. Before the Christmas carols had died away there were questions whether the Russians were indeed removing all their missiles and IL-28 bombers from Cuba, questions asking why the Russian troops weren't on the move? Rumors ran wild that both missiles and nuclear warheads were being tucked away in caves deep in the interior of the country.

The reports and alarms reached such a pitch that Kennedy and Robert McNamara decided to show correspondents the intelligence photographs on which the government based its conclusion that all the offensive weapons had been removed from Cuban soil. The interest in the background briefing was so intense that the showing was thrown open, and once again television carried an intimate view of administration into American living rooms.

McNamara, in his scratchy voice, opened: "In recent days

questions have been raised in the press and elsewhere regarding the presence of offensive weapons systems in Cuba. I believe beyond any reasonable doubt that all such weapons systems have been removed from the island and none have been reintroduced. It is our purpose to show you this afternoon the evidence on which we base that conclusion . . ."

For two full hours there followed one of the most remarkable briefings ever given in Washington. From thousands of pictures taken on more than 400 photo-reconnaissance sorties over Cuba a sequence of slides was flashed on a huge screen. The photographs showed conclusively how the missile sites had gone up and how they had come down, how the weapons and equipment had been taken to the Cuban coast and put on ships and sent back to Russia. While there still was some disbelief muttered on Capitol Hill, the briefing ended the loud outcries. The issue, at least for the time being, began to fade.

Yet, for the men who flew the jets with their cameras trained on the island, the Cuban matter remained starkly real —as this story came to the White House. In early February one of the reconnaissance planes flashed into Cuban air and began its pass from point to point with its cameras at work. Below the Cuban and Russian crews of the antiaircraft missiles came alive and scrambled for their guns. Radios began to crackle as the missile commanders tuned in one another. Above the reconnaissance planes, American fighters snarled, watching for any hint that the photo mission would be attacked. In the fighters' cockpits were tiny tape recorders tuned in to the ground radio messages of the Cubans. Monitoring stations on the coast of Florida could hear too.

First came the excited cries in Spanish from the Cubans to let them fire at the reconnaissance jet, to let them bring it down while they had a chance. But there were more commanding voices on the air—Russian voices.

"Hold your fire," came the stern commands, both in Russian and in Spanish. "Hold your fire. Don't shoot."

To Kennedy this was another bit of evidence to support his conviction that for the Russians to remove all of their troops immediately would be a risky business for the United States as well as Russia. The eager Cubans, left with the deadly SAM's, might fire at anything, and if any American plane were downed the United States would surely have to act, Russia would have to counteract and again there would be the real danger of escalation into a serious conflict. Once more Kennedy called on his reservoir of patience, in a sense allying himself with Nikita Khrushchev in favor of a moderately paced withdrawal of the Russian forces. But this kind of deliberate action was not consonant with the American character.

There were other irritants at work in the land.

Our relations with Canada and John Kennedy's own relations with Prime Minister John Diefenbaker were at an all-time low when the State Department chided the Canadians for not living up to a 1959 agreement to equip their jet interceptors and antiaircraft missiles with nuclear warheads. The ensuing storm caused the fall of Diefenbaker's government and all communication between the two governments was strained. To many State's public reprimand seemed unwise. Indeed, it was meant to prod the Canadians to make some kind of decision about their NATO commitment, a commitment supported wholeheartedly by the Liberals and their leader Lester Pearson. But the language of the statement was perhaps too blunt. Kennedy, upon reading of the incident, exploded over the clumsiness of the maneuver, which had been a joint undertaking by the State Department and the White House. But then he calmed down and hoped fervently that the new elections, set for April 8, would bring in Pearson.

Diefenbaker had been a constant problem. The Prime Minister had staged a most unpleasant scene with Ambassador Livingston Merchant when Pearson was invited to the White House to participate in the famous Nobel dinner, an occasion honoring all the living Nobel winners of this hemisphere, as well as other noted personalities. Kennedy had taken a few minutes out to talk to Pearson. Diefenbaker felt it gave his opponent an unfair advantage in the coming election. There were other minor incidents and these came to a climax later in the spring when the charge was made that Diefenbaker had an official paper left from the Ottawa meeting on which Kennedy had penciled a notation referring to Diefenbaker as "that SOB." [1]

Of all the difficulties that Kennedy had had with all the heads of state, he had never given up on any of them except one, said a close aide later. That one was John Diefenbaker, whose attacks on Kennedy became so bitter and so personal that the President finally decided he could not safely deal with the man. In the meantime, Kennedy gritted his teeth and waited for the election, trying a little humor to relieve his frustration. He jokingly decreed that the word "Canada" was not to be used around the White House until after the election. And casting an eye at the State Department, he observed wryly, "I suppose if this works out and Pearson is elected, those guys over in the State Department will think they were right all along."

The administration decision to drop the air-to-ground nuclear missile Skybolt had shattered the calm between Britain and this country because Britain had placed her faith in Skybolt. The Royal Air Force had spent 25 million dollars getting its Vulcan II bombers ready to take the missile, and now before the missiles were delivered they were being dropped. The future of Harold Macmillan's Conservative government seemed for the moment to hinge on this matter. McNamara had gone to England to try to work something out; then Kennedy and Macmillan had flown to Nassau, where in four days they hammered out a remarkable agreement to sell submarines and Polaris missiles to the English and to propose a multilateral nuclear force for Europe which would incorporate the Polaris weapons system. This had been done before Christmas, and it had been done with great fanfare after hours of secret talks on the shore of the Caribbean. But then had come the word from Charles de Gaulle. He had not only rejected the offer of the same deal given to Britain but also had then vetoed Britain's entry into the Common Market, presumably because she had turned to the United States for defense alignment rather than to France.

[1] Kennedy grew quite angry over this charge and on the morning it was reported he barked: "That's untrue. I'm not that stupid. I've been around long enough to know better than to do that. And besides, at that time I didn't know him so well."

At Nassau Kennedy had expected only that he and Macmillan would meet for several days, then go away and assign their technical staffs to work out the problems. Instead, Macmillan had been insistent on the detailed arrangement. He could not go home without it, he told Kennedy. Realizing that de Gaulle would not take kindly to this sort of dealing, Kennedy had made sure that the multilateral force concept be included, so that France would have equal chance to get a nuclear deterrent if she agreed to join Britain in a European force. De Gaulle had been invited to meet with Kennedy either before or after the meeting with Macmillan, but he had refused. And now he had dashed not only the nuclear force but Britain's trade hopes.

Beyond these huge troubles there were the aftereffects of *The Saturday Evening Post* article in which Adlai Stevenson was accused of wanting "a Munich" at the time of the Cuban blockade. The *Post* story, done by Stewart Alsop and Charles Bartlett, said that Stevenson had dissented from the consensus that counseled the final action. Bartlett's friendship with the President immediately became the basis for the interpretation that John Kennedy wanted to dump Adlai Stevenson. Kennedy's rather tardy declarations of faith in his ambassador to the United Nations and his coincidental efforts not to injure his friend Bartlett lent some credence to this belief, which lingered on for weeks.

With foreign aid in more trouble than ever, Kennedy unexpectedly accepted an offer of resignation from AID Director Fowler Hamilton. The stunned Hamilton went back to New York and the practice of law. Kennedy called in David Elliot Bell, Director of the Budget, and gave him the job, an assignment considered by many around Washington to be the most thankless in government.

In Latin America, the Alliance for Progress showed such slow progress that the President dispatched his brother for a frank talk with Brazil's President Joaõ Goulart about the need for reform in his government.

At home, even within the White House walls, there was little heart for another legislative assault to support the Medicare bill, a new farm bill, education bills and civil rights. The people seemed to be indifferent to these measures and their feelings were directly reflected in Washington. Added to this lethargy as a source of trouble was Kennedy's scary 98.8 billion dollar budget. It was so frighteningly close to 100 billion—an inconceivable figure—that Kennedy was again attacked for his spending. A final touch to his woes came when Kennedy went before the American Bankers Association and confessed that the most important part of his tax bill was the tax cut, not the tax reform. Up on the Hill the advocates of reform complained immediately and headlines trumpeted that Kennedy had changed his mind. Kennedy felt misinterpreted. The next morning he talked to his legislative leaders. "I don't want anybody to get the idea that I'm against reform," he said. But the fact was that Kennedy did feel reform was of secondary importance to keep the United States economy rolling, and he had long ago decided a tax cut was needed for that.

All of these difficulties and more piled up in the Oval Office. And one day, standing before 341 reporters in the State Department Auditorium, Tom Wicker of *The New York Times* in his courteous North Carolina accents, put the question just right.

"Mr. President, your policies in Europe seem to be encountering great difficulties. Cuba continues to be a problem. At home unemployment is high. The school bill seems far off. There seems to be more concern in the country over a budget deficit than for a tax cut. In view of all these things there is some impression and talk in the town and country that your administration seems to have lost its momentum and to be slowing down and to be moving on the defensive. Could you comment on this feeling in the country?"

Apparently Kennedy had some of the same thoughts too. His smile came a little too quickly; so did his answer.

"I have read that," he said. "There is a rhythm to a personal and national and international life and it flows and ebbs . . . we have a good many difficulties at home and abroad. . . . Some of our difficulties in Europe have come because the military threat to Europe is less than it has been in the past. In other words, whatever success we may have had in reducing that military threat to Europe brought with it in its wake other problems. . . . I prefer these problems to the other problems. . . . I would say our present difficulties in Europe, while annoying in a sense, or burdensome, are not nearly as dangerous as they were then . . . I think we have made it clear that we will not permit Cuba to be an offensive military threat. . . . I think we are making some progress in other areas, so that if you ask me whether this was the 'winter of our discontent,' I would say no. If you would ask me whether we were doing quite as well this winter as we were doing in the fall, I would say no."

For all his trouble, John Kennedy indeed had an inner serenity. Within the privacy of his office the hours went smoothly, his good humor remained. The fact was that the world was a calmer, more reasonable place in which to live in the early days of 1963. The troubles were mostly verbal; they were arguments of outlook and approach, conducted for the most part in civilized fashion rather than with tanks and the threat of nuclear destruction.

One day as the first signs of spring came to the Potomac, I watched the President balance lightly on the balls of his feet, his hands thrust deeply into his coat pockets. ("What the hell am I supposed to do with them?" he once asked when reminded of this habit.)

Six feet; 172 pounds; forty-five years old; a profusion of nondescript colored hair slightly out of control, strands of gray now on the fringes; gray-blue eyes; sharp furrows springing from the corners of the eyes and carrying back to the ears; longer, deeper marks across the brow; coarse and weathered skin with a fading trace of Florida sunshine; straight mouth; a vestige of a second chin—a single human out of the world's almost three billion, selected in this staggering lottery by the American electorate to control more power, either destructive or constructive—as he might choose—than any other man in history.

The responsibility of the President is so vast that it is incalculable by any terms we know. It is more than one man should bear; yet we have found no better way than to assign it to one man, a man we always hope is more than just human, but who never is, really.

The weaknesses of Kennedy's body were known. The bulge made by a small corset worn for a weakened spine showed through his shirt. The heel of his left shoe was built up a quarter of an inch because his left leg was that much shorter than the right leg. Every noon he dropped two white pills into his palm and swallowed them to compensate an insufficiency of his adrenal glands, which were impaired by earlier illnesses. But despite these troubles, Kennedy could work twenty hours without rest, could go sleepless through a night, could drive himself as far as any of the men around him.

His judgment could falter. There was the Bay of Pigs to prove it. But there was the Cuban quarantine a year later to show that it could be solid.

There was an awesome presence in that Oval Chamber, which was then quiet, cool, sunlit—the very heart of this nation—thirty-five feet long by twenty-eight feet, four inches wide. To an outsider the feeling of awe is always there. Any man who walks into that office senses it and I believed that the President did too, that even he never got fully used to it.

We stood on the gray-green carpet with the great American eagle woven in its center, just in front of his oak desk. On the curving walls were the naval paintings, ship models, the other mementos of a Navy man. And in the niches and on the tables and shelves were scrimshawed whales' teeth, an amazing collection which had poured in (some from places that do not have whales) when it became known he liked to collect them. There were eighteen teeth, half the complete denture of Moby Dick.

For a few seconds he stared out into the clear blue of the sky. Then he took his right hand out of his pocket and gestured toward the horizon. He had found the American people far calmer and their friendship far more enduring in his times of trouble than that of some of the lofty opinion makers, he said. He was thankful for that.

"I don't think the people are as mercurial out there as they are in Washington. Impressions are longer lasting out there. In Washington there is a terrific change of temperature with each issue. That is all they do here. Out there"—the hand came up again—"there are other things that are important."

"The country rather enjoyed the Cuban quarantine," he said, folding his arms and looking down. "It was exciting; it was a diversion; and there was the feeling we were doing something. But that was an easy one. They didn't have to go. It might have been a different story if there had been thousands killed in a long battle."

He walked to one of the couches in front of the fireplace and sat sideways, throwing an arm over the back and stretching his legs out over the cushions, a careless kind of position that showed his diligent exercise in the tiny White House gym had greatly strengthened his back. The Kennedy rocking chair stood, for the moment, empty on his left, a symbol of him and his administration. It now had the full status of F.D.R.'s cigarette holder and Ike's Stetson.

"In some ways we are better off, but in some ways we are not." He gave his cautious assessment in low tones from across the coffee table.

He had a deep pride in the state of our armed forces and that pride, plus his action in the Cuban missile crisis, underlay the sense of serenity. Our superiority in missiles, our improved conventional fighting capability and the new emphasis on guerrilla warfare, all carefully tailored by Robert McNamara, re-established confidence in our strength. In Southeast Asia the enemy had been engaged on his own terms, and though there still was no victory in Vietnam or Laos, we were no longer losing. There was a peace of sorts in Central Africa and Berlin had quieted. Though Latin America still was in deep trouble, there was new interest and what appeared to be new resolve by the Latin countries themselves to tackle their problems. We were at last competitors in the space race. And Russia now had new and serious political and economic problems to be solved by an aging and edgy Khrushchev. There were those around Kennedy who had concluded that the post-Sputnik Russian offensive had been turned back, that the USSR now was in the same kind of disarray in which the United States found herself in early 1961.

From all this the President could take heart. But there remained many problems, he reminded. Some of them were old problems that had simply changed character. There was the Russian presence still in Cuba. There was the discouraging fact of Charles de Gaulle's intractability, the confusion in the Atlantic Alliance and the disputes among the Common Market nations. At home Kennedy's tax program and his budget with its huge debt were under severe attack. Yet, to the President, the very fact that people could worry about such things rather than battles being lost in the Vietnam jungles or troops crossing the Autobahn to West Berlin was an improvement. In fact, no problem right then was so immediately threatening as to be called a full crisis.

The extent, diversity and complexity of United States involvement in this world still made Kennedy marvel.

"We have so many interests and we are tied up with governments in every part of the world. . . . How many people in this country had even heard of Yemen a few months ago? Yet what happens there affects us . . . we have a tremendous job in a world as varied as ours."

He was, he said, constantly baffled by the fact that many of the important people of this country were so sensitive over the disputes we got into with friendly countries and allies. There should be, he thought, a little more calm and patience as we tried to find our way in the complexities of this world. Too often, the President felt, when argument flared Americans assumed that their country was wrong.

He jumped up and walked to the French doors that look out into the flower garden. The doors were open to the air. Kennedy was mystically drawn to fresh air and sunshine. When he could he relaxed, he rested, he worked, in the sun and air.

"You've got to co-ordinate so many agencies," he went on, reflecting on himself and his government. "This is the burden of the White House."

He paced a bit, then he stopped and spoke again.

"Life is harsh in the undeveloped world. That is our most critical problem. Somehow we've got to change that. If the communists win once in those areas it is almost impossible then to throw them out."

His mind now was set on getting the tax cut. "The domestic economy is key," he said. "The tax bill is so important. I think we will get it but we are not getting as much help from business as we should . . . the problem is solvable if Congress will give us the power. . . . If we can get through 1964 without a recession . . ." He fell silent. It was too far to look just then.

*   *   *

But if frustration was the national ailment then there had been a few momentary escapes, some signs of good news to come.

In January in an elegant ceremony in the National Gallery of Art, the Mona Lisa, lent to the United States for a few weeks by France, was unveiled amid a glittering collection of the great and beautiful of Washington and the world. With Jackie, in a pink strapless dress, the President had added his own sure touch to a rare evening. Paying tribute to France as "the leading artistic power in the world," he went on to a humorous comparison between the painting's handling and the French position toward his own multilateral force proposed in the Nassau meeting. "In view of the recent meeting at Nassau," said Kennedy, "I must note further that this painting has been kept under careful French control, and that France has even sent along its own commander in chief, M. Malraux, and I want to make it clear that grateful as we are for this painting, we will continue to press ahead with the effort to develop an independent artistic force and power of our own."

From Moscow came a cautious letter to Kennedy. "The time has come now to put an end once and for all to nuclear tests. We are ready to meet you halfway." It was signed by Nikita Khrushchev. His proposal was for two or three inspections a year to investigate suspicious tremors, hardly the eight inspections we wanted. But it was an auspicious sign. Though not connected in any way with this proposal, the United States almost simultaneously announced that it would dismantle its Jupiter missile bases in Turkey and Italy. This maneuver had seemed almost like a deal with the Russians, but it was no such thing. Months before the Joint Chiefs of Staff had made plans to phase out these obsolete missiles and also some Thor missiles in England, to be replaced with Polaris-carrying submarines.

When Kennedy received from Marine Commandant General David M. Shoup an old Teddy Roosevelt order requiring that Marine Corps company officers be able to march fifty miles in twenty hours, double-timing the last 700 yards, Kennedy seized on the curiosity as a chance to divert the national mind from troubles. Replying to Shoup the President wrote: "President Roosevelt laid down such requirements not only for the officers of the Marine Corps but, when possible, for members of his own family, members of his staff and Cabinet, and even for unlucky foreign diplomats." Then Kennedy suggested that Shoup see if the Marines of 1963 could match their counterparts of 1908. But not only the Marines took up the challenge—the entire nation took to the road. The fad swept the campuses, the cities, the boondocks. Bobby Kennedy hiked up the C & O Canal tow path, secretaries from Capitol Hill followed. And then suddenly it got just a bit out of hand and the nation's doctors had to caution against such exertion for the unconditioned male. Kennedy himself, alarmed at the power of suggestion, issued a cautionary statement to hold down the overenthusiastic and finally the diversion began to fade when Pierre Salinger abandoned a proposed hike with White House newsmen. In an official statement, Salinger said: "My shape is not good. While this fact may have been apparent to others for some time, its full significance was pressed upon me as a result of a six-mile hike last Sunday. I have done little walking since then, except to go from my office to the White House dispensary. I may be plucky, but I am not stupid."

One by one Soviet ships came to Cuba and slowly Russian troops began to leave the island—but not nearly so fast as the Kennedy critics wanted. The intelligence estimates were that six ships would remove about 7,000 Russian troops, leaving 10,000 on the island. Kennedy still wanted these 10,000 out. He prodded his staff. "Do we have pictures of the Russian ships loading?" He wanted to see the photographs.

When Kennedy was asked about polls taken of United States prestige abroad, he at first ducked behind an excuse that they were secret. In his campaign, some of these "secret" polls had mysteriously been made public and they showed the same sagging United States rating which Kennedy had used against Richard Nixon. The initial Kennedy action to refuse to make the results public seemed to indicate the results again were not favorable to the United States. In fact, the findings showed this nation held in high regard. Objections to releasing the polls had been raised by the United States Information Agency because it was felt the results might cause embarrassment to the governments in whose countries they were conducted. But Kennedy was not one to let good news of such a nature languish in secrecy long. A friend in his office asked him what he intended to do. The President grinned. "They may leak," he said. Indeed, before too long *The New York Times* had a lengthy story, with the results given in detail.

Kennedy could even find time for some good humor at the annual dinner of Washington's Gridiron Club, an elite fraternity of Washington newsmen.

"Fellow managing editors," he began, when he was called upon to talk. The remark brought down the house because one of the many criticisms in this period was that he had been managing the news with more cunning than any other president in history. And then, using the names of columnists Doris Fleeson and Arthur Krock, the latter one of those who consistently needled the President, Kennedy said that Lyndon Johnson had complained recently to him about being picked on by Miss Fleeson. He had told Lyndon, said the President, "it was better to be Fleesonized than Krocked."

When spring came the Kennedy theory of cyclical changes in the emotions and fortunes of politics and government was proved again, for morale of the New Frontier once again was on the rise.

In San José, Costa Rica, Kennedy met with six Central American presidents while thousands in the streets pelted him with flowers and chanted "Kenn-e-dee" in ecstasy, and behind the closed doors he seemed to accomplish the main purpose of his mission—to satisfy the Central American presidents that the United States was keeping a close watch on Cuba and would help out any of the Central American governments in fighting communist subversion. He came back after three days with a smile and a Latin sun tan.

In Geneva at the disarmament talks came more drippings from the cold war thaw. The Russians agreed to Kennedy's proposal to hook up a direct line of communication between Premier Khrushchev and President Kennedy. It wasn't much, but it was something and it was John Kennedy's theory that if enough small gains could be made in easing the cold war, they someday would add up to quite a bit.

From Canada came the reassuring news that Lester Pearson had been elected prime minister over John Diefenbaker and a sigh of relief swept the White House. Now there was hope that Canada would fulfill its NATO commitments, that Kennedy could again deal with the Canadian government in faith and good will.

But then almost a year to the day that U. S. Steel's Roger Blough had shattered Kennedy's calm with news of a major steel price increase, came some more alarming news from the steel industry. In West Virginia the little-known Wheeling Steel Corporation, the nation's tenth largest producer, announced selective price increases in sheet and strip steel of $6 per ton.

For a few hours the White House was paralyzed, fearful that Wheeling was only the forerunner of an industry-wide boost. John Kennedy immediately called in his staff and began to worry. A scheduled departure for Palm Beach, Florida, was delayed a day as his men scurried to find out if indeed the industry had joined in a conspiracy against him.

Into the Cabinet room came the old team. Ted Sorensen was the co-ordinator and researcher. Walter Heller was there to furnish economic figures. Kennedy had asked Clark Clifford, attorney and friend of both business and the administration, to come over. Roswell Gilpatric, Deputy Secretary of Defense, and Douglas Dillon were on hand. The President was deeply concerned about his own position in case this was to be a major price increase throughout the industry, which was then silently praising Wheeling Steel for its guts. Kennedy at this time did not have the leverage he had had before. There had been no negotiations with steel companies or with unions on prices and wages. There had been no commitments either spoken or unspoken about steel prices. Kennedy could not afford another outburst against industry. One more SOB incident and much of the business community might be alienated for all time. The need at the moment was for more information and it was this task to which Dillon, Gilpatric and Clifford turned. In secret they placed calls to the top steel executives of the nation. The word came back that across-the-board price increases were not planned, that there was no apparent conspiracy. Further, the steel men made a compelling case for the selective boosts. Kennedy was satisfied and though his economic advisers were worried about the effects on the economy of the price increases, Kennedy considered the risk worth it. He could not risk another public fight with the industry, certainly not one that he might lose.

His answer was a stern and cautionary statement.

"I realize that price and wage controls in this one industry, while all others are unrestrained, would be unfair and inconsistent with our free competitive market—that, unlike last year, the government's good faith has not been engaged in talks with industry and union representatives—and that selected price adjustments up or down are not incompatible with a framework of general stability."

The pace changed again. On the heels of the steel statement came another announcement from Palm Beach. Jacqueline Kennedy was pregnant, expecting the new baby in August. For a few days all else was forgotten as correspondents spun out yards of stories about the Kennedy family. Jackie was only one of three Kennedy women expecting, the wives of Bob and Ted Kennedy also were pregnant.

The obstinacy of Congress began to show more than ever and the congressional lethargy continued to grow until by fall of 1963 it was one of Kennedy's biggest problems. And though Kennedy had bravely kept championing the Congress in his public statements, even he began in the spring to worry about the tortoise pace. One morning he came to his weekly breakfast meeting with his legislative leaders and with him he brought a slip of paper, a tally of the record of the Congress, so far showing that it was far behind normal schedules. Not even appropriation measures had been moving along. The great danger, Kennedy said, was letting the bills pile up in a log jam and then be faced at the end of the session with the necessity of sacrificing some of them to get others. "I think the country is getting impatient with Congress," Kennedy told his leaders. Several times he urged that they do what they could to make Congress "get going." He asked that each

committee chairman be approached to try to move the legislation faster. There was not only the tax cut bill but measures on mental health, feed grain, youth employment, mass
transit, aid to higher education. But for all the talk, congressional matters continued to get worse. The foreign aid
bill had never been in more severe trouble from both Republicans and Democrats, tired of doling out money to foreign
nations and then seeing them defy us or squander some of
the funds in useless projects or corrupt administration. Kennedy tried to soften the Congress. In groups of 10 or more he
invited the leaders of the Senate and House down for drinks
in the mansion late in the afternoons but there was no
visible softening. The Congress just did not want to budge
and there did not seem to be anybody around who could
change the congressional mind, including Congress' own leaders and the President of the United States.

In early May came the racial demonstration in Birmingham and John Kennedy's world changed again. Civil rights
from then on would do more to alter the tone and outlook
of the New Frontier than anything else the administration
had yet faced. For nearly a month the Negro demonstrations
in Birmingham had been on-and-off affairs, flaring occasionally, yet always seeming to die away. But Martin Luther King
had picked Birmingham for his crusade and Birmingham it
was to be. There the schools were totally segregated, so were
the restaurants, drinking fountains, toilets. The city was
under the lash of Public Safety Commissioner Eugene Bull
Conner, who had cowed Negroes for twenty-three years with
crude threats and the clubs of policemen. Now he had police
dogs and high-pressure fire hoses.

King had only his people but that was enough. Children
had joined in freedom parades for days and the jails were full
of kids when King sent groups to try to worship in white
churches. Four of the churches admitted the Negroes; seventeen churches turned them away. King called a mass meeting in the New Pilgrim Baptist Church, and when the thousand people came away from the church they found Conner
and his police drawn up, but this time Conner let them
through his lines as they gathered to pray. The next day there

came violence as 2,500 Negroes descended on downtown Birmingham. The dogs did their work perfectly and the pictures of them ripping the clothes off frightened Negroes shocked the world. The fire hoses with 700 pounds of pressure were equally effective and again over the wires flashed the alarming pictures of Negroes flung helplessly to the ground by the pressure of the water. The Negroes could not contain themselves; their leaders who preached nonviolence could no longer control the wrath, and the mob began to lob bricks and bottles at the police. But Bull Conner was too well prepared. Slowly he smothered the riot and the Negroes found themselves back in the church. "We will turn America upside down in order that it turn right side up," shouted King to his followers. Troops sent by Governor George Wallace came to the relief of Conner's weary men and for a few hours there was strained peace in the city.

By now Birmingham's city leaders were thoroughly alarmed and there began a series of meetings with Negro leaders and a team from Bob Kennedy's Justice Department. Martin Luther King had four demands; desegregate all public facilities in department and variety stores; give Negroes equal job opportunities; drop all charges against the rioting Negroes arrested during the demonstrations; set up a biracial committee to supervise reopening of the parks and other facilities which had been closed to avoid integration.

The Birmingham citizens' committee, at first refusing to be identified, gave halfhearted agreement to the demands but could not promise that the politicians would go along. Then a Negro home was bombed that night and again the Negroes surged through the streets of the city, and this time the frenzied rioters were more than a match for Bull Conner. Flames, bricks and screams ruled the night until some of Wallace's state troopers arrived.

When the worst had passed and uneasy peace returned, the country looked around for someone to blame and then blamed everybody from the President on down. Kennedy had watched the affair from the White House, being filled in by his brother and news dispatches. There were long talks between the brothers in the mansion, then at his midweek press conference the President attempted to explain his own position: "I have made it clear since assuming the presidency that I would use all the available means to protect human rights, and uphold the law of the land. Through mediation and persuasion and where that effort has failed through lawsuits and court actions, we have attempted to meet our responsibilities in this most difficult field where federal court orders have been circumvented, ignored, or violated. We have committed all of the power of the federal government to insure respect and obedience of court decisions, and the law of the land."

Many, however, disagreed that the President had done what he could. Harvard Law School Dean Erwin Griswold, a member of the civil rights commission, said, "It seems clear to me that he hasn't even started to use the powers that are available to him."

But nobody was very certain just what the President should do. However, the pressure was building for some new civil rights action by the federal government, presumably new and stronger legislation, and without it the moderate Negro leaders, who were trying desperately to keep control, might well be replaced by those who preached violence.

As the fire in Birmingham smoldered under an uncertain truce, flames licked at other cities—Greensboro, North Carolina; Nashville, Tennessee; Chicago, Illinois; Jackson, Mississippi; Cambridge, Maryland.

Kennedy decided to speak out some more and on a journey through the South he stopped at Vanderbilt University in Nashville and there he took direct aim at men such as Alabama's Governor Wallace, with whom Kennedy the same day shared a speaker's platform at Muscle Shoals, Alabama.

"This nation," said Kennedy at Vanderbilt, "is now engaged in a continuing debate about the rights of a portion of its citizens. That debate will go on, and those rights will expand, until the standard forged by the nation's founders has been reached—and all Americans enjoy equal opportunity and liberty under law. But this nation was not founded solely on the principle of citizens' rights. Equally important— though too infrequently discussed—is the citizen's responsibility. For our privileges can be no greater than our obligations. The protection of our rights can endure no longer than the performance of our responsibilities. Each can be neglected only at the peril of the other. All Americans must be responsible citizens, but some must be more responsible than others, by virtue of their public or private position, their role in the family or community, their prospects for the future or their legacy from the past."

While civil rights dominated the domestic scene, it could not halt the world. And from other quarters there was good news. Kennedy had gone to Hyannis Port for a meeting with Canada's new prime minister, Lester Pearson, and there on deserted Cape Cod in relaxed informality the good relations between Canada and the United States were restored. The two men dined on poached salmon and lobster, joked about the weather and baseball, came away with full understandings that Canada would live up to its NATO nuclear agreement, that the two countries would work out an agreement for sharing defense production.

Astronaut Gordon Cooper orbited the earth twenty-two times and Kennedy exulted: "This was one of the great victories for the human spirit."

And then there was Harvard night at the White House. To observe the end of his six-year term as a member of the university's board of overseers, he gave a stag dinner at the White House for the board and Harvard officials. Following cocktails and dinner the guests made speeches, and Kennedy also spoke. "It is difficult to welcome you to the White House," he said, "because at least two thirds of you have attended more stag dinners here than I have." When the laughter died, Kennedy noted that the White House and Harvard men had long had an affinity (John Adams, John Quincy Adams, Theodore Roosevelt, Franklin Roosevelt and now Kennedy). In fact, behind Kennedy on the mantel was an inscription taken from the first letter that John Adams, the first White House inhabitant, had written to his wife.

As Kennedy turned to read there was a thud and there on the floor at one end of the State Dining Room was Overseer Laurence Mallinckrodt. He had suffered a mild heart seizure. Among the other overseers were two doctors, James M. Faulkner and Robert F. Loeb, and they made Mallinckrodt comfortable while the ambulance sped to the scene. Meantime the rest of the men tiptoed out of the candlelit room and assembled in the Red Room, where the President finished his speech. After brandy and cigars and word that Mallinckrodt was not seriously ill, the guests drifted to the East Room and there a few of the hardy ones gathered around the piano for some Harvard songs.

The worry continued to be civil rights. Secretly Bob Kennedy went to New York for a meeting with a group of Negroes headed by the author, James Baldwin, who rounded up some white and Negro spokesmen who included singers Lena Horne and Harry Belafonte and playwright Lorraine Hansberry. It was an unusual group and notably absent were men from the NAACP and the Urban League. Tempers flared; the talk was emotional, almost weird. Bob had come to learn of the problems in the North, in fact to learn more about Negroes. The group warned him of racial explosions to come, shouted insults, criticized President Kennedy for not using all his power. Almost everyone but Baldwin left bewildered.

"Bobby Kennedy was a little surprised at the depth of Negro feeling," said Baldwin. "We were a little shocked at the extent of his naïveté." Later, Bob Kennedy confessed this meeting had been a mistake and a prominent Negro leader who supported the Kennedys complained, "If we can just keep Bob Kennedy out of any more secret meetings, we can make some headway."

In the streets and in the courts and in the minds and hearts of American citizens, the civil rights battle went on. Everybody talked about it. Secretary of State Dean Rusk called the crisis "one of the gravest issues that we have had since 1865." And Vice President Lyndon B. Johnson, speaking at the Gettysburg battleground, said, "The Negro today asks justice. We do not answer him, and we do not answer those who lie beneath this soil when we reply to the Negro by asking 'Patience.'" Frustration abounded and nowhere was it deeper than in the White House. John Kennedy had set a quiet course in civil rights from the start of his administration. And for a few weeks as violence spread he hoped that backstage meetings with business leaders, hotel owners, Negroes and governors might solve the problem. But it would not. There was no question about John Kennedy's moral commitment to equal rights but as President of all the land he had tried to keep southern support in Congress by not pushing for civil rights legislation, while at the same time holding his political sway with Negro voters by constant actions within his own executive powers to bring integration to schools and public facilities, to get Negro voters registered. Negroes demanded and needed more and the administration began to put together a civil rights bill. The meetings with the nation's powerful went on; the appeals from the Oval Office continued.

All of it seemed to build toward a new crisis when Negroes were to try to enroll at the University of Alabama in mid-June. Governor George Wallace had announced his intention to do everything in his power to block their entry. For weeks Bob Kennedy and the Justice Department had been preparing for this showdown. They had photographed the campus with military reconnaissance planes in order to be fully ready for any kind of difficulty. If they could help it, there would not be another Oxford, Mississippi.

A domestic crisis is a weird kind of drama in the White House that is watched and felt and listened to over television, phone lines and cables.

There is no direct contact with the enemy; there is hardly a break in the regular day's order. In the quiet of the Oval Office the decisions are made and the orders given in courtly style. On this day the blooms in the flower garden were beautiful. Here there is never the whine of a sniper's bullet, or the growl of police dogs, or the heat of mobs, or the rumble of troops on the streets. About the only thing that disturbs the surface calm is the urgent but subdued purr of the big black limousines that hurry up the back drive and brake impatiently outside John Kennedy's office. Yet somehow through the electronic ganglia some of the tension from far away comes to 1600 Pennsylvania Avenue.

When Kennedy had returned from Hawaii there was a wire from Governor George Wallace declaring his intent to go to Tuscaloosa and stand in the doorway to bar the entrance to the university of Vivian Malone and James Hood, both aged twenty. Kennedy's answer was swift. "The only announced threat to orderly compliance with the law . . . is your plan to bar physically the admission of Negro students . . ."

Early next day Kennedy was up before 8 A.M. The view down the south lawn was none too inspiring, for low gray clouds that had splattered rain on the city off and on all night long still clung to the horizon. The phone brought Bob Kennedy with the day's first report. It seemed as if there would be trouble in Tuscaloosa, Bob said. Nick Katzenbach of the Justice Department, who had flown to Alabama, Sunday, had concluded that Wallace meant what he said. The President listened, saying little, and then for a few minutes the two Kennedys talked about sending in federal troops. It was a very real possibility once again. Certainly they both felt that if they had to federalize the National Guard, then the President would have to go on nationwide TV to explain the action. They decided to plan it that way tentatively but June 11 was to be a day of watching and deep thinking.

Kennedy hurried on about his duties. Even then below him the Democratic legislative leaders were gathering for their weekly breakfast meeting. Before the President arrived the leaders chatted in the Red Room and some of the urgency of that day affected them. Hubert Humphrey reported the mounting concern of the liberals, their feelings that civil rights legislation would not go far enough. But others felt that any kind of civil rights bill that could be passed would be a major victory in a Congress as stubborn as the 88th. Larry O'Brien, who had been working furiously to weld some kind of coalition to get the tax cut through, was dejected. "After working all this time for a Democratic majority, now we can see it being blown all to hell," he said. For certainly southerners who had been persuaded to go along with the tax cut now would defect and hold their votes as a weapon against civil rights. At breakfast they talked it out some more and Kennedy warned that there might be trouble from Alabama that day. But he wanted to push on with his plans for a good civil rights bill. Already Mike Mansfield had set up a series of meetings with key senators so that they could be fully briefed on the civil rights ideas being considered.

Throughout the day Kennedy worked on a possible TV statement and kept abreast of the drama in Tuscaloosa. At

10:55 that morning the President pulled the legal trigger, ordering Wallace to step aside. He called Associate Press Secretary Andy Hatcher and said that he was signing the necessary proclamation ("I . . . John Kennedy . . . do command the Governor of the State of Alabama . . ."). Kennedy scribbled his signature and then quietly asked an aide to phone the proclamation directly to Katzenbach so that he could present it to Governor Wallace.

Before the next confrontation with Wallace, Kennedy had other things to do. He summoned the Republican leaders from the Hill to explain in general terms his ideas for legislation that would deal with public accommodations, school integration and voting rights. Even in these tense moments there were the signs of trouble ahead. Both Everett Dirksen and Charlie Halleck were skeptical. They needed more time, more information.

In the middle of this meeting a phone call came from Bob Kennedy. President Kennedy excused himself and walked from the Cabinet Room to his office. Bob reported that in a tragicomic sequence Wallace had stood in the doorway of the building on the campus used to register students. Katzenbach had turned away. Now the Alabama National Guard would have to be federalized to keep them out of Wallace's hands and to provide protection in case of violence. Kennedy's decision was instantaneous. The order would be issued as soon as he finished the meeting with the Republicans.

Kennedy, always fascinated by TV, had missed the broadcast of the confrontation. But when word came over the networks that it would be rebroadcast he went to the office of a secretary, Evelyn Lincoln, and turned on her set. He called Bob and the two watched the replay of the event, commenting to each other on the phone.

Four and one half hours after the first confrontation with Wallace, Katzenbach was back, but there was now another actor in the drama. Brigadier General Henry V. Graham, assistant commander of the 31st Infantry, an Alabama National Guard division, walked to Wallace, saluted and said gently, "It is my sad duty to inform you that the National Guard has been federalized. Please stand aside so that the order of the court may be accomplished." Wallace had a last bitter statement, but he walked away and in minutes the two Negroes were registered.

Kennedy decided he would go on TV that night with his message. Ted Sorensen hurried off down the hall to work on the speech, the President found a few minutes for a swim in the White House pool.

A short while before air time that evening his office was a scene of confusion. Kennedy waded through it to test the cameras. "The monitor is all right," he said, looking at the test TV picture. "But the camera ought to be brought up." Technicians hurried to oblige.

"Three minutes," a TV man said. Kennedy settled on the pillow in his chair. "Thirty seconds." There was silence; the President's nervous fingers played with the sheets of his speech text. "Stand by, Mr. President."

Kennedy's shoulders moved a few inches forward and his eyes narrowed a bit. "Good evening, my fellow citizens . . .

"This afternoon following a series of threats and defiant statements, the presence of the Alabama National Guardsmen was required at the University of Alabama to carry out the final and unequivocal order of the United States District Court of the Northern District of Alabama . . . It ought to be possible . . . for every American to enjoy the privileges of being American without regard to his race or his color . . . We are confronted primarily with a moral issue . . . a moral crisis as a country and a people. It cannot be met by repressive police action. It cannot be left to increased demonstrations in the streets. It cannot be quieted by token moves or talk. It is a time to act in the Congress, in your state and local legislative body, and, above all, in all of our daily lives."

The day had been Kennedy's, the speech had been only the final act. Now the telegrams and phone calls began to pour in, most of them complimentary. But there were still among them the cries of the extremists. "You ought to marry a Negro," said one. Others were obscene. When Kennedy saw one which read, "Mr. President, you couldn't be more wrong," he smiled a bit and commented, "Well, at least that is a fair criticism."

But if Kennedy won a victory in Alabama on June 11, he lost one in Jackson, Mississippi, that very night. Medgar

Evers, aged 37, father of three and a tough, dedicated NAACP field representative, was shot and killed near midnight in front of his home. The call to the White House came at 3 A.M. and it was decided not to wake the President until morning. But when the White House staff relayed the message to Kennedy he was shocked. "The President," said Hatcher later in the morning, "was appalled by the barbarity of this act." Yet two days later Dave Mack McGalthery, aged 27, went to the University of Alabama's Extension Center at Huntsville and registered for night classes in mathematics and Governor Wallace did not even show up.

The administration by its own admission was scrambling to keep up with the rising spectre. Day after day the conferences went on. John Kennedy's commitment to civil rights progress became total, deeper than any commitment he had made in his two and a half years. The feeling was best summed up one day when Kenny O'Donnell looked down at the floor in the corridor outside the President's office and said, "It's going to be a long, hot summer."

Kennedy wanted to see everybody on the issue. He asked Ike to come around for a visit. The General arrived early and fretted about being ahead of schedule. "Maybe he is not ready for me yet," he told a friend as he walked into an outer office to wait. But then the President saw him and came out. "I didn't know you were early," said Kennedy. "Come in." Lyndon Johnson came by for the meeting, in which Kennedy told Ike that he just wanted to bring him up to date on the civil rights matters since Ike had been the one to go through Little Rock. The General listened intently and he had a few wise words. "No one can be sure he's got the right answer," said Eisenhower. "No matter what you do you are going to be 'wrong' to a good many people. I know, I've been through it."

Kennedy called in businessmen, pastors, lawyers and labor leaders. They always assembled in the East Room, sat down gingerly on the gilt chairs that were usually used for more fashionable gatherings.

His appeal was for help. Typical was his talk to the labor leaders. "I want to give you a warm welcome," he said. "This is a very serious matter, it involves not only us who hold official position but all interested citizens who occupy positions of responsibility, and that includes all of you here. Most of all we would like to hear from all of you. We want to talk of what we can most usefully do about this matter."

One of Kennedy's best allies in this fight was Lyndon Johnson. It was the Vice President who detected the first real trouble on the Hill and cautioned against going too fast with a civil rights bill, of putting a program together without carefully consulting all the leaders. It was also Lyndon who dug up extraordinary facts about the Negroes—for example, in Brooklyn there were only 2.2 per cent of Negroes employed on federal projects while there were 65 per cent employed in Alabama.

"We'll get some civil rights legislation," predicted one Kennedy aide. "I think 50 per cent of what we propose is quite certain, the other 50 per cent less so. We will have to give some, but we will gain some."

The East Room seminars continued with women, mayors and governors. The conferences went on with the senators and congressmen. Finally, when the package was unveiled it proved to be the toughest civil rights program proposed in the twentieth century. The wisdom of some of it was questioned, but there it was. "I am proposing that the Congress stay in session this year until it has enacted—preferably as a single omnibus bill—the most responsible, reasonable and urgently needed solutions which should be acceptable to all fair-minded men," said Kennedy.

The program's six major provisos called for a law guaranteeing equal right of access and accommodation in lodging places, theaters, sports arenas, retail stores, restaurants, lunch counters and other such establishments substantially involved in interstate commerce; congressional authorization for the Attorney General to initiate school desegregation suits whenever requested; permanent status for the President's Committee on Equal Employment Opportunity; establishment of a National Community Relations Service to seek co-operation between the races; extra federal money for job training and adult education; provision that the federal government could withhold its funds from any program or activity in which discrimination occurred.

The start of the national debate on the bill was instantaneous. Some feared the accommodations clause would override the rights of private property and others complained that the cutting off of federal funds might deprive all citizens, Negro and white, of needed projects. For a civil rights bill there was a long, rough road ahead.

Nearly everybody concerned was worried. Negro violence continued to flare in both South and North and there was talk of a major demonstration in Washington as the civil rights program was taken up by Congress. From Congress came the reply that rioting in Capitol Plaza would doom any legislation for certain because it would harden southern opposition and probably produce an insurmountable filibuster. Then came an idea, not a new idea, but a great idea proposed more than thirty years ago by A. Philip Randolph, a Negro who is president of the Brotherhood of Sleeping Car Porters. It was for a peaceful march on Washington to dramatize the 1963 Negro revolution. It was suddenly an outlet for pent-up frustration, a way to avoid violence and yet a way for the Negroes to honorably protest their lot.

Marchers came in late August, nearly a quarter of a million, both black and white. They marched from the Washington Monument to the Lincoln Memorial, some singing, "We Shall Overcome," a swelling, haunting refrain that somehow told in tone what it was all about. They came in overalls and Ivy League suits, in beards and field shoes, and some wept as they walked. The famous and the unknown stood shoulder to shoulder looking at the brooding stone features of Abraham Lincoln as speaker after speaker talked. There was no violence, the 5,900 police assembled scarcely had to do anything but direct traffic, and the 4,000 soldiers and marines, at the ready nearby, did nothing all day but wait for a call that never came.

"We subpoenaed the conscience of the nation," Martin Luther King, Jr., said later. "We have developed a new unity among the leadership of the civil rights movement," added Randolph. "It is the first step in the building of a coalition of conscience," said Walter Reuther. All were right.

Though there were no bills passed or even promises made by official Washington, the great formless demonstration that stretched across the famous bottomland gave the Negro new power and dignity in the minds and hearts of the nation, the real civil rights battleground.

America and its President can only dwell so long on a single problem, and while the civil rights struggle had been the big business of spring and summer, it had been punctuated by other matters.

On May 29, for instance, the President became 46 years old. His staff decided it was time for a surprise party and late in the afternoon on the pretext that there was a call for him on the special scramble phone in the basement of the White House, McGeorge Bundy led a suspecting Kennedy to the White House mess. Pierre Salinger was master of ceremonies, and he handed Kennedy a speech to read. "We know you usually write your speeches, Mr. President," said Salinger. "But here is one which was written by a ghost writer and we would like you to read it." It was a take-off on Lincoln's Gettysburg Address (and began "Twoscore and six years ago there was brought forth at Brookline, Mass. . . .) as well as on a number of Kennedy's own speeches. A model space capsule was presented to the President. The card read: "Hope you have a good trip, Barry."

And midway in the proceedings a workman walked in with a huge basket of dead grass. It was Jackie's joke and the card read, "From the White House Historical Society—Genuine Antique Grass from the Antique Rose Garden," a rib at the President's fondness for the new flower garden, which he had ordered planted outside his office and which he showed to guests so proudly. It was a gay twenty minutes. That night the President with friends cruised down the Potomac in a final celebration.

In mid-June Kennedy had taken another step in international affairs that was to pay gratifying dividends later. From an inspection and speaking tour that had taken him to Hawaii, Kennedy streaked overnight back to Washington in order to keep a speaking date at the American University commencement on June 10. He had been at work a long time on this speech and it was to be vital. He was weary from the jet ride, the out-of-doors amphitheater was sweltering in June sun. But the words had profound meaning.

"Let us re-examine our attitude toward peace itself, too many of us think it impossible. . . . Let us re-examine our attitude toward the Soviet Union. . . . It is discouraging to read a recent authoritative Soviet text on military strategy and find, on page after page, wholly baseless and incredible claims. . . . But it is also a warning—a warning to the American people not to fall into the same trap as the Soviets, not to see only a distorted and desperate view of the other side, not to see conflict as inevitable, accommodation as impossible and communication as nothing more than an exchange of threats."

This was to be the Kennedy foreign policy doctrine for the summer. The President had been thinking hard about the continued thaw in Soviet-United States relations and he had decided that perhaps too many people were too pessimistic about peace, himself included. Peace is a very practical thing, reasoned Kennedy, to be gained step by weary step, event by prosaic event, detail by detail. This reflected a fundamental Kennedy concept that grand plans come only from attention to details.

For weeks Kennedy and Khrushchev had been examining each other's views in their own limited correspondence and through their embassies and the intelligence reports from other diplomats. As Kennedy studied the information he concluded that pressure was building in Moscow and indeed among communists around the world for Khrushchev to resume a tough line of talk and action against the West. Scheduled for June 18 was the Plenum, the full body of the Central Committee of the Communist Party of the Soviet Union. This Plenum session had particular significance since it preceded the July 4 meeting between the Soviets and the Red Chinese, who planned to discuss in detail their philosophical differences, now becoming bitter.

Kennedy concluded that the time had come to change our approach, to soften our words toward Russia. In his view too much of the talk recently had been negative. It was always about what we wouldn't and couldn't do. There had been no progress at all in the continuing talks about a nuclear test ban. In fact, just a few days before Kennedy was to give the American University speech, he and Harold Macmillan had sent another plea to Khrushchev for a new round of test-ban conferences. There was silence at first from the Kremlin and for a few hours Kennedy thought he would have to abandon his speech. Then came Khrushchev's acceptance and the President took new heart that his idea for a "soft answer" might indeed "turn away wrath." Certainly if Khrushchev was preparing to rise in the Plenum sessions and vent his anger against the United States, the Kennedy speech might give him pause and even cool him down. If it did not, Kennedy reasoned, then at least the Soviet Premier's words would have a hollow ring to the rest of the world, coming in the wake of Kennedy's own peaceful plea.

The world response to this speech was amazing. Some called it the best speech since his inaugural address and *Izvestia* and *Pravda* printed the text. More gratifying even than this was the secret word from intelligence sources that Khrushchev had been deeply impressed by the talk, that if Kennedy was willing to go before his own country, indeed the world, then he must be sincere. This was the beginning of the limited test-ban treaty which Kennedy would triumphantly sign in October, an achievement he rated second to none in his two and a half years in office.

June was travel month and Kennedy was off for Europe once again, bound for Germany, Ireland, England and Italy. He was alone this time because Jackie had given up all official activities to wait for her baby. It was for Kennedy a needed change of pace, and such trips were also a way to get the national mind off of all the home troubles.

In Germany with Konrad Adenauer at his side, Kennedy motorcaded through Cologne and on to Bonn. Thousands swarmed at the sides of the streets chanting "Ken-ah-dee, Ken-ah-dee."

"As a citizen of Boston," Kennedy told the people of Cologne, "I find it sobering to come to Cologne where the Romans marched when the Bostonians were in skins."

He attended mass in the great Cologne Cathedral and as he drove on he and Adenauer began to chat.

"Where did you get all those United States flags?" asked Kennedy, looking out at the tiny paper flags clutched by thousands of children.

"The same place you get them when you campaign in America," responded the wise old German with a smile. Adenauer, now ready to step out of office, was moved by the fact that Kennedy had carried through his visit to Europe despite all the troubles that beset him in America.

He turned to Kennedy and said, "You know, you could have easily put this off. You had so many reasons. The German people, who understand the subtleties of the situation, were worried you would not come." Then looking out of the Mercedes, still crawling slowly amid the cheering people, Adenauer waved toward them. "It is mild here compared to what it means to those in Berlin."

"You know," continued the Chancellor, "if you order them out like this they won't show up. Mr. President, you have to believe this is spontaneous because they know better than we do that their future is linked to yours." Again Adenauer marveled at the throngs, then he smiled again. "I even imagine the Cardinal in Cologne hasn't seen that good a crowd in church for some time." Kennedy chuckled out loud.

In the serious business in Bonn, Kennedy and Adenauer reached almost immediate agreement that for the time being the concept of the multilateral nuclear force was to be put on the shelf—there was too much uncertainty because of pending changes in governments in Germany, Italy and England. But both countries wanted to go ahead when the time came. Meanwhile, officials on the lower levels could proceed with technical talks. Defense was not Kennedy's big worry at these meetings. He was more concerned about the gold flow, the stability of the dollar, the Common Market.

"Our nuclear position is good," he said. "Our immediate troubles are economic." It was Kennedy's plea that these problems had to be looked at very broadly. If they took up, for instance, the problem of importation of American chickens alone and did not at the same time consider German tourism, said Kennedy, then "we run the risk of being ruined by the bookkeepers." Somehow, continued the President, the total picture had to be considered. Vice Chancellor Ludwig Erhard, who would soon take Adenauer's place, found he was in thorough agreement with this outlook and, indeed, had taken Kennedy's side in the Geneva trade talks. "By the way," said Erhard, "you ought to make me a dollar-a-year man because I am an expert on the subject."

Kennedy emphasized that the United States needed the help of the wealthy European nations, that they should assume more of the burden of maintaining the free world. If anything happened to the dollar, it would be bad for everybody, said Kennedy. Again the President found Erhard at his side and the Vice Chancellor said that if the dollar got in trouble "the disturbance would be like a disturbance in the planetary system."

There were light moments like the afternoon Kennedy wanted to bathe and change suits, and he retired to a small suite in the Palais Schaumburg set aside for him to use between business meetings. There was no hot water and the Germans ingeniously formed a bucket brigade up the back stairs filling the tub with steaming water.

While the press corps breakfasted on strawberries and champagne riding a train down the Rhine to Frankfurt, Kennedy took his helicopter in order to review American troops stationed there.

Again there was a motorcade and this time Erhard was beside Kennedy. The American had some political instructions for his companion. "Let's stand up and wave," he said. "*Was?*" asked Erhard, not yet used to Kennedy's style. But under the coaching of the President, he got on his feet and soon was following Kennedy's example, waving first with one arm, then the other, in order not to get either limb too tired. In front of Frankfurt's City Hall Kennedy urged him to get down with the people some more. "Let's go over and shake hands," he said, striding toward the barricades. Erhard came along and both of them did some politicking.

It was in Frankfurt's historic Paulskirche that perhaps the finest Kennedy message was delivered on the entire tour. In Bonn he had made plain to the Germans the United States' total commitment to Europe and to Germany. "My stay in this country will be all too brief but in a larger sense the United States is here on this continent to stay so long as our presence is desired and required. . . . Your liberty is our liberty, and any attack on your soil is an attack on our own." In Paulskirche (St. Paul's Church) he expanded and deepened the pledge in an eloquent address before the leaders of Germany. "The first task of the Atlantic Community was to assure its common defense. That defense was and still is indivisible. The United States will risk its cities to defend yours because we need your freedom to protect ours . . . the future of the West lies in Atlantic partnership—a system of cooperation, interdependence and harmony whose people can jointly meet their burdens and opportunities throughout the world. Some say this is only a dream, but I do not agree."

With France's Charles de Gaulle in mind Kennedy went on: "Those who would doubt our pledge, those who would separate Europe from America or split one ally from another, would only give aid and comfort to the men who make themselves our adversaries and welcome any Western disarray. It is not in our interest to try to dominate European councils of decision . . . I repeat again, so that there may be no misunderstanding: the choice of paths to the unity of Europe is a choice which Europe must make."

They rose to cheer the young President, the cheers echoing through the stark chamber where in 1848 the first all-German parliament had convened. The sun streamed through the tall windows, lighting the German state flags hung on the walls, and it was one of those moments when pride in the United States and her President touched all those who came with John Kennedy.

In Berlin the greatest human demonstration that Kennedy had ever seen was before him; mile after mile of packed streets, of cheering, waving people who stood ten and twenty deep to see the President of the United States. There were a million, perhaps two million, as Kennedy stood waving and smiling for more than four hours while his motorcade edged through the city. He stopped at the Berlin Wall. At the Brandenburg Gate, as his car pulled up, Kennedy turned and in silence stared at the low, ugly barrier. He walked to a special stand and looked over into a dead city. He was unsmiling; he thrust his hands into his pockets and hurried down. At Checkpoint Charlie he stood with clamped jaw and looked at the silence and lifelessness of East Berlin. He wanted to know where the tanks had come up in the tense days during his first year and Major General James Polk, commander in Berlin, pointed out the spot. As the President drove on, suddenly he looked out of his car far away into a grim, cold building where three women stood. They waved. "Isn't that kind of dangerous," wondered Kennedy, deeply moved by the sight.

In front of Berlin's City Hall were more massed thousands, and here Kennedy brought them to a roar. "There are many people in the world who really don't understand—or say they don't—what is the great issue between the free world and the communist world. Let them come to Berlin. There are some who say that communism is the wave of the future. Let them come to Berlin. . . . And there are even a few who say that it's true that communism is an evil system but it permits us to make economic progress. *Lass sie nach Berlin kommen.*"

The hard work of his tour was finished when Kennedy left Berlin. His stop in Ireland was for fun; his brief stay in England was more courtesy than anything else and his visit to Italy was ceremonial.

Ireland, of course, won his heart. At New Ross white-sweatered students lay down in the fields to spell out "Failte," the Gaelic word for "welcome." Rosy-cheeked children piped up "Kelly Killane" and then they sang a Kennedy favorite, "The Boys of Wexford." ("We are the boys of Wexford who fought with heart and hand to burst in twain the galling chain and free our native land.") Kennedy was entranced. "Another verse of the 'Boys from Wexford' would be just fine," he said. One of the children handed him a copy of the words and he sang with them. It was fun, indeed. Everybody laughed and cheered. Old folks, kids, mothers, ran beside the car to see John Kennedy. "Welcome home," read a sign.

Standing on the New Ross quay from which his great-grandfather had sailed for America, Kennedy said, "I am glad to be here. It took 115 years to make this trip and 6,000 miles, and three generations. When my great-grandfather left here to be a cooper in East Boston, he carried nothing with him except two things: a strong religious faith and a strong desire for liberty. I am glad to say that all of his great-grandchildren have valued that inheritance."

From the bearded mayor, Andrew Minihan, came the day's tribute. "We are proud of the fact that one of our race, you, Mr. President, has been chosen to lead the great American freedom-loving people."

In Dungan's town at the old family homestead the President found his cousin Mary Ryan and her two daughters waiting. The whole neighborhood turned out; the farmyard was freshly concreted, the house newly painted, and there were tables of cookies and cakes.

From the family doctor, Martin Quigley, came a sheepskin floor mat and the explanation: "This is to be put beside Mrs. Kennedy's bed for the arrival of twins in August."

Kennedy nibbled at a sandwich, helped cut the big welcome cake ("How about giving me a piece?" asked Mrs. Ryan), and then told the proud group, "We promise to come only once every ten years . . . We want to drink a cup of tea to all the Kennedys who went and those who stayed."

At the end of this day Kennedy stood before a crowd in Wexford. It was cold, and gray clouds spit mist at the 6,000 people in Redmond Place. Yet there was warmth, because the people after listening to Kennedy speak had begun to sing "The Soldiers' Song," the Irish national anthem. All was quiet except for the haunting tune. From the middle of the crowd came a clear tenor that floated above the other voices. The President of the United States looked out at these people and felt something. He lowered his eyes and smiled in a silent tribute to the moment.

In Cork the next day Kennedy was in his best form. He introduced Dave Powers, who had discovered seven of his own cousins. "He looks more Irish than they do," observed Kennedy. Then he turned to a priest beside him. "And then I would like to introduce to you the pastor at the church which I go to, who comes from Cork, Monsignor O'Mahoney. He is the pastor of a poor, humble flock in Palm Beach, Florida." The crowd roared with pleasure.

At Arbour Hill in Dublin Kennedy laid a wreath on the grave of the fourteen executed leaders of the 1916 uprising and he noted the moving exercise of his Irish honor guard. The day was gray, the grave was gray, so was the monument.

Somehow it fit, and again Kennedy was profoundly moved. He squinted to read the inscription on the wall behind the grave. "Irishmen and Irishwomen: In the name of God and of the dead generations from which she receives her old tradition of nationhood, Ireland, through us, summons her children to her flag and strikes for her freedom . . ."

The President became the first foreign head of state to speak before parliament and he was awarded two honorary degrees, one from the National University of Ireland (Catholic) and one from Trinity University (Protestant).

"I want to say how pleased I am to have this association with these two great universities. I now feel equally part of both, and if they ever have a game of Gaelic football or hurling, I shall cheer for Trinity and pray for National."

The warmth of Ireland lingered with John Kennedy as he flew on to see Harold Macmillan, Pope Paul and the heads of the Italian government. It lasted long after he returned to America and his many problems. Indeed, back in the Oval Office when his Irish visit was mentioned, he would give a broad smile and say, "It was terrific."

Kennedy's return to his desk was unusually harsh. He had just gotten off Air Force One and trudged into the Cabinet Room at mid-morning on July 3 when Secretary of Labor Willard Wirtz set the tone in a few short words. "We face a nationwide rail strike Wednesday."

After years of fruitless arguments and fruitless negotiations the dispute between the railroads and the unions about work rules—the "featherbedding" question—at last had come to a showdown. Management's right to instigate new rules had been upheld by the courts and the plans that management had which would eliminate some 65,000 railroad workers, were similar to those recommended by a government commission. Nevertheless, the rail brotherhoods threatened to strike when the new rules were put into effect. Kennedy sought and won more delay, but no solution to this problem was achieved until Congress finally voted compulsory arbitration.

But while the news at home was rather dim, that from abroad was once more good. Out of Moscow came the rather astonishing word that a limited nuclear test ban treaty with the Soviet Union appeared possible. When Averell Harriman and Viscount Hailsham had sat down for the first meetings in Moscow, Khrushchev had chortled: "We begin immediately with the signing." It was obvious that he wanted the treaty and so, indeed, did John Kennedy. It took only a few days more to iron out the details for an agreed ban on all tests except those underground. In Moscow Harriman initialed the treaty, still subject to the approval of the United States Senate, and in the United States President Kennedy went on TV with a note of caution.

"For the first time in many years the path of peace may be open," said Kennedy, but he went on to declare that the "treaty will not resolve all conflicts, or cause communists to forego their ambitions, or eliminate the dangers of war." Further, he said, the treaty would "bring new problems, new challenges from the communists, new dangers of relaxing our vigilance or of mistaking their intent." It would not be the "millennium," he argued, but it would be "a historic mark in man's age-old pursuit of peace." After three weeks of hearings and eleven days of formal debate, the Senate acted as everyone had known it would act and ratified the treaty, 80 to 19. In early October John Kennedy, using sixteen different pens, signed the document in the historic Treaty Room on the second floor of the White House. It was to John Kennedy one of his most gratifying moments.

Despite the urgency and heaviness of the national and world events there were moments of laughter. The President took up golf again, finding his back better than ever. One day he played a round with Pierre Salinger and the sequence on one of the tees was so remarkable the President passed it along to reporters. Salinger, who had for some years given up using woods in his game, had tried on this occasion to use a driver. He had somehow caught the ball on the head of the club and sent it crashing into part of the clubhouse, nearly 90 degrees from the intended path of flight. Undaunted, Salinger stepped up again and this time drove twenty yards off into some bushes. The President was both astonished and amused by this singular display and from then on began to coach his Press Secretary. Everybody enjoyed it except the President's fourteen-year-old caddie, Mark Salinger, who was somewhat embarrassed by his father's marksmanship.

On Kennedy's Hyannis Port weekends there was kite flying from the back of the "Honey Fitz," swimming in the ocean and hours of good lounging in the sun for the President in front of his rented home on Squaw Island. For a short while his life seemed pleasant. Then came more sadness. Jackie gave premature birth to a son, 4 pounds 10 ounces, christened Patrick Bouvier Kennedy. For thirty-nine hours the tiny baby struggled to live while doctors frantically worked over him, first at Otis Air Force Base where he was born, then at Boston's Children's Medical Center, where he was rushed in desperation. But at 4:30 one morning Pierre Salinger had to tell reporters, "Patrick Kennedy died at 4:04 A.M. The struggle of the baby boy to keep breathing was too much for his heart." The President took the gold St. Christopher's medal that Jackie had given him and put it in the white casket. The next day he sat alone in the first pew in a tiny chapel inside the residence of Richard Cardinal Cushing while the Cardinal read a Mass of the Holy Angels. Patrick was buried in a new family plot in Brookline marked by a lone stone which said simply: KENNEDY.

John Kennedy was in another slump. As fall came his Gallup poll popularity had fallen to 61 per cent. Racial unrest continued to plague the nation and the Republican presidential hopefuls, led by Barry Goldwater, rode to the attack week after week. The hopelessness of the Congress became even more pronounced. *The Congressional Quarterly,* a statistical publication, found at the end of July that some 38 per cent of the President's legislative proposals had received no action at all either in the House or Senate. It was no secret that the Congress had made plans to stay in Washington right up until Christmas and there was even talk that Kennedy's two top programs, the tax cut and civil rights, would not receive action until 1964. The Kennedy social measures like Medicare and aid to secondary education were hopelessly lost for yet another year. Congress was cutting the foreign aid authorization. And when the New Frontier proposed a bill calling for the Interstate Commerce Commission to arbitrate the railroad impasse, Congress brushed aside the suggestion and voted for straight arbitration. The defiance of Kennedy from the Hill had never been more pronounced. What was wrong?

Many of the New Frontier thinkers heaped the blame entirely on Congress and they got a lot of support from both Republicans and Democrats in and out of Congress. The machinery of committees, subcommittees, rules, seniority accession to committee chairs, had completely bogged down the governmental process, according to these men. "Something needs to be done like the old La Follette-Monroney Committee," said Arthur Schlesinger, Jr. "When a President can't even get his bills considered on the floor of the House of Representatives, something is wrong." The La Follette-Monroney Committee in 1946 had brought in needed streamlining to remedy similar sluggishness. But this present trouble seemed worse. Others felt that the Democratic leadership, including the President, was inadequate. Kennedy refused to get tough with Congress, feeling yet that he would only injure his cause more than help it by trying threats. Yet his friendly evening meetings with important senators and congressmen certainly had not mellowed them. There was the faint sensation that Kennedy did not really have his heart in his congressional relations. While Roosevelt and Truman seemed genuinely to enjoy dealing with Congress, and even Ike had a sincerity about him in his bouts with Democratic Congresses, Kennedy at times appeared to be going through motions only.

Some forgot, however, that in the early days of Roosevelt the only concern was his relations with Congress; his crisis was domestic; its solution depended upon legislation. Kennedy's field was far broader and far more complicated. It literally embraced the world and most areas of human endeavor. As if to underscore this point as November came, the President was again watching anxiously an extremely dangerous foreign development. The government of Vietnam was overthrown.

The vast communication tentacles of this nation terminate

in a wood-paneled room in the basement of the White House west wing. The room is called the situation room and there the unsleeping teletype machines clack out their messages. In the early hours of November 1, in short, blunt sentences from Ambassador Henry Cabot Lodge in Vietnam came the news. A coup was under way to oust President Ngo Dinh Diem and his brother and adviser Ngo Dinh Nhu. The coup was by the military leaders, now grown weary of the withdrawal of the Nhus from the people of Vietnam, of the senseless attacks on Buddhists and students, of what these military men alleged to be a slackening of the war effort against the real enemy, the communist Viet Cong.

The watch officer whirled and phoned McGeorge Bundy immediately. It was then just a few minutes after 2 A.M. Bundy heard the sparse report over the phone and hurried to his office. At 3 A.M. he was in the situation room poring over the new information and he was joined by Mike Forrestal, one of his assistants. It was obviously a serious effort and the delicate situation in Vietnam, which had for days been building to some kind of crisis, warranted waking the President. Bundy called Kennedy and gave him the news, then turned back to evaluating the intelligence reports. A cot was placed beside his desk and he finally lay down for a few minutes of sleep. At 6 A.M., however, he gathered what information he had and went to the President's bedroom to give Kennedy a more thorough briefing. A meeting of the top security men was scheduled for the morning, the Pentagon and State Department were fully alerted.

A few minutes before 10 A.M. the flotilla of black Cadillacs drove through the White House gates. Dean Rusk, Averell Harriman, Roger Hilsman and Robert Manning from the State Department. CIA's John McCone and Max Taylor, along with two briefing officers and their bulky charts, came in.

They met in the Cabinet Room and Kennedy studied the diagrams of Saigon that were set up across the table from him. The locations of the opposing forces, of the buildings, were clearly marked. Kennedy wanted to know about the loyalty of the troop units surrounding Saigon, whether Americans were in danger or not. Then there was little he could do but watch and wait. All day the dispatches came in from the American embassy and slowly the story unfolded. The coup, led by Lieutenant General Duong Van Minh (Big Minh) and Lieutenant General Tran Van Don, had succeeded and the Nhus were dead. Kennedy was shocked by the word of the deaths of two men who had been United States allies for years. Though he had been braced for a coup in Vietnam, he had hoped that the Nhus would be given safe conduct from the country. Indeed, Kennedy himself had set the stage for the coup. He had tried repeatedly to get Diem to make the necessary reforms in his government, so that the students, intellectuals, Buddhists and others alienated by the repressive measures would support the government. Kennedy wanted all the energies of the country focused on winning the war against the communists. The pleas went unheeded. Ambassador Frederick Nolting was withdrawn and Henry Cabot Lodge sent to replace him. The chief of the intelligence mission had been recalled too and some military and economic aid was cut off. Kennedy himself prodded the reluctant Diem on television, deploring his drift from reality and suggesting, indirectly, that it would be wise for him to get rid of his brother and sister-in-law, the fanatical Madame Nhu, both powerful influences on Diem and both instigators of many of the harsh measures. Kennedy's policy was not to directly promote a coup but not to oppose one if Diem refused to reform and the people organized an uprising. "Diem could have changed things at any time," said a top Kennedy man. "We were perfectly willing to work with him, but we couldn't under the circumstances he imposed on us."

The crisis eased, the generals remained in control and slowly began to form a government. Within a few days John Kennedy ordered that we recognize the new government.

Politics was suddenly in the air. And John Kennedy was again on the move, his spirits bounding as he indulged in his favorite sport. At the beginning of the year he had been convinced that Nelson Rockefeller would be his opponent in 1964, but the Governor's marriage to Mrs. Murphy dealt such a blow to the Rockefeller prestige that Kennedy began to talk about George Romney, Michigan's governor, as the

most likely candidate. Then quietly, but with an unsus-
pected force, Barry Goldwater's popularity mounted. At first
Kennedy did not believe that the Republicans would nomi-
nate a man of such conservative hue. He watched with fascination—occasionally with a twinge of pain—as Goldwater
sped around the country attacking the New Frontier. Finally
the evidence from the polls and the soundings of his own experts led him to believe that Goldwater might indeed win
the nomination by the simple process of winning the most
victories in the presidential preference primaries.

To counter some of the Republican headlines that Goldwater was receiving, the President headed west on a "non-
political" tour of inspection of key conservation projects
and natural resource areas. In fact, about the only natural
resource the President was looking for was the American
voter. But such amiable fiction is a presidential prerogative,
long practiced by presidents from both parties. Such arrangements save the party treasuries great amounts of money,
since on a "non-political" journey the taxpayer pays, while
the government must be reimbursed from the party's treasury for purely partisan junkets.

It was a jolly trip through Pennsylvania, Wisconsin, Minnesota, North Dakota, Montana, Wyoming, Utah, Washington,
Oregon, Nevada and California. Reporters called Kennedy
"Smokey the Bear" and "Johnny Appleseed," and he loved it.
He did indeed sniff the fragrance of balsam and view some
unspoiled wilderness. He even scanned the Grand Teton
Mountains at sunset, looking through binoculars for moose
along the Snake River. But he never lost sight of his mission,
and in Duluth, Salt Lake, Las Vegas and a dozen lesser stops
along the way he brought home the message of what he
thought John Kennedy had meant to the people. The message was peace and prosperity, and it went well with his audiences. He twitted Goldwater occasionally and discovered that
the folks applauded when he mentioned the test ban treaty.
He was experimenting, hunting for the phrases and sentences
that the people liked, looking for the format with which he
could feel comfortable and sound best. He started the tour
with his conservation message at the beginning of speeches, his
reminder of peace and prosperity at the close. But by the

time he finished the western swing he had reversed the order, and had all but eliminated talk of conservation. He flew to Palm Springs, California, for a rest over the weekend and he was visibly delighted with his performances.

On November 13 he called together his top political strategists. It was the first formal organizational meeting for the 1964 campaign. They met in the Cabinet room late in the afternoon, and the meeting went on for three hours and fifteen minutes. It was reminiscent of the famous Thanksgiving Day meeting in Hyannis Port in 1959, when Kennedy had set the strategy for his successful campaign for the nomination.

Around him at the big table were his brother Bob, Ted Sorensen, Larry O'Brien, Kenny O'Donnell, his brother-in-law Steve Smith, National Democratic Chairman John Bailey, Party Treasurer Richard McGuire, and Richard Scammon, Director of the Bureau of the Census and expert on where and how to get Democratic votes. There was an air of optimism in this meeting. World calm continued and there appeared to be nothing in the immediate future to disturb it to any great degree. The economy was booming; the nation was in its longest recession-free period since World War II; the gross national product was up 100 billion dollars above what it had been three years before; growth rate now topped that of Europe and Russia. In a few days Kennedy planned to visit Cape Canaveral and inspect the huge Saturn I rocket, which was scheduled to fly in December. If successful, it would be the most powerful rocket ever fired and it would put the greatest payload in history into orbit. Thus America's rocketry would finally surpass that of the Soviet Union, a dream Kennedy had cherished since the first months of his presidency, when he had helplessly watched the Russians lead the manned spacecraft race.

The business at hand during that meeting was a basic discussion of political plans for 1964. The call for the Democratic National Convention had to go out early the next year, and the apportionment of delegates, the language of the call and loyalty requirements had to be decided. The President wanted to make certain that those states which had given him the most solid support—both in the election of

1960 and in the electoral college—were given the most favorable representation at the convention. Several plans were discussed; they varied in detail but followed roughly the same ideas. Nothing was decided just then, because the President wanted more information.

One of his chief concerns was the convention; how to make it interesting, how to prevent boredom. The President had the idea that what was needed was a good film on the history of the Democratic Party. In 1956 Kennedy had gotten the big boost he needed to make him an active Vice Presidential candidate by narrating such a film. If the film could be done by good people, and they already had some talented volunteers for the job, he felt it would add interest to the convention.

He said also that one of his big disappointments was his failure to get across to the people the domestic accomplishments of the administration. He urged that there be a major film done on this.

The discussion then went on to the state organizations; who should have charge of co-ordinating the states in the campaign. They talked about getting a keynote speaker for the convention and Kennedy remarked, "I've never heard a really good keynote speech. I'd like to have one."

At the time of this meeting Kennedy still felt that Barry Goldwater would win the Republican nomination. But he cautioned the men around the table about making public predictions. "It would be unwise for any of us to talk about it," he said.

He was reasonably convinced that peace and prosperity would endure for him and the nation until the election. What he and the others wanted to know was what had been happening to voters. Where did the Democrats live these days; how much time should he spend, for example, campaigning in suburbia. This was a field in which Dick Scammon and Larry O'Brien excelled. Kennedy was fascinated by such discussions, and he asked Scammon for more information. Just where, for instance, was the breaking point in family income when Democrats became Republicans, and how long did party loyalty remain in a person even though his income had increased. It was Scammon's off-hand judgment that the breaking point was lower than many people thought, that it might be under $10,000 a year.

These political experts talked at some length about the South, and the racial problem in the election. It was Kennedy's feeling that even against Goldwater, the South was not entirely lost to him, that he would do better than many thought. In a few days he would campaign in Florida and Texas, and then he would have a better feel for the political temperature of the South.

Again during this meeting, as had been true in 1959, Kennedy amazed his own men with his detailed knowledge of the party machinery in the big states, of the names of key workers, of the political feelings in various regions of the country. It was a long and hard session but it ended with a lot of decisions made, a lot of requests for more information. The President asked that they meet again in two or three weeks. But this was not to be.

November 22 came gray and rainy, but the people were out anyway. By 7 A.M. 200 of them had gathered in the parking lot across from the Texas Hotel in Fort Worth. They were waiting to hear John Kennedy. This pre-breakfast appearance had been added at the last minute, when Texas Democrats objected that the President's major Fort Worth talk was to be before the Chamber of Commerce, an obvious Republican stronghold.

By speech time there were 3,000 in that crowd, and the drizzle persisted. Kennedy came out of the hotel with a wide smile, his chin up. He was hatless, and he thrust his hands into his coat pockets and strode straight to the people—the voters. Governor John Connally walked alongside. A multitude of hands reached out, and one by one the President gripped them. "Hello" . . . "Good to see you" . . . "Nice of you to come out." I stood beside Peter Lisagor of the *Chicago Daily News* and I marveled at how Kennedy could go through this performance day after day and still seem to enjoy it. I looked to my side and there stood Vice President Lyndon Johnson. On an impulse I reached out and touched his arm, and he turned and extended his hand. "Hello there," he said, and that was the last time I shook hands with Vice President Lyndon Baines Johnson.

"There are no faint hearts in Fort Worth," said the President at the microphone. "And I appreciate your being here this morning. Mrs. Kennedy is organizing herself." (There was a burst of laughter.) "It takes longer. But of course she looks better than we do after she does it." (More laughter, and Kennedy laughed too.)

He talked again with pride about the huge Saturn I rocket that he had seen in its gantry at Cape Canaveral the week before. "And in December—next month—the United States will fire the largest booster in the history of the world, putting us ahead of the Soviet Union in that area for the first time in our history."

Brigadier General Godfrey McHugh, the President's Air Force aide, standing beside me, turned and cupped his hand to whisper. "It had better go," he said. We both chuckled.

The President clenched his fist as he spoke and his jaw grew firm. "And in the final analysis," he said, talking of the nation's might, "that strength depends upon the willingness of the citizens of the United States to assume the burdens of citizenship. I know one place where they are to be found; here in this rain, in Fort Worth, in Texas, in the United States. We are going forward."

He walked back to the hotel the same way he had come, in the rain, searching the faces, smiling, waving in that short, understated manner. At breakfast they gave him a Texas hat and they asked him to put it on, but he refused. He never liked to be photographed in funny hats or riding horses or hamming it up. That wasn't Kennedy. He had declined sombreros and Indian headdresses and ten-gallon Stetsons from coast to coast. "I'll put it on in the White House on Monday, and if you'll come up there you can see it then," Kennedy joked as he handed the hat back.

They formed the motorcade in front of the hotel to go to the airport. Next stop, Dallas. Dave Powers stood beside his car waiting for the President to come down, and he was joking and talking. By now the sun was out, and promised for a fine day. Dave marveled at Jackie, who was persistently stealing the show all along the trip. When reporters polled the people standing on the streets, at least half, both women and men, confessed they were there to see the First Lady. "Just that smile and a little wave of her white gloves are enough to set them off," Dave said. Somebody kidded about his avid pursuit of home movies. Just the day before a professional photographer had complained that Dave got in his way. He laughed, but pointed out what an expert photographer he was becoming. The President recently had gone to the White House projection booth for a movie, and Dave had slipped in his homemade movies of the trip to Ireland. The surprised President had watched, then said to Dave, "These are terrific." On the sidewalk was Larry O'Brien talking with Senator Ralph Yarborough. Larry is an incurable politician, fascinated by the people and their candidates; the whys and wherefores of voters. Reporters stopped to question Pamela Turnure about the color of Mrs. Kennedy's suit. Raspberry pink was decided upon as the name of the color, amid a lot of laughter. This was the normal trivia of a campaign day.

In Dallas the sun was warm and so were the people, about 5,000 of them pressed against the airport fence. Jackie came out of the plane door first, a departure from protocol. It was indeed becoming Jackie's trip. She went with her husband to the fence, cradling a bouquet of red roses in her left arm, and there, smiling, she began to shake hands. The President followed, using both of his hands to greet the people. He seemed to feel especially proud then because Jackie was there. In her presence the crowds behaved a little differently. With the President they pushed and shoved and screamed and cheered and clutched. With Jackie they still shoved and pushed to get near the fence, but when she approached there were a few moments of restraint as they suddenly tried to show their respect for a lady. Then, as she passed on down the fence, they unbridled their exuberance again.

Governor Connally stood in the Lincoln bubble-top car and surveyed the scene with pleasure. Kennedy's trip to Texas was going well. Better than many had thought possible. Connally helped Jackie and his own wife into their seats in the

President's car, then Kennedy got in himself. There came the impatient roar of motorcycles, and John F. Kennedy's last motorcade was on its way.

It was all normal in those first miles, a fringe of people first that swelled to a packed crowd in downtown Dallas. A Goldwater sign was held by a grinning young man, but it was good sport. Reporters in the press bus looked for something different, and a local correspondent suggested that the motorcade route might go by General Edwin Walker's home. There was a thought that maybe the ultraconservative Walker would have a display of some kind in his front yard that would make good copy. But that hope died; the reporter was wrong about the route.

Minutes before 12:30 P.M. the cars went slowly down Main Street, and Texans jammed the sidewalks and spilled out into the street to see the President and his wife. It was still like a hundred cities all across the world that John Kennedy had visited—curious, cheerful faces by the scores, by the thousands. A lady reporter was more interested in seeing the famous Neiman-Marcus department store than in looking ahead at the bubble top.

The lead motorcycles rolled slowly toward Dallas' triple underpass. John Kennedy turned to his right to wave at the people on the curb, a bright green, grassy knoll behind them. Far back a reporter commented on the strange-looking red building ahead on the right. The Texas School Book Depository. Blue sky. Warm Texas sun.

Three shots. An era ended. A young generation lost its leader. The United States gave up its President. John Kennedy died.

Minds reeled in frenzy, trying to grasp some meaning and understanding, but there was none for hours, even days, perhaps not yet—or ever.

There was Jacqueline Kennedy's instant horror, and then something more enduring than even life itself rose with her. She cradled her husband's bleeding head in her lap, and she did not leave him until he was in his casket. He was buried on a hill in Arlington National Cemetery. And below lay the nation's capital, and far off, the vast horizon.

John Kennedy's eyes were often drawn toward the horizon.

He like Camp David because it lay on a forested lip of the Catoctin Mountains and commanded a view of long miles. He had looked over Narragansett Bay as evening fused earth, sun and sky. He would wander down a Cape Cod beach to feel the wind and look, think, beyond the moment. He used to gaze beyond the waves from his boat, and would stare from a plane window toward infinity. Now he was there.

INDEX